PRODUCING
THEATRE
A Comprehensive Legal and Business Guide

PRODUCING THEATRE

A Comprehensive Legal and Business Guide

by Donald C. Farber

Revised and Updated Edition

LIMELIGHT EDITIONS

New York 1987

First Limelight Edition September 1987

Copyright © 1981 by Donald C. Farber

All rights reserved under international and Pan-American Copyright Conventions. Published in the United States by Proscenium Publishers Inc., New York, and simultaneously in Canada by Fitzhenry & Whiteside, Limited, Toronto.

Library of Congress Cataloging-in-Publication Data

Farber, Donald C.
  Producing theatre.

  Includes bibliographical references and index.
  1. Theater—Production and direction—Law and legislation—United States. 2. Theater—United States —Production and direction. I. Title.
KF4296.F37 1987   343.73′078792   86-27312
ISBN 0-87910-074-5   347.30378792
ISBN 0-87910-103-2   (pbk.)

For my beautiful Annie,
who helped make it all happen

Gregrey W. Gorden has been a tremendous help in researching, writing, and updating certain parts of this book, specifically the part dealing with the union contracts. His contribution deserves special notice and much-appreciated thanks.

Contents

Preface

THE SECOND BOOK I wrote, now out of print, was entitled *Producing on Broadway: A Comprehensive Guide.* This book is an updating of *Producing on Broadway,* but it is more than that; it is intended as a text covering the business of producing theatre anywhere in the United States—that is, on Broadway, in resident theatres, stock, or other productions.

The first book I wrote, *From Option to Opening,* attempted to explain in nonlegal language all of the legal documents and relationships involved in the production of a play Off-Broadway. It was intended as a primer for those unfamiliar with theatrical producing; as many persons who produce Off-Broadway are, in fact, without any experience.

I still agree with most of the things I wrote in the preface to the first edition of *Producing on Broadway,* and, in fact, believe that what I said then is still valid today, so let me quote a portion of what I wrote:

> Many lawyers are too word conscious. I may seem a traitor to some in my profession (although I would be a good deal more correct to label it "my business"), and am certain not to endear myself to all my fellow attorneys, but I must make the observation that people are more important than words. I go to all of the trouble to analyze, digest, edit, and compile a book consisting of words about words, and then I have the effrontery to ask you to read them and learn them—but they may not be so important as what it is they intend to accomplish. Words are only

important to the extent that they are useful to people, either functionally or artistically. It may be necessary to bend certain words and change certain concepts that are so carefully stated in a contract to accomplish a given result which is good for everyone. The words are not an end in themselves. One accomplishes nothing if he wins the battle of the words and the contract words are inviolate, if he has destroyed the client's show in doing this.

One must also bear in mind the distinction between "facts" (if there is such a thing, since facts change and are also subject to interpretation) and "opinions." It is, for example, a fact that a limited partner's liability is limited to the amount of his investment, providing that the limited partnership has been properly organized in accordance with the partnership laws of the state of New York. It is an opinion that a dramatic show without a star should not go out-of-town on a pre-Broadway tour.

There are a lot of statements in this book that are something in-between facts and opinions. These statements reflect ideas that are in reality a consensus but are so widely believed that they are, in fact, facts—although they are not easily provable as such.

In all events, the reader will not find facts and opinions labeled. If something is a fact, there is no problem. If the comment concerns something about which there may only be opinions, and if there are important and respectable but divergent opinions, I have tried to express them. If there are divergent opinions, I have expressed the opinion of what I believe to be the most highly regarded thinking in the business on the subject, tempered with what I consider to be a good measure of common sense. Certainly you will find different opinions. You may even uncover different facts. But, for the most part, the facts set forth herein are unvarying facts, and the opinions set forth are, in my opinion, the best opinions.

Acknowledgments

WHILE I WAS UPDATING THIS BOOK, I was at the same time writing and editing four volumes of entertainment law forms, with appropriate commentary and background, for publication by Matthew Bender. The time involved was unbelievable. My family saw a lot less of me.

Thanks, respect, appreciation love and admiration go to my wife, Ann, who not only was very supportive of my writing endeavors but was understanding and patient when I had less time than I would have liked, for the family. My son, Seth, and my daughter, Pat, her husband, Nef, and their children, Justin and Miranda, all deserve my profound thanks and love.

My editors at Mathew Bender, Charles Knull and Allan Schwarz deserve special thanks, as some of the copy in this book was fine-tuned with their help in preparing their volume on theatre law. One more time, thanks to my first publisher, Ralph Pine. My associates, Debbie Gunset and Mitchell Lapidus, my secretary, Pam Markley, as well as my office assistant, Irene Fitzpatrick, were all helpful and have my thanks.

Special thanks and appreciation to my editor, Alice Kenner, and my helpful, sensitive, but still most practical, publisher, Mel Zerman.

Introduction

OF COURSE, THERE IS NO BUSINESS LIKE SHOW BUSINESS. That has to be the case, because the song says so. Many people accept this axiom without really fully accepting the fact that it is a "business." Show business is all kinds of things to all kinds of people. It represents excitement, glamour, and thrills for the uninitiated, at the same time representing backbreaking work, nervous anxiety, and emotional exhaustion for those on the inside. The business is an overcrowded, highly competitive business for most of the people who are in it. It's a business of feast or famine, and even the stars—with all the glamour and the big money—will, with a few exceptions, never know the financial security that the person taking home a regular weekly paycheck enjoys.

The actor, when he's starting, must play for a marginal salary in stock or Off-Broadway so that his work may be seen. If he is lucky and makes it big, then he may get work on Broadway, but it may add up to a total of six or eight weeks a year that he's paid. During this short time, he may earn big money, which must be spread out so he can live on it the entire year. With the tax bite and with the star having to live like a star even when he's unemployed, there are often huge deficits by the end of the year for those who enjoy the privilege of having their name above the title.

Tastes in theatre change. During the 1930s, the serious dramatic play was developing along with the musical theatre. The musical continued to develop and change, and the current Broadway hits consist mostly of musicals and comedies. The serious dramatic play is almost nonexistent on the Broadway scene. Even with a star of importance and prestige, the fate of serious drama is a questionable commercial proposition. Of course, we all hope that this will change. Whether there is no serious drama because the serious drama is not that good or whether there is no serious drama because the demand is not there is not entirely clear. This is the Broadway scene at the time of this writing. We must acknowledge it even if we don't willingly accept it.

Contract agreements with unions expire and are renegotiated; budget requirements change just as theatregoers' preferences change. No one can be certain that anything he or she writes on this subject, or any subject, is immutable. At the same time, we should realize that certain basic concepts are less likely to change, and if they do, the change will occur slowly.

Wherever a contract discussed in this book has a fixed terminable date, the date is noted. Changes that occur in a contract will, in most instances, be "nonbasic"—the kind of facts and details that are easily ascertainable. It is of primary importance that the framework and the basic concept of the various contracts, as well as the relationships and obligations of the various contributing parties, be understood.

If someone decides to go into "the business," he or she ought to know as much as possible about it. Contracts involved in producing a show are, in many instances, understood by too few people.

After many years of coping with the Dramatists Guild, Inc., Minimum Basic Production Contract (MBPC) as the most-used standard option for a Broadway play, the Guild and the League of American Producers and Theatres finally settled on a new contract known as the Approved Production Contract (APC).

This contract is not just a minimum contract, but rather a minimum and a maximum contract. It establishes terms that are fixed and immutable. The new contract is discussed in detail in this book (see Chapter 4). It is an improvement over the previous, little-understood contract, the MBPC.

It is possible, of course, to produce a show without knowing anything about the agreements. One can, for instance, hire a competent attorney, a manager, and an accountant. These three people—who should know the terms of most of the agreements—will deal with the various unions and parties. Ideally, however, the producer ought to know as much as he can about his *relationship* with the people he'll be working with. This relationship, being a contractual relationship, ought to be understood clearly in terms of the producer's rights, duties, and the obligations the producer has to the people he or she works with. There should be no need to wave one's contract under the other parties' noses, nor use it as a threat. But all parties should, however, understand it.

The APC, like the other agreements, will be discussed with the view that each contract be considered a single, cohesive unit, while understanding it in relation to other contractual obligations that will become legally binding when a producer begins producing a show.

In many instances, there are disputes as to the meaning of certain contract provisions. It will serve no useful function to examine the detailed arguments supporting each point of view. For our purposes at this time, it should suffice to know that there are discrepancies and disagreements in certain areas that are still to be resolved.

One should also bear in mind that what happens in reality is sometimes very far removed from the contract terms and provisions. In many instances, a contract is entered into on the union form and the parties signing are little aware of most of the terms.

There are also instances where, through custom, certain ways of doing things have developed that are in direct contradiction to the specific contract terms setting forth how something should be done. In such a case, the parties (if they even know the contract terms) have simply not bothered to comply with the contract, because following their own procedures is more suitable to accomplish the end. Little would be served by changing procedures to comply with a written document if the changed procedures did not serve some useful purpose.

After a careful study of this book, one would probably know more than most people in the theatre know about the contractual relationships involved in producing for the stage. As a practical matter, however, some of the contracts discussed in this book usually are drafted, after careful consideration and negotiation, by the attorneys for the producer and the other party. In other instances, there are contracts entered into by either the company manager, the general manager, or the house manager that the attorney for the producer doesn't handle. In fact, there are many contracts the theatre owners make with unions that affect the producer but that many people in the business, including attorneys, know nothing about or ever see.

This book discusses the contracts and the agreements that would be within the scope of experience of the producer, the attorney for the producer, the theatre owners, the house manager, the general manager, and the company manager.

It goes without saying, finally, that there is a vast amount of information that can never be learned from a book alone and will only be learned through the difficult but ever-rewarding process of acquiring experience through *doing;* that is, *producing.*

PRODUCING
THEATRE
A Comprehensive Legal and Business Guide

CHAPTER 1

Obtaining a Property

A N ORIGINAL WORK OF AUTHORSHIP, regardless of when it was created, is protected either by common law or by statutory copyright[1] unless the work has fallen into the public domain.[2] Copyright protection generally means that no one may use the work in any manner whatsoever without first securing the permission of the copyright owner or the person who acquired ownership of those rights through purchase, assignment, inheritance, or otherwise.[3] Failure to acquire permission can result in a lawsuit to collect the damages caused by the infringement, and can also give rise to an injunction to stop the unauthorized use. In order to avoid potential liability, and also to be fair to the owner of the work, a person interested in producing a copyrighted play in any manner—whether it be a Broadway production, an amateur production with free admission, or anything in between—should proceed first to acquire the performance rights. In so doing, the prospective producer must, among other things, determine if the rights are available and, if so, at what price and upon what conditions.

FINDING THE OWNER OF THE PROPERTY

In determining if the rights are available, the producer must find the person who has authority to deal with the property. If the author is alive, this can be done simply by contacting the author directly or by

3

contacting his attorney or other representative. The names, addresses, and phone numbers of these persons can be obtained from either the Dramatists Guild, if the author has had a play previously produced; the publisher of the play or music; the Writers Guild; or the Register of Copyrights in Washington, D.C.

If the play was previously produced in New York and was relatively successful, chances are good that one of the play-licensing companies has the work in its catalogue (i.e., Music Theatre International, Samuel French, Inc., Tams Witmark Music Library, or the Rodgers and Hammerstein Library). In this instance, a producer could contact the appropriate company rather than the author, his agent, or attorney.[4]

In all of the above cases, the process of finding who owns or controls the rights is usually quite easy; however, when the author is either deceased, foreign, or deceased and foreign, complications can be encountered.

A deceased author's works are most often controlled by his estate through a literary executor who may be the author's spouse, child, or other relative. The literary executor could also be the author's attorney, agent, or bank if the works are held in trust. Tracking down the right person can be very time consuming, especially if the author has been dead for many years. The spouse may have died also, transferring the work to someone else; children may have married or remarried and taken different surnames; the trust may have terminated—the difficulties in tracing the rights owner(s) are too numerous to mention. If the deceased author's play was previously produced, however, there is the possibility that a licensing company will be handling the rights on behalf of the estate, thus simplifying the procedure.

A foreign author is, in most instances, represented by a foreign agent, and sometimes the agent has a U.S. representative. The problems of distance and language differences oftentimes present obstacles in determining the identity of the person who controls the rights. At the very least, trying to contact the proper person in a foreign country will usually require more time.

Needless to say, if an author is both foreign and deceased, it's likely that nothing short of perseverence and steadfastness of purpose will bring forth the identity of the owner of the work. And even then there can be little assurance that the person found is indeed the true owner of the desired rights. For this reason (as well as others that will be discussed later in Chapter 2), the producer's representative should always insist that the contract for the rights to the play include language to the effect that the person granting the rights: (a) warrants and represents that he is the owner of the copyright in the work, and (b) that he has full right and authority to grant the rights he is granting.

In addition to the problems sometimes encountered in finding the owner of the needed rights, the acquisition of performing rights in music and lyrics presents yet another obstacle. The person to contact in order to acquire these rights depends primarily on whether the producer needs "grand" or "small" performing rights, and the determination to be made as to which of these rights is needed in a given situation depends on a number of intertwining factors.

Grand rights are those needed to perform the music in a dramatic fashion, while only small performing rights are required for nondramatic performances. The determination of what is dramatic and what is nondramatic is usually the essence of the problem, and in attempting a definition it becomes apparent that although the extremes are clear, the dividing line is not. If there exists a story connecting the songs together, the performance is considered a musical play and dramatic, thus requiring grand rights. If there is no story but just improvised patter connecting the songs, the performance may be more like a nondramatic nightclub act, requiring only small rights. But the kind of dialogue between songs is not the only basis on which to decide if a storyline exists. Sets, costumes, and props could, with the music and lyrics, create a dramatic sequence conveying a story, especially if one or all of those elements are similar to the sets, costumes, and props used in a play from which the songs were originally performed. Thus, although television, radio, nightclub, and concert performances of songs usually require only small performing rights, if a story is conveyed through any of the elements of dialogue, sets, costumes, and props, grand rights may be required. In certain instances grand rights are necessary if all the songs from a musical play are used in concert in the same sequence in which they were originally performed, even if none of the above elements are present. There are no definite rules that apply in order to determine whether a story is being told or not. However, if a producer has any question of which rights to acquire, it's always safer to get the grand rights, if possible, to avoid any lawsuits or injunctions for copyright infringement.

If the producer receives assurances from the apparent owner of the rights that the owner controls those rights that the producer needs, without specifying whether those rights are grand or small, the producer needing grand rights may be lulled into a false sense of security.

The producer may be made to believe either that the owner has the grand rights, when in fact he controls just the small rights, or that the grand rights are not needed for the production, when in fact they are. Therefore, the producer should always try to have the person or company granting the rights give him a warranty and indemnity on any losses he may sustain due to their granting the small rights, in the event the grand rights are in fact required. The indemnity should not be limited to the amount of money paid by the producer to the grantor of the rights for the use of the music. The amounts paid may be so small as to be of little value to the producer in the event of a lawsuit for infringement. It's the producer's obligation to make certain he or she has in fact acquired the grand rights if they are needed.

Small performing rights are usually licensed by either one of three major companies: ASCAP, BMI, or SESAC. Payment of either a designated fee per song or a blanket payment covering all the songs in the company's catalogue will authorize the use of the music. Although grand rights are safer to have, they are usually more expensive and sometimes more difficult to acquire than small performing rights.

The composer and lyricist of the songs will usually hold the grand rights to their compositions, but there are times when the music publishing company will be the owner. Songs written for the movies is one example of such ownership. These songs are usually considered works for hire (i.e., the film companies paid the composers and lyricist as employees to write the songs), and under the copyright law, the employer enjoys complete ownership in the works. Since many of the major film companies have publishing companies as subsidiaries, a producer wishing to acquire the grand rights to such songs would have to contact either the film company or the music publishers rather than the composers and lyricists.

Another example of complete ownership of a song by a publishing company is the situation where a young, unknown writer will sign an exclusive songwriter's contract with a publishing company that gives the writer an advance payment against future royalties. In exchange, the company owns all of the writer's musical output for the duration of the contract.[5]

In any event, whomever the owner may be, the cost for the grand rights for the music and lyrics will vary anywhere between $100 per song per performance week to a percentage of the gross weekly box-office receipts, as discussed later in this book.

It should be noted that this procedure of *separately* acquiring the grand performing rights to songs is only necessary when a producer intends to present on stage, and in a dramatic fashion, songs that were never part of a play, that were part of a play but did not merge with the play when presented, or that did merge with the play but have been released by permission.[6] The rights to the book, music, and lyrics of a musical play—either old or new—are usually acquired simultaneously.

DETERMINING HOW AND WHERE TO PRESENT THE PROPERTY

Before obtaining the property—in fact, even before determining who the owner of the rights is—the producer should have a clear idea of how and where he or she intends to produce the play (i.e., Broadway, Off-Broadway, stock, first- or second-class tour, regional or amateur theatre). This will be one of the factors determining whether the producer will acquire an exclusive option to produce the play, which should include the right to earn certain production rights and subsidiary rights income, or merely a nonexclusive license to present the play for a specified number of performances. In most cases, stock, second-class tours, and all amateur theatres acquire only a simple license. Broadway, Off-Broadway, and pre-Broadway tours, first-class tours, and some regional theatres will usually get options with the amount of additional and subsidiary rights varying greatly (this will be discussed in more detail in the next chapter).

The reason for granting an option rather than a license is based in part on the potential contribution the production will make to the play. If a producer intends to mount a first-class production to open on Broadway, the play will receive a great deal of exposure both by the number of people attending and the press coverage. This increases the future subsidiary market for the play in the stock, touring, and amateur circuit; and, in addition, can be the catalyst for the making of a movie, television series or mini series, and cast album. If the play is produced Off-Broadway, a future market is also created, although perhaps to a somewhat lesser degree since the play's exposure may be less.

The contribution made by the production would not be possible without the large contribution of money made by investors to produce the play. Since investors generally want to see their investment returned, they have learned to expect that the production company producing the play will participate in future profits derived from sales of the play to subsidiary markets. The investors' reason for this is simple: if they and the producer took an unknown property and made it into a successful play, which in turn caused it to make even more money by subsidiary uses, they should share in the author's receipts from those other sources. This advantage is achieved by the producer entering into an option agreement with the author, who will not be unwilling to give up a share of his future earnings from the play since he is aware that his play would have little future without a successful commercial production.

Generally, the more remote the production is from a first-class presentation, the less the author will be inclined to share in future earnings, since the chance of that production being the cause of future earnings becomes proportionately less. There are, of course, exceptions to this general rule for other than first-class productions performed in major theatres in major cities in the United States; however, Broadway and other first-class productions still reign supreme.

It should be added here that a simple license is almost always granted to a producer provided he agrees to pay the license fee. A license, however, may not be available if an agreement exists granting the exclusive production rights to another. This usually occurs when a producer holds the exclusive option to present the play, or when a play has been produced while under an option agreement, whereby the producer acquires additional exclusive rights to continue to produce the play. There are occasions when a producer who holds these exclusive rights will release them for use by another producer for a stock or amateur presentation, provided that such a production will not be within a competitive radius of one of the former's productions of the play.

In contrast to the often ready availability of a license, an option may sometimes be impossible to acquire even if the property is available and even if the producer is willing to pay an exorbitant price. The reason for this is that an author is sometimes more interested in having his or her work produced, directed, and acted by certain persons at certain times. If these persons are not interested or available at the right time, the author may lose interest or the play become unavailable. This situation will often be found with the estate of a famous deceased author, where the trustees or executors of the estate sometimes become overzealous in protecting the integrity of the author's works.

METHODS OF ACQUIRING RIGHTS TO A PROPERTY

A person wishing to produce a play can acquire the rights by one of several methods discussed below.

Produce a Play in the Public Domain

As mentioned earlier, all original works of authorship are protected either by common law or statutory copyright unless the work has fallen into the public domain. A work in the public domain is available to be used in any manner imaginable without the need to acquire or pay for rights. In order to understand how a work gets into the public domain, a basic understanding of the copyright law (both old and new) is necessary.

Under the old copyright law, prior to 1978, once a play was written it automatically enjoyed the protection of a common law copyright. If anyone misappropriates the work, the author can sue the wrongdoer in a court of law. This common law copyright can exist forever, provided the author does not "publish" his or her creation by distributing it to the general public.[7] If such publication[8] occurs, in order to have statutory copyright protection the author must comply with the provisions of the copyright law, providing that a "copyright notice" be prominently displayed on the work—i.e., © (or copyright) 1977 John Doe. Failure to affix this notice upon publication will usually cause the work to fall into the public domain. There are some rare exceptions to this rule which are written into the copyright law. For example, an inadvertent failure to affix the notice may not be fatal in certain instances.

Once the work was published with the copyright notice affixed, the common law copyright terminated and the work was then protected by statutory copyright under the old federal copyright law.[9] Although the common law copyright was perpetual, the statutory right under the old law granted protection for only a certain number of years. Prior to January 1, 1978,[10] the copyright term was twenty-eight years, with the opportunity of renewing the protection for an additional period of twenty-eight years, thereby bringing the total to fifty-six years. Since under the old law the federal copyright became activated when the work was published with a notice of copyright, the term of fifty-six years is measured from the date of publication. After the period of fifty-six years, the work falls into the public domain.[11] Furthermore, if the copyright was not renewed before the first twenty-eight-year term expired, the work would similarly become part of the public domain.

The new copyright law—effective January 1, 1978, for works created on or after that date—changed the term for the duration of copyright to the life of the author plus fifty years with no renewal term. The term begins from the date the work was created (if on or after January 1, 1978) and is not therefore measured from the publication date as under the old law. Furthermore, there is no longer any common law copyright since the new federal law preempted the area by providing statutory copyright protection upon creation of the work. Consequently, works created on or after January 1, 1978, no longer have a perpetual common law copyright until first publication. As under the old law, failure to publish with a copyright notice affixed will invalidate the copyright except under certain specific circumstances.

Although it may appear that determining if a work is in the public domain is simply a matter of adding fifty-six to the date of publication for a work created prior to 1978, such is not the case. The new copyright law provides many exceptions to the general rules mentioned above, and only a careful reading by a person familiar with the law will give an accurate answer. One such example of where the general rules do not apply (and where a producer intending to present a play in the public domain should proceed with caution) is with works whose renewal term (second twenty-eight years) was in existence in 1962, when the Congress began to write the new law. Since Congress quickly realized it was going to take a considerable amount of time to revise the old law—and that it would be unfair to penalize authors whose copyrights would expire by the time the new law became effective, thus depriving them of the benefits of its provisions—the Congress enacted legislation beginning in 1962 which extended the copyright of those works for a period of two years. Similar enactments (extending the copyright for one- or two-year periods) were made eight times more during the course of the revisions, extending those copyrights up until the date of effectiveness of the new law, January 1, 1978, which again extended all copyrights then in their renewal term to seventy-five years from the date the original copyright was secured. The effect of all these extensions is that works copyrighted anytime after September 18, 1906, whose copyright was duly renewed, now enjoy copyright protection for seventy-five years. Therefore, a less than fully informed person attempting to determine whether such work first published in late 1906 was in the public domain would add fifty-six to 1906, come up with 1962 as the last year of copyright protection, and incorrectly conclude that the work would be in the public domain and thus free to use.

The copyright office, for a fairly nominal fee, will make a copyright search to determine if and when a work in question was copyrighted and if and when the renewal registration was filed. The office will not, however, render a legal opinion as to whether a work has fallen into the public domain.

Although great care must be taken in determining if a work is actually in the public domain, a producer can save a great deal of money by producing such a play. There are no royalties to be paid, and no negotiations for an option. One of the drawbacks is that there is also no exclusivity. Anyone else can produce the same play in the theatre next door, and the producer will find himself in competition with the play he is producing. The chances of this happening, however, are somewhat remote, since the other producer would find himself similarly situated. Another drawback is that the producer and his investors will receive no income from the distribution of the subsidiary rights, since the work no longer enjoys the protection of a copyright; neither the author (if he is still alive) nor his estate have any rights to distribute. The work is free to be used by anyone without charge.

Commission an Adaptation of a Public Domain Work

The work in the public domain that attracts a producer's interest need not be restricted to a play. A novel, short story, or epic poem, for example, can be adapted into a stage play. Although the underlying work (i.e., the novel) may be free to use, the person commissioned to do the adaptation would usually hold the copyright on the dramatized version. In a rare instance, a producer may "hire" an adaptor as an employee. In such a case, the producer would be the owner of the copyright, since it would be considered a "work for hire." The normal procedure, however, is for the producer and author (as well as composer and lyricist, if it's to be a musical adaptation) to enter into a Dramatist Guild Approved Production Contract if mounting a first-class production is intended. If it is to be other than first class (such as an Off-Broadway presentation), an option agreement drawn by the producer's attorney will be used.[12]

Even if the producer's intention is to present the play as a second-class production in a remote location, the producer will still, in most instances, acquire some form of option rather than merely a license. This is so because the producer is offering to pay the author to write the adaptation, and if the producer does not get what he or she wants in return regarding a future interest in the play, the producer will simply not commission that author. Of course, the protection normally afforded to a producer by entering into an option (wherein he or she receives the exclusive rights to present the play) does not strictly apply in this case. Although the producer will have the exclusive right to produce the adaptation, the underlying work is in the public domain, and anyone else can come along and present a different adaptation—thus creating the competitive situation mentioned before. But, once again, the chances of this happening are somewhat remote. A problem which can more readily arise, however, whenever anyone uses a public domain work, is that if the production is successful, other producers around the country (or even the world) can produce a similar show and cut into the producer's potential stock, amateur, and other subsidiary markets. Furthermore, if a movie company thinks that adapting the work is a good idea for a film, it may not bother to negotiate a film deal for the producer's adaptation if it can do its own for a fraction of the cost. It is important to note in this context that although the idea for the adaptation may have been uniquely and originally that of the producer, an idea is not copyrightable. Therefore, others can use the same idea, provided they do not copy the producer's newly created version. In some circumstances, they can even use the same title, since titles—like ideas—do not enjoy copyright protection.[13]

Commission the Translation of a Public Domain Work

If the work in the public domain is a foreign-written play, and there is no need for a dramatic adaptation, commissioning a translation would be appropriate.[14] What was said in the preceding section concerning adapting a public domain work is equally applicable here. In this area, a producer may find it easier to hire a translator as an employee and thereby retain complete copyright ownership. This is, of course, a matter of negotiation and depends to a large extent on the reputation of the translator. Because a translation can be done by a person with little knowledge of the theatre, the final product may be awkward and unplayable, and the producer may own the copyright of a relatively useless translation. Paying more for a well-written-and-constructed translation by a talented translator will increase the chances of producing a good play.

Acquire the Rights to the Adaptation or Translation of a Public Domain Work

The previous two sections dealt with a producer hiring or commissioning an author, composer, lyricist, or translator. However, if a producer finds a previous adaptation or translation which he or she feels has chances for success, the producer can produce that version without commissioning a new version. The fact that the underlying work may be in the public domain does not mean that the adaptation or translation is also free to use. As stated before, any new versions are themselves protected by a copyright—unless, that is, they have also fallen into the public domain.

The same problems of competition attendant to producing other public domain works apply here.

If the producer intends to present the play as a first-class production, he or she would ordinarily negotiate and enter into a Dramatists Guild contract with the translator or adaptor. For other-than-first-class productions, there is no standard option agreement that is generally used. The producer's attorney will usually draft the producer's own contract.

Acquire the Rights to an Original Copyrighted Work

In contrast to public domain works, which are free to use without permission, are original works of authorship that enjoy full copyright protection. These works could be completely new and unproduced or could be old standards that have been on the boards many times. In either case, if the producer has in mind a Broadway or other first-class production, he will probably enter into a Dramatists Guild contract.[15] If other than first class, the option to be signed will vary as previously indicated. These options usually provide that the producer has the exclusive right to present the play, thereby eliminating the possibility of a competing production. Bear in mind that an idea cannot be copyrighted, therefore another author could write a different play based on the same idea.[16]

Depending on the reputation of the author, a producer may not be able to option the rights to produce a play unless he or she plans to put the play on Broadway, Off-Broadway, or in a major theatre in a major city in the United States. Since the author wants the production of his or her play to be the best possible if the producer is going to share in the author's future royalties, the producer will usually grant only a simple license to smaller theatre companies and producers.[17]

Acquire the Rights to an Adaptation or Translation of an Original Copyrighted Work

Just as a work in the public domain may be adapted or translated, so may an original copyrighted work. A producer desiring to present such a play would enter into the appropriate option agreement with the author of the translation or adaptation. Part of the option agreement should provide not only that the new version of the work is original with the author, but also that the author has full right and authority to grant the rights. This would include a warranty that the author had acquired the rights from the owner of the basic work to do the adaptation or translation, and a clause holding the producer harmless in the event the author breaches the warranty. In the event the producer is sued because he or she produced an unauthorized version of the basic work, the producer could in turn sue the author for breach of contract and recover any losses sustained as a result of the author's misrepresentation.

Acquire the Rights to Adapt or Translate an Original Copyrighted Work

Unlike a work in the public domain, a producer cannot legally commission an author to adapt or translate a copyrighted work and produce it without first obtaining the rights from the owner of the basic work. Provided the rights are available, the basic works such as novels, short stories, poems, plays, motion pictures, radio and television shows, and even comic strips can be translated, adapted, dramatized, or made into musicals. Usually the owner of the basic work will enter into an option agreement that will provide that the producer, upon exercise of the option, will own the rights in the basic work to adapt it for the stage in accordance with the terms of the literary purchase agreement annexed to and signed simultaneously with the option.[18] It is important that the agreement with the author of the basic work provides that the producer has the exclusive right to do the adaptation the producer desires and that the owner will not, during the term of the agreement, grant similar rights to anyone else. If the owner can no longer grant those rights to others, he or she will want to make sure of getting the best possible production in the best possible location.[19] For this reason, the owner of the basic work will not usually grant adaptation or translation rights to a producer who does not intend eventually to have a New York or other first-class production.

Commission an Original Work to be Copyrighted

A producer who has a unique idea can commission a playwright (preferably one with a reputation) to transform that idea into a play.

The terms of the contracts entered into between the producer and author will vary depending on the type of production, as previously stated. The contract will almost invariably be an option with additional rights rather than merely a license, since the producer is taking some risk in producing an unknown property and will want to provide investors with an added incentive to part with their money.

A possible area of interest in the commissioning of new plays is that of dramatizing the lives of famous people or certain interesting or unusual events in the news concerning people known or unknown. A producer desiring to commission the writing of such a play should first acquire good legal counsel, since such a production could give rise to a lawsuit under the right-of-privacy laws that virtually every state now has either by statute or court decision. The privacy statute in New York is found in the Civil Rights Law, Sections 50 and 51. Section 50 states "A person, firm or corporation that uses for advertising purposes or for purposes of trade, the name, portrait or picture of any living person without having first obtained the written consent of such person, or if a minor, of his or her parent or guardian, is guilty of a misdemeanor."

Section 51 states that the person so wronged can sue for an injunction and for money damages. The question of what is "for trade" is vague and has often come into conflict with the First Amendment guarantees of freedom of speech.

The statute has been further defined and refined by numerous court cases. The results of each case depend on the particular facts. Suffice it to say that if a producer intends to produce a play about a living person, he would be well advised to consult a knowledgeable lawyer.

Write or Adapt a Play to Produce

Since we are enumerating the ways to acquire a play to produce, we must not overlook the fact that the producer could, of course, write or adapt a play, or compose music and lyrics, or do any or all of these things. If a producer does any or all of these things, it would, perhaps, be prudent to find someone else to produce. If no one else wants to produce the work, one might observe that the producer is less than unbiased toward the writer's work, and the producer's objectivity and business judgment should be carefully considered. Perhaps there are people who can write well, compose well, direct well, and then also produce well. There just aren't many. Most people would do well to handle any one of these jobs with a degree of professionalism.

CHAPTER 2

The Option for Other Than a First-Class Production

AFTER THE PRODUCER has determined a desire to acquire the rights to a property, who controls the rights and where, and how he or she intends to produce the play, the producer must then negotiate the terms of the agreement to acquire the rights. If the producer is acquiring a license with no additional or subsidiary rights, the negotiation process and the terms will be relatively one-sided in favor of the author. The amounts due the author for a license are usually fixed at a percentage of the gross box office receipts or a flat fee, and the only variable is how much of an advance against royalties the producer need pay.

If, on the other hand, the producer is acquiring what is referred to as an "option," he or she should know what terms an option agreement can contain. This chapter will explain the most common terms found in option agreements, their purpose, and how they vary, depending on the bargaining power of the parties.

The Dramatists Guild, Inc. (the "Guild"), Minimum Basic Production Contract for an Off-Broadway show is almost never used. The contract for Off-Broadway was never fully negotiated. When the negotiations between the Guild and the League of Off-Broadway Theatre Owners broke down in the middle of negotiations, early in the seventies, the Guild decided to publish its own version in the hope that it would be accepted as a viable contract. It has never been used by knowledgeable attorneys and agents working in theatre, although some agents representing play authors have tried to force it on producers. The Off-Broadway contract the Guild would like to use is so unfairly pro-author that it would be difficult, if not impossible, to find financing for any play that is acquired by a producer pursuant to its terms.

After the reader has acquired a basic understanding of an option, the Approved Production Contract (which is a form of option most always used for first-class performances[1]) will be discussed in detail in Chapter 4.

OUTLINE OF CONTRACTUAL PROVISIONS

1. Warranties of author and producer as to ownership and originality of the property
2. Author's grant of rights
3. Noncompetition clause
4. Payments to author
5. Producer's subsidiary rights
6. House-seat allocation
7. Billing credits
8. Producer's additional rights to tour
9. Producer's additional rights to produce or move the play to Broadway
10. Producer's additional rights to produce the play in England
11. Producer's additional rights to produce other first-class productions
12. Approval of director, actors, and designers
13. Duration of right to produce the play
14. Right to assign option
15. Arbitration clause
16. Script changes
17. Legal clauses

A sample option agreement containing the basic language of these terms appears in Appendix G. You will be able to refer to the contractual language easily, since the numbers to the left of the terms cited above correspond to the same paragraph numbers in the contract.

Warranties of Author and Producer as to Ownership and Originality of Property

In Chapter 1, we discussed the necessity of the producer acquiring the rights to do the play to avoid a lawsuit. The language in this paragraph should serve to guarantee that the producer is, in fact, making a valid acquisition after finding the person who seems to be the owner of the property. The clause sets forth that the author or owner warrants and represents that the work: (a) is original and does not violate anyone's copyright (i.e., the author did not copy from another author); (b) does not violate any other rights of any person (this would include such areas as the right of privacy, defamation of character, libel, slander, and unfair competition); (c) is unencumbered by any claim made by someone against the author that adversely affects the play or the copyright (someone may be claiming a prior grant of the same rights being conveyed; this would be a claim that adversely affects the play. Producers want to option potential hits, not lawsuits); (d) is solely owned by the author, or owner, and that he or she has the right and power to enter into this agreement and to deal with the rights granted in the option.[2]

The author or owner also agrees to "indemnify" (pay) the producer for any losses the producer may suffer due to a "material" (substantial) breach of any of the above warranties. What is material may be a question for the court or an arbitrator to determine. If the court or an arbitrator finds the breach is material, the author must pay the producer's legal fees in addition to other damages, such as lost profits and any payments owing under contractual obligations that the producer undertook (i.e., fees for actors, designers, theatre, etc.) and that the producer cannot fulfill due to the inability to open or continue the play. The author also agrees to hold the producer "harmless" from any claims, demands, lawsuits, etc. This means that if the producer is sued by a third party, such as a real or a bogus owner of the play, the author must assume the responsibility so that the producer is not harmed by the claim.

If these provisions seem harsh and unfair to the author, one should realize that a producer spends great amounts of time and money to produce a play, and the investors would like to be assured that the already risky business of investing in plays is not made more hazardous by producing a play that infringes on someone else's rights, not to mention the fact that the author is, in reality, the one person who ought to know whether the material is stolen or whether it is original—and he should be willing to guarantee such facts.[3] The paragraph will also provide that the producer will similarly indemnify the author with respect to any material that the producer, director, stage manager, etc., puts into the play, for which the author suffers damages.

Although the author warrants that the play is original and owned by him or her, this warranty does not extend to the title of the play, since—as previously mentioned—a title cannot be copyrighted. Because the use of a title similar to one that has established a secondary meaning can be considered unfair competition, a producer may suggest that the author change the title to avoid trouble. If the author refuses, the producer will want to add a clause to the above provisions whereby the author warrants that the title will not infringe on anyone's rights.

Author's Grant of Rights

The producer purchases from the author or owner the right to produce the play within a specified period of time in a specified place. This is, in fact, the option, and if he or she does so produce, the rest of the agreement becomes effective. If the producer does not present the play within the option period, the agreement terminates and all rights revert to the author.

The amount the producer pays for the option will vary greatly, depending on numerous factors—including, among other things, the fame of the author and the amount of competition to produce the play. It is not unusual for a six-month option for an Off-Broadway production to cost $400, and the agreement may contain a provision for an automatic extension for an additional six months upon payment of $400 more, prior to the expiration of the first six-month term. It is possible for the option to cost up to $1,000 for six months. No matter what the option costs, the payments are most usually considered as advances against the royalty payments due to the author once the play opens.

Producers should try to negotiate the option terms so that they pay a smaller amount for the initial six-month period and a larger amount for the six-month extension. After the first six months, the producer should be in a better position to know if he will get the play financed and the cast he wants. If the show is close to coming together, the larger second payment can be money well spent and, in most cases, will be an advance against the royalties due the author when the show opens.[4] If, however, the producer finds that the show cannot be produced, his exposure will be limited to the smaller initial option payment.

A producer will always try to keep the option payment as small as possible, because if the play does not open, the option money belongs to the author and need not be returned to the producer. The option payment purchases the exclusive right to produce the work for a given period of time, during which time the author cannot sell the rights to another producer.

The producer will acquire the rights to produce the play in a definite location—i.e., New York City (on, or off, Broadway, or in a middle theatre[5]), a specific theatre, such as the Kennedy Center in Washington, D.C., or a specific kind of theatre (such as a stock or resident theatre.) The author will want this specified in order to know what kind of production it will be. Since the author is also under certain circumstances and conditions granting additional and subsidiary rights, he or she will want to make certain that the play will be presented in a manner that will create a future market. In order to help get a good production, the author may also grant the producer the right to present the play as a tour prior to its presentation at the designated location.

Bear in mind that the author may grant more than one extension and that the extensions may be more or less than six months. An original one-year option with a six-month extension is probably most common for New York productions, whether on, or off, Broadway. An author will rarely grant a producer an option and extensions that will add up to more than two years. If the producer cannot get the play on in two years, he or she probably cannot get it on at all, so the author will want to give it to another producer who can.

Noncompetition Clause

Although paragraph two in this clause states that the producer is acquiring the sole and exclusive rights to present the play in a certain location or a specific theatre or kind of theatre, it does not specify whether the author can grant the production rights in the play to another producer in another location. Paragraph three further provides that the rights granted to the producer are the sole and exclusive rights to produce the play throughout the United States and Canada.

The author usually agrees that he or she will not grant anyone the rights to do a movie version of the play that would be released either during the option period, the run of the play, or any period in which the producer may have any rights to produce the play in the United States, Canada, or the British Isles. A movie released during these periods would possibly directly compete with the play and could cause the play to lose business.[6] This clause protects the producer from such competition; however, it will permit the author to dispose of the movie rights provided the producer grants prior written approval, which will not be unreasonably withheld.[7]

The author may agree to not grant anyone the rights to perform the play in any media (except movies) in the United States, Canada, or the British Isles during the period the producer retains any rights or options to produce the play anywhere in the United States or the British Isles.[8]

Payments to the Author

In addition to the option payments received by the author, the producer also agrees to pay the author a percentage of the gross weekly box office receipts received from the sale of tickets. As mentioned earlier, the option payments are usually advances against these royalties and are therefore deducted from the first royalties earned by the author.[9]

The royalty to the author is usually a minimum of 5 percent of the gross weekly box office receipts, although this figure can and does vary. Some regional theatres have paid as little as 4 percent and some even get by with a flat fee of $100 or $125 per performance.

If the play is by a famous author, or if it is a play that more than one producer wants to option, the royalty may go above 6 percent of the gross weekly box office receipts but usually not over 10 percent. The royalties for a First-Class Production are set forth in Chapter 4, in the discussion of the Approved Production Contract (APC).

If the producer is presenting a musical, a 6 percent royalty is not unusual. It is usually divided 2 percent to the bookwriter, 2 percent to the lyricist, and 2 percent to the composer. Of course, if one of the collaborators is more famous than the other, or if his or her contribution is greater, that person may receive more than half of the gross weekly box office receipts.

The difficulty in raising money for theatrical productions has resulted in all kinds of "royalty pool formulas." The most common royalty structure at the present time will always have some element of a royalty pool formula, so that the investors may recoup their investment before the royalty participants make a killing. See the more detailed discussion of royalty pool formulas in Chapter 4.

The simplest, easiest, and most practical formula for an Off-Broadway or a middle theatre production is a waiver of half of the royalties by all royalty recipients until recoupment or 150 percent recoupment of the total production costs of the play, and adding an additional ½ percent, or 1 percent, of the gross weekly box office receipts to what the royalty would otherwise be, after recoupment.

For example, if the royalty is 5 percent of the gross, gross going to 6 percent after recoupment, under the royalty pool formula, it would be 2½ percent of the gross until recoupment and 7 percent thereafter. A musical might be 6 percent of the gross going to 7 percent after recoupment, and under the formula, it would be 3 percent of the gross going to 7½ percent after recoupment.

If you are a producer, don't let the author or the author's agent convince you to defer the royalty until recoupment. Waiver is necessary. A deferral doesn't help you with the major problem of getting investors.

It goes without saying that the same option agreement granting the producer the production rights should have an affirmative statement that the producer does hereby waive half of his or her producer's fee, until recoupment. This means that the fee, which is usually 2 percent of the gross, is 1 percent until recoupment and could go to 2½ percent after recoupment.

Another compromise is for the producer to give the author some percentage of the producer's profits. Since profits are relatively rare in producing plays, an author will usually opt for more concrete remuneration.[10]

If the producer[11] is presenting a musical adaptation of a copyrighted basic work, in addition to paying a percentage of gross box office receipts to the authors of the adaptation, he will most usually have to pay the owner of the basic work 1, 1½, or 2 percent of the gross weekly box office receipts. The payment for the right to adapt a basic work will include an option payment, which will usually range between $1,000 and $10,000 for two one-year options (and can be more or less). In the contract for the acquisition of the adaptation rights, the owner of such basic work will, in return for this sum, grant the producer (or whomever acquires the rights) a fixed period of time in which to complete the adaptation (usually one year) and an additional fixed period of time in which to produce the play (again, usually one year). The up-front option payment (or some part thereof) is generally considered as an advance against the 1, 1½, or 2 percent royalty earned by the owner when the play opens.

In addition, the owner of the basic work will want, and will be entitled to, an interest in the play's subsidiary rights. Usually, the owner of the basic work will receive that proportionate part of the author's share of receipts received from all subsidiary uses of the play[12] that his royalty bears to the total aggregate royalties payable to all of the creators of the new work, the adaptors (bookwriter, composer, lyricist), including in this total the payment to the owner of the basic work. The owner of the basic work should want a limit placed on the aggregate royalties for the purpose of this computation. The limit may be 10 or 12 or 13 percent so that the producer is not able to dilute the interest of the owner of the basic work. The adaptors may be more than the bookwriter, composer, and lyricist. For example, the producer might hire a talented director and choreographer whose work is so unique that their contributions qualify them as creators.[13] The director and choreographer would, as part of their contract with the producer, receive a percentage of the gross as an "author's" royalty, and would want to share in the subsidiary income as well. As the total aggregate royalty to the creative personnel increases, the percentage of subsidiary rights income payable to the owner of the basic work decreases. Therefore, the limit of 10 or 12 or 13 percent will at least guarantee a limit on the dilution of the share of the owner of the basic work.

For example, the proportionate share of subsidiary rights income of the owner of the basic work would be computed as follows: If the owner of the basic work were paid a royalty of 1 percent and all the creative personnel (bookwriter, composer, and lyricist) jointly receive 6 percent, then the owner of the basic work would share in receipts from subsidiary income by receiving one-seventh of the share of such receipts, since 7 percent is the total aggregate royalties. If there is a 10 percent limitation written into the contract and the owner of the basic work receives a royalty of 1 percent, then the owner cannot receive less than one-tenth of such subsidiary receipts even if the total aggregate royalties payable to the adaptors and owner of the basic work exceeds 10 percent of the gross weekly box office receipts.

The term "gross weekly box office receipts" has been frequently referred to. The contract defines it as all receipts at the box office from the sale of tickets, less: theatre party commissions, discount and cut-rate sales, all admission taxes presently or to be levied, Ticketron charges or the cost of any other automated ticket distributor, those sums equivalent to the former 5 percent New York amusement tax (the net proceeds of which are now set aside in pension and welfare funds of the theatrical unions and ultimately paid to said funds), any subscription fees, and actors' fund benefits.

The contract provides that the royalties for each week must be paid to the author usually by the Wednesday following that week's performances. The producer must enclose with the payment a signed copy of the box office statement. The author has the right to examine the books of the producer at any time during regular business hours upon giving the producer reasonable notice. To avoid unnecessary harassment, the producer will attempt to limit such inspections to not more than semi-annually.

It should be noted that the contract provides a waiver clause that is intended to assist the play to stay alive at critical times. In an effort to help keep the show alive, the author may agree to waive his or her royalty, but will want to waive only so much of it, if paid, as would cause the play to operate at a loss. An author may agree with such a waiver only if the producer agrees to waive the producer's fee, and all other royalty recipients, similarly, waive.[14]

Producer's Subsidiary Rights

As previously mentioned, the producer is acquiring only the rights to present the play with live actors on the stage. The producer's production will make a contribution to the value of the play for use in other media if it runs for a certain length of time.

In consideration of the contribution the producer makes to the play, the author agrees to share with the producer a percentage of the net receipts received by the author from the future exploitation of his work in other media.

A Broadway production probably contributes most to the value of a play in other media.[15]

The receipts from subsidiary rights in which the producer shares[16] are usually from the following sources: (a) worldwide—motion picture rights; (b) the continental United States and Canada—any of the following rights: radio and television; touring, stock, Broadway, Off-Broadway, amateur, and foreign-language performances; condensed tabloid and concert-tour versions; commercial uses; original cast album, tapes, cassettes, records, and video cassettes.

Although the producer shares in the receipts from all the above uses, he does not control the disposition of the rights. The author is the owner and controls the rights. The producer is a third party beneficiary and shares in what the author receives.

In the case of the original cast album for a musical production, the producer as well as the bookwriter, composer, and lyricist will negotiate and enter into the agreement. The fact that the producer is part of this agreement is not because of an interest in subsidiary rights, but rather because the original cast album will be made using the original cast— i.e., members of the show who are employed and furnished by the producer.

Even though authors control the future uses of their property, they must deal in good faith in disposing of those rights. Authors may not make a deal sacrificing any of the properties they have written, and in which the producer shares, so that they might make a better deal on another property in which no one shares. For instance, say an author has a play that a movie producer is anxious to make into a film and for which the author has been offered $100,000. In the event a producer produced the play and acquired an interest in subsidiary rights, the author should not be able to offer the movie producer the right to do the film for $75,000 on the condition that the movie producer will at the same time purchase another of the author's works for $150,000.

In other than a first-class production, later discussed, the number of performances the play has to run in order for the producer to share in the proceeds from the subsidiary rights may be computed in the following manner: 10 percent if the play has run for at least twenty-one consecutive paid performances; 20 percent for forty-two performances; 30 percent for fifty-six; and 40 percent for sixty-five consecutive paid performances. It is not usual for a producer to receive more than 40 percent.[17] The percentage is calculated on the author's net receipts earned from the disposition of subsidiary rights (less the agent's commission) if the contract for the disposition of such rights is entered into during a fixed period (usually seven, ten, or twelve years after the opening or closing of the original production), even though the receipts may be received after the fixed period expires. All the performances must be consecutive (without a lapse between performances) and must be for paid admission attended by the public.

Preview performances are paid public performances, but since they are prior to the critics reviews, their contribution to the value of the property may be less. If the play officially opens, up to seven paid preview performances may be counted by the producer in making this computation.

As noted above, the producer's participation in the author's receipts from subsidiaries is for a limited number of years after the last performance of the play in New York City (or more usually after the first performance). The producer will continue to participate in all receipts earned from any disposition of subsidiary rights for as long as those receipts are earned by the author, provided that the contract for the disposition was entered into within the agreed-upon number of years after the last or first performance. It is usually between seven and eighteen years, the extremes being three years or for the duration of the copyright in the play (fifty-six years under the old copyright law or the life of the author plus fifty years as under the new law). As a practical matter, the period is usually set on either side of ten years. An example of this is as follows: the option agreement states that the producer would share in the author's net receipts from any subsidiaries disposed of before the expiration of ten years from the date of the last public performance in New York City. The play opened on January 1, 1970, and ran consecutively until June 15, 1976. The author sold movie rights in July 1980 for $100,000. The producer would receive (earning 40 percent) $40,000. Although more than ten years transpired from the time the play opened, if the period is measured from the close of the play, then only four years and one month would have elapsed. If the author did not receive another payment from the movie company until July 1990, the producer would still get 40 percent of the new payment. Although the payment in 1990 comes more than ten years after 1976, the movie contract was entered into within the ten-year limitation period. It is for this reason that the contract contains the parenthetical phrase that the producer shall receive the percentage of net receipts *(regardless of when paid)*. The date of the contract, not the payment, is usually the controlling factor. The receipts of any contract entered into after the specified period (i.e., June 16, 1986, in the above example) will not have to be shared with the producer; however, all receipts from contracts entered into prior to that date continue to be shared.

The negotiations for subsidiary rights can be very important. If the play is a flop, the fight over subsidiaries may have been in vain.[18] However, since few people—including producers—can predict with accuracy which play will be successful and which will flop, every producer enters into negotiations with the thought in mind that the play will be a hit. The producer, the author, and, most importantly, the

investors know the value of subsidiary rights. If a producer does not get
a fair deal on the subsidiaries from the author, the author could have
a hollow victory. Investors may not invest, and without their money
neither the producer nor the author have a show.[19]

The previous breakdown of percentages per number of performances (10 percent for twenty-one, 20 percent for forty-two, 30 percent
for fifty-six, and 40 percent for sixty-five) is one of the common arrangements for an Off-Broadway production.[20] The APC, which is the contract approved by the Dramatists Guild, Inc. and the League of American Theatres and Producers, provides for the sharing of subsidiary
rights income in a more complicated manner. This is set forth in detail
in Chapter 4.

Elsewhere the numbers may vary. A New York City production can
negotiate a better subsidiary rights deal than a Kansas production. The
outcome of any such negotiations depends on various factors, probably
the most important of which includes the theatre, its location and size,
the prestige of the producer or producing company, the total cost of the
production, the eagerness of the producer, the stature of the author, the
availability of financing, and the sophistication of the investors.

An author will usually not object to granting an interest in the
subsidiary rights if it is for an important enough production. If an
Off-Broadway show is having a pre-New York tour, it may make sense
to count part of the pre-New York performances toward subsidiaries.
The parties, for example, may agree to count up to twenty-five out-of-
town performances. Thus, if sixty-five performances in New York City
would result in the producer getting a 40 percent interest, if the play
ran twenty-five or more performances in Boston or elsewhere, only
forty additional New York performances would be needed to get that
40 percent.

In selecting a property to produce, the producer may find that the
play was previously produced and that another producer has acquired
and continues to retain an interest in the author's subsidiaries. Since the
author does not want to give away another 40 percent of his or her
interest, and since the new producer will have difficulty in financing the
play without giving the investors an interest in subsidiary rights, a
compromise must be reached.

One method of resolving this problem is to convince the producer
of the first production to assign some part of his or her subsidiary rights
interest to the new producer if the new production runs for a required
number of performances. The original producer may not be unwilling

to do this in view of the fact that a successful new production could increase the value of the subsidiary rights for all concerned. In such a situation, the author may also part with some of his or her subsidiary interest as well in order to assist the new production. If the original producer—who had earned a 40 percent interest in subsidiaries—gives up one-half (a 20 percent interest), and the author—who has the other 60 percent—gives up a 10 percent interest, the new producer would have a potential 30 percent interest in the author's receipts from the disposition of subsidiary rights. The original producer would retain 20 percent and the author would still have 50 percent. See Chapter 4 for a discussion of how the APC deals with this problem.

House-Seat Allocation

One of the areas of an option agreement which generates less controversy is that of house-seat allocation (house seats are usually the best and most expensive seats in the theatre). The producer will usually offer the author a pair of house seats for all performances and ten pair for the night of the official opening. The reason for the absence of controversy is that house seats are not free, but they are valuable and everyone gets some. The tickets are held at the box office only until 6:00 P.M. of the day before each evening performance and 12:00 noon of the day before each matinee. If the author or his designee do not pay for and pick up the tickets by those times, the tickets become available for sale to the general public.

The attorney general of the state of New York has set forth rules and regulations concerning the use of house seats, and the author must agree to keep accurate records in accordance with the law.

Billing Credits

One area of sharp negotiations is that of billing credits. Everyone agrees that the author should receive credit, but where it should appear and how big it should be is open to negotiation. The author usually gets credit in all advertisements (except ABC and teaser ads),[21] programs, billboards, and houseboards wherever the name of the play appears. Sometimes the author will want to place a condition on the provision that he need not receive credit in ABC, shallow double, and teaser ads;

that condition being that his name need not appear provided no other name appears.

Depending on the bargaining power of the author, the size of his or her name will vary anywhere from one-third to 100 percent of the size of the title. If the author is famous, the producer will not raise much of an argument on the size of the author's name, since this will be what sells tickets.

Authors will usually want their names to be the biggest with only the title of the play being bigger. The producer may want to hire a director or star of prominence who, as part of their contract, will insist that their names be the largest. An author will often have to accept a clause that provides that no names will be larger than the author's except those of a star or director of prominence.[22]

In negotiating billing, in addition to the size of type used for the author's name, the style, boldness of type, and coloring of the type is established in relation to other names. Placement is also important. Authors usually insist that their names appear on a separate line beneath the title of the play.

When there are multiple authors, as in a musical, the names are usually listed as bookwriter, composer, and lyricist, in that order.

Producer's Additional Rights

If the play is produced in accordance with the terms of the option agreement, and if certain conditions are met—such as the play running twenty-one performances, or opening before a paid audience, or running for any number of performances that may be arbitrarily decided upon—then certain additional rights accrue to the producer.

The rights to tour the play, to produce the play in England, and to produce subsequent productions in different parts of the country are usually options that the producer acquires. These options must be exercised within a certain period of time after the opening or closing of the original production. It is not unusual that the rights must be exercised within six months after the first production of the play before a paying audience. In each instance, to exercise the option the producer must give notice and send an option payment to the author.

The agreement will usually provide that the option to produce the play for a tour of the United States, or in England, or for other productions must be exercised by sending the author notice and a payment of

$500 or $750 or $1,000 for each of the rights to open the play in any of these areas, within one year after the giving of the notice. Since it requires more time to set up a tour, it is wise to provide that the tour must be commenced within fifteen or eighteen months instead of a year. For each city in which the producer desires to produce the play other than a tour, he must make a payment of $500 or $750. The agreement will provide that the royalties in each instance will be in an amount the same as the royalties provided in the original option agreement.

The agreement will probably provide that the producer may move the play to Broadway at any time during the run of the play, or within six months (or one year) after the close of the original production of the play, by entering into an Approved Production Contract on the terms and conditions set forth.

Approval of Directors, Actors, and Designers

It is usual for the author to have approval of the director, actors, and designers, or some of them. The producer's representative will try to qualify the approvals to provide that they will not be unreasonably withheld by the author. Without such a provision, the author may be as arbitrary as he or she wishes with respect to the approvals. The provision that approvals will not be unreasonably withheld creates a litigatable or arbitratable issue that can be resolved by someone other than the author. A producer could then go ahead and hire the director even without approval, and at a later date, a court or arbitrator would determine whether the author was being unreasonable in withholding the approval. Without such a provision, the author could arbitrarily withhold approval of anyone for whatever whimsical reason he or she wanted.

Duration of Right to Produce the Play

The agreement will provide that the producer can produce the play during the continuous run of the play. The continuous run will usually be defined to mean that the run continues so long as there are no more than two, three, or four weeks between paid performances before a live audience. There are, of course, other ways of defining continuous run, but one should make certain that the agreement is clear as to the continuing right of the producer to produce the play and when those rights cease and terminate.

Right to Assign Option

The producer must have the right to assign the option, since, in all probability, he is going to assign the production rights to a limited partnership, which will be formed to produce the play. The author, on the other hand, has consented to this producer producing the play and will not want him to make a complete assignment to someone else and walk away from the production. The relationship between an author and producer is a very personal relationship, and although in many instances the successful author and the producer are not madly in love, it does make life simpler if they have mutual respect for each other and a working relationship. It is not unusual to provide that the producer may assign the contract to a partnership or a corporation in which he or she is one of the principals, without any other approvals, but if the producer wishes to make an assignment to an entity in which he is not one of the principals, then the author must approve of such assignment.

Arbitration Clause

If there is a dispute with respect to the contract, either party may ask a court of law to resolve the dispute. There is a better way of resolving disputes, however, that I feel is particularly applicable to theatre differences. It may be provided in the agreement that the dispute will be resolved by arbitration. The advantage of arbitration is that (1) the parties can select an arbitrator who is knowledgeable in theatre; and (2) most often a quicker decision may be reached. It is usual to provide that the arbitration will be in accordance with the rules and regulations of the American Arbitration Association.[23]

Agreements of this kind will sometimes provide that disputes may be settled by a party specifically designated by the parties to the agreement. For example, if there is a dispute of an artistic nature, the author and producer may consent that the director will cast the deciding vote. It there is a business dispute, the parties may agree that the dispute may be settled by either the attorney for the production or the general manager for the show.

Script Changes

Almost always the option agreement will provide that there will be no script changes without the approval of the author. Although rarely granted, it is usual to ask the author not to withhold such approval unreasonably with respect to the script. It is most usual to give the author sole and complete control even to the extent that he or she may be unreasonable.[24]

Legal Clauses

There are a few boiler-plate legal clauses usually added to the end of an option to produce a play. It may be provided that the agreement will be interpreted under the laws of the state of New York (or any other state where the agreement is being drafted), that this agreement is the entire agreement between the parties and anything previously said or written is invalid, that the parties are not to be considered joint venturers or partners, and such similar provisions.

CHAPTER 3

Movie Deals

INVESTORS EXPECT TO SHARE IN SALE OF MOVIE RIGHTS

MOTION PICTURE RIGHTS deserve special attention. As was pointed out, usually the investors in a show share in the proceeds from the sale of subsidiary rights if the play runs for a certain length of time. One of the most lucrative possible sources of income for a production, its investors, and its adaptors is a share in the sale of the motion picture rights. A distinction must be made between (1) the rights to deal with the motion picture rights in the play; and (2) the rights to base the play in whole or in part on the movie.

If a play is adapted from a work that has already been made into a movie, then the movie rights have already been disposed of and, unless the rights have reverted to the owner of the basic work (which is not likely in most instances), some kind of deal ought to be made with the company owning the movie rights.

FILM COMPANY MAY ALSO OWN BASIC RIGHTS IN WORK

A play and a movie may be based on the same basic work (a novel, a record, etc.), or a producer or adaptor may want to base a play on a movie (which, in this instance, would make the movie the basic work). The movie may have been an original, or it may have been based on another basic work that the motion picture company acquired all rights to, including the dramatic rights. In either event, appropriate arrangements should be made. The only basic difference in these two instances is that if the play is to be based on a movie, then the motion picture company will expect a larger payment. The reason for this is that in addition to permitting the adaptor to deal with the play to make a movie sale based on the play, they are also granting the rights to do the play based on the movie. If the movie is the basic work, the motion picture company is in a much stronger bargaining position than if it only owned the film rights and the film was based on another work. Why would anyone want the rights to base a movie on a play based on a movie? The answer is simple. The play, although based on the movie, might become a totally different property. If the play is a success, there is surely a market—especially if the play is a musical adaptation of a dramatic work.

One should always be prepared to bargain for the motion picture rights, so that if the play is a success it may then be made into another movie.

DRAMATIC RIGHTS

If the motion picture company owns the dramatic rights, that part of the negotiations is the same as negotiating with anyone else for the dramatic rights in a basic work, discussed in detail in Chapter 1.

FILM RIGHTS—OPTION OF FIRST REFUSAL

For the most part, aside from the dramatic rights, one may expect that the company owning the film rights will want an option of first refusal to make a movie based on the play for one-third less than any other bona fide offer. There may also be a fixed amount set forth in the agreement for which they may purchase the movie rights—such as $150,000 plus an amount equal to 2, 5, or 10 percent of the first year's gross box office receipts for the play, but in no event more than another fixed amount, which might be $1 million. These, of course, are hypothetical figures and could vary greatly in either direction.

SHARE OF SALE TO OTHER FILM COMPANY

In addition, if the motion picture company chooses not to make the film, and the rights are sold to someone else, the company will expect one-third of the proceeds of the film sale.

The motion picture company will expect a certain percentage of the box office receipts from the play—an amount such as 1, 1½, 2, or 2½ percent is not unusual. They might also insist upon a payment, at the time that the agreement is entered into, as an advance against the box office receipts, or merely as a fee. This amount may vary between $1,000 and $5,000, but very often is not even demanded, agreed to, or paid.

FILM COMPANY MAY WANT CAST ALBUM AND PUBLISHING RIGHTS

An owner of the motion picture rights may try to get the rights to publish the music and to make the original cast album if the play is a musical. Many of the major film studios have associated companies that do publishing and recording. It is not advisable for a producer or an adaptor to permit them to have these rights unless it is unavoidable. The producer may have to rely on an investment from a record or publishing company in exchange for the rights to the album, and if these rights have been tied up and are not available, he may lose this investment source. It is better to give the motion picture owners an option of first refusal on these rights, so that at the very least they will have to match any other bona fide offers.

Sometimes the motion picture owner will agree to cease distribution of the original movie, and sometimes not. In most instances, they will cooperate in every way, including making copies of the print available for viewing, for if a deal has been made at this point, they will in fact have a vested interest in the outcome of the play.

The negotiations would be similar whether the play will be a musical or a drama, except with a drama there would be no discussion of music publishing. A dramatic cast album is a possibility, but very unlikely, so that it is less a subject of sharp bargaining. The dollar amounts and percentages might vary, but not substantially. But, more important, bear in mind that most adaptations are for musicals rather than for dramas.

CHAPTER 4

First-Class Productions—The Dramatists Guild Contracts

Background

URING THE 1920s, a Dramatists Guild, Inc. ("Guild") contract was introduced that served as the legal basis for almost all the author-producer first-class stage productions in this country, including Broadway productions, until the early 1980s.[1] However, the Guild has had a difficult time insisting on the use of its author-producer contract because of the continuing question of whether playwrights, as independent contractors, are in violation of the Sherman Antitrust Act by virtue of their joining together in the Guild.[2]

The contract referred to as the Dramatists Guild, Inc., Minimum Basic Production Contract (MBPC) was used (1) to option original plays, and (2) to engage adaptors (bookwriter, composer, and lyricist) when a producer had acquired rights to do an adaptation of a basic work. For many years, there was a Guild agreement form that producers were required to sign, which contained the same contract provisions the producers also entered into with individual authors after 1961.

When the League of New York Theatres and Producers (the "League")—now the League of American Theatres and Producers—negotiated and signed an MBPC contract, it bound *all* members of the League to use that contract. After the Guild's troubles with the Sherman Antitrust Act, the League no longer signed the MBPC contract binding all its members. Despite this, individual producers usually signed the contract, not because they were bound to do so by the contract between the League and the Guild, but rather because of the bargaining power of the individual Guild members.

Periodically, the League negotiated changes in the contract with the Guild, even though its members had no League-imposed obligation to use the Guild contract. However, the contract was almost always used, because Guild members who were in demand had enough bargaining power to (1) insist on its use and (2) to force less-powerful members to comply.

The contract basically benefited playwrights, who received pittances as option payments but would get paid during the run of the play by a percentage of the gross weekly box office receipts. Under the contract, the straight-play minimum was 10 percent[3] of the gross weekly box office receipts, and the musical minimum was 6 percent. A straight play breaking even at $200,000 each week, would, if it grossed $200,000 one week, pay the playwright $20,000 that week. Investors would get nothing. Investors only shared in the net profits after all expenses were paid. They would then recoup their investment. With the heavy royalty payments, it was difficult to get to the point where there were net profits to pay to investors.

During the 1970s and 1980s, investors in theatre began examining the wisdom of investing in plays where the playwright could make money while the play itself was just breaking even, and before the investors saw a return on their investment.

THE ROYALTY POOL FORMULAS

The new approach began with the musical and spread quickly. The changes were known as "royalty pool formulas" and represented an attempt to use the initial weekly profits from a play in part to pay back investors.

The royalty pool formula reduced all gross weekly box office royalties (the author's, the director's, the choreographer's, the designer's, and the producer's fee) by one half (or some other agreed-upon figure) until the production costs were recouped. It used part of the weekly net profits to pay back the investors. The formulas varied; for example, in one formula, the royalty payments were increased after 100 percent recoupment, and again after 150 percent recoupment.

After the royalty pool formulas were embraced, the Guild was forced to give investors a break or find itself losing member support. (The League had commenced a lawsuit charging the Guild with violations of the Sherman Antitrust Act, and the Guild had counterclaimed with claims of violations of the same act by the League.)

THE *"GRIND"* FORMULA AND THE NEW GUILD CONTRACT

A new Guild contract was negotiated in earnest during 1984, with the goal of announcing the new contract effective as of January 1, 1985. However, an unforeseen event occurred. A producer not happy with the Guild recommendations was producing a musical play called *Grind.* He put together a formula that differed from what the Guild and the League had agreed upon. When four of the most important creative people in the business signed the *"Grind"* formula, the Guild, which had not been consulted, suspended the four members.

The Guild contract was not ready by January 1, 1985. In fact, it was not until March 1, 1985, that the contract was ready for acceptance, and even then, no copies were available for examination. Late in March 1985, the League was sponsoring seminars on the new contract, which had been labeled the Approved Production Contract (APC). Still, no copies of the contract were ready for distribution. There was a pervading question as to how viable the new APC would actually be, and the doubt lingered that it would be as universally used as the MBPC was.

The APC finally arrived in May 1985. The new contract still left much to be desired. For example, the first six pages of the APC for plays, not for musical plays, contains thirty-three cross-references. And the cross-references run into further cross-references: Section 2.04 refers to Section 9.01, which then refers to Section 11.01; Section 5.08 refers to Article XX, which refers to Section 7.01, Section 1.02 (c) (which refers to Section 2.05) and Section 8.01 (a) and (b). Section 4.02 refers to Article V, which refers to Article XX and Section 9.02. Many sections have cross-references within each section.

It seems clear that the dominant position the Guild once had with Broadway productions no longer exists. Important Guild members may realize that the other formulas are as good or better than the APC and will be willing to make exceptions to the Guild contract limitations. Even if variations of the APC are not used, when the APC is used, it represents a great improvement over the MBPC and will undoubtedly improve relations with investors. Regardless of how much the APC is used, it already has made a contribution by serving to settle the anti-trust lawsuit between the Guild and the League, and from the producer's point of view is a good contract. The net effect is sure to be an erosion of the strict control that the Guild has been able to impose on first-class-production contract terms in the past.

The Approved Production Contract is reproduced in its entirety in Appendices C and D of this book. The previously used contract, the MBPC, contained the minimum terms acceptable to the Guild, except that the Guild would consent to certain changes when requested by the producer's attorney or representative. Both sides acknowledge the APC to be a contract setting forth fixed terms—that is, terms that are minimum and maximum. The review of the contracts by the Guild and the League is intended to foster this concept and to permit any changes consistent with the existing APC terms. The thought is that any additions to the contract should clarify unclear terms or add any terms inadvertently omitted.

Since the Approved Production Contract came into effect, there have been a surprising number of clauses proposed to be included in Clause XXII intended to clarify or add to the contract without changing the nature of it as both a minimum and maximum contract.

Clauses dealing with "publishing rights," the "original cast recording," "warranties and representations," the amount of the "per-diem," "billing credits," and the like are some of the items that have received special treatment.

COMMENTARY ON THE DRAMATISTS GUILD, INC., APPROVED PRODUCTION CONTRACT FOR PLAYS

Initial Grant of Rights

Article I is similar to that of the previous contract in dealing with the granting of rights to produce the play and the services the author will furnish. As with the former agreement, what is most important about this article is that it gives the producer an "option": there is not a contractual obligation to produce the play.

Option Periods and Payments

The option periods as set forth in Article II are essentially the same as in the Minimum Basic Production Contract; however, option payments are larger. Section 2.04 is a new provision in that it extends the option during the presentation of a try-out, as a second-class performance, or as a developmental production of the play. The extension is for the number of days on which the play was presented plus an additional sixty days, up to a maximum of eight weeks. The acknowledgment of the Guild that it is sometimes in the author's interest to make concessions so that the play may have the advantage of a production to develop the play, without unreasonable expense, is a step in the right direction. This kind of concession is an awakening to the reality that the producer and the author have some common interests, and that their relationship, even on a monetary issue, ought not always be adversarial. Both the author and the producer have to fashion an agreement that will attract investor capital, or neither of them will have a play to produce.

Advance Payments

Deductions from Advance and Royalty Payments

Article III introduces a new concept, the "advance payment," as something separate from the payment for the options. Up until the use of the Approved Production Contract, the author was paid an option fee, that was usually a nonreturnable advance against the royalties, although on rare occasions part of the advance was considered a fee and not an advance against the royalties.

Under the APC, as set forth in Article VI, option payments for the first and second options are fees, not advances, against royalty earnings or against the advance payment. However, the payment for the third option period, if any, is to be deducted from the amount of the advance payment. All the advance payment provided for in Article III is a payment against the royalties, that is, the amount of such advance payment, reduces the first royalties earned by that amount.

The amount of the advance payment is related to the amount of the capitalization of the play and is fixed as 3 percent of the capitalization, less 3 percent of that sum. The maximum advance is fixed at $35,000.

For example, if a play is capitalized for $600,000, the advance would be 3 percent of $600,000, or $18,000, less 3 percent of $18,000, or $540.00, which would result in an advance in the amount of $17,460.

Royalties

Article IV sets forth the amount of the royalties, but states that some of the royalties are subject to the adjustments set forth in Article V. Section 4.01 defines the different kinds of performances, such as "out-of-town performances" and "preview performances." The significant contribution is in the definition and determination of the royalties for a fixed-fee performance.

Prior to the APC, the fixed-fee performances were dealt with in what was known as "Paragraph TENTH" of the MBPC, which was not part of the printed form and was the subject of negotiation for each contract.

With the APC, a fixed fee is paid to a producer when he sells the entire production for presentation by a local promoter, or local sponsor, who pays a flat fee for the entire show, which amount includes payment for the production rights. Since the payment received by the producer is not measured directly by box office receipts, there must be some other measure of the payment to the author for the production rights. Section 4.02 (d) fixes the amount of these payments.

The fixed-fee payments for a first-class performance are different than for other than a first-class performance. This is a somewhat complicated way to fix the fees payable to the author; but at least this is an attempt, and it will avoid the necessity of negotiating this item each time a contract is made.

Royalty Adjustments

Article V is the Guild's answer to the recognized need for a Royalty Pool Formula. It is an attempt to give the investors an opportunity to recoup their investment during a period when the author accepts a reduced royalty. The author's royalty increases after recoupment.

The adjustment for out-of-town, preview, and regular performances (with the exception of the first three consecutive seven-day periods following the official press opening of the play in New York City) is covered by Section 5.05. It provides that prior to recoupment of production costs the author will be paid a royalty of $1,000 per week, plus 25 percent of the weekly profits, but in no event more than 5 percent of the gross weekly box office receipts during weeks that the gross weekly box office receipts are not over 110 percent of the "weekly breakeven" as defined in Article V. The royalty provided is $1,000 for each of the first three consecutive periods following the official opening.

After recoupment of the production costs, the same kind of formula is used, but the 25 percent of weekly profits is increased to 35 percent during weeks that the gross weekly box office receipts are not over 120 percent of the weekly breakeven, instead of 110 percent. If the director of the play receives, during any week, an amount less than is provided for in the director's agreement, then the author's 35 percent of the weekly profits will be reduced on a pro-rata basis, but in no event less than 25 percent. Although it is not clear, it is presumed that the reference to "pro-rata basis" means that the author's share will be reduced in the same proportion that the director's share is reduced.

The adjustment for touring performances of the play covered by Section 5.06 is identical with the provisions on adjustments for regular performances (Section 5.05) discussed above.

A new addition is the provision that the royalty is fixed at a flat $1,000 per performance week, during any losing week of regular or touring performances. There is also a new provision in Section 5.09 that makes an adjustment that reduces the royalties payable for four weeks around the Christmas season. These are important provisions, because the play needs all the help that it can get during losing weeks, and traditionally plays suffer economically during the Christmas season. Unlike other businesses, theatre is a very seasonal business, and a play can experience several losing weeks or months, but if it can weather each storm, it may go on to run for a very long time.

General Payment Provisions

The general payment provisions of Article VII are similar to the provisions in the previous contract and merely designate to whom to make the checks and to whom to send them. That an adaptor of a foreign-language play must receive at least one-third of the compensation payable to the author is not new to this contract.

General Production Provisions

Most of the provisions in Article VIII are similar to provisions that were contained in the printed part of the old MBPC, or were added in Paragraph TENTH, which was the paragraph typed in with terms and conditions that were applicable to that particular play. The cast, director, and designers must be mutually agreeable to the producer and the author, and the straight play contract inadvertently includes "conductor, choreographer and/or dance director" when these would seem to be appropriate only in the contract for a musical play.

The significant part of this article appears in Section 8.01 (b) and (c), where it is provided that no one may change a word of the author's script without his or her approval; and, if there are any approved changes, they belong to the author no matter who contributed them. Although the producer may complain to the Guild that the author is arbitrary in not doing rewrites of the play, and the Guild may urge the author to do so, neither the Guild, nor anyone else, can force the author to make any changes unless he or she wishes.

The amount of the per diem paid to the author when he or she is away from home has always been typed in as part of the old Paragraph TENTH. Now this agreement attempts to make a provision that need not be negotiated, but does not really accomplish the purpose and it must now be set forth in Article XXII, which is the equivalent of Paragraph TENTH. If this provision is not added to Article XXII, the reference to "reasonable hotel and travel accommodations" of a class "equal to the greater of the class charged to the Company by Producer or Director" may be a source of disagreement and contention that interferes with the hoped-for smooth progress of the play. Ascertaining the "class" of the producer's accommodations is not always easy, since the producer is in charge of paying for them.

Section 8.06, concerning the author not using the designs without the consent of the owners of the designs, is a provision that the United Scenic Artists has insisted upon and that always appeared in Paragraph TENTH of the MBPC. This provision no doubt resulted from authors engaging licensing agents to license the stock and amateur rights and the licensing agents then wanting to designate the stage setup and the costume designs. A designer's work could then be copied in hundreds of theatres around the country and the designer would have no right to the income from such use. This section was intended to prohibit this practice.

"Billing credit," always a strongly negotiated item, is dealt with in Section 8.10, in an attempt to fix some parameters. One should have no trouble with the language as it is stated. An author usually expects that his or her name will be at least 50 percent of the size of the title, so that the 40-percent provision would, of course, be acceptable to the producers. The significant provision is contained in Section 8.10 (b) concerning the size of the author's billing credit, if the title of the play appears more than once in any one advertisement. This would seem to permit the producer to use a billing box, which has the title in much smaller type, and all credits are based on the size of the type in the billing box. Since it is provided that Section 8.10 may be modified or supplemented by a provision in Article XXII, one should make sure that this provision applies to posters, billboards, and the like; that is, the reference to "advertisement" must include such uses or it must be made clear that in addition to an advertisement, such other usage is permissible.

Use of part of the play for radio and television advertising is not a new idea. The amount of an excerpt from a play that may be used has variously been fixed at five minutes or ten minutes, so seven minutes seems a suitable compromise. There seems little doubt that an author, if approached later, would resist changing this to provide for a longer time, if the producer were willing to spend the money to arrange it or to have arranged for the kind of program that gives such advertising free as part of its programming.

It's nice for the original producer of the play to get credit as such in later productions and in other media, since billing credits are a very important part of the business and add to one's credibility in the business. Bear in mind that the author need only "use all best efforts" to make this happen, and it is not a contractual obligation that it occur.

House seats are still dealt with individually and are treated in the typewritten Article XXII. House seats, of course, are seats that must be purchased by the recipient.[4] The requirements of Section 8.14 were the result of the "ice scandal" investigation,[5] and the provision is intended to prevent a house-seat holder from trading-in tickets for a profit.

Article IX, titled "Additional Production Terms" is an attempt to clarify what up to now has been dealt with in a haphazard manner. In the previous contract, the MBPC, was an option for a "First-Class Production." Although there was sometimes a question as to just exactly what was meant by a "First-Class Production," nevertheless, the contract gave only first-class rights.

Most knowledgeable attorneys in the field would provide for second-class tours, in Paragraph TENTH of the MBPC, but there was not usually a provision that the contract covered all second-class productions. Off-Broadway also was not a part of the contract.

It worked the other way around. The Off-Broadway Contract, if properly prepared, provided that the producer could contract for a first-class production in one of three ways. He could:

1. Enter into an Off-Broadway contract containing an option to enter into a first-class contract, with a reference to the terms of such first-class contract.
2. Enter into an Off-Broadway contract, with the MBPC annexed, to be signed and become effective when the optionee gives notice and makes the payments required.
3. Sign both an Off-Broadway contract and an MBPC at the same time if the producer, at that time, believes that the play could be done in either arena, but is not certain which way to go either for artistic reasons or because he or she is not sure of being able to raise the larger amount of money required for the first-class production.

The new APC gives the producer the option to produce a second-class production, as well as a first-class production. A second-class production is defined as one that is other than stock, amateur and ancillary performances or Off-Broadway performances. It also sets forth the royalty terms for such a production.

Furthermore, if the producer's rights have "vested" (see below), the APC gives the producer the right to produce the play Off-Broadway, in the British Isles, Australia, and New Zealand.

Definition of "Vested"

In Section 11.02, the APC contains a definition of a concept that was employed throughout the MBPC. The term *vested* means that the producer's production has run a certain period of time so that from then on the producer acquires certain potentially valuable rights.

As in the previous contract, if the play runs the length of one of several specified times, then the producer becomes entitled to certain benefits namely:

1. The rights to produce the play in "Additional Territories," as they are defined in the "Agreement"
2. The right to reopen the play
3. The right to participate in subsidiary rights income and to be consulted on the disposition of such rights
4. The right to create, manufacture, and sell commercial use products, and at a later date to share in the income from such uses
5. A preferential bargaining position with respect to the motion picture rights.

There are several alternative ways for becoming vested, and the British Isles, Australia, and New Zealand are treated separately.

Participation in Subsidiary Rights

As in the previous contract the producer may acquire a participation in the subsidiary rights income[6] of the author. The producer will assign this potential income to the producing company that will produce the play. As was stated, first the play must run long enough to "vest." Fortunately, what is a "subsidiary right" is defined.[7]

Unlike the previous contract, which had but one plan set forth, the producer under the APC may elect one of four alternative plans for sharing the subsidiary rights income (in the musical APC, there are only three alternatives). If the producer does not elect one of the plans within the time set forth in Section 11.03 (c), then the author may elect one, and if he doesn't, within the time set forth, then Alternative III becomes applicable (see Appendix D). It is, of course, impossible to know which of the three or four alternatives will be most advantageous to the producer without knowing about the specific play. Obviously, some plays will do better as amateur performances, and others will do better in stock. Each play must be judged on its own particular kind of appeal, and a determination made of what is the best market for that particular play. Some plays will be difficult to present as stock or amateur productions.[8]

As before, the producer shares in the author's income, no matter when received, so long as the contract for subsidiary rights income is entered into within the specified period of time after the last performance of the play, pursuant to the Approved Production Contract.

The attempt to deal with "Revival Performances" is very helpful. Up until now, there has been some confusion concerning what rights the producer would have in the proceeds from a revival. It is also useful that the Approved Production Contract has finally tried to define the various kinds of productions, such as first class, second class, stock, amateur, developmental, out-of-town, and ancillary.

Commercial-Use Products

Unlike the previous contract, which simply gave a producer participating in subsidiary rights income a share of the income from commercial uses, the APC actually grants the producer the rights to exploit the commercial uses. After the producer's right to do so expires, the author controls these rights. When the producer has the rights, he or she shares with the author, and when the author controls these rights, he or she shares with the producer on any contract entered into before the expiration of forty years after the last performance of the play, wherever the producer has vested (British Isles, Australia, New Zealand, U.S.). In each instance, the percentage sharing is the same, 10 percent of the gross retail sales to the noncontrolling party and 50 percent of net receipts from such sales, as net receipts is defined in the APC contract.

It has always been important to a producer of a first-class stage production that he not be faced with competition from other stage productions and from other media. Section 11.07 attempts to more clearly define the limits of other uses of the play and expands the concept to include productions in other media.

Article XIII is a carry-over from the previous contract as is Exhibit B, the "Instructions to the Negotiator." The purpose of this article and Exhibit B, is to give some advantage to a film company that may finance the first-class production, but at the same time to make sure that there is no double-dealing.

An author bent on taking advantage of the producer could make a separate film deal in which he or she sells the film rights for something less than they are worth in exchange for the author's granting the motion picture company the rights to another play (in which he or she does not have to share the proceeds with a producer) for something more than the author would otherwise receive.

There is also the constant threat that a film producer will acquire the film rights from the author at a reduced figure, in exchange for the promise that his or her play will be produced. Bear in mind, that the APC, like the MBPC, is an option and not a contractual obligation to produce the play. In fact, there are an astonishing number of plays optioned that never get produced. So the promise of a production is an attractive lure to convince the author to sell the film rights for something less than they would otherwise be worth.

For these reasons, the APC provides for a film negotiator who is designated by the Guild and whose job it is to prevent such abuses and to make certain that any sale is on fair and reasonable terms for all parties.

Another important difference in the contracts is that the APC addresses audio-visual productions (Article XIII) rather than just motion-picture rights. Since the MBPC was first established, there has been technological development necessitating some of the changes provided in the APC. Television was invented, and then came audio cassettes and video cassettes, but if the producer's attorney was not knowledgeable in this area, he missed them. The new contract fills this gap.

The new provision that a producer of a revival, under certain circumstances, will share in the author's proceeds from a film sale is contained in Section 13.05. The new provision clarifies the terms if the revival is a first-class production and also now refers to a second-class revival. The author having given a 40 percent share of the proceeds from the motion-picture rights to the original producer, would not feel good about giving a similar percentage to the producer from the motion-picture-rights income of the author; there would be little likelihood of financing the revival.

Unfortunately, although Section 13.05 deals with this problem, it does not consider the sharing if the revival is Off-Broadway or in a "middle theatre." See discussion in Chapter 2 about a solution under such circumstances.

The APC provision for a theatrical conciliation council, provided for in Article XV, is something new. The council is to be composed of five author members and five producer members. The purpose of the council is to consider questions and problems that may arise from time to time during the term of the contract. If there is not a majority vote on any issue, the council selects one disinterested third party to resolve the dispute. If a majority cannot agree on the impartial party, the matter may be submitted to arbitration.[9]

What is most interesting is the reference in Section 15.01 to those specific sections that, in addition to the other contract sections, would be subject to consideration of the council. The specific sections singled out for mention are those covering (1) fixed-fee performance payments; (2) review of weekly breakeven and recoupment calculation; (3) author's billing; and (4) producer's lease, or license, of rights to produce the play in Australia or New Zealand.

Although the Guild still wants to certify the contract, there is, in addition to the certification procedure outlined, some very encouraging language as to the prospects of changing the contract terms under the proper circumstances.

It is a good thing that the Guild acknowledges that the terms of the APC are not etched in stone. They will consider reasonable modifications if necessary to counterbalance or neutralize special circumstances because of the nature of the play or its contemplated production, which circumstances could be expected to affect materially the producer's ability to "(a) finance the play, or (b) return to investors their capital contributions within a period then prevailing for other productions of similar size and type, or (c) obtain all the benefits to be accorded to the producer as contemplated by the APC." This is progress, the acknowledgment that the investors are an important part of the producing entity and that adjustments must be made to accommodate them.

There is also a method set forth in Section 16.05 for submission of the contract to a joint review board. If either the producer or the author do not agree with suggested revisions of the contract it may be submitted to the Board, which consists of one author member and one producer member selected from the Theatrical Conciliation Council.

Probably the most important thing that emerged from the negotiations for the APC is the awareness of the economic facts of 1985 theatre life, which resulted in an attitude on the part of the Guild that did not prevail during the time that the MBPC was being used. Although the MBPC provided for a General Advisory Committee to establish principles concerning the contract, it did little or nothing to improve the contract.

What happened, in fact, was that an attorney for a producer would negotiate with the Author's representative until an agreement was reached. Then the producer's attorney would submit the signed contract to the Guild for its counter-signature. If the Guild didn't like certain terms that were negotiated, they would instruct the attorney to have them removed from the contract. The attorney could argue with the Guild, but if they stood firm, and if their member author stood firm, the producer had no choice but to accept their edict or abandon the thought of producing that particular play.

With this background, it is no wonder that the theatrical business people welcome the concept of a theatre conciliation council and joint review board, but most of all the acceptance of the fact that the contract ought to be changed under certain circumstances at certain times. It is probable that the Guild had little choice but to accept this intrusion on its formerly held powers, the result of a combination of circumstances, such as the need to have a realistic royalty arrangement to attract investors, plus the awareness that some Guild members were quietly defying the Guild and making separate arrangements to get their plays produced. Sometimes such separate arrangements were made instead of using the MBPC, but most often an MBPC was entered into and then the representatives of the parties made some side letter agreements that the Guild never saw and never knew about.

The arbitration provisions are still part of the contract as set forth in Article XX, with some minor modifications.

Article XXI contains some miscellaneous provisions, two of which deserve careful reading and awareness of their existence.

Section 21.02 settles part of the hassle as to who is responsible for the payments to a not-for-profit theatre that presented the play prior to the producer's production.

It is most usual for such a not-for-profit organization to finance, in whole or in part, a workshop or showcase production, and in exchange, therefore, to receive some part of the gross receipts, and sometimes some part of the net profits of a future commercial production (see discussion in Chapter 2).

The not-for-profit organizations' pitch for a share of the net profits relates to their desire to have some part of the subsidiary rights income. It will be interesting to see whether this provision fixes the amount that is paid to such organizations as 1½ percent of the gross and 5 percent of the subsidiary rights income.

The provision for the gross payments is in a usual amount. The 5 percent of the subsidiary rights income would seem to be a reasonable substitute for the 5 percent of the net profits that was usually asked for and often agreed to.

COMMENTARY ON THE DRAMATISTS GUILD, INC., APPROVED PRODUCTION CONTRACT FOR MUSICAL PLAYS

Many of the differences between the APC for plays and the APC for musical plays involve: different numbers, both percentages and dollar amounts; adjustment because there may be three parties involved—the bookwriter, the composer, and the lyricist (although they may be only one or two persons)[10]; and the necessity of dealing with music and lyrics, publishing, and recordings.

In addition, there are a few conceptual differences which are based on the fact that a musical production will be presented in a theatre having a much-larger-potential box office gross than the gross for a straight play.

Section 1.06 sets forth a well-accepted basic principle, namely that the music and lyrics for a musical play belong to the composer and lyricist and they must be the copyright owners. (On some rare occasions a producer will try to encroach on these rights, but when this happens, it is most often a misunderstanding of the role of the producer, sometimes an honest mistake.) Music-publishing rights, small-performing rights, and recording rights belong to the composer and lyricist.[11]

In general, the main difference between the Musical Contract and the Play Contract is that the Musical Contract provides for larger advances and for smaller percentage royalty payments. That the percentages are smaller does not mean that the amounts paid are smaller. The following differences should be noted:

1. In Article II, the first-option period payment provided in the musical contract is $18,000 for twelve months and in the Play Contract was $5,000 for the first six months.

    The second-option period in the Musical Contract is $9,000 for a second consecutive twelve-month period and in the Play Contract is for $2,500 for the second consecutive six-month period.

    The third option period in the Musical Contract is $900 per month for a maximum of twelve consecutive months ($10,800) and in the Play Contract is $5,500 for up to twelve months, payable $2,500 for the first six months of such period and $500 per month thereafter.

2. A completed play is defined in Section 2.03 as at least 110 single-

spaced pages; in the Musical Contract is a book of at least eighty single pages and a score of music and lyrics for at least twelve songs.

3. The additional advance payments based on additional contributions to the capitalization are 3 percent in the Play Contract and 2 percent in the Musical Contract, as provided in Section 3.01 of the Musical Contract.

4. The maximum advance is $35,000 in the Play Contract and $60,000 in the Musical Contract, as provided in Section 3.02.

5. The out-of-town royalty and preview-performance royalty is a straight percentage in the Play Contract and is a fixed-fee-and-percentage arrangement in the Musical Contract. The regular-performance royalty is 5 percent until recoupment and 10 percent thereafter in the Play Contract and 4.5 percent until recoupment and 6 percent thereafter in the Musical Contract.

6. The fixed-fee performance royalty is 10 percent in the Play Contract and 6 percent in the Musical Contract as provided in Section 4.02 (d) of the Musical Contract.

7. The limitation on the producer's cash office in the Play Contract is $500 per week and in the Musical Contract is $1,500 per week, as provided in Section 4.04 (b) of the Musical Contract.

8. In computing the weekly breakeven amount, the author's royalties are considered to be $1,000 in the Play Contract, regardless of the amount actually paid, and are considered to be $3,000 in the Musical Contract, regardless of the amount actually paid, as provided in Section 5.01 of the Musical Contract. The weekly cash-office charge for this purpose is not to exceed $500 in the Play Contract and $1,500 in the Musical Contract. The producer's royalty for this purpose is limited to $250 in the Play Contract and $1,500 in the Musical Contract.

9. The "Adjustments for Regular Performances Post-Recoupment" in Section 5.06 (b) of the Musical Contract are applicable during weeks that the gross weekly box office receipts for any performance week do not exceed 115 percent of breakeven and is 120 percent in the straight-play contract. The limit on author's fixed-and-percentage royalty for this purpose is 10 percent in the Play Contract and 6 percent in the Musical Contract.

10. The adjustments for touring performances, pre-recoupment, as stated in Section 5.07 (a) of the Musical Contract is for a fixed royalty of $3,000 as opposed to $1,000 in the Play Contract. In no event can the author's fixed-and-percentage royalty exceed 4.5 percent of the gross weekly box office receipts for each week in the Musical Contract and 5 percent in the Play Contract.

The post-recoupment adjustment for any performance week of

touring performances refers to a maximum of 115 percent of weekly breakeven in the Musical Contract and 110 percent of weekly breakeven in the Play Contract. The fixed royalty is $3,000 in the Musical Contract and $1,000 in the Play Contract. In the Musical Contract, the author's fixed-and-percentage royalty won't exceed 6 percent of the gross weekly box office receipts and in the Play Contract won't exceed 10 percent.

11. During losing weeks, the author's royalty, as provided in Section 5.08 of the Musical Contract, is limited to $3,000 per performance week and is $1,000 per performance week in the Play Contract.

12. The Christmas-period adjustment provided in Section 5.10 of the Musical Contract provides for an advance to the author of $3,000 per performance week, and this amount in the Play Contract is $1,000.

13. Section 5.13 of the Musical Contract provides for a proportionate adjustment in the producer's royalty. For the purpose of calculating recoupment and weekly breakeven, the producer's royalty is computed as therein set forth but not less than $1,500. In the Play Contract, this amount is $250. In calculating the royalty, the reference to 6 percent in Section 5.13 (a) (i) of the Musical Contract and 10 percent in the Play Contract. The reference to 3 percent of the gross weekly box office receipts in Section 5.13 (a) (ii) of the Musical Contract is 2.5 percent in the corresponding clause of the Play Contract. The reference to Off-Broadway performances, with respect to the adjustment for the Author's royalty, is 6 percent in Section 5.13 (c) of the Musical Contract and 10 percent in the Play Contract.

14. Section 6.02 deals with deductions from royalties, and limits the amount of the deductions to $3,000 per performance week in the Musical Contract and $1,000 per performance week in the Play Contract.

Section 4.02 (d) (iv) of the Musical Contract does not appear in the Play Contract. It provides that, if the producer cannot in good faith arrange for fixed performance payments because the total royalty payments exceed 15 percent of the sums to the producer, the author defers part of the royalty payment so that the author receives the same proportionate share of 15 percent of the sum payable to the producer that he would receive from the total royalty, if paid. The balance over the 15 percent is deferred and payable from other designated receipts.

The Musical Contract, in Section 5.04, defines "Potential and Actual Gross Ticket Sales," and these definitions do not appear in the Play

Contract. The reason for the definition is that Section 5.05 of the Musical Contract provides for an adjustment in the "Royalty for Regular Performances in New York City Pre-Recoupment," if, in the first 21 performance weeks after the official opening, actual ticket sales in 17 of 21 of such weeks are equal to at least 87 percent of potential gross ticket sales. There is also an adjustment if, thereafter, for any three consecutive performance weeks, actual gross ticket sales fall below 87 percent of potential gross ticket sales. This is labeled the "87 Percent Formula."

The previous Dramatists Guild Minimum Basic Production Contract in the printed form made no provision for royalty adjustment. Producers' attorneys would put in provisions for reductions during losing weeks, if everyone earning a royalty took a similar reduction. The Guild took the position that when you need help with a royalty reduction you should come to them and ask for such help. In fact, reductions were then agreed to by the author and producer during the early weeks of many shows without the approval of the Guild, in fact without the Guild even having knowledge of the waiver of royalties by the author in many cases.

Section 5.07 (b) of the Musical Contract contains a provision not found in the Play Contract. It provides that, if the director for any week receives a payment less than the full royalty provided in his contract, the author will receive a reduced royalty on a pro rata basis, with limits as to the amount of the reduction.

The Play Contract provides that option payments for all but the third-option period are deducted from the advance payments made to the author. In Section 6.01 of the Musical Contract, it is provided that the option payments for all but the first-option period are deducted from the advance payment. Why there is this difference is not known, except that it is assumed that this is one of the compromises that resulted from the negotiations between the Guild and the League.

Whereas the Play Contract provides that the adaptor will receive at least one third of the compensation otherwise payable to the author, the Musical Contract, in Section 7.05, makes no such provision, and provides that, unless the adaptor is the English-language "bookwriter," he will not be considered an author or receive any part of the author's royalty.

Since the "author" of a musical (composed of a book, music, and lyrics) is usually more than one person, and the author of a play is usually one person, Section 8.03 in each contract has similar but different provisions. There is also a provision in the Musical Contract that, after three weeks from the first presentation in New York City, if approval for changes or replacements of the author who is bookwriter, composer and/or lyricist is requested and there is no response within seventy-two hours, the right to vote of such person failing to respond is forfeited. Why this same provision does not appear in the Play Contract is not known.

Sections 8.17 through 8.21 are not found in the Play Contract because they deal with items only important to a musical. Music publishing rights, musical scores, the cast album, and music and lyrics deleted from the musical are not proper subjects for a Play Contract. It should be noted however that, although cast albums of plays that do not have music are no longer popular, thirty years ago, play albums of straight plays were a very marketable item.

What is significant about sections 8.17, 8.18, and 8.19 of the Approved Production Contract are the references to what is provided in Article XXII. Article XXII is the provision that is not a part of the printed contract, but is added by the parties after negotiations. Although sections 8.17 through 8.19 deal with these items, there is still a great deal of leeway as to what will be negotiated and what will end up in Article XXII. The APC is intended to be a minimum-and-a-maximum contract and not subject to change for the benefit of either party. Except, however, these sections invite just such negotiation and change.

Traditionally, the producer shares 40 percent of the original cast album and the author 60 percent. The producer's share does not come from the musical running any given length of time, but rather from the producer furnishing the cast for the album. What has never been clearly defined is who has the rights to make the deal for the cast album. There have been various proposals in the past. Sometimes the author had the sole right, sometimes the producer had the sole right, and sometimes both parties would jointly share this right. In each case, of course, the outcome depended on the bargaining power of the respective parties.

What comes as a significant change is the agreement in Section 8.18 that the parties may agree in Article XXII on the terms for disposition of "various music publishing rights in the music and lyrics of the Play." The composer and lyricist have always held these rights in music publishing to be sacrosanct and not subject to encroachment by the producer. Through the years, some producers have tried to encroach on these rights. There is an acknowledgment in this section that, if the producer has the bargaining power, he may end up with some say so and perhaps even some monetary interest in the music publishing rights. This is the acknowledgment of a changed attitude. Whether any producers do in fact end up with any publishing income, or say so with respect to music publishing, remains to be seen.

The sharing of subsidiary rights income is different in each contract. The Play Contract gives the producer four alternatives and the Musical Contract gives the producer three alternatives. The percentages are different and the time for sharing is different. It is difficult to speculate which alternative is preferable from the producer's point of view. One can only assume that each play has its own future in different forms, and one must try to evaluate, or guess, where each particular play may be most successful.

The subsidiary rights provision (Article XI) in both contracts is a new concept. Previously, if the producer shared in subsidiary rights income, it was to the extent of 40 percent for the first ten years from the signing of the contract granting such rights, 35 percent for the following two years, 30 percent for the next two years, 25 percent for the next two years, 20 percent for the next two years, and nothing after the eighteenth year.

At this time, it is not known how important the APC will be in the future of Broadway productions. Since producers are not bound to use the contract, whether it will be widely used is still not known. Much will depend upon the authors themselves, as to whether they have the bargaining power to insist upon its use and whether they will feel inclined to do so. The next year or two should give some indication of the future use of this contract for both musical plays and straight plays.

ROYALTY POOL FORMULAS

The royalty pool formula agreed to for the production of one Broadway musical made an important contribution to the business of financing Broadway plays, particularly musicals. To understand the formula and its ramifications, one ought to have some knowledge of the various elements that go into making up a formula. They are:

1. The amount of any advance against the "contingent compensation," which is determined by all the variables that are set forth in the

formula and is usually payable from some percentage of the weekly operating profits or of the net profits of the producing company. The advance may be fixed at the time of the negotiations as noted below in (a), (b), and (c), or may be computed weekly as set forth in (d). The advance may be:

   (a) in a fixed amount, usually a dollar amount such as $250 for each 1 percent of the regular royalty to which the party is contractually entitled (for an Off-Broadway production), or $800 for each 1 percent (for a Broadway production), or some other amount;
   (b) computed as some stated percentage of the total capitalization of the play or of the potential gross weekly box office receipts;
   (c) any arbitrary amount arrived at by negotiation between the parties;
   (d) computed weekly based on the gross weekly box office receipts, such as an amount equal to half of the regular royalty for such weekly receipts.

2. The amount of any fee payable to any of the parties that does not constitute an advance against the contingent compensation
3. The designation of the parties who will share in the royalty pool formula in some proportion, almost always in the same proportion that they would share in gross weekly box office receipts, sometimes referred to as the pro rata share.
4. Any parties, such as the star and the "theatre" (theatre owner), who may share in the pool, but in some different way than the other participants, usually in a preferred position. (The "theatre" arrangement will often provide for the theatre to receive an amount to cover its expenses plus a percentage of the gross weekly box office receipts)
5. The parties, if any, who will not share in the pool, but receive fixed compensation
6. Any provision for minimum weekly guarantees, which may or may not be advances against the contingent compensation
7. A provision to pay the royalty pool participants pro rata from some percentage of the weekly operating profits (For example, they may be paid a maximum amount equal to half their royalty from 30 percent of such profits until 125 percent of recoupment)
8. An arrangement for increasing the royalty after recoupment of the production costs or some multiple of recoupment, such as 125 percent of recoupment, 150 or 200 percent (For example, the royalty pool participants may be paid a pro rata share from 30 percent of the weekly operating profits until 200 percent of recoupment and a pro rata share from 50 percent of such profits thereafter; provision

may be made for different payments to be made at different multiples of recoupment)

9. Any arrangement for payment of deferred royalties, which must also make provision for how the deferrals will be recovered. If a deferral is provided for, there is usually a provision that after recoupment of the total production costs, or 125 percent of 15 percent of recoupment, the deferral will be recovered pro rata by the pool participants from a percentage of some profits—perhaps 25 percent of the weekly operating profits or from the net profits of the partnership

10. It is also possible to provide a maximum weekly payment to any royalty pool participants

11. The royalty pool formula provisions may be fixed, or the producer may have the option during the first few weeks after the New York opening to pay the regular royalties or to invoke the formula

12. The formula may be based on the "weekly" operating profits (which term is, of course, defined, as are all the terms necessary to use the formula) or may be based on some other accounting period, such as every four consecutive weeks (The reasoning behind a four-week period is that a show may do great business for one week and then have three disastrous weeks, or vice versa. This is an attempt to balance the sharing of the loss or gain by an averaging process).

The different formulas sometimes use different terms to mean the same thing. These terms should be defined in the Limited Partnership Agreement. For example, the "total production costs," "100 percent of the production costs," "production expenses," "100 percent of the production expenses," "total production budget," and "100 percent of the total production budget" are intended to convey the same meaning.

In almost every instance, any of the above terms is followed by language to the effect that the amount is "exclusive of any bonds, deposits and other recoverables." In fact, if this statement is not included, one can be certain that the parties did not know what they were doing, or knew that what they were doing was a mistake. This is understandable when one realizes that the formula concept, and other previous attempts to make investing in theatre more attractive, was created to give the investors back their money before the production costs were increased. At the point that the investors can recoup their total investment is a good time to begin increasing royalties and other percentage payments. Even though the investors may not actually receive their investment back at that time, when this amount is attained by the producing company, they could be paid back in full. The bonds and other recoverables are assets of the producing company and profits are not necessary to cover such amounts in order to make the investors whole.

It is obvious from the above facts that royalty pool formulas may be as various as one's imagination. When structuring the formulas, the ultimate success of the formula will be in whether investors will be satisfied with it enough to part with their money.

CHAPTER 5

The Producing Company

PARTNERSHIP OR CORPORATION

Why a Limited Partnership?

Tax Benefits

FOR THE MOST PART, limited partnerships are used as the producing entity rather than a corporation, a joint venture, or a general partnership. Although there are various complicated schemes for using corporations to accomplish certain specific purposes, by and large the tax advantages of a partnership—namely that the profits are only taxed once, and in the event of losses, they will flow through and be deductible by the partners, subject to the passive-activity-loss rules of the Tax Reform Act of 1986—are advantages that most investors look for, expect, and sometimes even insist upon. With a corporation, the profits are first taxed as income to the corporation and then, when paid out to the investors as dividends, are again taxed to the investors. Moreover, any losses will not pass through a corporation to the shareholder, other than with a sub-chapter S corporation. Thus the loss would belong to the corporate entity and could not be used until the corporation had income to set off against the loss. A sub-chapter S corporation allows for the pass through of income and losses to shareholders (subject to the passive activity loss rules) the same as a partnership. There are reasons why a sub-chapter S corporation is not used for a theatrical production. Since the investors have purchased common stock in the corporation, any loss recognized on the sale of the corporation's stock is a capital loss, which can first be offset against capital gains, and the balance, if any, may then be offset against up to $3,000 of ordinary income. Most theatre investors have more need of a loss that can be offset against ordinary income than they have for a capital loss.

It is also possible to arrange for the investors to make loans to a corporation in which the producer is the sole stockholder. Up until 1942, when the Internal Revenue Code was changed, this was a common procedure. This was abandoned for the reason that a nonbusiness bad debt, unless by a corporation regularly engaged in the lending business, is considered a capital loss rather than an ordinary loss.

Limited Liability

A general partnership is seldom used as the producing entity, because it does not give the investors the protection of limited liability, which is the essential feature of a limited partnership. A limited partner's liability is limited to the amount of his investment.[1]

A "joint venture" is a fancy name for a kind of general partnership. The investors under such circumstances would be considered general partners with all of the liability of a general partner. There have been some producing companies (one rather well known) that have used joint venture agreements where the investors were led to believe that they enjoyed limited liability. Although he may not have to expend his own funds above the original investment, a joint venturer does not, as a matter of fact, enjoy limited liability and is exposed to the same liability as any other general partner in a general partnership.

Corporation May Be a General or Limited Partner

The laws of the state of New York were changed effective September 1, 1963, to provide that a corporation may be a general partner or limited partner. This, of course, means that it should be possible to combine the advantages of a corporation and the advantages of a partnership by having the producer or producers first organize a corporation that becomes the general partner of the limited partnership. In this way the investors, being limited partners, would have all of the tax benefits of a partnership; at the same time, the producer as well as the investors would enjoy the advantage of limited liability, since the corporate general partner would be exposed to general liability rather than the individual. If the corporation has large assets and is substantial, there may be good reason why one ought to do this.[2] If, however, a corporation is organized solely for the purpose of becoming a general partner of a limited partnership, and the corporation has no assets to speak of, then the Internal Revenue Service would consider the producing company to be a corporation for income tax purposes.

Of course, there is nothing to prevent an affluent producer from convincing one of his less-affluent co-producers to be the general partner of the limited partnership together with a corporation belonging to the affluent member. So long as there is an individual who is one of the general partners, there is no problem with any number of corporate general partners. The Internal Revenue requirements would be complied with if there is this single partner, and the partnership would be taxed as a partnership rather than a corporation, no matter how rich or how insolvent the individual partner is.[3]

Characteristics of Corporation for Tax Purposes

In order for the partnership to be taxed as a partnership and not as a corporation, it must have certain basic characteristics. There are four characteristics of a corporation which distinguish it from other entities: continuity of life, centralization of management, free transferability of interests, and limited liability.

1. It is for this reason that the Limited Partnership Agreement will generally provide that the partnership will end upon the death or insanity of a general partner or of one or more corporate officers. Such a provision is adequate to avoid continuity of life.
2. The agreement will almost always state that the management of the affairs of the partnership shall not be centralized in one or more persons acting in a representative capacity. In fact, the Internal Revenue regulations actually provide that a limited partnership organized under the laws of the state of New York does not have centralized management unless substantially all of the interests in the partnership are owned by the limited partners.

3. Under a limited partnership, if properly drawn, a partner may assign the right to receive a share of capital and/or net profits, but usually cannot grant the right to become a member of the partnership in his place. It is usually desirable to limit an assignment of a limited partner's interest by requiring the consent of the general partner. This limits free transferability.
4. The limited partners in a limited partnership have limited liability, and if the general partner is an agent acting on behalf of the limited partners, for tax purposes the partnership is deemed to have limited liability.

It is not easy to set forth fixed rules always applicable in determining whether the entity will be considered a partnership or corporation for tax purposes. Each of the characteristics of a corporation has relative importance, and in making a determination, all of the factors are taken into consideration. There is no doubt but that if all four characteristics of a corporation are present, it will be considered a corporation for tax purposes. If less than all four of the characteristics are present, it may or may not be considered a corporation, depending upon a number of factors which it is impossible to set forth here in detail. Suffice it to say that one must be aware of the problem so that the partnership does not inadvertently end up being treated as a corporation for tax purposes.

LIMITED PARTNERSHIP AGREEMENT

There is no standard theatrical Limited Partnership Agreement. There is a very old and dated printed form that some attorneys use and adapt for each particular show. The printed form omits some provisions that should be included, and the job of properly adapting it can be extensive. For this reason, most attorneys who do this kind of work use their own form, which will contain some of the provisions that are found in the printed form.

Basic Provisions

There are certain basics that most Limited Partnership Agreements used in theatre production have in common. It is usually these few important elements that the producer knows and discusses with the investor. Many investors who have invested in theatre before are aware of these basic provisions. For example, almost all theatrical limited partnership agreements provide that the first net receipts of the partnership are used to repay the investors their original investment, and after the investors have recouped their investment, all net profits are shared equally with the producer. The producer receives 50 percent and the investors share 50 percent proportionately, in accordance with the amount of their respective investments. Most limited partnership agreements provide that the investors will share in all of the profits of the producing company, including profits from subsidiaries. There are, however, instances where the producer will share only the box office receipts with the investors, just as there are rare instances where the producer will give the investors 60 percent of the profits, rather than 50 percent.[4]

The Limited Partnership Agreement is usually signed by the investor at the time the investment in the production is made. After all of the limited partners have invested and the production is completely financed, the attorney for the production will prepare a conformed copy of the agreement (a conformed copy is a duplicate of the original with the signatures of each partner indicated) and will forward a copy to each of the investors.

Usual Provisions

The discussion under "Definitions" below will cover most of the terms, items, and provisions found in most limited partnership agreements. Some things will be mentioned, however, which might not appear in all agreements.

One should bear in mind that each general partner assumes all of the obligations and liabilities of the producing company. Between them the general partners might have an arrangement for sharing the liabilities, but each is responsible for all of the obligations to creditors.

If additional funds are needed after the limited partners' money is used up, it must come from the general partner. In exchange for the obligations of the partnership, the general partner has the right to make all of the decisions for the partnership, and is—and should be—responsible as decision-maker.

The Limited Partnership Agreement will state that it is being made between the producer and those persons who sign the agreement as limited partners. It will set forth the main address of the partnership, as well as the name and address of the attorney for the partnership.

Definitions

Most Limited Partnership Agreements contain certain definitions.

"The Play"

Since "the Play" is referred to throughout the agreement, it is not unusual in the beginning to define the play as the specific play or plays that the partnership will be producing.

"Contributions of Limited Partners"

The term "contributions of limited partners" is generally defined in the agreements as the amounts that the limited partners contribute to the partnership.

"Aggregate Limited Contributions"

The term "aggregate limited contributions" means all of the contributions of all of the limited partners required to be made by them.

"Sinking Fund"

After a show opens, even if it is making money, the production company should not disperse all of the profits to the partners, because of the nature of the theatre business. It is not unusual to have a period of very successful business followed by several weeks or more of difficult times. If all of the profits have been paid to the partners, then there would be nothing in the partnership to get over the rough times. Accordingly, most agreements provide that a "sinking fund" may be established and retained by the partnership. The amount of the sinking fund is defined in the agreement and will usually be between $30,000 and $75,000 for an Off-Broadway play and between $100,000 and $250,000 for a Broadway play, the amount depending upon the play's total weekly expenses.

"Estimated Production Requirements"

The amount of money the producer intends to raise for the production is known as the "estimated production requirements." "Estimated production requirements" should be defined as the amount of cash that, together with any bonds or guarantees furnished, totals the specific dollar amount the producer will attempt to raise. As we shall see later, it may be possible for the production to commence with something less than the estimated production requirements, since it might be possible to produce the show for a smaller amount. However, under all circumstances the agreement should state the minimum specific dollar amount that must be raised for a production before the investors' money can be used. Investors want to know that when an investment is made, it will be used only if enough money is raised to produce the show.[5] The estimated production requirements of a dramatic play Off-Broadway will range between $100,000 and $250,000 and for a musical between $250,000 and $450,000. Such requirements for a Broadway dramatic play will be between $750,000 and $1,500,000 and for a musical between $3,500,000 and $6,000,000.

"Net Profits, Gross Receipts, Various Expenses"

In order to define "net profits," it is necessary to also define "gross receipts" and the various kinds of expenses: "expenses," "other expenses," "running expenses," and "production expenses."

Net profits is defined as the excess of "gross receipts" over all "production expenses," "running expenses," and "other expenses," as these terms are defined in the Limited Partnership Agreement.

The term *gross receipts* means all sums derived by the partnership from any source whatsoever from the exploitation of all rights in the play, including all proceeds derived by the partnership from the liquidation of the physical production of the play at the conclusion of its run, and from return of bonds and other recoverable items included in "production expenses."

The term *production expenses* is defined to include the fees of the director and designers; the cost of sets, curtains, drapes, costumes, properties, furnishings, electrical equipment, premiums for bonds and insurance, and cash deposits with Actors' Equity Association or other similar organizations by which—according to custom or usual theatrical practice—such deposits may be required to be made; advances to authors; rehearsal charges and expenses; transportation charges; cash office charges; reasonable legal and auditing expenses; advance publicity; theatre costs and expenses; and all other expenses and losses of whatever kind (other than expenditures specifically precluded by the contract) actually incurred in connection with the production of the play preliminary to the official opening. The agreement may further state that the general partner has incurred or paid, and prior to the inception of the partnership, will incur or pay, certain production expenses as set forth in the contract, and that amount, and no more, shall be included in the production expenses of the partnership, and if the aggregate limited contributions in full have been paid in, the general partner shall be reimbursed for the expenses paid by him.

The term *running expenses* means all expenses, charges and disbursements actually incurred as running expenses of the play including, without limitation, royalties and/or other compensation to or for authors, business and general managers, director, orchestra, cast, stage help, transportation, cash office charge, reasonable legal and auditing expenses, theatre operating expenses, and all other expenses and losses of whatever kind actually incurred in connection with the operation of the play and taxes of whatsoever kind and nature other than taxes on the income of the respective limited and general partner. The running expenses include payments made in the form of percentages of gross receipts as well as participations in profits to or for any of the persons, services, or rights referred to in the contract.

Other expenses is defined as all expenses of whatsoever kind or nature other than those referred to in the two preceding paragraphs hereof actually and reasonably incurred in connection with the operation of the business of the partnership, including but without limiting the foregoing, commissions paid to agents, monies paid or payable in connection with claims for plagiarism, libel, negligence, etc.

The term *expenses* includes contingent expenses and liabilities, as well as unmatured expenses and liabilities, and until the final determination thereof, the general partner has the absolute right to fix, as the amount thereof, such sums as the producer in producer's sole discretion deems advisable.

"Author"

"Author" is defined as the author, adaptor, and/or owner of the play and includes the singular or plural, as the case may be. A person may inherit or otherwise acquire the rights to produce the play, and would be the owner, although not the author of the play. An owner may sell the production rights to the producer.

Miscellaneous

There is usually a provision that states that the phrase "general partner" will be construed to mean the plural, if more than one person signs the agreement as general partner, and all pronouns are deemed to refer to the masculine, feminine, neuter, singular, or plural as the identity of the person or persons, firm or firms, corporation or corporations may require.

Representations and Warranties by the General Partner for a First-Class Production

The general partner warrants and represents (which, simply stated, means that he guarantees) that he or she has acquired the first-class production rights in the play by contract under the terms of an Approved Production Contract of the Dramatists Guild, Inc. Usually the agreement states that the limitations, restrictions, conditions, and contingencies of the partner's right to produce the play is as set forth in the Approved Production Contract, and that a copy of the contract is on file at the office of the attorneys for the partnership and is available for inspection by the limited partners.

For Other Than a First-Class Production

The general partner guarantees that he or she has acquired the rights to produce the play upon the terms and conditions set forth in the option agreement. The terms will, of course, vary depending upon the type of production, whether Off-Broadway, in a resident theatre, or in stock.

Warranties of Sufficiency

The general partner further warrants and represents that, in his or her opinion, the total cost of opening a first-class production of the play including all bonds, cash deposits, production expenses, and the cost of an out-of-town trial run, if anticipated, will not exceed the amount set forth as the estimated production requirements.

Formation of Limited Partnership

The agreement will state that the parties do form a limited partnership pursuant to the Partnership Law of the state of New York, for the purpose of managing and producing the play and for the purpose of exploiting all rights held by the partnership in the play. The rights that the production company owns are the rights that were originally obtained by the general partner when entering into the option agreement. The option agreement is assigned (an assignment is a transfer of rights and obligations) to the partnership after the partnership is formed by the general partner who acquired the rights.

Term of Partnership

The agreement will usually provide that the partnership will commence on the day when the Certificate of Limited Partnership is filed in the office of the county clerk and will terminate upon the death, insanity, or retirement of any individual general partner or upon the dissolution of a corporate general partner. The Certificate of Limited Partnership is a document that must be filed in the county clerk's office in the county in which the partnership is organized. The agreement usually provides that the general partner will file such a certificate. If the name of the partnership includes the words "Limited Partnership," the Certificate of Limited Partnership for a theatrical stage production need not be published once a week for six consecutive weeks in two newspapers, as is the case with all other certificates of limited partnership in the state of New York.[6] The partnership may also be terminated when all rights of the partnership in the play have terminated. Upon termination, the general partner must immediately liquidate the affairs of the partnership.

Death of Limited Partner

If a limited partner dies, the executors or administrators—or, if the limited partner becomes insane, a committee or other representative—

will have the same rights the limited partner would have under the agreement until the termination of the partnership. The share of such limited partner in the assets of the partnership is subject to all of the terms, provisions, and conditions of the agreement as if the limited partner had not died or become insane.

General Partner May Add General Partners

The agreement provides that the person who executes the agreement as general partner is the general partner of the partnership. However, the general partner may nevertheless enter into agreements with other persons to undertake the obligations and the privileges of general partners. The limited partners consent to the general partner entering into such an agreement, providing that the general partner is not relieved of any of his or her obligations under the agreement.

Rights in Play Assigned to Partnership

The general partner agrees to assign to the partnership all of the rights held or acquired by him or her in the play.

General Partner's Expenditures

The general partner is generally reimbursed for all legitimate expenditures made prior to the formation of the general partnership. The general partner may be reimbursed for the full cost of the option agreement, attorneys' fees, accountants' fees, script duplication costs, and similar expenses. The agreement may state an exact dollar amount that the general partner has expended to date, or it may simply state that he is to be reimbursed for those expenditures he may reasonably spend or incur, including but not limited to advances to the author.

Use of Funds Invested

Each limited partner in the agreement agrees to contribute a specific amount, which is set forth in the agreement; to the capital of the partnership, which money may be used by the partnership for the payment of production, running, and other expenses.

Investment of Bond or Theatre Guarantee

In lieu of a cash contribution, a limited partner may make an investment in the partnership by furnishing a bond to Actors' Equity Association, or one of the other associations, or by furnishing the theatre guarantee. The agreement provides that such an investment is the same as a cash investment by the limited partner. If the play closes before the limited partners' contributions have been repaid to them in full, and before the partnership has paid any of the obligations covered by the bond deposit, then each limited partner who furnished a bond must pay the partnership the full principal amount that was originally pledged by him as a bond or guarantee, less any amounts that he may already have been called upon to pay. There is an advantage to furnishing a bond or guarantee, since an association will accept an investment in a savings bank account if it is given together with an assignment to the association to be held as security. Under such circumstances, a party putting up bond money does not lose the bank interest, whereas all other investors in the producing company would receive no interest on their investment. This provision of the agreement is not intended to substantially discriminate in favor of such bond-furnishing investors, but it does. In the event that the play closes and the other limited partners have lost part or all of their investment, a proportionate share will be taken from the bond-furnishing limited partners to the extent that the bond is not used and is returned to them.

There is also a provision in most agreements that the general partner may arrange for the deposit of bonds or other deposits based on an agreement that provides that the first net profits received shall be paid to the association or theatre holding the bond for the purpose of releasing the bond to the investor who put up the bond. This would mean, in effect, that such an investor would have a distinct advantage over the other investors in that his or her funds are returned first. It is most usual for the contract provision to provide that such an arrangement may not reduce the percentage of net profits payable to the other limited partners. This means that the general partner will have to compensate those persons who furnish bonds by giving them a share of the producer's profits. If a producer is having difficulty raising the last money needed for the show, and is very close to being financed, he or she may under such circumstances make such an arrangement for the furnishing of the bond. Most general partners do not want to prefer one limited partner over another, but if it means getting the last $50,000 necessary for the production to go on, and it might not otherwise go on, then the general partner might be more inclined to make such an arrangement.

Use of Funds—Smaller Capitalization Finally

The general partner agrees not to use the funds received from the limited partners until a specified amount of money—whatever the producer states is sufficient to produce the show—has been raised.

The amount sufficient to produce the show is usually stated as the "estimated production requirements" (see page 69), and there may be a maximum and a minimum set forth. The producer may try to raise $300,000, which is set forth as the "maximum estimated production requirements," but may be able to produce the play for $250,000 with a somewhat smaller reserve or by reducing the advertising budget. The amount of $250,000 is the "minimum estimated production requirements." The partnership agreement will provide that the partnership may use the invested funds when between $250,000 and $300,000 has been raised and that under no circumstances may an investment of a limited partner be used without prior written approval from such limited partner, until at least $250,000 has been raised. If the amount necessary to produce the play is not raised within the period of the option to produce the play, the general partner agrees to return to the respective limited partners all of the funds collected.

The Arts and Cultural Affairs Law of the state of New York, with the rules and regulations promulgated thereunder by the attorney general of the state of New York will not permit the difference between the "minimum" and the "maximum" amount raised for a play to be in excess of 25 percent of the amount of the maximum to be raised.

If the play is finally capitalized for less than the maximum estimated production requirements, then instead of returning money to the investors, each limited partner will end up with a larger percentage of the show for his investment. For example, if a limited partner invests $3,400 for a 1 percent interest in the profits of a $170,000 show, and if the producer later decides to capitalize the show for $155,000, then the $3,400 investment would purchase 1.09 percent of the net profits of the production, and the investor would receive this share. An investor is investing a fixed dollar amount, and may get more than 1 percent for the $3,400 investment in such case, but the investor may not get less than 1 percent for such an amount.

Overcall

The partnership agreement may provide that each limited partner must, upon demand of the general partner, make an additional contribution of 10 percent, 15 percent, or 20 percent of his or her original contribution. This is called an "overcall."

An overcall provision in the agreement is not recommended. If there are a large number of investors, it can be difficult to collect the overcall from all of them. If one or more refuses to honor the overcall, what is the general partner's obligation? The agreement may provide that the general partner may collect the amount not paid by a limited partner from the other limited partners, which is sure to make the general partner very unpopular with those having to pay. Or the agreement may provide that the general partner is responsible for any delinquent payments, which is also not a preferable position for the general partner. The general partner can sue for the overcall not paid, but this is both expensive and inconvenient.

Books of Account

The general partner agrees to keep or cause to be kept full and faithful books of account in which all the partnership transactions will be fully and accurately entered. The books of account as well as the box office statements received from the theatre (or theatres) are available for inspection and examination of the limited partners or their representatives. The general partner further agrees to deliver to the limited partners a complete statement of production expenses not later than sixty days after the official opening of the play, a monthly unaudited statement of operations, and such other financial statements as may be required by the New York Arts and Cultural Affairs Law and Regulations. The limited partners are furnished with all information necessary to prepare their federal and state income tax returns.

General Partner's Services

The general partner agrees to render the services customarily and usually rendered by theatrical producers and to devote as much time as necessary to the production. It is understood that the producer may engage in other businesses, including other theatrical productions.

The agreement will state that the general partner has complete control of production of the play and the exploitation of all rights in the play. The limited partners' liability is limited, but so are the limited partners' rights with respect to management of the production.

General Partner's Fee and "Cash Office Charge"

For his services, the producer is paid a producer's fee, which is usually in the amount, of 1, 1 ½, or 2 percent of the gross weekly box office receipts. The producer will also reimburse himself for office facilities furnished to the production; this includes office space, secretarial services, telephone service, stationery, and the like. The amount that the producer takes as reimbursement is known as the "cash office charge" and is usually an amount between $100 and $250 each week for an Off-Broadway show and between $750 and $2,000 each week for a Broadway show. The cash office charge does not cover long-distance telephone calls, and if there are unusual expenses that would cause the producer's cost to exceed the amount set forth as the cash office charge, the producer would usually be entitled to reimburse himself for these additional charges.

The producer will generally receive the cash office charge and his producer's fee beginning two or three weeks prior to the first rehearsal and continuing through the week after the close of the play. Of course, if the producer's fee is based upon a percentage of gross box office receipts, he would not receive the producer's fee until there are box office receipts.

Fee and Cash Office Charge If More Than One Company

In the event that there is more than one company, the fee and cash office charge is also payable for each additional company for the period beginning two or three weeks prior to the first rehearsal of such additional company and continuing until one week after its close.

Additional Limited Partners

The agreement will very often provide that additional persons may become limited partners either before or after the aggregate limited contributions have been obtained. If after, and the general partner needs money above the original amount intended as the total capitalization, he or she may not take additional limited partners and reduce the respective shares of the original limited partners, so the general partner must pay such additional limited partners from the general partner's share of the net profits, just as the general partner would pay for a bond deal from his or her share of the profits.

Advances and Loans

The agreement will usually provide that the general partner has the right to make or receive loans to the partnership, and these loans will share a certain advantage. If all of the production money has been expended and additional funds are needed to get the show on or to keep the show running, then the general partner may make a loan to the producing company or obtain a loan from someone else, which may be repaid in full prior to the return of any of the contributions of the limited partners. It is most usual, however, for the agreement to provide that the partnership may not incur any expenses in connection with any such loan or advance, and that the percentage of the net profits payable to the limited partners must not be affected by such an arrangement.

Additional Services by Producer

The Limited Partnership Agreement should contain a provision that if the producer finds it necessary to perform any services that would otherwise be performed by a third person, then he may—if he so desires—receive reasonable compensation in the amount that the third person would have received for such services. It may happen, for instance, that the producer has to fill in and direct the show, or act as stage manager, or serve in some other vitally important capacity, and unless this provision appears in the agreement, he could not be paid for such services no matter how well performed and no matter how important to the company.[7]

Share of Profits

As was previously stated, it is most usual for the limited partners to share the profits equally with the producer after they have recouped their total investment. The agreement usually states this in the following way: each limited partner shall receive that proportion of 50 percent of the net profits that his contribution bears to the aggregate limited contributions, excluding, however, from such limited partners all persons who may be entitled to compensation as limited partners only from the share of the general partner in such net profits and excluding from such aggregate limited contributions, the contributions as limited partners so made by such persons. Simply stated, this means that each limited partner shares the 50 percent of the net profits with the other limited partners, pro rata in accordance with the size of the investment of each limited partner. The excluded limited partners for their excluded contributions, as we have stated, would receive compensation from whatever part of the general partner's profits the general partner has agreed to pay them.

In lieu of returning any part of the capital contribution of a limited partner to cover the contingency previously referred to—in the event that the play is finally capitalized for less than the estimated production requirements—the percentage of the net profits of each investor is accordingly increased so that each will receive that proportion of 50 percent of the net profits that the contribution made by the limited partner bears to the reduced aggregate limited contributions, excluding the same limited partners (and their contributions) who are compensated from the producer's share of the profits. This means simply that if the capitalization of the show is less than anticipated, then the limited partners' specific dollar amount will purchase a larger percentage than originally anticipated. Each limited partner still shares part of the 50 percent of the net profits, and his or her share is pro rata in accordance with the size of the investment; however, if the total budget decreases, this same dollar amount invested is then a proportionately larger percentage of the smaller reduced capitalization. It will be remembered that this was discussed previously under the heading "Use of Funds—Smaller Capitalization Finally," where it was pointed out that $3,400 purchases 1 percent of the net profits of a $170,000 production and the same $3,400 purchases 1.09 percent of the net profits of a $155,000 production.

Limited Partners' Limited Liability

The agreement specifically states that limited partners will not be personally liable for any debts, obligations, or losses of the partnership except from the capital contributed by them.

Payments in Cash

Unless agreed to, the limited partners have no right to demand and receive property other than cash in return for their contributions.

Return of Contributions

Contributions of the limited partners are returned to them after opening of the play after the partnership has accumulated a cash reserve in the amount of the sinking fund (plus a reasonable amount for initial expenses in the event that the original company is sent on tour, and plus an amount for any additional company or companies that the producer wishes to organize to present the play), and after the payment of all expenses and provision for contingent expenses. If an investor, instead of investing cash, has given an obligation to Actors' Equity Association or to a similar organization, then in lieu of paying that particular investor's share to him, the partnership will set aside the amount of each distribution until there is a sum sufficient to release the bond to the limited partner, and will then substitute the amount for the limited partner's obligation and release the bond security to such limited partner.

Distribution of Profits

The agreement will provide that after the limited partners' contributions have been returned to them, after accumulating the cash reserve in the amount of the sinking fund plus any reasonable amount for additional companies, and after payment of all expenses and provision for contingent expenses, the net profits are to be paid monthly to the limited and general partners in accordance with their respective interest in the profits. The monthly financial report prepared by the accountants for the partnership is used to determine whether or not any contributions are to be repaid or net profits distributed.

Distribution upon Closing

Upon the closing of all companies and abandonment of further intention of producing the play, the assets of the partnership are liquidated as promptly as possible. The cash proceeds are used first for the payment of all debts, taxes, and obligations, for the creation of reserves for all contingent obligations, and then for the repayment of the capital contributed by the limited partners if they have not been repaid. The balance is then divided among the limited and general partners in the proportion that they share in the net profits.

The agreement will probably provide that all physical assets of a salable nature belonging to the partnership must be sold at public or private sale, but that no assets other than the physical assets have to be sold. Any limited and/or general partner may purchase the physical assets at such sale.

After the completion of the run of all companies under the management of the partnership, the general partner has the right to sell or otherwise dispose of the production rights and the partnership's interest in the subsidiary rights other than the motion picture rights. The limited and/or general partners may be the purchasers at any such sale provided that the amount paid by them as purchasers is a fair and reasonable price. The agreement will sometimes provide that if there is a dispute as to the fairness and reasonableness of the offer, the president of the League of American Theatre Owners and Producers will make the determination.

Return of Contributions or Profits to the Company

Most limited partnership agreements provide that if any contribution or distribution of profits is returned to the partners and funds are thereafter needed by the partnership, the general partner may demand

the return of any part of the profits or contribution distributed. The
general and limited partners must first repay any profits received by
them, and if such profits are insufficient, then the limited partners must
return their capital contributions. The return to the partnership of
profits and contributions by each partner is in proportion to the respective amounts received as profits by the parties.

Abandonment

The partnership agreement will provide that the general partner has
the right, whenever he deems it necessary, to abandon the production
at any time prior to its opening for any reason. In such an event, the
production will liquidate all of its funds or accounts and the gross
receipts will be distributed in the same manner that they would be
distributed if there were no abandonment of the production. This provision is an essential part of any agreement, because although the producer agrees to produce the show and fully intends to do so, show
business, like no other business, has unpredictable possibilities that
could preclude proceeding with a production.

If the general partner, after the first public performance of the play,
determines that continuation of the run is not in the best interests of
the partnership and should be abandoned, he or she has the right to
make arrangements with any person to continue the run of the play on
such terms that he or she feels are in the best interests of the partnership.

Substitute Limited Partner

A limited partner may assign his or her interest in the partnership
to someone else who would be then known as an assignee. It is not
unusual for a partnership agreement to provide that the assignment
may only be made once and only with the producer's approval and may
further provide that an assignee may not become a substitute limited
partner in the place of his or her assignor. Under the partnership laws
of the state of New York, there is a provision that one may become a
substitute limited partner in accordance with certain procedures. The
producer must be in a position to choose his or her limited partners and

would not want to end up with a limited partner who is undesirable, hence the limitation appears in most agreements.[8]

Additional Company to Produce Here or in Great Britain

Use of Company Funds

The partnership agreement may provide that the general partner may organize an additional company or companies to present the play in the United States, Canada, or Great Britain (if the rights to produce the play in Great Britain accrue to the partnership). Under such circumstances the net profits are not distributed until there is further accumulated in the bank account in addition to the reserve (sinking fund) provided for, a sum that, in the opinion of the general partner, will be sufficient to pay the production expenses of each such additional company. In the event that there is more than one company being presented at the same time, the reserve (sinking fund) provided for shall be maintained for each separate company before the repayment of contributions or distribution of net profits.[9]

General Partner's Involvement in Other Company

It is not unusual for the agreement to also provide that the partnership may enter into an agreement concerning the disposition of the British production and subsidiary rights of the play with any partnership, corporation, or other firm in which the general partner may be in any way interested, provided that such agreement must be on fair and reasonable terms.

There is also likely to be a provision that the general partner may be associated with any person, firm, or corporation which produces or co-produces a second company of the play and may receive compensation for doing so, without any obligation to account to the partnership or to the partners of the original producing company, provided that the original company receives from any such person, firm, or corporation the customary fees and royalties payable to it as the producer of the original company.

The general partner may have the right in the contract to make arrangements to license the road rights to any other party or parties the general partner may designate, provided that the partnership receives reasonable royalties, or other reasonable compensation, and the partnership assumes no obligation in connection with any loss or expenses of the company to which the license is granted. The limited or general partners are not disqualified from participating in the company to which the rights are licensed by investing their funds, or otherwise, as a separate enterprise. A general partner may render services to the entity licensing the rights in connection with the exploitation of such rights.

General Partner's Acquisition of Rights After Termination of Partnership

If, after the termination of the partnership, the general partner purchases the production rights of the play for the United States or Canada, either with or without the physical production of the play, and with or without the partnership's interest in the proceeds of the subsidiary rights of the play, then the amount which the general partner pays for such rights must be the fair and reasonable market value, or an amount equal to the best offer obtainable, whichever is the higher price.

Motion Pictures

It is not unusual for the agreement to contain a provision to the effect that the parties acknowledge that one or more of the limited partners may be a motion picture company, or person nominated or otherwise controlled by a motion picture company, and that such company may acquire the motion picture rights in the play. In such event the partnership must be free to deal with the motion picture company without liability on the part of the motion picture company to account to the partnership or to the general partner or limited partners for any profits it may derive from, or in connection with, the rights which it acquires.

Execution of Agreement

There are certain provisions in the agreement that are designed to simplify the execution of the agreement and the filing of the necessary documents. For example, there is a provision that the agreement may be executed in counterparts, all of which taken together shall be deemed to be one original. This avoids the necessity of all partners actually signing the same copy of the document. Each of the partners agrees that the original of the agreement (or set of original counterparts) may be held at the office of the partnership; that a Certificate of Limited Partnership be filed in the office of the county clerk and a duplicate original (or set of duplicate original counterparts) may be held at the office of the attorney for the partnership; and that each partner shall receive a conformed copy of the partnership agreement. In addition, the limited partners give any one of the general partners a power of attorney in his place to make, execute, sign, acknowledge, and file: (1) the Certificate of Limited Partnership and to include in the certificate all information required by the laws of the state, (2) such amended Certificates of Limited Partnership as may be required, and (3) all papers which may be required to effectuate the dissolution of the partnership after its termination.

Arbitration

The limited partnership agreement will almost always contain an arbitration clause which provides, in effect, that if there is a dispute in connection with the making or validity of the agreement, or its interpretation, or any breach of the agreement, then such dispute is determined and settled by arbitration in New York City (if that is the location of the parties or at least the party with the most bargaining power) pursuant to the rules of the American Arbitration Association. Any award rendered by the Arbitration Association is final and conclusive upon the parties and a judgment may be entered in the highest court of the forum, state or federal, having jurisdiction. Such a provision cannot, however, affect the rights of the limited partners under the federal securities laws (later discussed), which govern the offering of a security (a limited partnership interest is considered a security) to the public for sale.

CERTIFICATE OF LIMITED PARTNERSHIP

The Certificate of Limited Partnership previously referred to is the document that is filed in the county clerk's office in the county where the partnership will have its office and do business. The partnership agreement usually provides that the partnership will come into existence when the certificate is filed.[10]

The certificate and any amendments to the certificate must be signed by all of the partners, both general and limited. The limited partnership agreement contains a specific provision designed to simplify the signing of the certificate by the limited partners, for if there are forty or fifty limited partners, it could be a troublesome chore to obtain all of their signatures. For this reason, the Limited Partnership Agreement contains a provision that the limited partners appoint one general partner as their attorney to sign the Certificate of Limited Partnership, any amendments, and the Certificate of Dissolution of the partnership. So the general partners will sign as general partners, and one general partner will sign for all the limited partners pursuant to this power of attorney.

Contents of Certificate in New York State

The certificate will contain the following information:

1. The name of the partnership.
2. The nature of the business of the partnership, which is usually stated to be: to act as theatrical producer and to turn to account all rights held in the play.
3. The principal place of business.
4. The date that the partnership commences business and the date of termination.
5. The time when the contribution of each limited partner is returned to him or her.
6. The name and place of residence of each member, general and limited partners being respectively designated, the amount of cash and a description of and the agreed value of any other property contributed by each limited partner, and the percentage of individual profits to be received by each limited partner.
7. Additional contributions, if any, agreed to be made by each limited partner and the times at which, or events on the happening of which, they will be made.
8. If a limited partner may substitute an assignee as contributor in his or her place, then this must be set forth together with the terms and conditions of the substitution.

9. The right, if given, of partners to admit additional limited partners.
10. The right, if given, of one or more of the limited partners to priority over other limited partners as to return of contributions or as to income and the nature of such priority.
11. The right, if given, of the remaining general partner or partners to continue the business on the death, retirement, or insanity of a partner.
12. The right, if given, of a limited partner to demand and receive property other than cash in return for his contribution.

CHAPTER 6

Co-Producers and Associate Producers

E ITHER BEFORE OR AFTER the option is acquired, the producer may decide to produce the play together with a co-producer. Producing a show is a large venture, and it may be advisable to have assistance in the raising of the money, in handling the business details, and in the many areas of decision.

What one gives the co-producer and what one receives in exchange depend upon the relative bargaining power of the parties.

Co-Producer As General Partner

Bear in mind that a co-producer will ultimately also be a general partner of the limited partnership. As a general partner, he or she may bind the partnership. Furthermore, each general partner, as stated, in obligating the general partnership, obligates at the same time all of the general partners personally to the payment of a debt. The partners, as between themselves, may agree to share the obligations of the partnership in any fashion, but a creditor of the partnership may seek payment in full from any one of the general partners.

Co-Producers Operate As a Joint Venture

Before the limited partnership comes into existence, the producer and co-producer will be operating as an entity—usually a "joint venture." A joint venture is a kind of a partnership and each of the joint venturers is a general partner, and thus personally liable for all of the acts of the joint venture.

Joint Venture Agreement

Basic Terms

The Joint Venture Agreement will state that the co-producers own a property they wish to produce, that they are going to endeavor to raise the money for the production, and that when the money is raised, they will be the general partners of a limited partnership that will produce the play. This agreement will set forth the basic terms that will be incorporated into the Limited Partnership Agreement. There will also be set forth the amount of the budget, the method of sharing profits and losses by each of the partners, whether the partners' profits are related to the amount of money that each producer raises, how the producers' fees are to be shared, how the cash office charge is shared, and so forth.[1]

Sharing of Profits by Co-Producers

The co-producers may agree that they will share equally in the profits of the company irrespective of which partner is responsible for the raising of most of the money for the show. On the other hand, sometimes co-producers wish to relate the share of the profits more directly to the amount of money that each one raises. If one is going to relate the sharing of the profits to the amount of money that each co-producer raises, one ought also to relate the other important contributions to the production to the sharing of the profits. For example: the partner who discovered the property could claim a larger percentage of the profits for this contribution, the party influencing the star could claim something extra for that, and so on. The next logical step is an attempt to balance all of the items that each of the co-producers contributes, and to relate the share of the profits to the relative importance of each contribution. Very often when co-producers sit down and try to balance the contribution that each one makes to a production, they discover that the importance of each contribution is difficult to measure. As a result, they end up sharing equally in the profits and losses, with all parties agreeing to contribute their best efforts to the production in all ways.

Who Makes Decisions

The Joint Venture Agreement will also set forth how decisions are to be made and what happens if there is a deadlock. It is very important that there be some quick resolution in the event that there is a disagreement. In the case of an artistic decision, two co-producers may provide that, in the event of a dispute between them, the director will make the final determination. they may also provide that in the event of a business dispute, the question will be settled by the attorney, the accountant, or anyone else whose business judgment both producers would respect. Other possibilities exist for settling such disputes and are as various as one's imagination.

Who Signs Checks and Agreements—Billing Credits—Arbitration

The agreement should also set forth who may sign checks and who may sign other obligations of the joint venture. The ever-prevailing question of billing credits must be dealt with in this agreement—that is, whose name comes first. It is usual to provide that wherever the name of one co-producer appears, the name of all co-producers will appear in type of the same size, prominence, and boldness. Billing credits are usually in alphabetical order in the absence of other more pressing considerations. An arbitration clause may be included, which, as we know, means that in the event of a dispute, rather than going to court, an impartial person would make the determination.

Personnel Agreed Upon

The Joint Venture Agreement should also set forth the personnel the producers have agreed upon who will be employed by the show, namely the attorney, the accountant, the general manager, and any other personnel agreed upon at this stage.[2]

Termination of Joint Venture

The joint venture will cease upon the organization of the limited partnership unless the parties abandon the play and decide to terminate it sooner.

Associate Producers—Money

An associate producer may sometimes be utilized by a production, which almost always means that he makes a contribution of money. Associate producers rarely have any say-so in the business, although a smart producer will always consult with the associate, even if he ignores the associate's advice or suggestions.

The associate, in addition to getting billing credit,[3] will generally get a percentage of the producer's profits. It is not unusual to give the associate 1 percent of the producer's share of the profits for each 4 percent (it could be for each 3 percent or 5 percent—4 percent is usual) of the producing company purchased by an investment for which the associate producer is responsible.

Front Money

Amount Needed and Uses

It may be necessary or advisable for a producer to take a co-producer or an associate producer to assist with the raising of the "front money" (see "Front Money Arrangements" below). Usually one may expect to need between $15,000 and $50,000 in front money for an Off-Broadway play, and between $50,000 and $150,000 for a Broadway play, the amount depending upon whether the play is a straight play or a musical, and other factors. Front money is used for the production prior to the receipt of the total capitalization and release of the investors' funds. It is generally used to acquire the property, to engage an attorney and general manager, to print scripts and to do the other usual pre-production work. The Attorney General of the state of New York has issued rules, pursuant to the Arts and Cultural Affairs Law, which specifically set forth what front money may be used for.

Producer Reimbursed for Front Money Not Used to Raise Money

Front money expended is reimbursed to the producer after the play is financed to the extent that the front money was used for properly budgeted items and was not used to raise money. One may not reimburse oneself for money spent to raise money. Thus, the cost of auditions and the like must be borne solely by the producer and may not be recouped as a pre-production expense.

Agreement Should Set Forth Facts

Sometimes a co-producer will contribute all of the front money if, in exchange, the other producer furnishes the property. The facts should be set forth in the "Co-Production Agreement" as to which producer is responsible for the front money, and what the party receives for it.

Front Money Arrangements

The term front money as used herein shall mean funds which may be used only for the following preproduction expenses of the proposed production: fees; advances; deposits or bonds made for the purpose of purchasing options on a book, play or other underlying materials; engaging creative personnel; securing a theatre; retaining legal, accounting and other professional advisors; preparing offering documents; the costs of a workshop to be presented by the issuer or other purposes reasonably related to the production for which the front money was raised.[4]

One should be cautious about the meaning of "or other purposes reasonably related to the production for which the front money was raised." This would probably include the costs of reproducing scripts, but ought not be extended to include the buying of dinner and drinks at Sardi's—or trips to the West Coast to consult with the author or director.

An arrangement for front money must not be confused with the assignment of profits in exchange for raising capital for the production. Front money is risk capital and, as stated, can be used prior to the capitalization of the show. If the show is not produced, then the front money investor loses the money spent by the producer. The person furnishing the front money will usually get 1 percent of the producer's share of the net profits for each 1 percent of the producing company that that particular amount of money would buy from the limited partner's share of the net profits.

A front money investor might also be given associate producer

billing in addition to the percentage interest. Of course, if the front
money is left in the production after the budget is raised—that is, if the
amount of the budget is reduced by the amount of the front money and
that front money was used for properly budgeted items and not used
to raise money—the front money investor will receive a share for the
amount of the front money from the limited-partner's profits, as well
as what he or she receives from the general partner's share. If front
money investors want their money returned to them at the time the
show is fully financed, then they are left only with their share of the
producer's profits, since they leave none of their money in as an investment as a limited partner.

Raising Money—Ne Filings—The Securities and Exchange Commission and Attorney General

THE SECURITIES AND EXCHANGE COMMISSION AND ATTORNEY GENERAL FOR A PRODUCTION IN NEW YORK STATE

IF FUNDS WILL BE RAISED from the public outside of the state of New York,[1] the production must file certain documents with the Securities and Exchange Commission and with the attorney general of the state of New York before any fund-raising occurs. If funds are to be raised solely in the state of New York, then filing with the SEC is unnecessary, but one must still file with the attorney general.

If a producer is making an offering under the federal securities laws in interstate commerce, to satisfy the federal securities laws, he or she may have several options:

1. Make the offering pursuant to Regulation D pursuant to Rule 506 as a private offering, or pursuant to Rules 504 and 505 as small offering exemptions.
2. Make the offering as a small offering pursuant to Regulation A, as a Regulation A exemption from registration.
3. Make the offering as a Form S-1 Full Registration.
4. Make the offering as Form S-18 Full Registration.

the offering exceeds $1½ million, a full registration is required
accordance with what is known as Form S-1 or Form S-18. The full
registration is a detailed, complicated chore and requires careful preparation, because it is important that there be no misleading statements
in the documents filed with the SEC.

If the total offering price does not exceed $1½ million, then instead
of a full SEC registration in accordance with Form S–1, or S–18,
it is possible to file for an exemption from registration pursuant to
Regulation A. The fact that the offerer is "exempt" from registration
does not mean that the offerer is exempt from filing. The filing that
must take place is a simpler and less-complicated kind of filing
than the full registration and usually may be accomplished in less
time.

It bears repeating that if funds are being raised outside the state in
which the business is to be conducted, and if the funds are being raised
from the public, then one must either file a full registration or, if the
offering is for less than $1½ million, an exemption from registration.
The SEC presumptions favor a conclusion that an offering is being
made to the public if there is any doubt as to whether or not it is a public
offering.

The penalties for noncompliance with the Securities Act are severe:
in addition to possible criminal penalties, for example, a producer may
be held responsible for the total budget if there is noncompliance. This
means that he may raise money, open the show, close the show, lose
the entire investment for the investors, and then have to reimburse the
investors for the total budget. For this reason, if there is any doubt as
to whether a filing should be made, it is wise to resolve the decision in
favor of filing.

The SEC is careful to point out that they do not actually approve
of the facts as submitted to them. What the SEC does is accept or reject
a filing. If it is not accepted, appropriate changes must be made in the
documents submitted so that the documents will be accepted. They
must accept the documents before an offering may be made to the
public. However, the SEC makes the fine distinction that acceptance of
a filing does not constitute "approval" of the filing.

A person should bear in mind that no sales material of any kind may
be given to a prospective investor unless it is filed and accepted by the
SEC. Each prospective investor must be given an offering circular or
a "prospectus," as it is sometimes called.[2]

REGULATION A
SEC EXEMPTION FROM REGISTRATION

Documents to Be Filed

In order to obtain an exemption from registration, certain documents must be prepared and filed with the SEC: (1) Form 1-A—Notification under Regulation A; (2) the offering circular; (3) a copy of the Limited Partnership Agreement; (4) a consent and certification by the attorney; (5) any other pertinent documents or agreements.

Form 1-A—Notification Under Regulation A

The "Notification Under Regulation A," like all of the other documents, is submitted to the SEC in quadruplicate.

This document must set forth the name of the producer, the name of the producing company that will be organized to produce the play, the date that the company will be organized, the state in which it will be organized, and the state in which the principal business will be carried on.

The offerer must set forth any predecessors, affiliates, and principal security holders of the issuer as well as their addresses and the nature of the affiliation. The name of any person owning 10 percent or more in the producing company must be set forth as well as the amount of such interest.

The name and residence of each director, officer, and promoter of the offering company must be set forth. Since the offerer is a limited partnership, in most instances, there are no directors or officers, and many parts of the application are inappropriate.

The Prospectus or Offering Circular for a Regulation A Exemption

The offering circular—which is prepared, filed, and used in an exemption from registration—as well as the prospectus—which is used for a full filing pursuant to S-1—are intended to detail the terms of the agreement between the investor and the producer. Hence, one may discern a good deal of repetition in the discussion of the prospectus in that it restates the Limited Partnership Agreement terms (discussed in detail in Chapter 6). In addition to the Limited Partnership Agreement terms, the prospectus is intended to inform the prospective investor of the inherent risks in investing in theatre.[3]

The offering circular which must be filed with the SEC is patterned after a form which was arrived at as a result of discussions between the SEC and the League of New York Theatres (now the League of American Theatre Owners and Producers). The present form of offering circular leaves much to be desired from a theatrical point of view, but it is a vast improvement over the circular previously used, which was created for the purpose of protecting investors from dishonest promoters of oil wells, nonexistent steel companies and the like, but did not have any relationship to the theatrical business and its own peculiar attendant insecurities.

Front Cover

In the present form of the offering circular, in addition to setting forth the amount of money that is being raised, the name of the company, and the name of the play, the following must appear on the outside front cover page in capital letters and in type as large as that generally used in the body of the circular:

THESE SECURITIES ARE OFFERED PURSUANT TO AN EXEMPTION FROM REGISTRATION WITH THE UNITED STATES SECURITIES AND EXCHANGE COMMISSION. THE COMMISSION DOES NOT PASS UPON THE MERITS OF ANY SECURITIES NOR DOES IT PASS UPON THE ACCURACY OR COMPLETENESS OF ANY OFFERING CIRCULAR OR OTHER SELLING LITERATURE.

The Offering

The circular will set forth the name of the producer and the fact that he will be the general partner. It will state what financial contribution, if any, is made by the general partner and how the profits and losses will be shared. It will state the minimum amount that each limited partner may invest and the maximum amount that will be raised. If the partnership may be formed before the total budget is raised, then this must likewise be set forth.

The name of the attorney for the production is usually set forth also.

The Risk to Investors

The offering circular must set forth the fact that the risk of loss is especially high in this business and the investor should be prepared for the possibility of a total loss. It will state the fact that during the last season a certain percentage of plays resulted in loss to investors; depending upon the season, this will vary between 70 percent and 80 percent. Information must be furnished as to how long the play must run at capacity to return to the limited partners their initial contributions. The percentage of plays that have run this long during the last season must also be set forth.

Usually about twenty or more separate risk factors must be included in the offering circular. These clearly emphasize the fact that investment in theatre is a risky business. And, of course, it is. Because of the risk, however, if a play is successful, the returns are commensurate with the risks.

Subscriptions

The agreement sets forth to whom the investment is to be given and the fact that the funds will be held until an amount sufficient to present the play has been raised. It is usual to state that if the amount necessary to present the play has not been raised by a certain date, all funds will be returned to the investors.

It usually says that an investor may consent to the producer using his funds prior to the total budget being raised. If this is stated, it is also pointed out that there is no advantage to the investor in giving this permission and, in fact, there may be a disadvantage.[4] The producer reserves the right to pay any investor an additional percentage of the profits so long as it is paid from the producer's share of the profits.

Overcall

A Limited Partnership Agreement, as noted in the discussion of such agreements, will sometimes set forth the fact that the limited partners must contribute an additional 10 percent, 15 percent, or 20 percent above the initial investment if called upon by the producer to do so. If this is the case, it must be set forth in the offering circular.

The Producer

Detailed facts are set forth concerning the producer. The SEC is careful to make sure that only ascertainable facts are set forth and that there are not any misleading statements or superlative adjectives. Information must be given about all previous plays produced by the producer during the previous five years, and it must state the names of the plays, the opening and closing dates, the number of performances, and the percentage of gain or loss per dollar invested.

The Play

A brief outline of the play or other details about the play must be set forth.

The Author

Details about the author and his previous works must be set forth. If this is the first play produced by the author, then it must be so stated. The payments to the author will also be detailed here.

The Director

Information about the director and past works must be set forth, if the director has been hired. The offering circular must also state the fee payable as well as any royalty payments—or estimates, if the director is not signed.

The Cast

The names and information about any important cast members who are signed must be set forth together with the details concerning their salaries.[5]

Theatre

If a contract for the theatre has been entered into, all of the details must be set forth. If not, it must be stated what the estimated capacity of a probable theatre will be and what the estimated costs will be.

Scenic Designer

Appropriate information about and the compensation of the scenic designer must be set forth if he or she has been signed, or an estimation is made.

Compensation of General Partner

This section must state the amount of the producer's fee, the amount of the cash office charge, and the fact that the producer will receive 50 percent (or whatever percentage is to be received) of the net profits of the company, as well as any other compensation to which the producer would be entitled. It is wise to set forth the fact that if the producer does perform any services of a third person, then the producer may, if he or she so desires, receive reasonable payment in the amount that the third person would have received for these services. In the absence of such a provision, if the producer with directing ability found it necessary to direct the show to save it, he or she could not be compensated for the directing.

Use of Proceeds

A detailed production budget must be set forth showing the proposed expenditure of the funds raised.

Estimated Weekly Budget

The total weekly costs at capacity must be set forth as well as the number of weeks that the play must run at full capacity to return the original investment.

Net Profits

Net profits are defined and the offering circular here sets forth any payments from the gross weekly box office receipts that are deducted in the computation of net profits. Since the limited partners will receive net profits, they should want to know if a large percentage of the gross box office receipts will be payable to a star, author, or director and thus deducted from the gross receipts in computing what constitutes net profits.

Return of Contributions—Share of Profits

The circular must set forth how the profits are shared, which is usually 50 percent for the limited partners and 50 percent for the general partner. It will also state when the contributions will be returned to the partners.

Production and Subsidiary Rights

It will briefly be stated what rights in the play the production owns and the extent of the interest in subsidiary rights.[6]

Other Financing

The circular must state whether anyone has advanced anything of value toward the production of the play.

Financial Statements

Since the partnership will later be formed, there are no financial statements available to furnish to prospective investors and this will be stated. A statement will also be made that the limited partners will be furnished with all financial statements required by the New York law. The name of the accountant and attorney will be stated.

Production Personnel

The offering circular will sometimes set forth the names of the general manager, the press agent, and the production supervisor or stage manager.

In addition to the notification, the offering circular, and the Limited Partnership Agreement, the submission will include a document signed by the attorney consenting to being the attorney and any other exhibits that are pertinent, such as any contractual arrangements entered into. (See pages 116-117 for items that must be part of every offering investment agreement and in offering circulars.)

RULE D

A "Rule D" offering is a private offering. Rule D, like all of the other provisions of the federal securities laws, requires that the offerer comply with the state laws in each state in which the offering is being made.

Although the transactions under Rule D are exempted from the registration requirements of Section 5 of the Securities Act of 1933, such transactions are not exempt from the antifraud, civil liability, or other provisions of the federal securities laws.

- Rule 504 of Rule D, applies to offerings not exceeding $500,000, within the 12 months before the start of and during the offering of the securities.
- Rule 505 applies to offerings not exceeding $5,000,000, during such period, and
- Rule 506 applies to offerings exceeding $5,000,000, during such period.

SEC FULL REGISTRATION PURSUANT TO FORM S-1

The registration statement consists of a facing sheet of the form, the prospectus, containing certain specified information required that is largely inapplicable to a theatrical financing, and the exhibits.

The Facing Sheet

The facing sheet sets forth the name of the issuer—that is, the name of the limited partnership and the general partner or general partners, since it is the limited partnership, through the general partners, which is offering the securities (limited partnership interests). In addition, the nature and amount of securities being offered is indicated. Thus, for example, if the partnership is capitalized at $5 million, $5 million in limited partnership interests would be stated. If the general partner is entitled to 50 percent of the net profits of the company and the limited partners the other 50 percent, then the price per unit is, for convenience, figured on the basis of 50 units. In a partnership capitalized at $5 million, each 1 percent interest in the limited partnership would cost $100,000. The filing fee and the name and address of counsel to the issuers are indicated and a statement is added that the approximate date of the proposed sale is as soon as possible after the effective date of the prospectus (the date of clearance with the SEC).

The Prospectus

The prospectus (also referred to as an offering circular), being the basic sales document used in connection with the sale of securities to the public, must contain all of the relevant facts concerning the offering, and no sale can be made unless a prospectus is shown to the potential investor prior to the sale. The prospectus must be prepared with great care and accuracy since misstatements, even though unintentional, may be serious.

Although no sales may be made until after the prospectus has been accepted for filing by the SEC, while the SEC is processing the offering a "red herring" prospectus may be distributed to potential investors. After the prospectus is initially filed with the SEC, a legend in bold red ink is printed across the top of the first page as follows:

PRELIMINARY PROSPECTUS—ISSUED

A registration statement relating to these securities has been filed with the Securities and Exchange Commission, but has not yet become effective. Information contained herein is subject to completion or amendment. These securities may not be sold nor may offers to buy be accepted prior to the time the registration statement becomes effective. This prospectus shall not constitute an offer to sell or the solicitation of an offer to buy nor shall there be any sales of these securities in any State in which such offer, solicitation or sale would be unlawful prior to registration or qualification under the securities laws of any such State.

This red herring prospectus (which may be used with a full registration but not with a Regulation A Exemption from Registration) may be sent to potential investors to advise them that an offering is being processed and that sales will be made in the future. It is important that a detailed record be kept of when and to whom the "red herring" is distributed, as such information will be requested by the SEC.

Contents of the Prospectus

The prospectus will contain all of the facts of the partnership agreement, information about the persons involved in the production, and facts that the SEC Regulations require and that are designed to give the investors complete information so there is a full and fair disclosure.

Introductory Statement

Initially there is stated a set of statistics concerning the speculative nature of the offering: approximately 80 percent (this figure may vary from year to year) of the plays produced in the past year resulted in loss to investors; based on estimated expenses, this play would have to run "X" (the number is inserted depending upon the facts) number of weeks at capacity merely to recoup the capitalization and "X" percent (the percent amount is inserted depending upon the facts) of the plays produced in the past year failed to run that long; of those that did, most did not play to capacity. The investor is reminded that there is no ready market for the partnership interests being offered, that no assignee of a limited partner may become a substituted limited partner, and that there is no right to withdraw from the partnership except in the event the entire capitalization is not raised by the outside date set forth in the Limited Partnership Agreement.

Some general statements are made concerning the nature of the partnership: the limited partners furnish all of the capital of the partnership and bear all of the losses up to the amount of their partnership contributions, in return for which they are each entitled to their proportionate share of 50 percent of the net profits of the partnership; if there is to be an "overcall," that is stated; the general partner, who makes no cash contribution to the partnership, receives 50 percent of the net profits, a percentage of gross receipts as a management fee (usually from 1 to 2 percent), and a weekly office expense charge for each company presenting the play; limited partners take no part in the control of the business or affairs of the partnership, and the general partner makes all decisions relating to the conduct of partnership business. The investor is advised that to an extent the success or failure of a play depends on the ability of the producer to secure suitable talent and a suitable property and that considerable competition exists among producers in the acquisition of talent and properties. The investor is further reminded that ultimately it is the professional drama critic and the audience who determine whether the production will be a commercial success or failure.

The Producer

The name and principal place of business of the producer is indicated. In addition, a brief outline of the producer's background in the theatre and his past record is set forth. The record indicates, in table form, the plays he or she has produced during the last ten years, their opening and closing dates in New York, the number of performances in New York, and the profit or loss to the investors per dollar invested.

Acquisition of Property

A few sentences briefly stating the nature of the play appear here, with an indication of the size of the cast that will be required and the number of major roles.

The date and parties to the Dramatists Guild, Inc., Approved Production Contract (APC) or other rights acquisition agreement, are set forth in addition to the royalties payable to the authors (which would include the bookwriter, lyricist, and composer if it is a musical). In addition, if the play is based on a book or a movie or some other underlying work, the date and parties to the underlying rights agreement are given together with the royalty payable to the owners of the underlying rights. A general outline of the Dramatists Guild APC, or other rights acquisition agreements, with respect to the right of the partnership to share in subsidiary rights income is also set forth. There is a statement that the contracts are on file and available for inspection at the offices of the attorney for the partnership, and that copies are on file with the SEC in Washington, D.C. Finally, reference is made to the fact that, upon formation of the partnership, the general partner will assign the contracts to the partnership.

Estimated Cost of Production and Aggregate Contributions Being Offered

A statement is made as to the estimated total cost of producing the play (usually the capitalization of the partnership). Reference is made to an overcall, if there is to be one, and a statement is made that if funds are required in addition to the capitalization of the partnership, the general partner may make loans to the partnership, without interest, which are repayable prior to the return to the limited partners of their contributions.[7]

An explanation of the share of net profits to which each limited partner would be entitled is again included and also an indication of the minimum amount that may be invested by each limited partner. "Net profits" are defined usually as the excess of gross receipts in excess of all production expenses, running expenses, and other expenses, as defined in the Limited Partnership Agreement.

Return of Contributions if Partnership Not Formed

A limited partnership contribution is payable at the time of execution of the partnership agreement. All contributions are held in a special bank account in trust until employed for production or preproduction purposes or until returned to investors. (This clause is essential in the Limited Partnership Agreement, as it is a requirement of the New York State Attorney General's Regulations.) If the entire capital is not raised by a specific date, each limited partner's contribution is returned unless it was expended pursuant to written consent specifically waiving the return of the contribution. It should be stated that the limited partner's contribution will be returned "without interest." Monies advanced by the general partner personally for partnership expenses are deemed a cash contribution to the partnership if the general partner elects not to have the money reimbursed to him.

General Nature of Offering

Plan of Offering Interests to Public

The prospectus will state how the contributions will be offered to the public. That is, it will usually say the offering will be made through the mails, by telephone and personal solicitation by the producer. It may sometimes state that the producer intends to solicit motion picture and record companies for contributions to the capital of the limited partnership.

Subscription to Limited Partnership

This section of the prospectus will state that, in order to subscribe, the limited partners must sign copies of the Limited Partnership Agreement and deliver this together with the amount of the investment to the producer. The producer has the right to accept a subscription or not.

Restriction on Right of Limited Partner to Withdraw from the Partnership

The offering circular will state that, upon signing the partnership agreement, the party is obligated to become a limited partner of the partnership and has no right to withdraw from the partnership or reduce his contribution. If the total budget is not raised, then, of course, the contributions will be returned to the prospective limited partners.

Rights of Assignee of a Limited Partner

There will be set forth the fact that an assignee of a limited partner will not have the right to become a substituted limited partner. It may also state that the partnership is not bound by any assignment of a limited partner unless the general partner consents to the assignment, or whatever the proposed limited partnership agreement provides on this item.

Use of Proceeds

There is here set forth a pre-production budget stating how it is estimated that the proceeds will be used. It will also usually state that the estimate is not necessarily based on any bids of third parties, and the general partners are not limited in their use of the funds as set forth, but may make changes in the allocation which may be deemed necessary or advisable. There is likely to be a statement also that the estimate includes some expenditures that have already been made and others to which the general partner is committed.

Purpose of Partnership

The prospectus will state the purpose of the partnership, and the language used will probably be to the effect that the purpose is to manage and produce the play and to exploit and turn to account all rights at any time held by the partnership in connection with the production of the play.

Commencement of Partnership

It will be stated that the general partner will form a partnership in accordance with the partnership law of the state of New York, and will open up a special partnership bank account in which all of the funds of the partnership will be deposited. The partnership monies will be used solely for the business of the partnership. There may also be a reference to the effect that the monies invested prior to the formation of the partnership are to be held in a special account in trust, as described in another section of the offering circular.

Contracts and Assignments Thereof

There will be here set forth all agreements that have been and will be entered into in connection with the production of the plays, as well as agreements that are anticipated. It is stated that the producer will assign to the partnership all of the contracts entered into in connection with the play.

Sources of Partnership Income

The prospectus will state that the partnership income will come from turning to account all rights in the play.

If there is a pre-production recording or other contract, all of the terms of such contract will be set forth.

Expenses of Conducting Business

"Production expenses," "running expenses," and "other expenses" are defined later in this section. Attention is called to the fact that running expenses, in addition to certain stated items, will also include any percentage of the net profits or of the gross receipts that are payable to an author, member of the cast, scenic designer, costume designer, director, choreographer, or any other person offering services for the play. Running expenses will also include the percentage of the gross receipts paid as the producer's fee, as well as the payment to the producer for the weekly cash office charge.

Disposition of Partnership Income; Return of Contributions; Profits and Losses

The prospectus will here set forth the terms outlined in the limited partnership for the repayment to the investors of their contributions pro rata after payment of all expenses and establishment of a cash reserve in a stated amount. There is also herein set forth the fact that losses are borne entirely by the limited partners, in proportion to their respective contributions, until net profits have been earned, and after net profits have been earned the general partners and limited partners share losses in the same proportion that they are entitled to share in the net profits. There is also the statement contained in the Limited Partnership Agreement that contributions and profits paid to the partners may have to be returned to the partnership if required.

Net Profits

It is here pointed out that the producer may enter into contracts providing for payment of shares of the net profits, and the remaining net profits are then divided between the limited and general partners. It is not unusual to have to pay a percentage of the gross receipts or net profits to the star, the theatre, or the director, and sometimes the choreographer and designer.

As of the date of the prospectus, there is set forth the specific percentage payments of gross weekly box office receipts and net profits that will be deducted prior to computing the net profits payable to the partners.

Effect of Federal Income Taxes

The prospectus may have an opinion of counsel for the partnership as to the tax status of the producing entity, or it may alternatively advise all potential investors to seek tax assistance to answer their specific needs.

Additional Funds

The offering circular may state that the general partner or others, if additional funds are needed, may lend money to the partnership or borrow money from others for this purpose. Such loans may be repaid prior to the repayment of contributions to the limited partners. Also, union and theatre bonds and guarantees may be furnished instead of using partnership funds for this purpose, and the amount of such bonds and guarantees may also be repaid prior to repayment of the limited partners' contributions.

Additional Companies[8]

If the Limited Partnership Agreement contains provision for the partnership to produce other companies of the play, then these facts must be set forth. It may state that funds of the original company may be used for this purpose.

Theatre Tickets

A complete detailed list of everyone entitled to purchase house seats is set forth in this section of the offering circular.

Control by General Partner

It will here be stated that the general partner has complete control of the production and agrees to render such services as are customarily rendered by a theatrical producer. A general partner may, of course, engage in other businesses, including other theatrical productions.

Remuneration of General Partner

There is here set forth the fee payable to the producer. It is not unusual for the producer's fee to be an amount ranging between 1 and 2 percent of the gross box office receipts. If a royalty pool formula is in effect, the producer will accordingly reduce his or her fee.

Reimbursement of General Partner

There will be here set forth the amount that the general partner has laid out for the production, for which he will be reimbursed after the partnership is formed.

Interest of General Partner in Certain Transactions

There is here set forth the fact that the general partner will furnish office facilities and what these will consist of, as well as a statement that he will be reimbursed by payment to him of a specified amount known as the cash office charge. If the Limited Partnership Agreement authorizes the partner to deal with the partnership or to function in any way so that his interests are adverse to the interests of the partnership, then these facts must be set forth.

Abandonment of Production

The general partner may abandon the production at any time prior to the opening for any reason whatsoever, and this fact is set forth in the offering circular.

The Creative Elements

The names and biographical credits of the author, composer, lyricist, director, choreographer, and star are detailed as well as information about any other creative personnel who are signed for the production.

Termination of Partnership

There is here set forth details as to when the partnership will terminate and the fact that if the limited partner dies the partnership may continue, with his or her executors or administrators having the same rights that the limited partner would have had.

Underwriting

Any facts concerning arrangements for underwriting all or any part of the investment must be set forth in the prospectus in detail. Underwriting is not usually a part of a theatrical offering.

Miscellaneous

The name of the attorney for the production is set forth. It is also stated that there are no financial statements available since the company has not yet been formed, but that, upon formation of the company, the limited partners will be furnished with financial statements as required by law.

There is a large mass of information that must be accumulated and furnished to the SEC for their purposes, which does not appear in the prospectus. Much of this information is intended to inform the SEC about the conditions surrounding offerings other than theatrical offerings and is particularly applicable to corporate offerers. For this reason, many of the items are inapplicable to a limited partnership, and especially inapplicable to a theatrical production, so the information is furnished by stating that the items are inapplicable. The exact information required is carefully prepared by the attorney for the production, and a detailed itemization is beyond the scope of this book.

FILINGS: WHERE MADE; ADVANTAGES AND DISADVANTAGES

A "Regulation A" filing is made at the regional office of the SEC, where the business will be conducted, and not in the Washington office as is the case of a form S-1 filing. A Form S-18 filing may be made in the Washington office or in the regional office where the business will be conducted. There is a distinct advantage if one files in the New York office, because there are numerous filings in this region and the personnel working at the New York SEC Regional Office are familiar with the very special problems that are part of the theatre business.

A Regulation A filing requires less time for the attorney to prepare, costs the client less money, and can be accepted for filing within three or four weeks after the initial filing, which means that the client can start raising money about five or six weeks after he or she comes to see the attorney for the production.

A "Form S-1" filing in Washington usually takes about six to ten weeks to complete. The time referred to in this and the preceding paragraph are not absolute but vary depending upon the backlog in the SEC offices; however, these are fairly good estimates of the average time required. The Form S-1 will take the average lawyer about twice the time to prepare for filing, so if you count on finishing the work in a week for a Regulation A filing, you can count on two weeks to complete the Form S-1.

A "Form S-18" filing will require about the same time to prepare as a Form S-1 filing. There is a distinct advantage in being able to file with the regional office, if your business happens to be in New York City. The regional office there, as has been stated, is familiar with theatrical filings, more familiar than the Washington office or any other regional office in the country. Because of this, one is likely to get prompt, understanding treatment of the filing. It is possible to get a response to a Form S-18 filing within four weeks. This, of course, also depends on how busy the SEC office is at any given time, and how complete the documents are that are submitted for filing.

THE ATTORNEY GENERAL

If the money for the production is going to be raised only in the state of New York, an SEC filing may be avoided. In all cases, however, there must be a filing with the office of the attorney general.

New York, like all of the other states in the union, has what are known as "blue sky laws" (security laws designed to protect investors). In addition to the New York law, there are the New York state theatre financing regulations that govern a theatrical financing. It may be necessary to file in other states in which money will be raised. The production attorney will make this decision as to where filings are necessary.

If a filing has been made with the SEC, the filing with the attorney general is greatly simplified, since the attorney general will accept the offering circular filed with the SEC with one or two minor additions that will have been included at the time the SEC filing is made.

If there is no SEC filing and money will be raised solely in the state of New York, and if the offering is for $250,000 or less, the producer may file and use a prospectus (an offering circular) and a Limited Partnership Agreement, or may choose to simply file and use a Limited Partnership Agreement setting forth all of the terms of the agreement with the limited partners. If more than $250,000 is being raised, an offering circular must be filed and used. If it is possible to avoid the use of an offering circular, I usually recommend it, as the attorney general's offering circular, like the SEC form, must contain some provisions likely to discourage investment.

If the offering is to be made to less than thirty-six persons, it is possible to avoid filing with the attorney general if each of the investors expressly waives, in writing, the right to have offering literature filed and the right to receive information that would be contained in such an offering circular.[9]

Front Money for Developmental Production

A producer may, without filing with the attorney general, make an offering to fewer than five persons for the sole purpose of raising "front money." Front money may only be used for the specific purposes hereinafter set forth. This provision is very specific in that the offering may only be *made* to four persons or fewer.

The important contribution of the amendment to the regulations effective January 16, 1985, is the inclusion of "the costs of a workshop" as a proper use of front money. "Front money" is now defined in the regulations as ". . . funds which may be used only for the following pre-production expenses of the proposed production: fees; advances; deposits or bonds made for the purpose of purchasing options on a book, play or other underlying materials; engaging creative personnel; securing a theatre; retaining legal, accounting and other professional advisors; preparing offering documents; the costs of a workshop to be presented by the issuer or other purposes reasonably related to the production for which the front money was raised."

The importance of this new definition stems from the fact that, on occasion, a producer may want to have a workshop or other developmental production of a play, which under the Actors Equity Workshop Code can be produced for about one-eighth of what an Off-Broadway production would cost, and for about one-twentieth of what a Broadway production would cost. By first doing such a production, the producer gets an opportunity to see the play, and to develop it less expensively, and at the same time gets the opportunity to expose potential investors to the play on the stage. The arguments against doing such a production first is that it is a rather expensive "backer's audition," and second, if the producer merely did a reading in someone's home, or in a hotel room, it would serve the same purpose of exposing the investors to the property.

What is significant is that, if a producer now wants to do a workshop or other developmental production, since he or she can properly use the front money for this purpose, the front money investor can end up with a percentage interest in the play as finally capitalized for the Broadway or Off-Broadway production. For example, if the Off-Broadway show is capitalized for $500,000, $10,000 will purchase 1 percent of the Limited Partnership that will be formed to produce the play. If a front money investor invests $20,000, then in addition to whatever he or she would get from the general partner for furnishing the front money, the investment can be considered an investment in the producing company that will produce the play Off-Broadway, and he or she will be entitled to 2 percent of the profits from the producing company.

Under these circumstances, it is usual for the producer to have completed the necessary securities filings when the workshop or other developmental production is presented, so that he can pass out the offering literature to prospective investors at the showcase production and actually take their investment at that time, rather than having to wait until some later date to receive the investments.

Six Items Required in Every Investment Agreement

The law provides specifically that all investment agreements must contain the following six items, and the first two must be included in all offering literature used. Filings with the Securities and Exchange Commission are usually accepted as filed by the Office of the Attorney General if the following items are properly included:

1. A statement that all monies raised from the offering and sale of syndication interests shall be held in a special bank account in trust until actually employed for pre-production, or production, purposes of this particular theatrical production or until returned to the investor or investors.
2. A statement that financial statements will be furnished to all investors and the Department of Law pursuant to the provisions of Article 23 and the regulations issued by the attorney general thereunder.
3. A representation that the producer has acquired the right to produce the theatrical production that is the subject of the offering, the date on which such right was acquired, and the expiration date of such right.
4. A statement that, where authorized by investors, contributions may be used for pre-production or production purposes prior to the completion of the offering. If the producer intends to use the interest earned on investors contributions, when permitted to do so, this option must be fully explained. If investors wish to authorize the use

of contributions or interest earned thereon prior to completion of the offering, the authorization must be set forth in boldface roman type, or if typed in capital letters, with underlining.

5. There must also be disclosed the total amount of expenses that have been advanced at the date of filing the agreement with the Department of Law, which are to be reimbursed out of the capitalization, with an itemized breakdown and the conditions of repayment of such advances.

6. The producer's residence must be set forth, but it is not necessary to disclose information concerning previous theatrical experience.

Exemption from the Accounting Requirements

The Arts and Cultural Affairs Law and the regulations thereto provide in detail the requirements of accountings for plays, including the necessity of furnishing a "certified statement." A "certified statement" can be very costly, and there is a provision for exemption from the accounting requirements if the production is capitalized for $250,000 or less or if the offering is *made* to fewer than thirty-six persons. The producer must still comply with all the other requirements of maintaining extensive books and records.

CHAPTER 8

The League of American Theatres and Producers

T HE BROADWAY PRODUCER must deal with a number of different craft unions and associations. The producers and theatre owners founded their own association on January 30, 1930, which is now known as the League of American Theatres and Producers. The League has offices at 226 West 47th Street in New York City. Whether a person owns one theatre or seventeen theatres, and whether the theatre owner is the producer of one show or seven shows, the theatre owner is entitled to only one membership in the League.

Purpose of the League

Generally, the objectives of the association as stated in its bylaws, are to conserve and promote the general welfare of the legitimate theatre and the common interests and welfare of theatre owners, lessees, or operators and producers of plays, and to afford an organization which enables them to act for their common purpose and interest. The primary duty of the League is to act as bargaining representative for theatre owners and producers with the various craft unions and associations. Each contract is negotiated and entered into for a specified limited period. There are usually some changes, often minor, when each contract is negotiated.

Dues

The dues paid by producers and theatre owners is $250 per week during each week that a show is running in a first-class theatre in New York City and first-class theatres in other cities around the country.

Collective Bargaining Agreements

The League has negotiated and signed collective bargaining agreements with many associations and craft unions, which may be divided into three categories:

- Agreements between the unions and the theatre owners or lessees.
- Agreements which are entered into by the unions with both the theatre owners or lessees and the producers. Those contracts between the theatre owners and unions are, of course, as important to the producers as the contracts that the producers make directly with the unions. All contracts directly affect the producer.

Agreements for Theatre Owners or Lessees

The contracts negotiated by the League for the theatre owners or lessees are with the following:

- Theatrical Protective Union, Local No. 1, IATSE, represents the basic house crew of a theatre covering the carpentry, electrical, property, and other related work including "taking in" and "taking out," handling, assembling, and dismantling all equipment used in the show. This covers the curtain men, sound men, fly men, carpenters, electricians, property men, and the like.
- Treasurers and Ticket Sellers Union, Local No. 751, as its name implies, represents treasurers, assistant treasurers, and other box office personnel involved in ticket selling. Ticket Takers and Telephone Operators Union, Local No. 751 is aligned with Treasurers and Ticket Sellers.
- Legitimate Theatre Employees Union, Local No. B-183, represents the employment of usher, directresses, chief ushers, front doormen, ticket takers, and backstage doormen.
- Theatre, Amusement, and Cultural Building Service Employees,

Local No. 54, represents building service employees such as porters, elevator operators, cleaners, and matrons.

- Local Union No. 30, International Union of Operating Engineers, affiliated with the AFL-CIO, represents employees engaged in the operation and maintenance of heating boilers, heating systems, mechanical refrigerating systems, air circulation (which is part of the mechanical refrigerating system), standpipes, and fire pumps.

Agreements for Producers

The contracts of unions with the producers negotiated by the League include the following:

- Actors' Equity Association, covering actors and stage managers.
- Theatrical Wardrobe Attendants Union, Local No. 764, covering the wardrobe crew of wardrobe supervisors and dressers.
- The Society of Stage Directors and Choreographers, covering directors and choreographers.
- The United Scenic Artists, covering set designers, lighting designers, costume designers, and assistant designers.
- The Dramatists Guild, Inc., Approved Production Contract, previously discussed in detail, is also negotiated by the League for the producers, but a contract is not signed by the League and the Guild. (See pages 39 and 40 in Chapter 4.)

Agreements for Both Theatre Owners and Producers

The contracts of unions with the producers negotiated by the League include the following:

- Association of Theatrical Press Agents and Managers, Union No. 18032 AFL-CIO, which, as the name states, covers press agents (often hired by the producer or the theatre owner but most usually the producer alone), company managers (hired by the producer), and house managers (hired by the theatre).
- Associated Musicians of Greater New York, Local No. 802, American Federation of Musicians, which covers the musicians. The number of musicians required in a particular theatre varies, depending upon whether the show is a drama or a musical. If the production is a drama, the number of musicians employed depends upon the amount

of live and taped music used in the production. If the production is a musical, the number of musicians employed depends upon the size of the house. However, musicians in excess of the contractual minimum may be employed if deemed necessary for artistic considerations.
• Make-Up Artists and Hair Stylists Union, Local 798, IATSE, AFL-CIO, which covers make-up artists and hair and wig stylists employed in the production of legitimate shows.

Employer and Employee Also Sign Agreement—Term of Employment

The League has entered into a bargaining agreement with all the above-listed associations and unions. Those with a bargaining agreement still have separate agreements that must be entered into by the employee and the employer. The theatre owners generally hire their employees under a one-year contract during each season, usually the period from Labor Day to Labor Day. A producer enters into an agreement with an employee for a particular production.

The contracts entered into with the theatres will be discussed separately from those entered into with the producers and those entered into with both the producers and the theatres.

Terms in Common

Union Sole Bargaining Agent

All the contracts have some terms in common. For example, all the agreements—with one exception—have language to the effect that the producer (producer is referred to as "manager" or "management" in many of these agreements) recognizes the union as the sole and exclusive bargaining agent for all employees who perform work under the jurisdiction of the union. (The one exception where there is not a recognition clause makes it quite implicit even though it is not specifically stated.)

Employee Must Join Union—No Strikes or Lockouts

All the agreements state in similar language that an employee doing the kind of work covered by the union contract must become a union member within a specified time, usually within thirty days after such employment. The contracts almost always provide that there will be no strikes, walkouts, or lockouts.

Scope and Jurisdiction

All agreements have a clause setting forth the scope of the agreement and the jurisdiction of the union. Of course, the language differs with each agreement, since each union or association has a different jurisdiction. That is, some are applicable only to legitimate theatre while others cover revues, nightclub acts, ballet, and other performances. The geographic jurisdiction of the different unions and associations also varies.

Pension and Welfare Rates

The schedule of rate payments differ as do the hours of employment. There are provisions for welfare payments and/or pension payments in all the agreements.

Business Agent May Enter Theatre

Some contracts provide for a payment of dues (check-off) by the theatre and producer directly to the union. It is usual to find a provision that the business agent of the union (or other representative) may be admitted to the theatre at all times for the purpose of verifying conditions.

Grievance Procedure and Arbitration

All the contracts have a provision for grievance procedures or arbitration or both to settle any disputes. The contract dates vary from one to ten years. In several contracts, there are provisions for vacation benefits to employees.

Pension and Welfare Tables

Tables 1, 2, and 3 will be helpful with respect to certain items contained in all contracts on which comparison can be made.

TABLE 1 CONTRACTS WITH THEATRE

	Local #1 Carpenters, Electricians, Property	Local #751 Treasurers and Ticket Sellers	Local B-751 Mail and Telephone Order Clerks	Local B-183 Ushers, Directresses, Front and Back Doormen	Local #54 Building Service Employees, Elevator Operators, Matrons, etc.	Local #30 Heat and Air-conditioning Maintenance
Contract Dates	August 1, 1986 to July 31, 1988	Sept. 1, 1985 to August 28, 1987	Jan. 22, 1986 to Jan. 21, 1986	Sept. 3, 1984 to Sept. 6, 1988	Sept. 3, 1984 to Sept. 6, 1987	Dec. 22, 1985 to Dec. 21, 1988
Pensions	7% gross earnings	8% gross earnings		$1.13 per day per employee paid monthly	5% gross earnings	$14.20 per employee per week
Welfare	7% gross earnings	5% gross earnings	6% gross earnings	6½% gross earnings	$600.00 per employee semi-annually	$15.00 per employee per week
Vacation	9% gross earnings paid yearly by separate check	8½% gross earnings	7% gross earnings	6½% gross earnings	24 weeks' work first year gets 1 week's paid vacation	8% gross earnings
Annuity	13% gross earnings	12% gross earnings	$.50 per day per employee			

TABLE 2 CONTRACTS WITH PRODUCER

	Actors' Equity Association	Local #764 Wardrobe Supervisors and Dressers	Society of Stage Directors and Choreographers	Local #829 United Scenic Artists
Contract Dates	June 30, 1986 to June 25, 1989	August 30, 1985 to September 1, 1988	October 1, 1986 to December 31, 1988	March 20, 1978 to December 31, 1989
Pensions	8% gross earnings up to $5,500.00	6% gross earnings	$500.00 initial contribution; $45.00 weekly contribution; $40.00 each additional company	11% of contract fee not to exceed $1,441.00
Welfare	$31.00 per actor per week	7% gross earnings	$1,000 initial contribution; $75.00 weekly contribution; $50.00 each additional company	
Vacation	4% to a maximum of $52.00 weekly	8% gross earnings		
Annuity		7% gross earnings		

TABLE 3 CONTRACTS WITH THEATRE AND WITH PRODUCER

	Association of Theatrical Press Agents and Managers Union No. 18032	Local #802, American Federation of Musicians	Local 798, Make-Up and Hair Stylists
Contract Dates	January 1, 1983 to December 31, 1985	September 10, 1984 to September 13, 1987	August 1, 1985 to July 31, 1988
Pensions	8% gross salary	5% gross payroll	$25.00 per week per employee
Welfare	$65.00 per week per employee	$10.00 per week per employee	6% of gross earnings
Vacations	8% of gross weekly salary	6% of gross weekly salary	6% of gross earnings
Annuity	—	—	2% of minimum scale

DEPARTMENT OF SPECIAL PROJECTS

In 1973, the League formed the Theatre-Industry Committee. The committee decided that the League must expand to deal with the various problems that confront the legitimate theatre. In late 1975, on the committee's recommendation, a department of Special Projects was created. Special Projects was directed to address, among other concerns, the following priorities: urban environment, computerized ticket selling and marketing, and public relations.

Urban Environment

The League, recognizing the importance of the Times Square theatre district's impact on the theatre-going public, is taking an active stance on the current laws, rules, and regulations affecting the theatre and theatre district. The Department of Special Projects works daily with the federal, state, and city agencies with jurisdiction and responsibilities in the Broadway area. Special Projects encourages the enforcement of laws and regulations on the books as well as the maintenance of the region. Specific concerns have been to urge the development of statutes or ordinances dealing with loitering, the licensing of massage parlors, peep shows, and liquor licenses for topless bars. In addition, Special Projects has endorsed a rigid enforcement of existing laws concerning prostitution, peddling and vending, building-code violations, and littering. Special Projects and the League have undertaken efforts to improve the physical appearance of the Broadway area by providing trash receptacles in heavily traveled areas and in developing decorative planting projects for public spaces.

Special Projects has also researched real estate developments projected for the Broadway area and has taken positions pro or con on behalf of the League. These include the redevelopment of Eighth Avenue, Manhattan Plaza, Manhattan Project–Theatre Row, a convention center, a major hotel development, and the Times Square redevelopment.

Public Relations

Special Projects has taken strong affirmative action in the field of public relations. A major effort has been and is being made to promote the importance of the Broadway theatre to New York City, New York State, and the entire country. Politicians and public officials at every level of government are provided data and urged to consider laws directly or indirectly involving the Broadway theatre. Special Projects undertakes to produce statistical information to demonstrate the economic and cultural importance of the Broadway theatre to the American economy and way of life. In the 1983–84 Broadway season $227 million in ticket sales were tallied. It is estimated that in that same season $378 million in theatre-going-related expenditures were generated, having a theatre-related economic impact in the New York metropolitan area of some $750 million. In addition, the commercial theatre expanded $243 million, for an additional impact of $630 million.

Special Projects has taken these statistics and joined with New York City and New York State to promote tourism and the Broadway theatre. Several distinctive campaigns have been mounted featuring the cast of major Broadway hits and the special allure of the city and Broadway. The "I Love New York" campaign has been chief among these.

The Antoinette Perry ("Tony") awards focus the attention of millions of Americans on the Broadway theatre each year. Special Projects involves itself with the promotion of the awards show as well as its planning. From promotional brochures to the creation of a Broadway theatre museum, educational projects in New York school districts, and lobbying on behalf of the Broadway theatre, the League's Special Projects department is expanding the League's abilities to serve Broadway's theatre owners and producers.

Funding for Special Projects is shared by the producer and theatre owner on a prorated basis. A musical is assessed $600 per week and a dramatic play is assessed $480 per week.

CHAPTER 9

Contracts with the Theatre

IN HIRING THE CREW, a producer ought to try to find a group that is compatible socially as well as on a working basis. There are persons in the business who usually work together. A certain electrician may work with a particular carpenter most of the time as a team, so a producer would hire both. This is desirable since it is to the advantage of a production to have persons on the show who know the working habits of their fellow workers. Liking the people one works with is also most helpful, especially in theatre when often the work is under extreme pressure and in close quarters.

THEATRICAL PROTECTIVE UNION, LOCAL 31, IATSE

Jurisdiction

This union has jurisdiction over carpenters, electricians, and property men, and includes "taking in" and "taking out," handling, assembling, and dismantling of any and all equipment, property, chairs, seats, furniture hardware, all electrical fixtures and appliances, staging, scenery, masking, unloading, loading of vehicles, and the like. The minimum basic house crew for each theatre consists of a head carpenter, head electrician, head property man, and curtain man, and in the Mark Hellinger, the Minskoff, the Gershwin, and the Winter Garden the basic crew in addition includes an assistant electrician.

Term of Employment

Although the employment is for the term of the agreement with the union, the employee need not be paid during the period that the theatre is dark, subject to any other specific provisions of the contract.

Work Week

The work week commences on Sunday and ends with the following Saturday night's performance. All employees work on a weekly salary basis with a few minor exceptions specifically set forth in the agreement.

Take-in and Take-out

There are detailed terms covering the taking in and putting on of an attraction as well as the taking out of an attraction. The take-in provisions include, for example, the fact that all employees must be called for not less than a minimum call of eight hours on a take-in and put-on of a show during the first day, and all calls after that must be for not less than a minimum of six hours. The employees must receive one hour off for meals between twelve noon and 1:00 P.M., and between 6:00 P.M. and 7:00 A.M., or be paid double the hourly rate for such hours.[1]

Regular Work Week Hours

The contract states that during the regular attraction, the work week for heads of departments and assistants consists of eight performances: six evening performances occurring during the hours of 7:30 P.M. to 11:30 P.M. Monday through Saturday evenings, plus two matinee performances occurring during the hours of 1:30 P.M. to 5:30 P.M. on Wednesdays and Saturdays. The hours are slightly less for other persons. The heads of departments must work as well as direct the department. A carpenter cannot operate the curtain but may assist the curtain man in one-scene shows.

Wage Rates

The wage scale provided in the agreement is as follows:

	August 1, 1986 to July 31, 1987
Heads of Department	$743.84
Assistants	$656.30
Fly Men, Front Light Men, Laser Operators and Sound Men	$619.83
Portable Board Operators, Public Address Men, House or Traveler Curtain Men, Flying, Rigging, Traps, Turntable or Winch Men and all other men	$568.90

Minimum Hours and Repertory

All calls, unless otherwise specifically provided for in the contract, shall be for a minimum of four hours' duration.

When any theatre operates under repertory conditions—that is, two or more shows playing within the repertory season—the pay scales will be 10 percent above the normal rates. Giving two one-act plays as part of a single performance is not repertory. The repertory scale is applicable only to performances, not to "put-in" and "take-out."

Extra Performances and Sign Work

The agreement contains specific provision for nine or more performances per week and seventh-day performances, as well as regular Sunday, special Sunday, holiday performances, and midnight performances.[2] It is also provided that an employee must be paid a full weekly salary even if an attraction operates on a fixed policy of less than eight performances per week. There are special provisions covering work on theatre signs.

Vacation and Temporary Closings

Employees on vacation must be replaced by the union during their vacation. They must be paid one-half of their regular salary during a period of voluntary closing, which is considered the interruption of a show in order to permit a star a leave of absence and other similar reasons.

Fireproofing and Inspections

There are specific provisions that the respective head of a department must be employed on at least a four-hour call for fireproofing of scenery, drops, props, equipment, or material; that the three heads of departments and the curtain man must likewise be employed on a similar call for annual fire inspection; and that the head electrician will be given a six-hour call to obtain or renew the standpipe license or permit for the theatre.

Discharge for Cause—Severance Pay

Except in the case of discharge for drunkenness, dishonesty, or incompetence, heads of departments and assistants employed for at least one year are entitled to severance pay in the event of termination of their employment. They are entitled to one week's pay at the rate being received at the time of termination for each year of service, with a minimum of fourteen weeks' pay.

Rehearsals and Construction Work

There are detailed provisions concerning rehearsals at rehearsal halls and theatres, as well as detailed terms concerning closing performances.[3] The rates of pay for theatre rehabilitation and construction work are set forth in detail. This includes work in the pit, platforms, stage work, flooring, rigging, loading and unloading of cars, etc.[4]

Dark Houses, Safe Conditions, and Photos

The agreement also covers work in dark houses and the reduction of manpower as a result.[5] There are provisions that the working conditions will be safe. Specific provision is also made for the taking of all commercial pictures, television taping, and filming.[6]

TREASURERS AND TICKET SELLERS UNION, LOCAL #751

Jurisdiction

As the name implies, this union governs the hiring of treasurers and ticket sellers within the five boroughs of the city of New York. The League members must negotiate special terms, wages, and hours for theatres outside this area.

Wage Rates

The wage scale provided in the agreement is as follows:

	Sept. 1, 1986 to Aug. 30, 1987
TREASURERS, for week of six (6) days (Monday to Saturday inclusive) not less than	$756.86
ASSISTANT TREASURERS, for week of six (6) days (Monday to Saturday inclusive) not less than	$664.73

SUNDAYS, Box Office is to be open from 12:00 Noon to 10:00 P.M. A minimum of four (4) members of the Box Office Staff shall receive, in addition to their weekly salary not less than one-quarter (¼) of weekly salary for two performances, and a minimum of three members of the box office shall receive not less than one-sixth (1/6) of weekly salary for one performance, without any offset or deduction for taking a substitute day off during the week.

MIDNIGHT PERFORMANCES, not less than one-sixth (1/6) of weekly salary.

The above scales provide for up to eight (8) performances from Monday through Saturday. One-eighth (⅛) extra shall be paid for any performance in excess of eight during that period.

Advance Sales—Extra Attractions
Other than Current Attraction

TREASURERS, when performance
given on Sunday (regardless
whether tickets sold in advance
or not): For one performance,
not less than $126.15
For two performances, not less
than $189.21
When performance given on
Sunday (regardless whether
tickets sold in advance or not)
for one performance, not less
than $110.79
for two performances, not less
than $166.18

Advance Sale and Benefits

For handling the advance sale of a current attraction on weekdays and for a weekday matinee, the salary may not be less than one-sixth of the weekly wage for each day. The parties must also be paid a salary, prorated at the weekly rate, for advance sale and for benefit performances during a period that the theatre is normally dark.

Refunds

If more than $400 has to be refunded, the treasurer and assistant treasurer must be retained for that purpose and must be paid at the rate of one-sixth of the weekly salary for each day, but in no event longer than one week unless the employer decides to retain the staff. After the amount of the refund is reduced to less than $400, further refunds may be handled without additional compensation at any box office which is staffed by members of the union. If the theatre has a following attraction, then the treasurer and assistant treasurer must make refunds with no extra compensation to them, providing that continuity of employment is not interrupted.

Contract for Season

A standard individual contract is entered into with each employee. It names the theatre at which he or she is employed and the period of employment, which may not be less than a season (as defined), except in cases of extra box office help. There is also an exception in that the employment may be for less than a season if the lease of the employer terminates before the expiration of the season and/or the employer loses control of the theatre. In such event, the contract of employment is for that portion of the season that the employer is in control of the theatre. The employer must designate the box office staff not later than August 1 of each year that the theatre is open, and if the theatre is dark, the employer must designate the box office no later than September 1, regardless of when the theatre opens thereafter. Although the hiring is seasonal—even during the season, unless otherwise specifically provided in the contract—the employee is not paid if the theatre is closed.

Season, Box Office Staff, Subscription, and Benefits

"Season," as it is used in the contract, means such time as the theatre is open from September 1 to August 31 the following year. The box office staff of each theatre consists of a box office treasurer and at least three assistants, except that during a refund week it consists of those staff members under contract. A negotiation procedure outlined in the agreement determines whether theatres seating over one thousand should be required to employ yet another assistant treasurer at assistant's salary. No person other than the treasurer or his assistants may handle ticket sales to the public or a broker. Extra help may be engaged to handle subscriptions and benefits at places other than in the box office. All reservations at the theatre must be handled by employees covered by this agreement. The employer or his or her representative, the producer or his or her representative, the treasurer or his or her assistant treasurer and ticket sellers are the only ones permitted in the box office.

Minimum Hours

Treasurers and assistant treasurers must be called to service at least one week prior to opening of the play, and one day must be added to the one week for each paid preview in advance of the public opening. The treasurer outlines the hours of the box office employees, and these may not exceed eight hours in any one calendar day, of which one hour must be a meal period. Work for advance sales less than a full week is prorated. Time and a half is payable for certain holidays as set forth in the agreement, and the employees receive an additional one-sixth of their weekly salary for "settlement" at the end of a run.

Bonding of Treasurers and Assistants

Box office treasurers and assistants must be bonded and the bond is paid for by the employer. The money and tickets for which the treasurer and his or her assistants are responsible can be handled only by them.

Termination of Employment

Either party, by written notice, may terminate the contract of a box office employee during the first week of employment. This, however, may not be done where that box office employee was employed for the previous season by the same employer and did not receive notice of termination before May 31; he or she is automatically reengaged for the following season.

Transfer of Theatres and Closing Notice

House staff employees may be transferred from one theatre to another during the season, providing that the continuity of the operation is designated in the individual contract of employment. If the attraction has run more than four weeks, then closing notice given by the employer to the box office employees before the closing of the box office on Monday night shall be effective to constitute one week's notice of closing as of the following Saturday night. If the employer fails to give notice, he or she must pay one week's compensation in lieu thereof. If the attraction has run four weeks or less, then notice of closing is not necessary. However, if the attraction closes during a calendar week, the box office staff is entitled to a full week's compensation.

Discharge for Cause

An employee may be summarily dismissed for cause without prior notice. Cause means intoxication on duty, dishonesty in the discharge of duty, disorderly conduct in the performance of duty, or inability to secure a bond. There is provision in the contract for review of a summary dismissal.

Notice if Theatre Is Sold

If the theatre is sold, the box office employees' employment may be terminated on two weeks' notice or two weeks' pay in lieu of the notice.

Miscellaneous

There are specific provisions in the contract for negotiations in the event that the theatre is leased for less than a year by the same employer or by a different employer for other than legitimate theatre purposes. Employees are not paid during the period that a production is closed because of fire, accident, strikes, riots, acts of God, the illness of the star or a principal featured performer, or action of a public enemy, which could not be reasonably anticipated or prevented.

Ticket Cannot Be Sold for More than Stated Price

The contract specifically states that neither the employer nor the employee may accept any charge or fee in excess of the amount designated on the ticket as the ticket price.

LEGITIMATE THEATRE EMPLOYEES UNION, LOCAL #B-183

Jurisdiction

This union agreement controls the hiring of ushers, ticket takers, directors, head ushers, and doormen. The union shop provision is to the effect that the union will supply the employer with applicants in the operation of "legitimate" theatre or theatres and vaudeville or motion picture theatres or theatres having a "reserved seat" policy, as distinguished from a "grind" policy in the city of greater New York. If the union cannot supply help, then the employer may engage help in the open market.

Term of Employment

If an employee is retained for four weeks, the employee may not be replaced before the following Labor Day except for just cause. If there is a dispute as to what constitutes just cause, which the theatre and the local union cannot settle, then the League and the general office of IATSE (the parent union) will settle the matter.

Prior employees must be recalled for the following season unless they are given notice of termination at least thirty days before Labor Day.

Although the hiring is for the season, the employee need not be paid during a period when the theatre is closed unless otherwise specifically provided for in the contract.

Wage Rates

The weekly and daily wage rates are as follows (minimum wages per performance in parenthesis):

Effective Sept. 8, 1986

Ushers	$168.01 ($21.00)
Directresses	$178.65 ($22.33)
Head Ushers	$206.51 ($25.19)
Ticket Takers	$254.80 ($31.86)
Doormen	$268.07 ($44.68)

Eight-Performance Week

The scale of employment is based on an eight-performance week (except doormen), and employees substituting for regular employees are paid a proportionate share of a week's work. Performances in excess of eight are at the rate of time and a half, except where a show opens with a policy in excess of eight performances.

Doormen's Week

Doormen's work week is six days but not exceeding forty hours in a week. Over forty hours per week is paid at the rate of time and a half with a minimum overtime call of seven hours. Doormen receive no extra compensation for extra performances.

Overtime (Other than Doormen)

Extra time required for ushers, head ushers, directors, or ticket takers, in excess of the regular hours, is paid at the hourly rate, with a minimum of one hour. All midnight performances are paid at the rate of time and a half.[7]

Program Insertions and Cancelled Performances

Employees are paid $2 extra per week whenever they insert printed material (other than cast changes or show publicity) into the theatre programs. In the event of a cancellation, employees on a regular eight-performance week are paid for eight performances even though they may work less.[8]

Time Employees May Leave Theatre

With the exception of opening night, one-half of the employees (excluding doormen) are permitted to leave work twenty minutes after the curtain goes up. If a theatre has only one ticket taker, this does not apply to him.

Special Uniforms

If the producer requires that an employee wear any special uniform, such apparel must be furnished by the producer. White collars for ushers must also be furnished by, and laundered at the expense of, the producer.[9]

Notice of Discharge

An employee on a weekly salary must be given two weeks' notice in writing of discharge, and employees wishing to terminate must do the same. If the theatre closes or the policy of the theatre changes, only one week's notice is required. If an attraction closes after having run less than four weeks, no notice is necessary, nor is it necessary for an employee discharged for drunkenness or dishonesty.

THEATRE, AMUSEMENT, AND CULTURAL BUILDING SERVICE EMPLOYEES, LOCAL #54

Jurisdiction

This agreement covers custodians, roundsmen/porters, elevator operators, twenty-six-hour custodians, and matrons. In 1986 Local 54 had about 400 members working in Broadway theatres.

Wage Rates

The minimum weekly wages are as follows:

Head custodian (if the theatre has only one porter, he shall be considered head custodian) shall receive:
A minimum weekly wage of $341.50 for the period commencing Labor Day 1986.
Custodians shall receive:
A minimum weekly wage of $319.44 for the period commencing Labor Day 1986.
Roundsmen shall receive:
A minimum weekly wage of $319.44 for the period commencing Labor Day 1986.
Elevator operators shall receive:
A minimum weekly wage of $319.44 for the period commencing Labor Day 1986.
Head twenty-six-hour custodians shall receive:
A minimum weekly wage of $222.03 for the period commencing Labor Day 1986.
Twenty-six-hour custodians shall receive:
A minimum weekly wage of $202.45 for the period commencing Labor Day 1986.
Matrons shall receive:
A minimum weekly wage of $206.45 for the period commencing Labor Day 1986.

Basic Crew

The basic crew employed in a theatre is the same number of employees employed in the theatre on the first day of August 1955, or, if closed on that date, the last open date before then. New theatres opened since then have a basic crew consisting of the number of employees used on the opening of the theatre.[10]

Discharge for Cause

An employee may not be discharged except for intoxication while on duty or an act of dishonesty. The contract contains provision for investigation and review of a discharge.[11]

Sunday Performances

The entire crew (normal complement of workers) must be employed in the event of a Sunday performance or performances. If the Sunday is the seventh consecutive day of work, the employee receives time and a half.[12]

Hours of Work

Standard Week and Overtime

Custodians work a standard forty-hour week consisting of six days not exceeding eight hours per day. Overtime for work in excess of eight hours per day, or forty hours per week, is at the rate of one and one-half the regular straight time hourly rate. If a custodian is required to work in excess of three evening performances a week, then he or she must be paid time and a half for all hours worked during such performances. The regular head custodian of the house must be at the theatre when the box office is open to the public, even though the house is not in operation.

Twenty-Six-Hour Custodians' Standard Week and Overtime

Twenty-six-hour custodians work a standard week of twenty-six hours consisting of six days not exceeding four hours each day performed between the hours of 7:00 A.M. and 1:00 P.M. with one additional hour each matinee day at the conclusion of the matinee performance. The overtime rate for twenty-six-hour custodians is one and a half times the regular rate and is paid after four hours of work per day, or after six days per week, or after twenty-four hours per week, except when there are matinee pick-ups, in which event overtime commences during that week after twenty-six hours.

Matrons' Standard Week and Overtime

Matrons' standard work week consists of eight performances per week within a six-day period. The maximum time of each performance is four hours. All time worked in excess of eight performances per week or four hours per performance is considered overtime and is paid at the rate of time and a half.

Uniforms and Equipment Supplied

The uniforms, work clothes, and equipment required to be worn or used by the employees is supplied and maintained by the employer.

MAIL AND TELEPHONE ORDER CLERKS UNION, LOCAL B-751

Jurisdiction

This agreement covers all mail clerks, telephone operator and head mail clerks, and head telephone operators employed in any and all theatres.

Wage Rates

The minimum weekly wages effective January 22, 1985, are as follows;

Mail Order Clerks	$340.93
Telephone Operators	$352.57
Head Mail Order Clerk and Head Telephone Operator	$394.16

Scope of Work

The mail order clerks and telephone operators assist the treasurer and assistant treasurer in servicing mail and telephone ticket orders. If three or more mail clerks or three or more telephone operators are employed, one of them will perform the functions of a "head" as agreed to by the treasurer of the theatre and the business representative of the union.

Hours of Work

The basic work week for heads shall be five days or 35 hours per week. Time and one-half will be paid after 35 hours. The mail order clerks basic work week is five days, 7 hours per day, for a total of 35 hours per week, excluding meal hours. The basic work week for telephone operators is six days. Approximately 6 hours per day for a total of 35 hours per week. All time worked in excess of 6 hours in a day or 35 hours per week or on a seventh day will be paid for at time and one-half. Overtime is computed in one-hour segments.

The basic work week for all employees excludes Sunday. Work on Sunday is paid at time and one-half, in addition to the basic weekly salary.

Holidays

Employees who work on any of the following holidays receive a day's pay for such work, in addition to their other compensation: New

Year's Day, Lincoln's Birthday, Washington's Birthday, Independence Day, Labor Day, Columbus Day, Election Day, Thanksgiving Day and Christmas Day. If an employee is not required by management to work on any such holiday, the employee is given credit for the day.

Safety

At no time is an employee required to work in a theatre alone.

Termination

An employee may be dismissed only for just causes and then only upon notification to the union in writing within twenty-four hours after the dismissal specifying the reasons for the discharge. Except for the closing of a show during preview weeks or the week of the official opening, one week's notice of layoff or one week's pay in lieu thereof is paid to laid-off employees.

LOCAL UNION #30 OF THE INTERNATIONAL UNION OF OPERATING ENGINEERS

Jurisdiction

Local #30 is the collective bargaining agent for employees engaged in the operation and maintenance of the heating and air-conditioning systems in the theatres.

Work Week

The work week consists of five straight-time days and a sixth day at the rate of time and a half. All work in excess of eight hours in any day or in excess of forty hours during a week is at the rate of time and one-half.

Wage Rates

The minimum wages of the employees covered by this agreement, effective December 22, 1986, is an hourly rate of $11.93 \times 40 = \$477.20$ plus eight hours for the sixth day at time and one-half or $17.90 \times 8 = \$143.20$. The weekly salary for a forty-eight-hour week is $620.42.

Holidays and Vacations

The employer agrees that employees will be paid for New Year's Day, Independence Day, Labor Day, Memorial Day, Election Day, Lincoln's Birthday, Washington's Birthday, Thanksgiving Day, and Christmas Day. Employees required to work on a holiday must be provided with eight hours work at double the regular rate, plus time and one-half for everything in excess of eight hours. The employer further agrees that a replacement will be hired to replace each employee while he or she is on vacation.

Season

Employees are employed on a seasonal basis from October 15 (unless the theatre opens later) to April 15, which is the guaranteed employment period. An operator must also be hired during the air-conditioning season to operate the equipment.

CHAPTER 10

Contracts with the Producers

ACTORS' EQUITY ASSOCIATION

Casting

USUALLY THE STAGE MANAGER, the casting director, and the choreographer (if one is hired) take charge of the casting, so that the director, author, and producer are insulated from seeing persons totally impossible for the parts. The good possibilities are brought back for the director, author, and the producer to see, and a decision is then made. The decision, as it should be, is largely the director's, but the entire cast must be approved by the author (and composer and lyricist if it is a musical) and the producer, who does the hiring (see Article VIII of the Approved Production Contract for Plays, Appendix D).

In most instances, the negotiations for the cast are carried on by the general manager for the production. Equity requires that there be an open call at which any Equity member so desiring may audition for any part.

Star and Director

Probably the most that a star will be paid is $30,000 per week. (The term *star* is defined to mean performers whose names appear above the

147

title of the show or carrying the label "starring" or "also starring" before their names.) A star might also get a smaller amount as payment against a percentage of the gross box office receipts, and perhaps also a percentage of the net profits, so that the star on good weeks could end up getting paid something more than the flat $30,000 per week.

If a director or star gets a percentage of the net profits, although it is a share of the "net" profits, it nevertheless comes off the top and is considered an operating expense. It is thus not payable from just the producer's share of the profits but from the profits before they are shared by the investors and producer.

Three Standard Contracts

The Actors' Equity Association Contract covers the hiring of the cast and stage managers. There are four basic contracts: (1) a Standard Minimum Contract for principal actors, (2) a Standard Minimum Contract for chorus, (3) a Standard Stage Manager's Contract, and (4) a Standard Run of the Play Contract. The minimum contract for principals and the minimum contract for the chorus are almost identical, with a few minor differences.

Contracts Include Agreement with League and Equity Rules

The Actors' Equity contracts are very simple one-page documents. The standard minimum contracts and the run-of-the-play contracts are 8½-by-11-inch paper. The type is small but easily readable. However, each of these agreements states on it that all the provisions contained in the basic agreement entered into between Equity and the League, and the Equity rules governing employment, is part of the agreement as if it were set forth at length. The Equity rules governing employment are set forth in a small pamphlet of 120 pages. The rules are very detailed and set forth most of the provisions governing the employment of an actor.[1]

Deputies

One of the members of the cast is elected as the deputy to represent the Equity members in dealing with the producer in connection with any breach of the agreement or other employment terms. If a chorus is employed, then there is a deputy for chorus singers and deputy for chorus dancers.[2]

Minimum Salaries

The minimum salaries that became effective June 30, 1986, are as follows:[3]

	Point of Origin	Away from point of origin out-of-town expense payment
Actors		
1986/87	$740	$490 per week

(Rehearsal expense money is the amount of the minimum salary, no matter what the actor's contract salary is.)

Stage Manager—Dramatic		
1986/87	$1,013	$490 per week
Stage Manager—Musical		
1986/87	$1,200	$490 per week
1st Assistant Stage Manager—Dramatic		
1986/87	$845	$490 per week
1st Assistant Stage Manager—Musical		
1986/87	$950	$490 per week
2nd Assistant Stage Manager—Musical		
1986/87	$790	$490 per week

Point of Origin

The contract has designations for either New York, Los Angeles, Chicago, or San Francisco as the points of origin for a show. In the case of any other city, Equity has the right to designate the point of origin. While performing in the city designated as the point of origin, New

York conditions apply. In all other cities, road conditions apply. The point of origin remains the same after it is designated.[4]

Rehearsal Payments

The producer agrees to pay rehearsal expense money for a period of eight weeks for a dramatic production and nine weeks for a musical production and revues for principal actors, and up to ten weeks for the chorus in musical productions and revues.

Before or During Rehearsals

The producer must notify the actor and Equity in writing of the first date of rehearsal. If the beginning rehearsal date is not fixed in writing, the actor may terminate at any time prior to the commencement of rehearsals without penalty; the actor may also terminate, whether or not he or she has received notification of the first rehearsal date, without penalty at any time prior to two weeks before rehearsals commence. The actor may not give notice within two weeks of the fixed first-rehearsal date or during the rehearsal period, except with Equity's consent. Likewise, the Standard Minimum Contract may be terminated by the producer before the opening by giving written notice to the actor and paying him or her a sum equal to two weeks' compensation plus rehearsal salary due.[5]

Certain Extra Payments for Chorus

Dance captains must be paid not less than an additional $120 per week.[6] If a member of the chorus is required to play a part, speak lines, sing a song, or do a dance that is individual in its character and which is understudied, then such person must be paid an additional $15 per week.[7]

Televising, Recording, and Motion Pictures

Equity prohibits the televising, broadcasting, visual and sound recording, motion picture filming, and video taping of any production, in whole or in part, without its expressed permission. Applications for televising, broadcasting, filming, taping, and recording must be received thirty days in advance, and the terms and conditions under which this televising, broadcasting, filming, and recording will be done must be negotiated with Equity.

The union will permit the filming, taping, and recording of television or radio commercials for in-flight or theatrical use of three minutes or less in duration if the actors involved have signed the applicable SAG or AFTRA contracts. A film or video tape may be taken of a production only for use on a television newscast, review, or feature story. This filming or taping must conform to a number of Equity prescribed conditions depending on whether it is shot during rehearsal or during a performance.

Original Cast Recording

On the recording of a musical album, the producer must employ, under the appropriate AFTRA contract, the actor who sings or verbalizes the part in the show. A producer must give Equity at least three days' notice of the making of a recording. A day's recording session is limited to eight out of nine hours, with a one-hour break after no more than five hours, and must be completed not later than 6:30 P.M. when it occurs on a day of an 8:00 P.M. performance.[8] The stage manager must be employed for the recording session.

Number of Performances

Eight performances constitute a week's work and may be given only during a period of six out of seven consecutive days.[9] A week's work consists of eight performances in no more than six days, even on road tours. The actors must be paid a week's compensation even if less than eight performances are given in any week, and they must be paid a sum equal to two-eighths of the weekly compensation for each performance in excess of eight during each week. If admission is charged (except bona fide benefits endorsed by the Theatre Authority or by Equity), then they are counted and considered as performances for which the actor is to be paid.

If more than two performances are given or begun in any one day, the third performance is paid for as an extra performance even though

the total number of performances given during that week is eight or
less.[10] Any performance begun before 1:00 P.M. and/or after 11:00 P.M.
is counted as an extra performance and is paid for at the rate of
two-eighths of the actor's weekly salary. Actors must have at least one
full day of rest in each calendar week free of rehearsals and performances.

Performances Lost

There is specific provision in the contract for the payment of actors
in the event of performances lost as a result of an act of God, riot, public
enemy, fire, or accident.[11]

Rehearsal Hours and Recesses

During Rehearsal Period and Prior to New York
or Road Tour Opening

During the rehearsal period there must be a recess of 1½ hours after
each 5 consecutive hours of rehearsal. The chorus and principals working with chorus must be given a 5-minute break during each hour.[12]

During each calendar week of rehearsal period, the actors must be
given one day off, except during the last seven days prior to the first
public performance when none is required.

Rehearsal hours prior to the New York or road-tour opening must
not exceed 7 out of 8½ consecutive hours a day, which includes the
1½-hour recess above referred to.[13]

Final Week of Rehearsals Prior to First Public Performance

The maximum rehearsal time above described does not apply during
the final week of rehearsals prior to the first public performance. During
that week, the rehearsals must not exceed ten out of twelve consecutive
hours a day including recesses, except for the final day before opening.
If the company does not rehearse for the full week before opening on
the twelve-consecutive-hour basis, then when it returns to New York
it may use that number of unexpected days of the week prior to the New
York opening on a twelve-consecutive-hour basis, provided that there
is still unexpired rehearsal time.

After First Performance but Prior to New York Opening—Maximum Hours

After the first public performance outside New York City, and before the New York opening, rehearsals including recesses and performances must not exceed twelve hours on any one day while the company is out of town. If there is unused rehearsal time, there is provision—with certain limitations—for using it upon the return to New York.[14]

Rest Periods

The company must receive a regular rest period of twelve hours at the end of the day (ten hours for principal actors on days before matinee days). The rest period preceding the call on the day of the first paid performance must be no less than nine hours.[15]

Company Calls

After New York Opening—Half-Hour Call

After the official opening in New York City, the company may not be called sooner than the one-half hour call on the day following the scheduled day of rest, except in emergencies or in case of a replacement of a star or major featured principal on the day of his or her first performance in the part.

After New York or Road Tour Opening—Chorus Hourly Limit

After the New York or road tour opening, chorus rehearsals—except those necessary for emergency cast replacements—are limited to eight hours weekly for routine rehearsals, or twelve hours weekly for understudy rehearsals or new material or numbers. In no event can the total rehearsals for the week exceed twelve hours unless overtime is paid.[16]

After New York or Road Tour Opening—Principals' Hourly Limit

After the New York or road tour opening, principal actors' rehearsals, except rehearsals necessary for emergencies and cast replacements, are limited to eight hours weekly, or twelve hours weekly for understudy rehearsal; however, during the first two weeks after the New York or road tour opening, and for emergencies or in cast replacements, rehearsals may be five hours per day (two hours on matinee days).[17]

Overtime Pay

Overtime Pay for Rehearsals

If the actors rehearse more than the hours stipulated, they must be paid an additional $21.50 per hour, or part thereof.[18]

Overtime Pay for Travel

On a day of travel, rehearsal and travel time combined must not exceed ten hours excluding rest periods.[19] When it does exceed ten hours, overtime must be paid. The overtime pay for travel is $20 per hour.

Terms of Employment

The Standard Minimum Contract and the Run-of-the-Play Contract both provide that an actor must be guaranteed no less than two-weeks'-consecutive salary plus any rehearsal expense money due.[20]

Guarantees—Minimum and Run-of-the-Play Contracts

The Standard Minimum Contract for principals and chorus both provide that the actor will be paid a minimum of two weeks' salary. This salary must be paid after the date of the first public performance or the opening date specified in the contract, whichever occurs first.

The Standard Run-of-the-Play Contract is distinguished from the Standard Minimum Contract in that, under the Run-of-the-Play Contract, the actor is guaranteed a minimum of two weeks' employment during each theatrical season. At the time the contract is entered into, the producer and actor agree that he or she will be employed (if the show runs, of course) during a certain number of seasons, and the contract sets forth the number of seasons. If the contract is for more than one season, the producer guarantees that the actor will be paid a minimum of two weeks' employment for each season contracted, unless notice is given as provided in the contract. The notice provided for must be delivered to the actor and to Equity not later than five weeks after the first public performance in New York City (which date cannot be later than fifteen weeks after the opening performance) or five weeks after the opening of the road tour (if the contract is for a road tour), and the notice must state that the producer does not intend to present the play during any season following the current season. If the notice is delivered, together with payment for all of the seasons contracted after the second season, then the producer does not have to pay the guarantee for the second season. The notice, however, must be given simultaneously to all actors in the cast holding Run-of-the-Play Contracts for more than one season or year.

If a play continues its run, an actor signed to a Run-of-the-Play Contract must be paid his or her salary for every week during the season(s) that he or she is signed for, but in no event for less than two weeks. This is so even if the actor is replaced in the part.

The producer and actor may agree to a layoff during the months of July and August, providing that the producer gives at least four weeks' written notice of such layoff to the actor and designates a reopening date not later than September 1, or fourteen days after the layoff, and also guarantees the actor at least two weeks' employment upon the reopening.

The advantage of a Run-of-the-Play Contract is obvious in that the producer can know for certain that an actor will be with the show if it has an extended run. On the other hand, the actor can know that he or she will be paid for each week of the season signed for if the play runs. The price that the producer must pay is the guarantee for the minimum number of weeks in each season. If, for example, a producer wanted to make certain that a particular performer would be with the show if it ran for five years, then, if the show closed without the notice discussed above) having been given to the actor, he or she must receive a minimum of two weeks' salary for each of the five years or a minimum of ten weeks' salary. If the show closes after the notice has been given and the payment is made with the notice, the producer could save the guarantee for the second year and would only be obligated to pay the total of eight weeks' salary; that is, two weeks for the first year and for each of the third, fourth, and fifth years.

It should be noted that an actor signed on a Run-of-the-Play Contract is entitled to be paid for the run of the play unless his or her employment is terminated in accordance with some provision of the contract.[21]

Converting Standard Contract of Principal Actor to Run-of-the-Play Contract

It is possible to sign a principal actor to a Standard Minimum Contract and then convert the contract to a Run-of-the-Play Contract.

Increased Salary and Written Notice

A principal actor signed to a Standard Minimum Contract with a salary of $1,000 or more may agree to convert the Standard Contract to a Run-of-the-Play Contract. In order to exercise this option and convert, the producer must deliver personal written notice to the actor before the fifth consecutive performance of the actor in the play.

No Probation and Five-Week Guarantee for Principal Actor

The rider that gives the producer the option to convert must also provide that the five-day probationary period in the contract is deleted, so that there is no probationary period for the actor. Also, the rider granting the option to the producer must provide that the actor is guaranteed not less than five weeks' employment, rather than the minimum two weeks' employment that would otherwise be provided for if this rider were not added to the Standard Contract.[22]

Chorus Six-Month Run-of-the-Play Contract

There is also provision for hiring a member of the chorus on a six-month Run-of-the-Play Contract. The rider, which is added to the contract, must provide that: (1) the rider will apply to the road tour or point of organization and run only through the tryout period included;

(2) neither party may give notice of termination of the contract prior to twenty-four weeks from the opening of the play; (3) the rider must be signed by the parties before the first day of rehearsal; (4) if the member of the chorus obtains a contract to play the part of a principal during the six-month rider, then the chorus member may terminate his employment upon two weeks' notice; (5) the rider may only be used if the chorus member is paid at least $60 per week above the minimum, not including payment for any extras or other duties for which extra compensation is provided.[23]

Extensions of Chorus Six-Month Run-of-the-Play Contract

The producer may also sign a chorus member under a contract that gives the producer the option to convert to a six-month run-of-the-play rider, provided that the producer exercises the option prior to the first day of rehearsal. If this rider is used, the chorus member is paid at least $60 more per week than the minimum salary, not including payments for any and all other duties.

Conversion to Chorus Six-Month Run-of-the-Play Contract

The producer may also sign a chorus member under a contract that gives the producer the option to convert to a six-month run-of-the-play rider, provided that the producer exercises the option prior to the first day of rehearsal. If this rider is used, the chorus member is paid at least $60 more per week than the minimum salary, not including payments for any and all other duties.[24]

Extra Chorus Payment

A member of the chorus designated to swing a number in a production, who is not hired solely as a swing performer, must receive $12.50 per week in addition to the regular weekly salary. (A swing performer is a chorus member who may be called upon to perform in a number as a replacement if a chorus member is out.) The chorus member may perform in several numbers and "swing" on another number if he or she is needed.[25]

Number of Chorus Members

The rules make specific provision as to the number of chorus members that must be retained. Following the first day of rehearsal this number may not be reduced in any way.[26]

No Pay for Actors' Fund

The rules provide that an actor must perform without compensation for one performance during the first three months of the play's run, and for one performance every twelve months thereafter for the Actors' Fund Benefit. There are specific terms covering the notices, rehearsal, and procedure for an Actors' Fund Benefit.[27]

Paid Previews Before Opening Count Toward Minimum Guarantee

If a show gives paid previews immediately preceding the opening—that is, where there are no intervening days, rehearsals, or unpaid previews—and if the play closes within two weeks of the opening, then the producer may claim the pro rata salaries paid to the actors for the previews as a credit and offset against the minimum guarantee provided for in the contract of employment. The producer need not pay rehearsal-expense money if the actor is not required to rehearse more than four hours on the day of a paid preview. Any sums paid to the actor for rehearsals, whether at full salary or as rehearsal-expense money, or any sum paid for unpaid previews or for paid previews not immediately preceding the opening performance, may not be credited against the minimum guarantee specified in the contract. The point is that credit is given only for salary payments immediately preceding opening and only in the event that there are no intervening days.

If an actor is paid rehearsal-expense money in addition to payment for the preview, the producer may have an additional day of rehearsal for each such preview for payment of only rehearsal-expense money. Payment for such previews, however, may not be used as a credit against the minimum-contract guarantee.[28]

Termination After Opening

Individual Termination After Opening

The producer or the actor may terminate the contract at any time upon or after the date of the first public performance of the play by giving two weeks' written notice to the other party. If a company is closed in accordance with the notice of closing to the entire company, the company notice will supersede any individual notice then outstanding.

Termination by the Company After Opening

The producer may close the play and company upon one week's written notice or upon payment of one week's contractual salary in lieu thereof, if the Equity actors have been paid for all of their services rendered to the date of closing, in no event less than two weeks' salary plus rehearsal expense money.

Termination by Actor After Opening

If the actor wishes to terminate the contract after the play has opened, the producer has no responsibility for the return transportation. The chorus member's successor must not be engaged at a lesser salary than that of the chorus member replaced unless the chorus member terminated solely for the purpose of fulfilling another engagement.

Payment Where Actor Does Not Work Out Notice

If the actor is not allowed or required to work out any notice given to him under the contract, he or she must be paid immediately and may accept other employment. If the producer gives individual notice of termination, the producer must pay the actor the cost of transportation and baggage back to the point of organization whether he returns immediately or not.[29]

Termination—Run-of-the-Play Contracts

Notice of Closing

The producer must give all actors signed to a Run-of-the-Play Contract one week's individual notice in writing of the closing of the production and company or pay one week's salary in lieu thereof.

Run-of-the-play contracts terminate on the date stipulated in the individual contract of employment without further notice. A principal actor engaged under a Run-of-the-Play Contract may agree to continue with the production after the expiration of the contract without entering into a new contract, but he or she will be deemed to be employed under all the terms and conditions of the Standard Minimum Contract.

Exceptions to Foregoing Closing Provisions

There are certain exceptions to the foregoing. They include:

1. Termination of rehearsals as a result of fire, accident, riot, strikes, illness, or death of the star or prominent member of the cast, act of God, or act of a public enemy. Under such circumstances the actors must be paid one-seventh of the out-of-town living expenses for a maximum of two weeks. If the layoff has continued for two weeks, the producer may pay half the contracted salary for two further weeks and may terminate the contract without penalty.
2. Where an actor absents himself from rehearsal for ten days due to illness, the producer may terminate the contract at the end of the ten days. Equity may consent upon appeal to reduce this period.
3. If the play is abandoned before opening, the producer must pay the actor an additional two weeks' salary.
4. If an illness or an injury other than injury in the course of the actor's employment prevents the actor from performing and the illness continues, or appears that it will continue, for ten days or more, Equity may, at the request of the producer, modify or terminate the actor's contract on such terms as it considers just.
5. An actor may be discharged for inability to perform due to intoxication or similar cause. There are provisions for arbitration as to whether it was for just cause.
6. If an actor's part is cut out, the producer may terminate the contract by the payment of a sum equal to four weeks' contractual salary in addition to any other sums due for services rendered, plus an addi-

tional four weeks' salary to the extent that the play runs more than four weeks after the actor's part is cut out or the contract is terminated.

Closing Notice

A closing notice given at or before the end of the performance on Monday night is considered to be one week's notice effective at the end of the following Saturday night, and notice effective at the end of the second Saturday following is deemed to be two weeks' notice. If a show is playing a schedule of Tuesday through Sunday, then notice given on Tuesday is effective at the end of the following Sunday-night performance as one week's notice, and effective the Sunday after that would be considered two weeks' notice. Except as just stated, a week's notice is considered to be seven calendar days. A notice of closing must be posted for the entire notice period unless it is initialed by every member of the cast. If the notice is posted after the half-hour call (half-hour before curtain time), it must be promptly called to the attention of the cast.[30]

Hiring "As Cast" and "Understudy As Cast"

If the part to be played by a principal actor is not specified, then he or she is only required to appear and perform in the part in which he or she makes a first public appearance. If a principal actor is employed to appear "as cast," then—except in revues—he or she is not required to appear and perform in any part or parts other than the part or parts he or she appeared in during the first two weeks of the run of the play. When hired "as cast," the producer must designate at least one half of the roles "as cast" on the actor's contract. An actor hired "as cast" may terminate during the rehearsal period without penalty by giving the appropriate termination notice. If the principal actor is employed to "understudy as cast," then—except in revues—he or she may not be required to appear and perform in any part or parts other than the part or parts he or she was assigned to understudy up to the date following the first two weeks after the opening of the play in New York City, or four weeks after the out-of-town opening, whichever is sooner. An actor may not be required to understudy unless his or her contract specifically provides that he or she will understudy, and if the actor and producer have agreed to a specific understudy part or parts in the original contract of employment, then such provisions as set forth in the contract would be applicable. Hiring "as cast" is not applicable to revues.[31]

Juvenile Actors

Juvenile actors are paid the same as other actors. A juvenile under the age of fourteen may, at the time he or she signs his contract, agree to a six-month Run-of-the-Play Contract. The producer is required to provide the services of a tutor while on tour or an out-of-town tryout as well as a rehearsal supervisor.

Extras

An "extra" is defined as one who may not be identified as a definite character either singly or within a group—i.e., an actor who provides atmosphere and background only. An extra may not be required to change makeup but may, however, be required to make a single costume change. Extras cannot be rehearsed for more than two weeks before the first public performance and may not speak except in "omnes" (in a group), may not sing, dance, understudy, and may not tour except with a pre-Broadway tryout of eight weeks or less.

Extras are paid no less than half the minimum salary of an actor. During a pre-Broadway tour, they must be paid one-seventh of out-of-town expenses per day for each day they spend out of town in addition to their regular salary. Extras receive hospitalization and medical coverage. After the New York opening the extra may be rehearsed for two weeks, the same as principal actors. After the two weeks, extras must be paid $20 for any hour or part of an hour. An extra gets a one-week guarantee of salary from the date of opening of the play, and one-week's notice of termination of the contract; no probationary period is provided for in the contract.[32]

Understudies

Dramatic Plays

In dramatic plays, all parts for which contracts are issued, except those of star and bit players, must be covered by understudies.

Extra Payment for Performance—Principal Actor

No understudy can perform in a role that he or she covers without additional compensation, A performing actor must be paid $33 per week per role understudied, up to three roles. A general understudy may understudy up to five roles, for which the actor will be paid $33 for each role understudied.

One-eighth of an actor's own contractual salary will be paid to the understudy for each performance of the role understudied. A cast member understudying a star billed over the title, if receiving less than $150 over the minimum, will be paid at least $150 for each performance given in place of the star.[33]

Chorus—Extra Payment Under Contract

If a member of the chorus understudies a principal, he or she must be paid not less than $33 per week in addition to weekly salary. If a member of the chorus understudies another member of the chorus (involving understudy rehearsals), he or she must be paid a minimum of not less than $12.50 per week in addition to his or her other salary.[34]

Understudies Present at All Performances

Understudies must be present at each performance unless the producer consents otherwise.

Time of Hiring and Commencement of Performance As Understudy

Understudies must be hired no later than one week before the first paid public performance, for road tours, and two weeks after the first paid public performance for pre-point-of-origin tryouts or previews, where the show is opening cold at the point of origin.[35]

Understudy parts assigned to chorus must be assigned with new contracts or riders and with salary adjustments no later than two weeks after the first public performance of the production, or at the time of the official New York opening.

Where the contract of a chorus member is amended so that additional compensation is agreed upon, based on the assignment of the understudy work, the producer may, within two weeks of the first public performance in New York, withdraw said understudy work and additional compensation and assign it to another chorus member. This does not apply, however, where the understudy work and compensation is part of the original contract of employment.[36]

An understudy cannot be required to perform until one week after he or she is engaged. The producer must use his or her best efforts to provide the understudy with scripts and/or sides and music no later than two weeks after the New York opening. Understudies may be in only one company at a time.

Termination of Principal Actor and Replacement

If a principal actor's employment is terminated, a contract for replacement must be negotiated and signed between the producer and the understudy or other replacement no later than two weeks after the principal's last performance in the production.

Stage Managers and Payment

There must be at least one stage manager and one assistant stage manager on a straight dramatic show and at least one stage manager and two assistant stage managers on a musical show. The stage manager must be engaged and paid the contractual salary at least two weeks before the beginning of rehearsals. The assistant stage manager must be hired and paid the contractual salary at least one week before the beginning of rehearsals. When a stage manager or assistant stage manager is called to perform services in productions, either prior to the week before rehearsals begin or after the production is closed, he or she must be paid no less than one-sixth of the applicable minimum weekly rate for each day. Stage managers and assistant stage managers must be members of Equity in all companies in which an Equity member is employed.

A replacement stage manager in a musical must also be hired one week prior to the date he or she is to take over the production. All stage managers and first assistant stage managers in musicals are not permitted to act or understudy, except in an emergency.[37]

Layoffs

If the actor has worked for two weeks, the manager may lay off the company during Holy Week and/or for no more than seven consecutive days during the fourteen-day period before Christmas Day, providing that the actor receives two consecutive weeks of employment after the layoff. The producer must give four week's written notice in the event of such layoff. During the layoff, the actor need not give any services except a run-through rehearsal on the day of reopening. If there is a change in cast, or illness of a star or prominent member of the company, then Equity may allow additional rehearsals. If the company is outside point of organization, then the minimum salary plus out-of-town expense money must be paid during the layoff.[38]

Death of Star or Illness

The contract sets forth detailed terms and provisions in the event of the illness or death of a star, or if there is no star, in the event of the death or illness of the first featured actor who is playing a leading role.

Part Cut Out of Show

If the actor is on a Run-of-the-Play Contract and if the part is cut before the official opening, the producer may terminate the contract by payment of an amount equal to four week's contractual salary in addition to all sums due for services rendered, plus four additional weeks after the actor's part is cut out or terminated. In no event may an actor, on a Run-of-the-Play Contract, whose part is cut out receive less than payment for the guaranteed period specified in his or her contract of employment.[39]

Billing

The contract provides that wherever houseboards are maintained, and within the limitation of the existing facilities, the names of the principal actors in the cast must be listed on the houseboards in front of the theatre in letters no less than one-half inch in height. Where there is no houseboard outside the theatre, the producer must agree to place one prominently inside the lobby. There is also provision for removal of an actor's name and pictures in the event that he or she leaves the cast, and a specific provision for notification of the producer of any breach of the billing clause. If a breach of this clause is not corrected within seven business days, the producer must pay a sum equal to one-eighth of the actor's salary for the first week of the breach, two-eighths for the second week, three-eighths for the third week, etc.[40]

Billing If Understudy Plays Part

Specific provisions are set forth for program billing in the event that an understudy takes the place of a principal actor.[41]

Clothes and Makeup

All wardrobe must be furnished for all actors. All wigs, hats, gowns, footwear, and wardrobe must be furnished for all actors and must be new if they are modern and conventional wear. All costumes or clothing furnished by the producer must be freshly cleaned when delivered and cleaned thereafter when necessary, but at least once every month and within one week before the show goes on tour. Ordinary and conventional makeup is furnished by the actor, but anything that is unusual must be furnished by the producer. If the actor must use body makeup, the producer must furnish a regular linen towel service for removal of the makeup.

The chorus must be furnished with their costumes, including footwear. The producer must furnish one pair of toe shoes for each member of the chorus who must dance on toe.

If a principal actor wishes to wear his or her own clothes instead of those supplied by the producer, the actor may do so only with the producer's consent. Under no circumstances may a chorus member wear his or her own clothes. A principal actor will not rent or lend any wardrobe to a producer for use in any production unless the terms of the rental or loan are stated in the actor's contract of employment and are approved by Equity.[42]

Transportation and Baggage

There are detailed rules concerning transportation of the actor and baggage, including specific provisions covering rail, bus, and air transportation. The rules are very detailed concerning the times, the amount of baggage, when the parties may travel, overtime travel, and the like.[43]

Photographs and Publicity

There are specific provisions set forth in the rules for the taking of photographs and publicity with stated limitations upon picture calls.[44]

Alien Actors

If a producer wishes to import alien actors for a production, he must obtain the approval of Actors' Equity Association, which approval may be applied for in three different ways.

Individual Actor—or Less than the Entire Cast

If a producer wishes to import an actor or actors for a production, he must first submit the application, a copy of the script, and other pertinent information to Equity.

Upon receipt of the application, the Equity Alien Committee has fifteen days to consider the application and render its decision.

If the producer is dissatisfied with the Alien Committee's decision, he may appeal, and present his case to the Equity Council at its next meeting, at which time the council will render its decision.

If the producer is still dissatisfied, the matter may be submitted to an impartial arbitrator who will, within one week's time, render a decision binding on both parties. The arbitrator is instructed to use as a criteria certain definitions contained in the Actors' Equity Association agreement and rules governing the employment of nonresident aliens.

An alien actor may qualify if he or she meets all the criteria set forth in one of two categories—if he or she is a star performer or an actor providing unique services—or if he or she is part of a unit company or special character cast.

Star Performer

The producer must submit documents testifying to the current widespread acclaim, international recognition, playbills with star billing, receipt of internationally recognized prizes or awards for excellence, and documentary evidence of earnings commensurate with the claimed level of ability.

Actor Providing Unique Services

The producer's application must document that the actor whose services are sought will be providing unique services that cannot be performed by any existing members of Equity; that there are no persons in the United States capable of performing such services; and that a diligent search has been made in the United States to find such an actor.

Unit Company

If a producer desires to bring over a repertory company, then the application is made to Equity. Equity will approve of the application, providing that it is a true repertory company. They must do at least two shows in repertory and the company must appear for a limited run—that is, not over twenty weeks in each city in which they appear.

Special Character

It is possible to make an application to Actors' Equity Association to approve of an entire cast, based on the fact that the play is of such a unique character that, by design or by the nature of the play, the entire alien cast must be kept intact to preserve the particular quality of the play; that it is impossible to do the play here with local actors. Whether or not a play is of such a special character is determined solely by the Council of Actors' Equity, which is the governing board of this group.[45]

THEATRICAL WARDROBE ATTENDANTS UNION, LOCAL #764

Jurisdiction

This agreement is applicable to every New York production, and every production originating in New York, and governs the employment of wardrobe supervisors, assistants, and dressers. Each show must have a minimum wardrobe crew of one wardrobe supervisor, except on: (1) "one-man shows" and (2) on special shows where no wardrobe other than the performers' street clothes are worn and no wardrobe changes requiring the assistance of any other person are to be made.

Wardrobe supervisors and assistants may not perform dressers' duties, and dressers engaged in a production may not perform the duties of supervisors or assistants except in places of extreme emergencies, limited to one performance. A performer may not assist another performer in dressing nor may the stage manager or his or her assistants perform the duties of a dresser.[46]

Wardrobe, Stars, Duties Defined

Wardrobe is considered to be all clothing, hats, shoes, and the like, worn in the production, whether personally owned by the performers or purchased or rented. The term "stars" is defined to mean performers whose names appear above the title of the show or carry the label "starring" or "also starring" before their names. The duties of employees covered by the contract include maintaining, cleaning, dying, pressing, sorting, handling, distributing, hanging, packing, repacking, repairing, altering, transporting, and the general supervision of all items, costumes, wardrobes, and costume—wardrobe accessories, as well as the dressing of, and making changes for, all performers. The duties also include making, executing, fitting, and remodeling of such items, as well as the control, disposition, and organization of costumes and wardrobe for their efficient and artistic utilization.

Stars' Dressers

Stars may personally select their own dressers, but any dresser so selected, whether on the payroll of the production, the star, or both the production and the star, is subject to the provisions of this agreement and must be or become a member of the union. Star dressers shall have the right to negotiate additional pay for any extra services required. A letter or contract shall be signed between management and the star dressers.[47]

Changes in the Law—May Reopen Negotiations

The agreement provides that if the Labor Management Relations Act of 1947, as amended, is further amended or repealed, or in the event that there are new rulings or legislation covering permissible union security forms other than presently allowed, or should the National Labor Relations Board (NLRB) issue a decision or advisory opinion declining to exercise jurisdiction over the League of American Theatres and Producers or over the business of its members, then the union shall have the option on ten-days' written notice of reopening the agreement for the limited purpose of negotiating modifications to the extent authorized by any such change in the law.

Rates of Pay—Hours of Work and Overtime

The schedule of minimum rates of pay provided in the agreement is as follows:

	September 1, 1986 to August 30, 1987
Wardrobe supervisors	$559.40
Assistant supervisors	$512.82
Overtime hourly rate	
Wardrobe supervisors	$20.98
Assistant supervisors	$19.23

Seventh Day
    Wardrobe supervisors   Double-time of one-sixth
    Assistant supervisors   of gross weekly salary

Sunday performances $26.54 additional
2nd & 3rd performances   for each performance

Performances in excess of eight (8)
    Wardrobe supervisors   Double-time of one-eighth
    Assistant supervisors   of gross weekly salary

Holidays
    Wardrobe supervisors   Double-time of one-sixth of
    Assistant supervisors   gross weekly salary

        Lincoln's Birthday
        Washington's Birthday
        Memorial Day
        July 4th
        Labor Day
        Election Day
        Christmas Day
        New Year's Day
        Columbus Day
        Veterans Day

Dressers:
    Per performance $45.86
    Per week $366.88

    Holidays (per performance)
        Lincoln's Birthday
        Washington's Birthday $91.72
        Memorial Day
        July 4th
        Labor Day
        Columbus Day
        Election Day
        Veterans Day
        Thanksgiving Day
        Christmas Day
        New Year's Day
        (Hourly rate for above holidays—$26.18)

    Broken time per four-hour call $52.63

    Dressers per hour $13.09

| Overtime per hour (Time and one-half) | $19.64 |

| Overtime per hour (Double-time)
(12:00 midnight—8:00 A.M.) | $26.18 |

| Packing during performance (additional) | $22.91 |

All broken-time calls are for a minimum of four (4) hours.
All daytime picture calls are for a minimum of four (4) hours,
except as otherwise specifically set forth.

Eight-Performance–Six-Day Week and Overtime

Six days constitute a regular work week and the seventh day is a rest
period. Any work performed on the seventh consecutive day shall be
paid for at time and one-half (one-sixth of the weekly salary in the case
of wardrobe supervisors and assistant supervisors). When employees
are required to render services for more than eight performances of an
attraction within any regular work week, the employee gets paid double-time of his regular rate for each such additional performance. For
a single performance on Sundays, dressers shall be paid the regular
straight time rate unless it is seventh-day work or performance in excess
of eight.[48]

Dressers

Dressers' Work Time

Dressers are required to report thirty minutes before curtain time.
If there is a change in the advertised curtain time, the producer must
notify the wardrobe personnel of the actual time for the next performance within the first hour of the previous performance. Dressers are
required to give their services for the payments above set forth provided
that the performance does not exceed 3½ hours, including the thirty
minutes prior to curtain time.

Dressers' Hours and Overtime

Where the work of hanging costumes at the end of the performance
does not exceed fifteen minutes after curtain time, and where the per-

formance time does not require an excess of 3½ hours work, then no overtime payment need be made. Where under such circumstances there is an excess of 3½ hours work, excluding fifteen minutes after curtain time as above referred to, all time worked in excess of 3½ hours is paid for at overtime rates. A full hour's overtime must be paid for any fractional hours worked. This does not, however, apply to opening night in New York.[49]

Dresser Minimum

Any dresser ordered to report for a performance or for maintenance work who reports at the specified hours is guaranteed the minimum call as set forth in the schedule.

Dressers Accompany Wardrobe

Dressers are required to accompany all wardrobe removed from the theatre for any reason whatsoever, from the time of removal until the return of the wardrobe to the theatre. If no dresser is available, the wardrobe supervisor or assistant acts in the dresser's place and is paid at the broken time rate set forth in the schedule. This does not apply to wardrobe removed from the theatre for washing, cleaning, or repairing.

Rehearsals

Wardrobe personnel are not paid additionally during put-ons, rehearsals, and run-through if there is no commercial tie-up involved.

Number of Employees and Minimum Hours

After the New York opening, the necessary number of wardrobe personnel agreed upon between the business manager of the union and the producer is required, and each must receive a minimum call of four hours.[50]

Closing—Wardrobe Supervisors and Assistants

When a production closes out of town, wardrobe supervisors and assistants are paid from the time of closing of the show until their return to New York.

Rest Periods

All employees who are part of the maintenance crew in the theatre when a performance is not being given must get rest periods of five minutes for each hour or twenty minutes for every four-hour period.

After Midnight

If a performance commences before midnight and runs after midnight, all wardrobe employees must be paid at the double-time rate for such performances. They receive waiting time at the broken-time rate from the fall of the curtain on the previous (regular) evening's performance unless no regular performance was given that day.

Wardrobe Supervisors Packing for TV

Wardrobe supervisors receive additional compensation at the rate of one-sixth of their weekly salary for the service of packing and returning the wardrobe to proper condition for use in a production when a wardrobe is sent to a television studio for use in a television show. If no dresser is available, the wardrobe supervisor or assistant will act in the dresser's place.

TV at Theatre

If a production is televised from the theatre during the regular performance, all employees are paid at the prevailing television rate in addition to their regular pay.

Publicity Pictures

Wardrobe supervisors, assistants, and dressers are paid an hourly rate as provided in the contract for their services involved in the taking of all commercial or publicity pictures. This does not apply to non-commercial pictures. Commercial pictures are defined as those where the pictures are exploited in connection with an advertised product or when the producer derives compensation for such pictures.

As a continuity of employment, pictures may be taken (on an hourly basis) one hour before or after a performance, and in such instances all the wardrobe personnel must be employed.

For taking of all pictures after the performance (whether commercial pictures or pictures for general publicity), those employees involved are paid at the overtime rate in addition to their regular pay.

Working Conditions

The League agrees to use its best efforts to see that a suitable wardrobe room with a window, or other means of proper ventilation, is provided, as well as proper sanitary conditions, toilet facilities, wash-basins, etc. Personal clothing of the members of the wardrobe crew must also be safeguarded. All sewing and other equipment furnished by the employees must be insured against fire and theft at the producer's expense, or, in lieu thereof, the producer is required to reimburse the employees for any loss or damage to their equipment.

Equipment Furnished

The producer agrees to furnish sewing machines for proper repairs and irons and/or ironing boards, and if the employee is required to furnish any such equipment, a weekly rental, as agreed upon between the employee and the producer, is charged.

Making a Costume

If a costume is made, produced, or executed by a wardrobe employee, whether it be a duplicate or not, the employee is paid compensation in addition to the regular salary at an agreed upon sum.[51]

Layoffs and Reductions and Dismissal for Cause and Replacement

All contract wardrobe employees must be given two weeks' notice in writing by the producer of any layoff or dismissal, and one week's notice of closing. Dressers must be given one week's notice of layoff, dismissal, or closing. Except in the event of a closing, written notice of any layoff or dismissal must also be given to the union. Contract wardrobe employees must give the producer two week's notice in writing for resignation, and dressers must give the producer one week's notice of a resignation.

No reduction in the number of dressers is permitted after one week of performances in New York City unless there has been a sufficient reduction in wardrobe to warrant it.

Dismissal for Cause

Replacement of laid-off, dismissed, or resigned wardrobe employees is mandatory. An employee may not be discharged without just cause, which means intoxication, dishonesty, or failure to abide by any of the terms of the agreement between the League and the union.

If the producer wishes to lay off the entire company for Christmas or Holy Week, the producer must give the wardrobe personnel at least two consecutive weeks of employment prior to the layoff and two consecutive weeks of employment after the layoff. Wardrobe employees on tour for any such layoff period are paid full expense money or a week's salary, whichever is greater.

Termination and Renegotiation

The parties agree that at least sixty days prior to the expiration date they will meet and confer to negotiate the terms of a new agreement.

Endangered Theatres

The Ritz, Belasco, Nederlander, Biltmore, and Lyceum have been designated endangered theatres, and when a production opens cold—that is, without an out-of-town tryout—the union has agreed to certain concessions in their contract. For example, the wardrobe supervisor is allowed to perform three changes in addition to costume pre-sets. These kinds of concessions are meant to allow producers using these theatres to reduce the manpower requirements of their productions and thus their operating costs.

SOCIETY OF STAGE DIRECTORS AND CHOREOGRAPHERS

Directors—Extra Payment for Rewriting

Nowadays directors pick up extra money by participating in the writing of the show. Although a director may not get program writing credit, he or she may get as much as 1½ or 2 percent of the gross receipts for the writing, in addition to the directing fee. The minimum director's fee, as will be noted, is $15,000 plus 1½ percent of the gross receipts. However, if he or she is a "big-name" director, the fee will be between $15,000 and $30,000, and between 2½ percent and 4 percent of the gross receipts, as a directing fee; he or she may also receive up to 10 percent of the net profits of the company. In addition, the director who helps with the writing would share in the writer's receipts from the movie sale as well as from the sale of the other subsidiaries. This could mean big money.

Jurisdiction

The collective bargaining agreement of the Society of Stage Directors and Choreographers governs, as the name implies, employment of directors and choreographers in first-class productions in the United States. First-class productions do not include vaudeville-type shows, concert-type shows, readings, nightclub acts, theatre restaurants (Las Vegas shows, however, is considered first class where so classified by Actors' Equity as part of a road tour), ballets, symphonic and musical importations, and any production not under the jurisdiction of Actors' Equity. In exchange for recognition of the Society for first-class productions, the Society has agreed that it will not attempt to seek recognition to bargain with the producers for other than the first-class presentations just noted. A theatrical production, to be covered by this agreement, must also be presented on the speaking stage in a first-class theatre.[52]

The Society agrees to admit members on a nondiscriminatory basis and agrees that its constitution and by-laws will provide that any initiation fee or similar charge will be reasonable and be required of all applicants and members. The current initiation fee is $1,000, with annual dues of $125 as well as 1½ percent of the member's annual gross.

Producer/Director or Producer/Choreographer

The contract does not cover a producer not previously a member of the Society when such producer is acting as a producer/director or a producer/choreographer, nor will such person be induced, coerced, or otherwise required to become or remain a member of the Society. Any producer/director or producer/choreographer who was previously a member of the Society remains a member and the contract would be applicable.[53]

One Waiver of Royalties Permitted

A producer may not request that a director or choreographer waive any of the terms of the agreement without the consent of the Society; however, a reduction of royalties of up to four weeks (which need not be consecutive) may be made without the consent of the Society provided that the agreement in writing for the reduction is signed by the producer and the director or choreographer and is filed with the Society within one week after the reduction is agreed upon.[54]

Director and Choreographer Terms

Fees

The minimum fee payable to a director of a first-class production is not less than $15,000, and for a choreographer not less than $11,500. Not less than 25 percent of the fee in either case is paid directly to the director or choreographer on signing of the contract and is nonreturnable, and the balance of the fee is payable in three equal payments at the beginning of the first, second, and third weeks of rehearsal, or not later than one week before the first performance, whichever is sooner. If a production is abandoned, there is no liability for fee payments after the date of abandonment; however, those fees accrued prior to the abandonment must be paid to the director or choreographer.

Royalties

In addition to the contract fee, the director of a first-class dramatic production must be paid a royalty of not less than 1½ percent of the gross weekly box office receipts, and the director of a musical must be paid a royalty of not less than three-quarters of 1 percent of the gross weekly box office receipts. The choreographer of a first-class musical must be paid one-half of 1 percent of the gross weekly box office receipts. In all instances the weekly payments must be made no later than ten days after the week for which the weekly payments are due.[55]

Gross Box Office Receipts Defined

Gross weekly box office receipts are defined in the agreement as the receipts from the box office less:

1. All admission taxes levied by any governmental agency on gross receipts.
2. Pension and welfare deductions exercised as a result of the New York City tax abatement program.
3. Theatre party commissions and discounts, and cut-rate sales.
4. Subscription fees.
5. Actors' Fund benefits.
6. Any deductions similar to the ones listed above.

In bus-and-truck operations where a guaranteed lump sum is paid to the producer, the lump sum less booking commissions is the basis for the computation of royalties in lieu of gross box office receipts. Any sum received by the producer in excess of the guaranteed lump sum shall also be included in computing royalties.[56]

Option to Direct Future Companies, and Payments

The director and the choreographer are given an option to direct all future companies presenting the play, in the United States, in which the producer is interested. If the director or choreographer accepts the employment with the additional company, then he or she will receive, for each additional company, one-half of the original fee. In addition, a director will receive no less than 1½ percent of the gross weekly box office receipts for a dramatic production, and no less than three-fourths of 1 percent of the gross weekly box office receipts for a musical production; the choreographer will receive no less than one-half of 1 percent. If the director elects not to direct the additional company, then he or she will receive no fee but will receive no less than three-fourths percent of the gross weekly box office receipts for a drama and three-eighths percent of the gross weekly box office receipts for a musical. If the choreographer does not elect to exercise the option, he or she will not receive any fee, but will receive no less than one-fourth of 1 percent of the gross weekly box office receipts derived from any and all such companies. The director and the choreographer have ten days to decide whether or not to do the additional production.[57]

Length of Employment

A maximum of eight consecutive weeks in the case of a drama and ten consecutive weeks in the case of a musical, after the first public performance out of town, is the limit of the director's or choreographer's obligation prior to the official New York opening. If additional time is required during out-of-town tryouts, the director or choreographer must continue to work if available and uncommitted by virtue of any other professional engagement.[58]

Strike—Lockout—Fire—Flood—etc., and Suspension Rates

If a production is suspended because of strike, lockout, fire, flood, act of public enemy, or act of God, the period of suspension is not considered part of the consecutive employment periods above referred to. When a suspension occurs prior to the date the production opens in New York, if the director or choreographer is available he or she will continue to serve, and if unavailable, additional directorial or choreographer's royalties are reduced as follows: (1) production not in rehearsal—no royalties; (2) production in rehearsal for at least two weeks—one-third of royalties; (3) after out-of-town opening—two-thirds of royalties.[59]

Billing Credits

The agreement provides that the director and choreographer must each receive billing in all programs and houseboards. The director's credits must appear on a separate line in an agreed size, type, and position on which no other credit will appear. For each company choreographed by the choreographer, he shall receive billing in all programs and houseboards.[60]

Dismissal for Cause

A director or choreographer may not be dismissed (except where the director or choreographer is guilty of breach of contract) without full payment, as provided in the contract.

After-Opening Supervision

The director and choreographer must supervise and maintain the quality of the production after opening. Each of them must see the production at least once every eight weeks unless prevented from doing so by other contractual obligations. If additional direction or rehearsal is necessary, the director and choreographer must do so without additional compensation. If either the director or choreographer neglects to supervise and maintain the quality of the production as set forth in the contract, then that director or choreographer would forfeit one-half of his or her royalties until the work is done.[61]

Terms Applicable Solely to Choreographer

The choreographer's agreement has certain provisions in it that are not applicable to the director.[62]

Assistant Choreographers

For example, it is provided that the choreographer may have an assistant of his or her choice during the entire rehearsal period and during part or all of the out-of-town tryout period. The length of the assistant's employment and compensation must be negotiated by the assistant and the producer, as the assistant is not covered by the provisions of the agreement between the producer and the Society or between the League and the Society. The choreographer may waive this requirement.

Dance Captain

The choreographer has the right to designate a captain or replacement among the dance company, who—after the show has opened in New York—will have authority to call necessary rehearsals and rehearse understudies and replacements to maintain the quality of the dancers' performances.

Approval of Rehearsal Pianist

The choreographer will select or approve a dance rehearsal pianist who will be at the choreographer's disposal for the rehearsal, road, and tour period. The duration of the dance captain's employment and compensation, and the duration of the rehearsal pianist's employment and compensation, will also be negotiated by the respective parties and the producer, as neither of them is covered by the provisions of the collective bargaining agreement between the League and the Society.

The choreographer has first call on the services of the pianist. However, when the pianist is not occupied with dance routines, the pianist is available to the rest of the company.

UNITED SCENIC ARTISTS, LOCAL #829

Jurisdiction

The United Scenic Artists, Local #829, Agreement applies and is limited in its application to scenic designers, costume designers and lighting designers, and assistant designers employed by or engaged in a theatrical production produced for Broadway. If an individual designs the scenery and/or the lighting and/or the costumes, he or she must have a separate contract for each.

Definition of Services

Scenic Designer

The scenic designer designs the production and completes either a working model of the settings to scale or completes color sketches or color-sketch models of the settings and necessary working drawings for the constructing carpenter. The designer also supplies the contracting painter with color schemes and designs, and selects or approves properties required for the production, including draperies and furniture, and designs and supervises special scenic effects for the production, including projections. The designer will also supply specifications for the constructing carpenter, supervise the building and painting of sets and the making of properties, and, at the request of the producer, discuss estimates for the set construction with the bidding contractors. In addition, the designer will be present at pre-Broadway and Broadway set-ups, technical and dress rehearsals, the first public performances and openings out-of-town, the first public performance and opening in New York, and will conduct scenic rehearsals for these as may be required.[63]

Costume Designer

The costume designer designs the costumes and will submit a costume plot listing costume changes by scene for each character in the cast; provide color sketches of all costumes; and supply the contracting costume shop complete color sketches of all costumes or outline sketches with color samples attached. The designer will participate in not more than three estimating sessions with costume shops of the producer's choice. If the designer is required to obtain more than three estimates for the same costumes, extra compensation, agreed upon by the designer and producer and subject to the union's approval, will be paid.[64] The designer selects and coordinates all contemporary costumes, including selections from performers' personal wardrobes when the situation arises. The supervision of all necessary fittings and alterations, the selection and approval of all costume accessories (such as headgear, gloves, footwear, hose, purses, jewelry, umbrellas, canes, fans, bouquets, etc.), and the supervision and approval of hair styling and selection of wigs, hairpieces, mustaches, and beards are responsibilities of the costume designer. The designer should be present at pre-Broadway and Broadway technical and dress rehearsals, the first public performances and openings out-of-town, the first public performance and opening in New York, and will conduct costume rehearsals when required.[65]

Lighting Designer

The lighting designer designs the lights, provides a full equipment list and lighting plot drawn to scale, showing type and position of all instruments, and provides a color plot and all necessary information required by the contracting electrician. A control plot showing allocation of instruments for lighting control must be provided by the designer. The lighting designer will supervise and plot special effects and supervise hanging and focusing of the lighting equipment and the setting up of all lighting cues. Up to three estimates may be obtained by the designer for the producer. If the producer requires the designer to obtain more than three estimates, extra compensation will be paid as agreed upon between designer and producer subject to the union's approval. The designer will be present at pre-Broadway and Broadway set-ups, technical and dress rehearsals, the first public performances and openings out-of-town, the first public performance and opening in New York, and will conduct lighting rehearsals as may be necessary.[66]

Minimum Scenic Design Fees

As of January 1, 1985, designers in all design categories employed by a producer are to be paid at least the following minimum fees for dramatic and musical productions and for any other type of theatrical productions other than so-called concert presentations, which will be discussed separately. The rates for scenic designing a dramatic single set is $3,961; a dramatic multi-set is $5,762, and a dramatic unit set, with phases, is $7,203. The scenic designing of a musical single set is $3,961; a musical unit set with phases is $7,203; and a musical multi-set is $12,964.

A unit set is a set that stays in view of the audience at all time. One may bring in items or remove items from the basic set, but if the basic set remains in view, it is a unit set. Each change is called a "phase."

Minimum Lighting Design Fees

The minimum lighting design fee for a dramatic single set is $2,449; a dramatic multi-set is $3,609; and a dramatic unit set with phases is $4,610. For the musical single set the minimum fee is $2,881; a musical unit set with phases is $4,322, and a musical multi-set is $6,481.

Minimum Costume Design Fees

Costume design fees are determined on two different scales. The fee for a design for a dramatic play is determined by the number of characters in the play and whether the setting of the play is considered "modern" or period. "Modern" is defined as five years either way of the current date. For a dramatic play with one to three characters the minimum fee is $2,160 with the fourth to seventh additional character at an additional fee of $180 each. For a dramatic play in a modern setting, with eight to fifteen characters, the minimum fee is $3,601. If the play is period it is an additional $720. The sixteenth through twentieth character is again an additional $180 each, regardless of period or modern setting. A design for modern dramatic plays with twenty-one to thirty characters demands a fee of $5,041, with an additional $1,081 for a period setting. Again, an additional $180 is charged for the thirty-first through thirty-fifth character, regardless of period or modern setting. The design fee for a dramatic play with thirty-six or more characters in a modern setting is $6,481. If the play is period, there is an additional fee of $1,441. A fee for a design for a musical play is based upon the number of persons who appear on stage in costume. The minimum for the musical play in which one to fifteen persons appear on stage in costume is $4,322; beyond fifteen persons, it is an additional $217 each, up to twenty persons. A musical with twenty-one to thirty persons who appear on stage in costume has a minimum fee of $8,643 with each additional person on stage, to a total of thirty-five, at an additional $217 fee each. A musical with thirty-six or more persons appearing on stage in costume has a minimum designer fee of $12,964.[67]

Payment of Designers' Contracts

An individual agreement must be signed by the producer and the designers for scenic design, for costume design, for lighting design, and for assistant designers. All individual agreements must be signed and filed in triplicate with the union for its approval before work can commence. When the individual agreement is filed with the union, the producer deposits with the union a cash bond in an amount equal to 25 percent of the design rate payable to the designer, or $1,441, whichever is greater. The remaining 75 percent will be deposited with the union when painting or construction of sets commences in the shop, or on the first day of full cast rehearsal, whichever occurs first.

The union will pay the designer his fee from this bond according to the following timetable:

1. Not less than 25 percent of the design rate or $1,282, whichever is greater, on the filing of the individual agreement.
2. 25 percent of the design rate when painting or construction of sets commence, or on the first day of full cast rehearsal, whichever occurs first.
3. 25 percent of the design rate on the first public performance.
4. The balance shall be paid on the official New York opening or road tour opening, whichever is applicable.[68]

Out-of-Town

The producer will provide the designers and any assistants with round-trip transportation expense whenever they are required to travel outside New York City. The producer will pay designers and assistants not less than $72 per day for living expenses for each day they are required to be outside New York City in connection with the production.[69]

Postponement

On the opening date of a production these payments shall be made as if the production had been carried out and opened on the originally named date so long as the designer has completed the necessary working drawings and color sketches or plots (sets, costumes, or lighting). If the opening is postponed for four weeks or more, the designer shall perform the remaining services only so far as hi contractual commitments permit.[70]

Abandonment

If a production is abandoned prior to the first public performance, and the designer has completed the necessary working drawings and color sketches or plots (sets, costumes, or lighting), the designer shall receive three-quarters of the originally agreed upon payment.

If a production is abandoned and the designer has not completed the designs agreed upon, the designer and producer shall negotiate the remaining payment due, but in no event will the designer receive less than one-half of the originally agreed upon payment.[71]

Duties and Obligations

The specific requirements of each of the designers varies. The scenic designer must either construct a working model of the settings to scale or complete sketches; supply the contractors with color schemes or color sketches; design, select, or approve properties required for the production, including draperies and furniture; design and/or supervise special scenic effects for the productions, including projections; supply specifications for the constructing carpenter to build and paint the sets; participate in three estimating sessions; attend the first out-of-town and New York openings and dress rehearsals; and attend public performances from time to time for the purpose of conducting "normal check."

The lighting design contract provides that the lighting designer must furnish a full equipment list and a lighting plot, drawn to scale, showing type and position of all instruments necessary to accomplish the lighting; provide color plot and all necessary information required by the contract electrician; provide color plot showing the allocation of instruments for lighting control; supervise and plot special effects; supply specifications and solicit estimates of the same; supervise the hanging and focusing of the same; supervise the hanging and focusing of the lighting equipment and the setting up of all lighting cues; attend the first out-of-town and New York openings as well as dress rehearsals; conduct the lighting rehearsals for each performance; and attend performances from time to time for the purpose of conducting a "normal check" of the lighting.

The costume designer must submit a costume plot of the production, listing costume changes by scene for each character in the cast; complete all sketches of costumes designed for the production; supply the costume shop with complete color sketches or outline sketches with color samples attached, including drawings or necessary descriptions of detail and its application; solicit estimates from three different costume shops; be responsible for selection of all contemporary costumes or selection from the performers' personal wardrobe where appropriate; supervise all necessary fittings and alterations; design, select, and/or approve all costumes accessories, such as headgear, gloves, footwear, hose, purses, jewelry, umbrellas, canes, fans, bouquets, etc.; supervise and/or approve hair styling and selection of wings, hair pieces, mustaches and beards; attend dress rehearsals and the first out-of-town opening; and attend public performances from time to time for the purpose of conducting a normal check of the costumes.

Transportation and Other Expenses

The producer agrees to reimburse the designer and assistants for all authorized out-of-pocket purchases made for the production and for authorized work transportation involved in New York and out-of-town.

No Design Alterations and Additional Payments

The producer agrees in the contract that he will not alter, or make substitutions for, the work created by the designer without the designer's approval. If additional work is needed over and above what was originally contracted for, the designer must be paid additional sums of money for the additional work.[72]

Strikes—Fire—Acts of God

There is a provision that the designer's obligations are subject to delays due to strikes, acts of God, fire, or other causes beyond the control of the designer, and that the designer is not responsible for damages that result from the failure or inability of contractors, builders, painters, or other persons who are hired to carry out the execution of the plans.

Title to Designs

The title to all drawings, designs, and specifications remain the property of the designer, who, however, may only use them for exhibition or use other than sale for use in another production. The producer and designer may agree to share in the proceeds of any sale of these designs to a gallery.[73]

Kickbacks Forbidden

The designer agrees not to accept any compensation, commission, gift, or other remuneration or payment from persons, firms, or corporations employed or engaged to carry out work in connection with the production.

Concert Presentations

A concert presentation, whether musical or dramatic, is defined in the agreement by way of example: the productions of *Darrow* (Henry Fonda) and *Will Rogers U.S.A.* are not concert presentations, while the Hal Holbrook production of *Mark Twain* is considered a concert presentation.

When a bona fide pre-existing concert presentation is brought to Broadway, no fee is required. If any additional work is required, a mutually negotiated fee may be agreed on.

However, if the concert presentation is prepared solely for the purpose of making its appearance on Broadway, or Broadway prior to road show, the following fees apply: where work is actually required in any design category, a minimum of $2,160 is paid for that category for concert presentations in the Broadway, 46th Street, Imperial, Lunt-Fontanne, Majestic, Mark Hellinger, Minskoff, Palace, St. James, Shubert, Gershwin, Winter Garden, and new or renovated theatres of comparable size; a minimum of $1,296 for each category in all other theatres. Pension and welfare contributions are paid on all work performed.

A standing committee of six members, three selected by the union and three selected by the League, will review on an on-going basis a production's designation as a "concert presentation."[74]

Assistants

Assistants to lighting, costume, and scenic designers are hired by the producer at the request of the designer. The work of the assistant is to assist the designer in his or her work. A separate agreement must be filed with and approved by the union for each assistant. The assistant's fees, including required pension and welfare payments, must be filed with the union similarly to the designer's fees. All designer's assistants are employed at not less than weekly. If an assistant is on the road for less than five days, he or she is paid for each day at a rate prorated at one-fifth of his or her weekly salary plus the $72 per diem.[75]

Billing

The producer agrees to give the designers billing on the theatre houseboards, the theatre program, in the initial New York City newspaper display advertisements, and in other New York City newspaper display ads of similar content prior and subsequent to the New York opening. Billing is also given to designers on window cards and three sheets where billing is given to any other creative participant in a production other than the author, starring actors, directors, and star choreographers. If the producer gives billing to more than two of the four categories mentioned, billing must be given to the designers.

The size of billing and format is negotiated between the producer and designer. Under no circumstances will the billing be less than clearly legible in relation to the use of the medium. The designers' credits must be of equal size with each other and grouped together and placed in the traditional position in relation to the director or choreographer of a musical show and to the director of a dramatic show.[76]

Subsequent Productions

The original designer has the right of first refusal for any subsequent reproduction of the company by the original producer. The designer has a minimum of two weeks to accept.

If the original designer declines to perform the work, the producer selects a substitute designer subject to the approval of the original designer. The fee of the original designer will be reduced by the amount of the fee paid to the substitute designer.[77]

Importation

Importation, whether domestic or foreign, of scenery or scenic designs, lighting or lighting designs, or costume or costume designs are permitted. If work is not required to make the scenery, costumes, or lighting ready for Broadway, a designer need not be employed. The standing committee, described in the section on concert presentation, determines if work will be required. The committee will also determine the fee to be paid to the designer employed to perform the necessary work. The producer must notify the League at least ninety days prior to the anticipated importation.[78]

Other Uses or Designs

The producer cannot assign, lease, sell, license, or otherwise use, directly or indirectly, any of the designs and/or settings, costumes, or lighting for use in motion pictures, television, television cassettes, live broadcasts, simulcast, tapes or film, film cassettes, or any other use without the prior written approval of the designer and without negotiating with the designer for such use. Where the designs or any settings or parts of settings, costumes or parts of costumes, or lighting are used for reproduction for television broadcasting (whether live, filmed, or any other process, the producer will, prior to such use, deposit in the office of the United Scenic Artists a cash bond. For any single use in any closed-circuit television or subscription television (whether by closed-circuit or air broadcast) the amount of the designer's fee for those designs actually used are negotiated on a case-by-case basis; in commercial (free air broadcast) television, 50 percent of the designer's original design fee for those designs actually used; and in noncommercial (free air broadcast, such as PBS), 35 percent of the designer's original design fee for those designs actually used. The television rights granted under this provision are limited to a single broadcast and no rights are granted beyond this initial broadcast (except for PBS, when the broadcast rights are limited to one week following the initial broadcast), nor is any right granted to reproduce this television broadcast or showing by means of Kinescope, film, electronic tape, or other means, except upon written agreement with the designer and upon the payment of a fee for each broadcast. If used for promotional purposes and no one connected with the production is paid (other than actors at the applicable actors' minimum), no payment is made to the designer.[79]

CHAPTER 11

Contracts with the Producers and Theatres

Association of Theatrical Press Agents and Managers, Union #18032

Jurisdiction

THE ASSOCIATION IS COMMONLY KNOWN as ATPAM and covers the employment of press agents and managers. Managers include house managers employed by the theatre and company managers who are employed by the production.

In fact, the agreement specifically provides that a contract of employment must be entered into with each employee and that a press agent, a house manager, and a company manager must be employed at all times that a production is playing within the union's jurisdiction.

The agreement states that the jurisdiction of the union is intended to include not only stage productions, but variety and vaudeville attractions, summer theatre, burlesque, road show picture presentations, theatrical entertainment, opera, musical presentations, concerts, ballets, carnivals, circuses, sport expositions, and similar exhibitions and events.[1] The jurisdiction is not confined to the New York metropolitan area.

Wage Rates

The minimum weekly wage scale for the period commencing January 1, 1987, to December 31, 1987, is as follows:

House Managers/Company (All Cities)	$942
Press Agents	$1,074
Company Managers (Dramatic Tour)	$942
Company Managers (Musical Tour)	$942
Press Agent (Tour)	$1,074

Doubling Prohibited

An employee may not double. For example, one employee may not be both the house manager and company manager except in a stock company.[2]

Work Week

The work week consists of six working days from Monday to Saturday inclusive, with not more than eight performances during the six days. For each additional performance during a week, the house manager and company manager must receive an additional one-sixth of their respective weekly salaries. If a production is performed seven days a week in New York City (defined in the contracts as the five boroughs of the greater city of New York), then the company and house manager must be paid for the seventh day at two-sixths of contractual weekly salary, in addition to any other compensation.

Time of Salary Payments

Salaries payable to managers and press agents must be paid no later than 6:00 P.M. on Friday of the week in which the services have been rendered, and expense statements must be paid at the same time if the statements are rendered sufficiently in advance for the payments to be made.

The employer must pay all transportation charges. All plane travel is to be made on scheduled first-class flights on major airlines. Non-scheduled flights are not permitted.

Summary Dismissal

An employee may be summarily dismissed for intoxication on duty or dishonesty in the discharge of his employment.

Production of Radio, TV, Motion Picture, or Industrial from Theatre

The house manager and company managers must receive one week's salary in addition to their regular salary when a radio, TV, motion picture performance, taping, or recording of substantially the entire production originates in the theatre. When a radio, TV, motion picture performance, taping, or recording of a portion of the entire production originates in the theatre—exclusive of radio or TV news programs, such as critical reviews—the house and company manager must be paid one-half week's pay, in addition to their regular salary. Such partial taping or recording must require not more than three days. The company manager and press agent must receive one week's pay in addition to their regular salary when a television performance of all or part of the production originates outside of the theatre. The house manager must receive not less than one-half week's regular salary whenever an industrial show performs one or more performances in the theatre during the week.[3]

Recording of Albums

The company manager and the press agent must receive one week's regular salary for each production album recorded.[4]

Closing Run of Less-than-Four Weeks

An employer may close a play and terminate the employment of all members of the union engaged if the play runs for four weeks or less.

They must, however, be paid the minimum; a company manager for a musical must be employed for at least five weeks prior to the Monday of the week in which the first public performance takes place (four weeks for a dramatic production), and a house manager must be employed at least one week prior to the day in which the first public performance takes place and for at least two weeks. This does not affect the tenure of the house manager, who is, as stated, entitled to tenure after one week's employment.[5]

Closing Run of Over-Four Weeks

If the play has run more than four weeks, the employer must give one week's notice of closing. If the production closes on a Saturday night, the company manager and house manager must be paid at least one day's additional pay for the purpose of finishing the detail work in connection with the closing of the show. If either the company or house manager is called upon to render up to three day's service, he or she must be paid one-half week's salary; from four to six days, he or she must be paid one full week's salary.[6]

Fire—Strike—Riot—Etc.

If the show cannot be performed because of fire, accident, strike, riot, the public enemy, act of God, the illness of the star or a principal or featured performer, or if the employee cannot perform on account of illness or other valid reason, the employee is paid only up to the date of the closing of the attraction, if such be the case, or to the date of the employee's incapacitation.

Termination of Employment—Notice—Company Manager or Press Agent

If an employer wishes to terminate the employment of a company manager or press agent prior to the closing of a show, the employer must give the company manager or press agent at least two weeks' notice in writing if he or she has been employed for twelve weeks or less, and must give four weeks' notice in writing if the employment has been for more than twelve weeks but less than twenty-four weeks. A company manager or press agent who wishes to terminate his or her employment must give the employer at least two week's notice in writing.[7]

Midnight Performances—Holiday Pay

House staff employees and company managers must also receive additional pay in the amount of one-fourth of the regular weekly salary for midnight performances. House and company managers will be paid an extra one-sixth of weekly salary for the holidays of New Year's Day, Christmas, Thanksgiving, July 4th, Lincoln's Birthday, Election Day, and Labor Day, and one-twelfth of weekly salary for Washington's Birthday, Memorial Day, Columbus Day, and Veterans' Day.[8]

Managers—Specific Terms

Minimum Term of Employment—Company Manager

A company manager for a musical production must be employed at least five weeks (four weeks for a dramatic production) prior to the Monday of the week in which the first public performance (paid or otherwise) takes place.[9]

Minimum Term of Employment—House Manager

A house manager must be employed at least one week prior to the day in which the first public performance takes place. The house manager must be on service at all times when the theatre is open to the public. A house manager must receive at least two weeks' salary, even if the production closes within the first week of its engagement. If a house manager is hired, he must continuously remain until the attraction is postponed or abandoned, and until he is given proper notice in accordance with the agreement.[10]

Limited Engagement—Company Manager

If a limited engagement in New York City is booked and played as a road tour after the original engagement in New York City, then the company manager must be paid his or her contracted salary as a company manager on tour throughout the New York engagement, rather than his or her salary as part of a New York engagement.

Sunday—Extra Pay—House and Company Managers

House managers and company managers are entitled to receive additional compensation for Sunday performances at the rate of one-sixth of the regular weekly salary for one or two performances. These additional payments are not made if Sunday is part of the regular six-day week.

House Staff Employees

House Staff Defined

"House staff" means the house manager and house press agent, if there is a house press agent. A house manager must be employed, but a house press agent is optional.

Seasonal Employment

House staff employees are hired for a season (unless the lease, if the premises are leased, terminates before the end of the season), which runs from Labor Day to the Saturday night preceding the following Labor Day. Although the hiring is seasonal, subject to other specific contract provisions, a house-staff employee is not paid during a period that the theatre is dark. A house staff employee under contract for seasonal employment may accept other employment while the theatre is dark, provided that his or her new engagement does not interfere or conflict with his or her contract for seasonal employment.[11]

Dismissal During First Week

A house manager employed for the first time may be dismissed by an employer during the first week without the consent of the union but after the first week the house manager has tenure and cannot be dismissed, except in accordance with the terms of the agreement.

Automatic Renewal

A house staff employee is automatically engaged for the following season unless he is otherwise notified in writing not later than May 31 of the current season.

Severance Pay

A house manager is entitled to receive four weeks' severance pay if he has up to three years of employment with the same management or same theatre, and six weeks' severance pay if over three years. A signed contract in any season is considered a year of employment. The employee cannot receive credit for more than one year during any season. There is no severance pay if the employee is discharged for just cause.

Ownership Change—Severance Pay

If the ownership or the control of the theatre changes and the house staff is not continued, the employee must be paid severance pay due at time of sale or lease. The employer agrees, however, that he will exercise every reasonable effort to continue the same house manager on the job for the balance of his contract. Notice of any sale or rental of the theatre must be given to the union.

Press Agents

Minimum Term of Employment

A press agent must be employed four weeks prior to the Monday in which the first paid public performance is given when the attraction opens cold in New York City. If the attraction opens out of New York City on a pre-Broadway tour, a press agent must be employed at least five weeks prior to the first paid public performance.

If an attraction goes on tour after a New York City engagement, the employer must employ a press agent at least five weeks prior to the day of the first public performance on tour. This does not relieve the producer of the obligation to employ a press agent until the end of the New York engagement.[12]

Part Time

If the employer engages a press agent on a part-time basis prior to the times set forth above, then the press agent must be paid a one-half week's salary for part-time work during the fifth, sixth, seventh, and eighth weeks before the week in which the opening occurs in New York City, and one week's salary for part-time work for any four-week period prior to the eighth week before the week in which the opening occurs in New York City. A press agent may not be discharged unless he has received the equivalent of two weeks' full salary for such part-time work. The part-time arrangements are applicable only in New York City and, of course, are not applicable if the press agent is required to devote full time during any of the weeks. Oddly enough, the agreement provides that the union is the sole judge as to whether or not the employment is part time or full time.

Opening Postponed—Abandonment

If the opening is postponed or abandoned, the union and the employer will make arrangements for compensation to the press agent during the period that he does not render services, but the press agent must have received at least two week's full salary before the week in which the attraction was scheduled to have opened.[13]

After-Opening Closing

If the press agent does not have a Run-of-the-Play Contract, and the producer wishes to close the show, he or she may terminate the press agent's employment during the first week after the opening of the play and pay him or her for each day's compensation at one-sixth of the regular weekly salary on the condition that the play actually closes on the Saturday following the notice to the press agent. If notice is given before noon, the press agent need only be paid up to and including the day preceding the notice. If notice is given after noon, he must be paid up to and including the day that the notice is given to him. If the play continues beyond the Saturday, the press agent resumes work and receives a salary for the period of the layoff.

Temporary Closing

If a production is temporarily closed and reopens in the same city within four weeks, then the same press agent must be employed at least one week prior to the reopening. If the closing is longer than four weeks, the same press agent must be hired at least four weeks prior to the Monday of the week of the first paid public performance (the number depending upon whether the show is opening cold in New York City or out-of-town pre-Broadway), the same as stated above for a new production.[14]

Exclusive Services

The employer and press agent may mutually agree that the press agent's services are exclusive. An associate press agent's services are limited to engagements within the city of New York or pre-Broadway tours. No press agent on tour after the New York engagement, or after six weeks of a pre-Broadway tour, may handle more than one attraction, nor may a press agent handle more than one production on pre-Broadway tour at the same time.

Advertising Agency

After the press agent is hired, the producer will have to give consideration to the selection of an advertising agency. The advertising agency, as distinguished from the press agent, handles all of the paid advertising; the agency works in conjunction with the press agent. The agency does not cost the producer any additional money for placing the advertising, as an advertising agency is paid a percentage of the billing by the periodical or newspaper in which the advertising is placed. The agency is, of course, paid for art work.

The advertising agency will help with all of the art work and the ad layouts, will work up the logo, will advise where and when and how much to advertise, and will do this for the producer together with the advice of the press agent, who is, in fact, in charge of the entire advertising campaign.

Endangered Theatres

ATPAM and the League agree that the Ritz, Belasco, Nederlander, Biltmore, and Lyceum will, for the duration of their current contract, be considered endangered theatres. They have developed a formula that reduces the operating costs of mounting a production in one of these endangered theatres. The League hopes that these endangered-theatre agreements will make these theatres economically viable. ATPAM has agreed to reduce the salaries of their members employed by endangered theatres based on the weekly gross ticket sales. For example, if the gross income from actual ticket sales before any deductions divided by the potential gross is 70 percent or less, the ATPAM member's salary will be 80 percent of the contractual minimum.

ASSOCIATED MUSICIANS OF GREATER NEW YORK, LOCAL #802 AMERICAN FEDERATION OF MUSICIANS

Hiring of Musicians

All musicians are hired by the theatre, that is, they are signed by the theatre even though the payment of the musicians may be shared by the theatre and producer as discussed in the chapter on the theatre license agreement. A contractor selects and hires the musicians and signs the contract with the theatre. Very often the composer or conductor has someone that he would like in the orchestra, so this will influence the actual selection.

Jurisdiction

The League of American Theatres and Producers has entered into a collective bargaining agreement with the musicians union that sets forth the minimum rates of pay as well as other provisions of employment.

Minimum Number of Musicians—Musical

The minimum number of musicians required in a musical show is set by contract. The following minimum number of musicians were employed at the following theatres until the Sunday following Labor Day 1987 (all figures include the leader):[15]

Broadway, Mark Hellinger, Majestic, Imperial, Shubert, and Palace—26

Lunt-Fontanne, Winter Garden, St. James, and 46th Street—25

Minskoff and Gershwin—24

Neil Simon—20

Virginia, Martin Beck, and Nederlander—16

Broadhurst—15

Biltmore, Longacre, Ambassador, Barrymore, New Apollo, Music Box, Eugene O'Neill, Lyceum, Belasco, Cort, Plymouth, Royale, and Brooks Atkinson—9

Circle in the Square, the Golden, the Booth, and the Ritz are determined by the executive board of the union in consultation with the producer involved, with a maximum limitations of six. Every musical show must have an associate conductor who receives 30 percent additional over and above the minimum scale.

Minimum Number of Musicians—Dramatic

If a dramatic show includes less than four minutes of music, whether recorded or live, no musicians need be employed. However, if four to twenty-five minutes of recorded music is used, four nonplaying musicians are required. If four to twenty-five minutes of live music is used, four must be employed. If over twenty-five minutes of recorded music is used, six nonplaying musicians will be employed. If over twenty-five minutes of live music is used in a dramatic show, at least six playing musicians must be employed.[16]

Electronic Musical Set-Ups

Electronic instruments such as the Moog, RCA Synthesizer, etc., are not to be used without the express permission of the Local 802 Executive Board. Permission may be granted if the use of such electronic instruments does not diminish the earning capacity of any musician.

Out-of-Town Break-In

For a week's work during the out-of-town break-in, all musicians receive the prevailing wage scale plus a separate check for expenses in the amount of $504 per week for the term of the contract.

Work Outside Pit

Orchestra members who are required to play in view of the audience and anywhere outside the pit receive $34.84 per week in addition to their regular weekly salary. If the musician is in costume, an additional $23.23 payment is paid.[17]

Week's Work Defined

A "week's work" consists of eight performances or less during six out of seven consecutive days.

Minimum Rates

The minimum salary for any playing musician is $720 per week. The minimum salary for a nonplaying musician is $400 per week.[18]

Contractor Paid Extra

The contractor receives 150 percent of the minimum salary, and the conductor receives 175 percent of the minimum salary for a playing musician.

Librarians Paid Extra

Librarians shall be paid an additional one-eighth of basic scale per week.

Rehearsal Rates

2 1/2 Hours or Less Up to 6:00 P.M.

For rehearsals terminating not later than 6:00 P.M., the rate for 2½ hours or less, per musician, is $40.63.

Overtime

Overtime for rehearsals referred to above is paid for at the rate (for each thirty minutes or less of such overtime), per musician, of $8.13.

For One-Hour Rehearsal After Night Performance

For a one-hour rehearsal before an evening performance, the rate paid, per musician, is $24.38.

For One Hour on a Two-Performance Day, or After Matinee

Per musician: $29.38.

After Midnight

Rehearsals starting at, or after, midnight, for one hour or less are paid for, with overtime, in fifteen-minute segments, per musician: $28.44.

During Break-In Period

During the break-in period of a show, a three-hour rehearsal may be substituted in lieu of a performance. When such a rehearsal occurs in the afternoon and is followed by an evening performance, it is terminated no later than 6:30 P.M. The evening performance following begins no sooner than 8:00 P.M., allowing 1½ hours for dinner. Such performances are either rehearsal or performance but not a combination of both.

Rehearsal Pianists and Audition Musicians

Rehearsal musicians for all shows preparatory to opening, and not in conjunction with the full orchestra, are paid at the following rates for a six-day, forty-hour week, exclusive of Sundays:

Per musician—$749.03.
Overtime prior to midnight: for each fifteen minutes or fraction thereof—$4.84.
Rehearsals on the Seventh Consecutive Day: for six hours or less are paid for at the rate of $116.13.

No more than eight hours' playing is permitted within a period of twelve hours in any one day, and must terminate no later than midnight.

Rehearsal musicians employed by the day are paid at the following rates:

Day Rate—two hours or less, terminating not later than 7:00 P.M., is $58.06.

Night Rate—night rehearsals, three hours or less, terminating not later than midnight—$87.10.

Overtime continuing before midnight for one-half hour or less—$14.52.

Overtime continuing after midnight for each fifteen-minute segment—$9.29.[19]

Doubling Rates

No member of an orchestra or stage band can perform on more than one instrument unless he or she receives additional compensation. If the musician plays an additional unrelated instrument, he or she must be paid an additional one-eighth basic scale per week, and if he or she plays two unrelated additional instruments, he or she must receive a further sum of one-sixteenth of the basic scale per week. Doubling charges need not be paid if he or she is required to play certain instruments that are set forth in the contract as being very similar. That is, for example, a musician may play more than one member of the saxophone family, or the bassoon and contrabassoon, or the tuba and sousaphone, etc., at no additional charge.[20]

Notice of Closing

Musicians must be given at least one week's notice of the closing of the show unless members of other unions, such as Actors' Equity or Stage Hands, must get more than one week's notice, in which case the musicians must get the same.

Temporary Layoff

The show may be temporarily closed, and the musicians laid off temporarily, only for certain conditions set forth in the contract. If the star's contract permits a vacation, then a layoff for up to two weeks is permitted during any one year, provided that twenty-five weeks have accrued for each week of layoff. If the show is to be closed down temporarily because of poor business, a layoff of up to, but not exceeding, eight weeks may be made during the months of June, July, and August, but only if the consent of the union is obtained, which consent will not be unreasonably withheld. The musicians must be given two weeks' notice of layoff if a show is closed for poor business, and they may leave the engagement. If the show does not reopen after such a layoff, the musicians must be guaranteed at least two weeks' employment.

Dressing Rooms

The musicians must be furnished with convenient dressing rooms, rest rooms, lockers, and sanitary washroom.

Musicians Cannot Invest in Show

The agreement specifically provides that employers who are producers will not engage any musicians who invest in the producer's show.

Pay TV

In the event that there is a closed circuit or pay television production during the period commencing with the tryout period and ending sixteen weeks after the end of the New York run, the employer must offer employment for said production to the orchestra that played the original show.

Original Cast Album

If an original cast album is made, the musicians who have been employed for the run of the show, and extra performing musicians, must be the ones who record the album.

Schedule Changes

Show schedule changes must be sent to the union as well as notification four weeks in advance of an Actors' Fund performance.

Music Preparation

Extensive terms, conditions, and payment schedules governing the arranging, orchestration, copying, transposing, and proofreading of music are attached to the AFM collective bargaining agreement.

MAKEUP ARTISTS AND HAIR STYLISTS UNION, LOCAL 798, IATSE, AFL-CIO

Jurisdiction

The contract recognizes Local 798 as the sole and exclusive bargaining agent for makeup artists and hair stylists employed in the presentation of legitimate shows in the Broadway area. Membership in Local

798 is not a condition of hiring an individual; however, once employed by the production, the individual must join the union.

Minimum Salaries

The minimum weekly salaries for the period beginning August 1, 1986, to July 31, 1987, are as follows:

Heads of Departments	$580.25
Assistants	$527.50

Minimum daily rates are one-sixth of the above, plus 10 percent. Minimum hourly rates are $15.83 for this period.

Hours

The contracts provides that employees shall work eight performances each week, 3½ hours per performance. The first half hour is to be used as set-up time.

Holidays

Labor Day, Thanksgiving, Christmas Day, New Year's holidays for weekly employees. If the employee must work a performance on Thanksgiving or Christmas he or she is paid an additional one-sixth of weekly salary for that day's work.

TV, Taping, or Filming

If a production is taped or filmed for television, the makeup, hair, and wig stylists are paid on the basis of the applicable television, film, or commercial agreement between Local 798 and the employers in the television, film, or commercial industry.

CHAPTER 12

Out-of-Town Pre-Broadway

Purpose—Audience Response

UP UNTIL THE EARLY 1960s, almost every Broadway show would go out-of-town for a pre-Broadway run prior to the Broadway opening. The purpose of an out-of-town try-out was to get audience response so that the show could be fixed before it was subjected to the grueling attention of the Broadway critics. Since taking a show out-of-town is an expensive operation, someone eventually came up with the idea that it wasn't really necessary.

It Depends on the Play

In fact, there are some plays that definitely should be tried out-of-town, and others where it would make little difference. If a play does not have a pre-Broadway tryout, it will probably preview on Broadway for a longer period of time so that the Broadway preview audience response may be utilized to fix anything that needs fixing, to the extent that it can be fixed, in the available time.

Dramatic Show Differs from Musical

A dramatic show probably should not go out-of-town unless there is a star in the show, a star with out-of-town drawing power. The dramatic show without a star on a pre-Broadway tour is likely to have difficulty finding that audience from which a response is to be measured.

A musical, without a star, likewise should not go out-of-town on a pre-Broadway tour unless there is a subscription audience waiting to see the show when it arrives. If the theatre wants the show, then the theatre will make arrangements for you to take advantage of the subscription patrons that some theatres have, which can mean guaranteed box office receipts. The Fisher Theatre in Detroit, the Mechanic in Baltimore, the O'Keefe in Toronto are theatres, for example, that have subscription patrons.

A show—dramatic or musical—with a star, or a musical with a subscription ticket sale, should most usually plan on a pre-Broadway tour.[1]

How Long on the Road—And Previews

Most usually a straight dramatic show will stay on the road for from four to six weeks before coming to Broadway, and a musical will generally stay out for between six and ten weeks. After the show comes in to New York, it may preview for a few days or a week, or, if it is in trouble and needs a lot of fixing, for several weeks if the money holds out. The very least is a run-through the dress rehearsal prior to the official opening.[2]

If the show does not go out-of-town, it may preview in New York for between one and three weeks. If it does not go out-of-town, it is likely that there is not an excess amount of money; in most instances, then, it will be difficult to preview the show for more than a week or two, as this costs money. Do not count on making money during the previews. It can happen, but only if you have that big-box-office-drawing star, or if the play is written by a currently "hot" or famous author, or some other such unusual situation.

There have been instances recently where big musicals with superstars have gone on the road for extended tours of a year or more, and they have done big business. The object in such instances is to have such a successful run on the road that by the time the show comes to Broadway it has recouped the entire investment in the production. Sometimes this works. Sometimes it doesn't and the show has flopped.

Sets and Props Moved by Truck or Train

Although the cast and crew may be flown between stops, the sets and props are almost always moved overland. If it is a big hop, it is possible that the sets and props will also be flown, but this is not usual on most moves. It is not usual to risk the chance of bad weather in transporting the sets, for a certain amount of time is required to set up after arrival. Overland means that a certain number of hours will be required from the time the play is out of the theatre; most likely the last truck will leave at about 8:00 A.M. following the last evening performance. There is no assurance if the sets are flown that they will arrive in time to be installed and ready to go for the next scheduled performance.

Desirable Musical Houses

The most desirable musical houses are the very large houses. Weekly operating expenses for a musical are so great that unless the show is in a large theatre there is little chance of making money. The O'Keefe Theatre in Toronto and the Fisher in Detroit are ideal, since they are immense and can easily gross over $500,000 a week if you come in with a hot property.

Moving a Show—Deck Complicates Move

Moving a show is an expensive, complicated procedure. The main complication arises from the fact that the last thing out of the theatre has to be the first thing into the next theatre. The last truck to arrive with the floor (or deck, as it is called) must be the first to go into the new house. What sometimes happens is that some of the other parts of the set can be unloaded and flown while the deck is being put down.

A deck is a platform (usually eight-inches deep) that contains all of the turntables and winches. Although some shows do not require a deck, almost all musicals—and many dramatic shows—need one.

Some Shows Own Two Decks

Sometimes a successful road company will own two decks, so that one can be disassembled while, at the next stop, the other is being installed.

Out-of-Town—Union Requirements

The union requirements are different in each theatre out-of-town. One pays more for the cast and there is a per diem expense payment that must be made to the cast and crew.

Out-of-Town Advertising

While it is out-of-town a show advertises in all of the major dailies, as the cost is relatively small. All of the out-of-town advertising for a large musical during a three-week stay in a city, for instance, might amount to a total of $100,000.

New York Advertising

In New York City, at the present time, the only really important newspaper for theatre advertising is the *New York Times*. Some small amount is sometimes spent on the *New York Post* because it is an afternoon paper, and because it has an audience that, in some instances, responds to a particular kind of show.[3]

Out-of-Town—When to Fold—When to Get Help—Etc.

A show will never close out-of-town unless the producer runs out of money and has to close, or unless, in that most rare instance, a producer with loads of money decides that the show is so bad that it hasn't a chance and, for his reputation's sake, he must deliver the *coup de grace*.[4] There are countless show-biz tales of out-of-town flops going on to become theatre history greats, so producers generally keep their shows alive and bring them in to New York for the opening night reviews if at all possible.

Musicians—On the Road

Usually a musical will carry five or six musicians and pick up enough others on the road to make twenty-five or twenty-six in all. The union does not really care whether the production carries the musicians with them or hires them on the road; however, since some of the out-of-town houses have contracts with the local musicians' union to hire a certain number of musicians, it is wise to leave room for the hiring of that number to fulfill the requirements. Then, too, it is more costly to carry the musicians with the production, and usually unnecessary, especially when very competent musicians may be employed in all of the towns booked into. There are usually between twenty-five to thirty musicians on most musicals.

Out-of-Town Advance Man

The advance man on a show that goes out-of-town is the press agent. If the show is on a road tour, the advance man never sees the company, since he is always a week or two ahead of them. His job is to make sure that as many people as possible learn of the show's coming. To accomplish this, he sets up press interviews for the stars and does whatever else he can to obtain publicity.

On a pre-Broadway tour, the advance man will go out of town two or three weeks ahead of time, but will usually only stay for a day or two in each town. He may come back for any important interviews and will come back for opening night. In his absence, the press agent will ask the company manager to act as the clearing house for the local newspaper and radio people. This may be difficult in some instances, for it is not always easy for the company manager to go to a star, who may at the time feel harassed and overworked, and ask him or her to get up an hour early for an interview with a newspaper reporter the star has never heard of and that one cannot know the possible results of.

Out-of-Town License Agreement

The out-of-town license agreement is discussed in detail after the discussion of the Broadway license agreement, in Chapter 13. If one has an understanding of the Broadway license agreement, it is easier to understand the out-of-town license agreement.

CHAPTER 13

Broadway and Out-of-Town Theatre Licenses

Theatre Arrangement

THE THEATRE should be arranged for as soon as possible after one is certain that the production will proceed. If there is a theatre jam-up, it is possible for a show to wait around for one or two months for a theatre to open up. This could be expensive.[1]

BROADWAY THEATRE LICENSE AGREEMENT

License Agreement—Not a Lease

The agreement to use a Broadway theatre is not a lease as one would expect, but rather a license agreement. Theatre owners, not wanting to have the occupancy of their property burdened with the large number of "landlord and tenant" laws that are tenant-oriented, have opted for a license agreement to avoid this.

The Theatre License Agreement for many years traditionally provided a modest weekly guarantee plus a payment to the theatre of 25 to 30 percent of the gross weekly box office receipts, or some combination of amounts in this neighborhood. There were also elaborate arrangements for sharing certain of the expenses of the theatre, usually at the same percentage rate as the sharing of receipts. The sharing was for different periods of time for different items. These included a sharing of the take-in and take-out, advertising of various kinds, the musicians, ticket sales—that is, extra personnel needed in the event of a smash hit—and such items. At that time the theatre owner and the producer were more partnered than they are now.

The theatre owners in the late seventies decided that if they wanted to invest in the production they would do so by giving the producer cash or the equivalent thereof, but that they did not want to be, in a sense, a co-producer of every play that came into their theatre. Hence, the theatre owners increased the amount of the weekly guarantee to cover all of their weekly expenses of running the theatre and decreased the amount of the weekly gross that was shared. The concept of sharing expenses also mostly disappeared.

The Broadway theatres are owned by three entities, the Shubert Organization, Inc., Nederlander Associates, Inc., and Jujamcyn Theaters Corporation.

The license agreement of each entity is different in some respects, but each has many similar provisions. Some of the terms are negotiable, and the producer's lot is dependent upon the attractiveness of his play compared to the desirability of other plays that are angling to get into the theatre at that particular time.

A license agreement for a Broadway theatre is set forth in the Appendix of this book. There is also a form for a somewhat unique situation. Sometimes a smaller theatre will be licensed on an arrangement that if less than 500 seats are used the license fees will be something less than otherwise. This arrangement usually provides that the producer may at a later date utilize more than 499 seats, and at that time the license fees will change. This would permit the producer to produce the play for a smaller amount and to operate at a smaller weekly operating cost. If the play turns out to be successful and 499 seats are not enough, the producer can then increase the number of seats that are available.

As noted above, some of the items are negotiable. The following are those clauses that need clarification or are the subject of negotiation:

- The amount of the guaranteed payment that must be made to obtain the license. The guarantee is usually an amount equal to twice the weekly guarantee. It is usual that the weekly guarantee to the theatre will cover all of the costs of operating the theatre. However, sometimes the producer can convince the theatre owner to delay the giving of a guarantee up front.

- The amount of the weekly rental, or fixed fee. Whether the payment is labeled a fee or rental is unimportant. The thing to bear in mind is that the rental and fee and all other payments for expenses of the theatre will be in an amount that is sufficient to cover all of the operating and running expenses of the theatre, as can be seen in the provisions in the forms.
- The percentage of the box office receipts that the theatre will claim. The percentage of the gross box office receipts is the theatre's profits and will usually be 5 percent, or something between 5 and 10 percent.
- The length of time that the producer has to remove his or her belongings at the termination of the agreement. The producer usually has 48 hours to vacate the premises at the termination of the license, but this can be as little as 6 hours or as much as 72 hours. The time will depend upon whether or not the theatre has a backup production waiting to occupy the theatre.
- The amount that triggers the "stop clause." The stop clause can be triggered by varying amounts. This amount depends entirely on the bargaining power of the parties (see the forms for examples of this amount). Although the stop clause may be invoked by either party, it is mostly for the protection of the theatre, since the producer has other ways of terminating the agreement. The paragraph refers to the dollar amount falling below a certain specified amount for any week. This can be negotiated to two weeks, and maybe even to two consecutive weeks, depending upon the producer's bargaining power.
- The number of house seats that the theatre will get (see the forms in the Appendix for numbers that are typical).
- The theatre owner must employ the box office personnel as the theatre license issued by the state of New York requires this. The legislature of the state felt it would be wiser to have the theatre caring for the money received for tickets, rather than the producer, many of whom are believed to be more transient than the theatre owners with their existing real estate.
- What the producer will furnish. There is sometimes a provision that could be very important to the theatre owner, the identity of the "star." Theatre owners make money when the theatre is occupied for a long period of time. Thus the hit shows mean more money, and the theatres strive to bring in hits. Although a star cannot alone make a hit, under certain circumstances the presence of a particular star may make the difference between a hit and a flop. For this reason, the

theatre owner wants to know who the star will be and that the star represented to be part of the production will in fact be part of the production.

- The amount of the security deposit with the theatre. This is usually a figure not too far from the weekly guarantee multiplied by two. Sometimes the agreement permits the producer to substitute securities satisfactory to the theatre in lieu of cash as the security deposit. This is very important, because the usual theatrical Limited Partnership Agreement makes provision for special treatment to one furnishing a bond or security deposits (see reference to bond or security contained in the discussion of the Limited Partnership Agreement).
- Provision for an additional payment for the air conditioning ($200 per performance is not unusual).
- The time for presentation of the play, which is a negotiable item and may be extended to a period more than two weeks after the preview date.

A producer should try to get reciprocal provisions in the agreement with respect to: (1) violations; if caused by the theatre they should promptly remove them, and (2) indemnification to the producer for theatre's noncompliance with violations.

The provision appearing in one of the forms that the theatre in its sole discretion may determine whether the producer has sufficient funds and, if not, may terminate the license, is harsh and ought to be modified.

It is important to the producer that the theatre be responsible for complying with all governmental rules and regulations for the theatre, namely that there is a valid Certificate of Occupancy for the purpose it is being licensed and that the theatre will continue to keep the premises in condition so that there will be no violations.

The result of the negotiations will be dependent upon the availability, or scarcity, of theatre space at the time that the negotiations take place.

Simply stated, the present arrangement provides that the theatre owner will recoup all of the expenses required to maintain the theatre and will receive a share of the gross box office receipts in addition, which will be the theatre owner's profit. Thus the theatre has no risk, except that the theatre will be unoccupied.

The amounts set forth in the forms are actual amounts negotiated for plays that have been produced during the last year, some of which are still running on Broadway.

OUT-OF-TOWN LICENSE AGREEMENT

Sharing of Gross Receipts

The out-of-town first-class Theatre License Agreement is very similar to the Broadway License Agreement. It is most usual that the producer pays $25,000 guaranteed (to cover the theatre expenses) plus 10 percent of the gross weekly box office receipts.

Guarantee and Deposit

The amount of the weekly guarantee and the amount of the security deposit vary with the size of the house, whether it is a musical or a nonmusical coming into the theatre, and other factors. The weekly guarantee will vary between $7,500 and $15,000, and the security deposit is usually the amount of the one-week guarantee.

Stop Clause Not Usual

There is no reason to have a stop clause, since in most instances the play tries out out-of-town only for a very limited engagement.

Equipment Must Comply with Laws

The electrical equipment brought into the theatre by the producer must comply with all local statutes and laws.

P.A. System Furnished but Not Operator

The producer may use the public address system in the theatre at no additional charge; however, it is most usual for the producer to pay for the operator who operates the P.A. system.

Souvenir Book Sales

The license agreement sets forth the maximum that may be charged for souvenir books, and also provides that the theatre must be given either a 10 or 20 percent commission, which is paid to the house concessionaire. All other concessions are reserved for the theatre.

Penalty to Producer If Star Out

In the out-of-town license agreement, there is also a penalty provision in the event that the star or featured player leaves the show or cannot perform.

Theatre Furnishes Treasurer and Assistant

The theatre will furnish a treasurer and assistant treasurer, but if it is necessary to engage a second assistant treasurer in the box office, the salary of the second assistant is shared by the parties in the same percentage that they share the receipts. Any additional box office help required is paid for solely by the producer.

Theatre Use Before Opening

Some out-of-town license agreements will provide that for a stated period prior to opening, a fixed licensing fee is paid. This may be between $1,500 and $2,500 per week. When a fixed sum is paid for the theatre prior to opening, the producer must usually also pay for the cost of electricity during that period. Bear in mind that the theatre must (or ought to at any rate) be used for rehearsals for a few days prior to the opening.

Theatre Designates Newspaper for Advertising— Insurance—Fireproofing Sets—and Miscellaneous

It is not unusual to provide that the theatre may designate the newspapers in which the advertising appears. The theatre maintains jurisdiction of the sale of the tickets at all times. The producer agrees that he will carry liability and compensation insurance during the time that the play is at the theatre. Scenery and paraphernalia must be fireproofed. An out-of-town lease also contains certain limitations on the appearance of the company in clubs, restaurants, or other places patronized by the public. If the show closes for further rehearsals, or due to sickness or inability of the principal performer, there is a provision that the producer must pay a fixed amount each week that it is closed.

CHAPTER 14

Pre-Opening—During Run—After Opening

PRE-OPENING

Star and Director—Raising Money

WITH BUT ONE OR TWO EXCEPTIONS, having a particular star or director helps very little in raising money for a production. The one or two exceptions are those very rare persons whose names have become household words and who cannot possibly do anything that does not make money, even if the production is something somewhat less than good.

Record Company Financing

Record companies have in the past invested large sums of money in musicals in exchange for the right to do the original cast album. Original cast albums are no longer in vogue, and investments by record companies are almost nonexistent.

Film Company Investing

Some film companies do make investments in and do actually produce plays. Such a company expects a preferred bargaining position on the film rights (usually an option of first negotiation and an option of first refusal). Sometimes a film company will make an outrageous offer for the film rights of a play in exchange for the investment, and sometimes they don't get it.

Insurance

Most Broadway producers will find it advisable to have the following insurance coverage:

- Workman's compensation (this coverage is mandatory).
- Disability insurance (mandatory in New York).
- A theatrical floater policy. This is an all-risk policy (with some minor exceptions) covering costumes, electrical equipment, sets, and basically all the other personal property of the show except buildings and improvements.
- Business interruption coverage. This is coverage for an indirect profit loss caused by loss of the theatre, loss of sets, or some other similar happening.
- Personal effects insurance (required by Actors' Equity Association). This is an Inland Marine Form Policy, which covers the actors' and stagehands' jewelry, clothing, furs, and personal property.
- Liability insurance insuring injuries to the public and the cast and crew. The coverage includes bodily injury and property damage.
- Nonappearance coverage for a star. If the star does not appear for one reason or another, the producer may suffer a large loss. This insurance coverage may range between $200,000 and $500,000.
- Of course, there are many other kinds of insurance to cover special things and special events.

The theatres will, in most instances, have the following insurance coverage:

- Workmen's compensation for all theatre personnel.
- Fire and allied peril coverage on the building.
- Fire and allied peril coverage on the contents of the building.

- Boiler and machinery insurance covering the heating and air-conditioning equipment.
- Business interruption (rental insurance) to compensate for the theatre being dark because of fire or other peril.
- Broad form money and securities coverage inside and outside, which would cover box office hold-up and payroll hold-up.
- Fidelity bond.

There is a large variety of miscellaneous insurance policies which a theatre owner might carry to cover glass, signs, marquees, and numerous other parts of the theatre. In most cases, however, there is a very small market for this kind of insurance, and, in some instances, it is not easy to place it.

Bonds Required

Before the show goes into production, the producer will be required to furnish certain bonds and guarantees that have been previously discussed. The following will be required:

- Actors' Equity Association—two weeks' salary.
- ATPAM—two weeks' salary.
- Stagehands, payable to IATSE for Local No. 1—one week's salary.
- American Federation of Musicians—one week's salary.
- American Federation of Musicians, Arrangers and Copyists—bond varies in amount, usually between $2,500 and $5,000.
- Wardrobe Attendants, Local No. 764—one week's salary.
- United Scenic Artists—payment for the entire set, costume, and lighting design must be made in advance to the union.
- The theatre—a deposit usually in the amount of one or two weeks of the guaranteed rental.
- The union guarantees are for the minimum salaries provided for in New York City.

Independent Booking Office, Out-of-Town Booking

Up until March of 1985, the Independent Booking Office, a not-for-profit corporation, arranged for the booking of tours, took care of the contracts and the other details of a pre- or post-Broadway tour. The office charged a regular weekly fee payable by both the theatre and the producer, but it wasn't enough. The fees were too low for too long and it was inevitable that insolvency would force them to go out of business. The void that was created was filled by the League of American Theatres and Producers.

The Independent Booking Office had certain information that had been accumulated through the years, and this formed the basis of the Theatre Specifications File in the League's computer. The League did not take over the function of booking tours, but the information in the computer was the information needed by producers to book tours. With the help of the information in the computer the tours are booked through the producer's office, by a staff member or the company manager, or by one of three booking agents who charge a fee based on the weekly receipts. The booking agents are Columbia Artist Theatricals, National Artist Management Company, and Road Works Productions.

The Theatre Specifications File contains the following useful information for the major theatres and art centers throughout the country which present Broadway tours and tryouts:

- seating capacity
- stage dimensions
- electrical configurations
- stage and pit dimensions

- information on in-house laundry facilities to comply with union requirements.
- location of sound booth
- location of dressing rooms
- showers
- information on star dressing rooms

- taxi companies available
- in-house doctors

The League's providing this information serves a useful purpose for producers wanting to take their shows on tour or outside of New York for tryouts.

Play Doctor

Payment

Rarely does a production call someone in to rewrite a show, as most doctoring comes from directors or persons acting as directors. Generally what is needed is a point of view about the script, and this comes from the director, and not from rewriting. If a top director is called in to doctor a show, it can cost as much as $2,000 per day for his services. Expensive, yes, but if it means saving the show, it is money well spent. Usually the doctor-director will be paid $20,000 or $30,000 as a fee plus 1 or 2 percent of the gross receipts. Directors have also done doctoring for different considerations. On one occasion, the "doctor" was given a well-known European sports car for the job. (It happens to have been a used car at that!) Other gifts are sometimes settled on.

Billing

The billing credits are often a hassle when there is a director replacement. Often the new director does not want his name on the billing, and often the original director agrees with him. If the new director wants billing and the original director will not permit the removal of his name, the producer has just one more problem to deal with and to settle. But then this is a producer's role.

Advertising

Most usually the first big ad for a show is run during the second or third week of rehearsal; however, if the show has a big star, the first big ad might be as early as four or five months before the scheduled opening.

Advance Sale

The treasurer handles the money and is personally responsible if there is a shortage or if the show closes, and there are insufficient funds to make refunds for the advance sale. Although tickets are printed as far in advance as needed, on a dramatic show it is unlikely that they would be printed further in advance than ten weeks (sometimes six weeks, or something between six and ten) unless the show has a lot of theatre parties signed. A musical show would most likely start with tickets for twelve weeks in advance, unless there is indication of a huge advance sale and a long run.

A large advance sale by itself is not enough to provide a producer with a great feeling of security. What is important is how far the advance sale is spread out. Even a two million dollar advance on a big musical might not by itself spell success. In a theatre grossing $500,000, that would mean that the equivalent of four weeks' tickets are sold in advance. If the equivalent of four weeks' tickets is spread over thirty weeks or more, and there is little sale at the window, the show would be in big trouble—two million dollar advance sale notwithstanding.

Ticket-Sale Deductions

There are no amusement or other taxes on the sale of theatre tickets. The only deduction is the 5 percent that used to be for the New York City amusement tax, is now used for the union pension-and-welfare plans and shared by the unions in accordance with an arbitration award in April 23, 1963.

Ticket Brokers

The box office personnel deal with the ticket brokers. By and large, ticket brokers can do very little to make or break a show, since they more or less cater to the demand for tickets rather than being a very moving force in creating the demand.

Theatre Parties

In a Shubert house, the theatre takes care of the theatre party arrangements. In other houses, the general manager or the producer arranges an audition for the theatre party agents. It is then necessary to find out what dates each may want and shuffle things around so that everyone is happy.

A theatre-party contract will specify the name of the star, and if that star does not appear in the show, then the party may be cancelled and the money must be refunded.

DURING RUN

Range of Production Costs

The range of cost of a dramatic show is between $750,000 and $1,500,000, and a musical between $3,500,000 and $16,000,000.

Potential Weekly Gross and Weekly Net

One can plan on a dramatic show grossing between $250,000 and $350,000 at capacity, depending upon the size of the theatre, and a musical at capacity grossing between $450,000 and $500,000. A dramatic production will likely break even when it grosses between $150,000 and $200,000, and a musical between $250,000 and $300,000.

AFTER OPENING

Reviews—What to Do

The morning after the opening there is customarily a meeting in the office of the advertising agency to plan the expenditure of money for advertising. The producer, the press agent, the general or company manager, and sometimes the attorney are present. If the show gets raves, the job is an easy one. If the show gets unanimous plans, although painful, the job is once again an easy one. The difficult area is when a play gets mixed reviews, and there is a chance that it could make it, but it's hard to tell how good that chance is and therefore difficult to know how much money to spend to try to keep it alive.

When to Close

It is not an easy decision to close a show if there is the possibility of business developing at a later date. One has to weigh the amount of the advance sale and the number and size of the theatre parties against the current box office sales and try to come up with some kind of divination of what the future holds. It isn't always easy. Usually when a show starts downhill there is very little chance that it will make it, and often ego, or what have you, motivates keeping it open.

National Company

If a show is a big hit in New York, then there is no problem at all with a national company, since the show will probably get guarantees of a certain amount everywhere it goes.

Generally, the production must be simplified technically—that is, the scenery and props—so that it may be moved in and out of towns with some degree of speed. The staging is most generally a duplication of the Broadway production. Usually the stage manager puts the show together, and then the original director comes in for the last week of rehearsals and takes it out-of-town through the opening night.

Most often the show will have a dress rehearsal with the Broadway set before it leaves New York, with an invited audience, for the first performance out-of-town is generally with a paid audience.

As with the pre-Broadway tour, the independent booking office sets up the bookings and is paid, as with the pre-Broadway bookings, $75 each week by the producer and another $75 by the theatre.

Producer

A producer ought to do what the name implies, "produce." Strangely enough, show biz happens to appeal to a wide assortment of people. Sometimes people go into the business for the wrong reasons. Playboys should restrict their activities to other than theatre. Sharpies who want to cash-in-quick should stick to the racetrack. One ought not practice being a dilettante while producing. Producing means making a lot of difficult decisions and carrying them out. Painful as it may be, it sometimes means firing your favorite star, or even your favorite person, if he or she happens to be the director and is not right for the show.

A producer has to be in a position to select wisely, raise money, hire, fire, influence people, convince people that they should or should not do something, mediate disputes, encourage and assist people to work together and to get along together, buy wisely, sell sharply, hold hands and soothe heads, comfort the sick, assist the needy, and to be all things to all people. In a word, to "produce."

APPENDICES

APPENDIX A

Front Money Agreement

CLAUSE

(Name and address of organizer)

January 2, 1986

Dear *(name of investor):*

1. We plan to organize a limited partnership (the "Partnership") under the laws of the *State of New York* to present and produce, *on Broadway in New York City* and elsewhere, a musical stage play currently entitled, *(title),* based on the *novel.* We are writing the *book, music and lyrics* and are the anticipated general partners of the Partnership, although others may be admitted as such. The limited partners of the Partnership will share pro-rata in *fifty-percent (50%)* of the net profits of the Partnership, and the general partners will receive *fifty percent (50%)* of such net profits, all to be defined in the Partnership agreement. The amount of capital to be raised by and for the Partnership is yet undetermined, but will likely exceed *$4 million.*

2. You have agreed to advance to us the sum of *(e.g., $80,000)* which shall constitute front money. We shall have the right to use these funds immediately, but only in connection with the Play, for the following pre-production expenses of the proposed production: fees; advances;

deposits or bonds made for the purpose of purchasing options on a book, play, or other underlying materials; engaging creative personnel; securing a theatre; retaining legal, accounting, and other professional advisors; preparing offering documents; the costs of a workshop to be presented by the issuer or other purposes reasonably related to the production for which the front money was raised.

3. (a) In consideration of the foregoing, if and when the Partnership is formed, and the offering of Partnership interests is allowed to commence, you may be designated as a limited partner thereof, at your option, to the extent of the amount of front money so advanced by you, and you shall be entitled to such portion of the limited partners' share of the net profits of the Partnership as your investment bears to the total capital raised for the production of the Play. For example, you will receive *(e.g., one percent) (1%)* of the net profits of the Partnership, if any, if an offering of $4,000,000 of Partnership interests were to be made.

(b) In addition, you shall be entitled to an interest in the Partnership's net profits equal to your portion of the limited partners' share of the net profits of the Partnership, but payable only from the general partners' share of such net profits as, when and if received by the general partners (and subject to all rights of refund, rebate and return as are applicable to the general partners' share under the Partnership agreement).

(c) If you elect not to be designated as a limited partner of the Partnership, prior to exercising your option to be so designated, you will (a) receive a full refund of your front money contribution, without interest, in the event and at such time as the Partnership is fully capitalized; and (b) in lieu of the consideration referred to in subclauses "a" and "b" of this Clause "3," you will be entitled to receive such portion of *fifty percent (50%)* of the net profits of the Partnership as your front money contribution bears to the total capital raised for the production of the Play, but payable only from the general partners' share of such net profits as, when and if received by the general partners (and subject to all rights of refund, rebate and return as are applicable to the general partners' share under the Partnership agreement).

4. You understand that the front money advanced hereunder is high-risk capital and that if the Play is abandoned, at any stage, for any reason whatsoever, our only obligation will be to account to you for the funds spent, and to return to you, and the other parties advancing money, any unused balance of such funds on deposit, pari passu. We agree to furnish you with an accounting for all front money advanced

to us hereunder, but not more than once every *six months* and then only until such money has been fully expended, or the Play abandoned, and the provisions of this Clause "4" fully satisfied.

5. At such time, if any, as the Partnership is to be formed and you elect to be designated as a limited partner thereof, you hereby irrevocably authorize, nominate, and appoint each of us as your attorney-in-fact to execute the Partnership agreement on your behalf, to the extent of the amount of front money advanced by you under Clause "2" above, and to take any and all further steps which we may deem necessary or appropriate to effectuate your investment in the Partnership in accordance with the foregoing provisions. You will be furnished with a copy of the definitive offering documents, if required by law, the Partnership agreement and any other offering material at that time.

6. You are aware that while offering literature may be filed with the Securities and Exchange Commission and the *Department of Law of the State of New York,* the Partnership's offering has not yet been declared effective or allowed to commence by these securities agencies.

7. Your liability in respect to the Play shall be limited to the amount of front money advanced by you under paragraph "2" hereof. We agree to indemnify you against any and all claims, liabilities or expenses, including reasonable attorneys' fees, arising out of any claim by third parties asserting that you are liable for any sum beyond such amount.

8. Except as herein specifically set forth, you shall not have any rights by reason of your making this advance of front money.

9. This letter, when countersigned by you, shall constitute a binding agreement between us which shall be construed in accordance with the laws of the *State of New York.* Our agreement hereunder may not be modified orally.

If this letter correctly sets forth your understanding, please sign and return a copy of same.

Very truly yours,

_____

_____

AGREED TO AND ACCEPTED:

_____

Social Security or
Federal I.D. #:

_____

Literary Purchase Agreement*

AGREEMENT made as of this   day of   , 19 , by and between   , residing at   (hereinafter sometimes referred to as the "Purchaser") and   , residing at   (hereinafter sometimes referred to as the "Owner"), with respect to the original literary work entitled   .

In consideration of the covenants and conditions herein contained and other good and valuable consideration, it is agreed:

FIRST: The Owner does hereby warrant and represent that:

(a)   is the sole author of an original literary (type of work) entitled   (hereinafter sometimes referred to as the "Work"); that the Work was registered for copyright in the Copyright Office on the   day of   , 19 , under Entry No.   , in the name of   .

(b) The aforesaid copyright was renewed in the Copyright Office in the name of   on the day of   , 19 , under Entry No.

*The agreement is for a literary property in which the television and motion picture rights have already been sold. The purchaser, in such a case, must find the owner of and negotiate the option and rights to purchase the motion picture and television rights in the newly created musical stage play. Without such rights, it is not likely that a top bookwriter, composer, and lyricist would want to work on the play. Very often the literary property agreement is for all rights, including the stage, film and TV rights. If such is the case, the use of the film and TV rights is conditioned upon the play running a certain period of time, usually the time needed to "Vest" as provided in the Dramatists Guild, Inc., Approved Production Contract. Of course, the owner's royalty will be less than if the film and TV rights were also included.

(c) Motion picture and television rights in the Work have been conveyed to

(d) The Owner has full right and authority and is free to enter into this Agreement and to grant, upon the terms and conditions hereof, the rights herein granted and no right, title, and interest now valid or outstanding for or to the Work or the rights herein granted by which such rights or the full enjoyment and exercise thereof might be encumbered or impaired heretofore has been conveyed or granted to any other person, firm or corporation by the Owner or his predecessor in interest.

(e) No adverse claim has been made on him with respect to the rights herein granted in the Work, and he knows of no claim that has been made that the Work infringes upon the copyright in any other work or violates any other rights of any person, firm or corporation, and the Work was not copied in whole or in part from any other work.

(f) The Owner has the sole unencumbered, unrestricted and lawful right to enter into this Agreement and to make the grant hereinafter provided for and has the full right, power and authority to make, enter into and to fully perform this Agreement in each and every respect; no consent or permission of any authors' society, performing rights society, firm or corporation whatsoever is required in connection with the grant in this Agreement made, or in connection with any of the subject matter of this Agreement.

(g) At the present time there are outstanding no rights to present a stage adaptation or radio production and the only rights (other than the publishing rights) which are still in effect are the motion picture and television rights heretofore referred to.

(h) There is no claim or litigation concerning or purporting to affect the Owner's right or title in or to the Work as herein presented or conveyed.

SECOND: The Owner does hereby convey, grant and assign to the Purchaser the sole and exclusive rights to use, adapt, translate, subtract from, add to and change the Work and the title thereof in the production of a legitimate musical stage presentation, and to use the Work or any part or parts thereof and the title and any similar title and any or all of the characters and characterizations of the Work in connection with such legitimate musical stage presentation (hereinafter sometimes referred to as the "Play") based upon the Work; together with the further sole and exclusive rights, by mechanical or electrical means, to record, reproduce and transmit sound, including the spoken words, dialogue, music and songs, whether extracted from the Work or otherwise, and to change such spoken words, dialogue, music and songs in or in connection with or as part of the production, performance and presentation of such Play; the sole and exclusive right to make, use, license and vend any and all records required and desired for such purpose; to produce or cause the musical Play to be produced upon the regular speaking stage throughout the world, and to use, sell, lease or otherwise dispose of the musical Play and all rights of every kind and nature therein now or hereafter ascertained and to authorize others so to do for any and all purposes and by any and all means throughout the world, subject further, however, to the rights in the Work previously granted as hereinabove set forth; and, subject to the reservations of rights or reverter to the Owner hereunder, the exclusive right to copyright the Play in the name of the Purchaser or his nominee, and to obtain extensions and renewals of such copyright. The right to use the title is granted exclusively only for and in connection with the Play, based in whole or in part upon the Work, and the Owner makes no warranty with respect to the rights of the Purchaser so to use such title, except insofar as same is affected by Owner's acts or omissions.

THIRD: The Purchaser will cause a completed musical play to be written and composed, and upon completion of the Play, any and all rights therein, whether presently known or hereafter ascertained, of any kind, nature and description, including but not limited to, television, radio, motion picture, foreign, commercial, second-class touring, stock, amateur, tabloid, sequel, remake, shall become the sole and exclusive property of the Purchaser.

FOURTH: The Purchaser has paid to the Owner, upon the execution hereof, the sum of $ as a non-returnable advance payment on account of the following royalties, also to be paid the Owner:

(a)   percent of the gross box office receipts from all first-class stage presentations of the musical in the United States of America, the Dominion of Canada and Great Britain, authorized or licensed hereunder as provided in the Dramatists Guild, Inc., Approved Production Contract for a musical, and in addition   percent (making a total of   percent of the gross box office receipts from the production of the Play, after the total production costs of the Broadway Play have been recouped.

(b) That proportion of the Authors' ("Author" and "Authors" as used in this agreement refers to the bookwriter, composer, and lyricist collectively) share of all proceeds, emoluments and other things of value received from the sale, lease and disposition of any and all other rights in the musical, including, but not limited to, motion picture, publication of libretto, radio, television, stock, amateur, foreign, commercial, operetta, grand opera, second-class touring, "remake," "sequel" and condensed tabloid versions and all other rights now known or hereinafter to be known in the proportion that   percent shall bear to the total percentage of gross box office receipts payable as royalties to the Bookwriter, Composer, Lyricist and Owner, however, in no event less than an amount equal to   percent of the total of such net proceeds received by Bookwriter, Composer, Lyricist and Owner.

(c) Anything to the contrary herein notwithstanding if the Authors and all other royalty participants, including the Purchasers with respect to the Producer's fee, agree to a royalty waiver in accordance with the terms of a Royalty Pool Formula, then Owners agree that they will accept a waiver of royalties that is in the same proportion that the Authors waive in accordance with the terms of the formula. If there is a dispute as to what constitutes a reduction in the "same proportion," the decision of the Accountant for the Production Company shall be binding upon the parties.

FIFTH: The rights herein granted shall cease and terminate and shall automatically revert to the Owner without any obligation of any kind to the Purchaser:

(a) Unless the Purchaser shall have written or cause to have written a completed play based on the Work.

(b) Unless the Play is presented on the stage, before a paying audience, on or before the day of   , 19 .

Nothing herein contained shall be deemed to obligate the Purchaser to produce the Play. The time period herein provided may be extended as hereinafter provided for in Paragraph "SIXTH" of this Agreement.

SIXTH: The Purchaser shall have the option of extending the time within which to cause the completed Play to be produced, as hereinabove provided, for an additional year, that is, until   , upon serving written notice upon the Owner of the exercise of such option on or before   , and by paying to the Owner the additional sum of   as a further non-returnable advance against royalties.

SEVENTH: It is mutually agreed that:

(a) The Author shall be deemed to be the sole Author of the musical for all purposes hereof and shall have full and exclusive rights and privileges as Author with respect to all matters relating to the production of the musical (such as, but not limited to, choice of cast, director

and sale of motion picture [if not in conflict with any existing contracts concerning the motion picture rights] and other subsidiary rights, etc.).
No signatures of the Owner shall be necessary in connection with any of the foregoing, provided, however, that the Author will furnish to the Owner fully conformed copies of each Agreement made regarding any sale or other disposition upon the execution of any such Agreement.

(b) Commencing with the date hereof and continuing until the termination of all the Purchaser's rights hereunder, the Owner will not grant the right to adapt or redramatize the Work or any part thereof in any form and will not sell, lease, license, assign or otherwise dispose of any performing rights in or to said story.

(c) Upon the presentation of the musical for the number of performances that would cause the rights to vest in the Producer, in accordance with the terms of the Dramatists Guild, Inc., Approved Production Contract (the "APC"), the musical and the Work shall be deemed merged forever and in perpetuity in the sense that the Owner shall not convey or dispose of any rights in or to the Work, including the copyrights therein and thereto, without the prior written consent of the Author. Under no circumstances shall the sale of the Work be limited anywhere. Notwithstanding any such merger, however, the Owner and their assignees and licensees may continue exclusively to exercise their respective rights of publishing and selling copies of the Work (as distinguished from the musical) in any and all territories of the world and to derive and retain for their account all royalties and proceeds therefrom, and, in this connection, the Owner's rights in the copyrights of the Work or any part thereof shall continue to be vested in the Owner, subject, however, in all respects, to the terms and conditions of this Agreement. If the Work shall merge in the Play as herein provided, then the Author shall have the sole right to sell, lease, license or otherwise dispose of the motion picture and subsidiary rights therein (*subject, of course, to any previous grant by the Owner*). In extension and not in limitation of the foregoing, it is specifically understood and agreed that the Author's rights in motion picture, subsidiary rights, British Isle production rights and other related rights shall be effective upon a merger of the Work and Play as herein provided. If the original run of the musical shall terminate prior to the aforementioned minimum period, the Owner shall thenceforth be completely free to exploit any and all of his respective rights in such story for the sole and exclusive benefit of himself, his successors, licensees and assigns.

(d) All leases, licenses or other dispositions of any right or interest in or in connection with the musical and/or the subsidiary and/or the motion picture rights thereof shall be in writing and made in good faith on the basis of the best efforts and interests of all concerned.

(e) All contracts executed by the Purchaser and Author of the musical in connection with any of the rights in the musical or pertaining thereto, which are the subject of this Agreement, or the rights of the Owner therein or herein, shall acknowledge the interest of the Owner pursuant to the terms of this Agreement. In instances where the Owner is entitled to any of the proceeds, Purchaser will exercise his best efforts to provide in any contract that express provision shall be made for payments directly to the Owner through his agent as hereinafter provided and copies of all such contracts relating to the rights herein, confirming, affecting or relating to any of the Owner's rights hereunder shall be furnished to the Owner through his agent, as hereinafter provided, promptly upon the execution thereof.

(f) The Owner shall not be entitled to receive any share from, nor to receive any accounting for, any and all royalties and other compensation from publication of the original lyrics and music in and of the musical, mechanical reproductions and original cast album and other recordings including statutory and copyright royalties, and so-called small rights arising out of the music publication and recording contracts by the Purchaser or anyone else for his original music and lyrics, and all royalties and dividends, etc. that may be derived by the Purchaser or anyone else, as lyricist(s) and composer(s), from such organizations as the American Society of Composers, Authors and Publishers; Broadcast Music, Incorporated; and other similar organizations. It is understood, however, that any sale or disposition of synchronization rights for use in connection with the making of a motion picture and/or of a television program shall be deemed a disposition of motion picture and/or television rights, as the case may be, and the Owner shall share in the proceeds therefrom in accordance with his rights to share in the disposition of motion picture and television rights as herein provided for.

EIGHTH: If the musical shall not be produced on the legitimate speaking stage, pursuant to the terms hereof, on or before the date herein provided for, as the same may be extended pursuant hereto, or if the rights do not merge as herein provided, then,

(a) All rights in the Work granted to or acquired by the Purchaser hereunder shall forthwith revert to the Owner with the same force and effect as if this Agreement had never been entered into.

(b) All rights in such portion of the musical as shall not be contained in or taken from or incidental to the Work shall forthwith revert to the Purchaser.

(c) The Purchaser shall be free to make such use and disposition of his original music and lyrics of the musical as he sees fit, but it is expressly understood and agreed that the Purchaser or his assignee shall not have any right to retain or use the name of the Play (or any title of which such name or title is part) as the title of any works or rights which may revert to them hereunder, or in any way have the right to capitalize on the fact that such right and/or music and/or lyrics were once a part of the musical and/or associated with any version of such play.

NINTH: The Purchaser agrees that the name of   shall appear in all advertising and publicity issued by or with the consent or under the control of the Purchaser wherever the Author's name shall appear, with the same size and prominence as Author's name. If the title   is not used as the title of the Play, then that title will appear in the credits as the story on which the Play is based.

TENTH: The Purchaser agrees to hold in the name of the Owner two (2) pairs of house seats for each performance of the Play in New York City (except theatre parties and benefit performances), which seats shall be held until noon of the day preceding the performance with respect to a matinee performance and until 6:00 P.M. of the day preceding with respect to evening performances, which seats shall be paid for at the regularly established box office prices therefor. The Owner shall also have the right to purchase four (4) pairs of house seats for the New York opening.

ELEVENTH: Subject to the terms and conditions hereof, the terms of this Agreement shall be for the period of the copyright of the musical.

TWELFTH: Purchaser will advise or cause the Owner to be advised in writing, in full and complete detail, of all offers for the purchase of the motion picture and/or television rights to the musical as soon as possible after the receipt of such offers but not later than forty-eight (48) hours prior to the acceptance of any such offer.

THIRTEENTH: Purchaser will keep and maintain, or by contract cause to be kept and maintained, full and correct books and records relating to the presentation of the musical hereunder and all transactions in which the Owner may have an interest hereunder and the proceeds derived therefrom. Such books and records will be kept in New York, New York. The Owner and/or his agent and/or representatives shall have access to such books and records during all regular business hours and may take or cause to be taken excerpts and/or extracts therefrom. Payments herein required to be made to the Owner shall be made at the same time and in the same manner as payment to Author and pursuant to the terms and conditions of the Option Agreement. Payments to the Owner shall be accompanied by copies of all such statements as are required to be furnished to Authors by the Dramatists Guild, Inc., Approved Production Contract and such rules and regulations.

FOURTEENTH: The addresses of the parties herein shall be for all purposes as follows:
Copies of all notices shall be mailed to Donald C. Farber, Esq., Tanner Gilbert Propp & Sterner, 99 Park Avenue, New York, New York 10016. All notices required to be given hereunder shall be in writing and sent by certified mail addressed as above provided, except as may, from time to time, be otherwise directed in writing by the respective parties.

FIFTEENTH: Any claim, dispute, misunderstanding or controversy or charge of unfair dealing arising under, or in connection with, or out of this Agreement, or the breach thereof, shall be submitted to arbitration before one arbitrator to be held under the rules and regulations of the American Arbitration Association. Failure by the Producer to pay any amount claimed to be due by the Owner is evidence of a dispute entitling the claimant to an arbitration. Judgment upon the award rendered may be entered in the highest court of the forum, State or Federal, having jurisdiction. The arbitrator is empowered to award damages against any party to the controversy in such sums as they shall deem fair and reasonable under the circumstances. The arbitrator is also empowered to require specific performance of a contract, or in the alternative money damages, and have power to grant any other remedy or relief, injunctive or otherwise, which they deem just and equitable.

The arbitrator is also empowered to render a partial award before making a final award and grant such relief, injunctive or otherwise, in such partial award as they deem just and equitable. The arbitrator may determine and indicate in his written award by whom and in what proportion the cost of arbitration shall be borne.

SIXTEENTH: The Owner hereby acknowledges that (name of agent or attorney) (hereinafter referred to as "the Agent" or "the Attorney") has acted for the Owner in the negotiation and consummation of this Agreement, and the Owner therefore agrees that so long as the Owner or their assignees shall have any rights under this Agreement or any extensions of renewals hereof or under any agreements amendatory hereof or in substitution hereof or under any first-class dramatic production agreement which may proceed from this Agreement,   shall be the sole exclusive and irrevocable agent of the Owner with respect to the Owner's interest in this Agreement and in the rights and privileges granted herein, with the sole and exclusive right and power to deal therewith for the Owner and, further, that as such agent, shall be entitled to receive any and all monies due the Owner pursuant hereof and to deduct and retain for itself ten percent (10%) thereof, except where such monies are applicable to an exercise of the amateur rights of the musical, in which case it may deduct and retain for itself twenty percent (20%) of such monies. This designation of   as sole and exclusive agent for the Owner shall be irrevocable and Purchaser hereby is directed by the Owner to make payment to   of any and all sums payable to the Owner hereunder. The Owner acknowledges that all such payments by the Purchaser to   , when made, shall be deemed to be payments by the Purchaser to the Owner hereunder.

SEVENTEENTH: This Agreement, irrespective of its place of execution, shall be construed and interpreted in accordance with the laws of the State of New York as though, and with the same effect, as if it had been actually executed and delivered within such State.

EIGHTEENTH: This Agreement shall be binding upon and shall inure to the benefit of the parties hereto and their respective heirs, executors, administrators, personal representatives, successors and assigns.

NINETEENTH: Purchaser shall have the right to assign this Agreement, provided, however, that the assignee shall in all respects be subject to, and assume in writing directly to the Owner each and every term, provision, condition and obligation herein contained.

TWENTIETH: This Agreement constitutes the entire understanding between the parties hereto and no warranty, representation, inducement or agreement not contained herein shall be binding on the parties. This Agreement can be modified only by a written instrument duly authorized by the parties hereto or the authorized representatives of each of the parties.

IN WITNESS WHEREOF, the parties hereto have executed this Agreement as of the day and year first above written.

_____
Owner

_____
Purchaser

Co-production Agreement

AGREEMENT made as of this   day of   , 19   , by and between John Jones (hereinafter sometimes referred to as "Jones") and Henry Smith (hereinafter sometimes referred to as "Smith").

FIRST: The parties hereto do hereby form a Joint Venture to be conducted under the firm name of   (hereinafter sometimes referred to as the "Joint Venture"), for the purpose of producing and presenting in New York City the   play "   ," written by   (hereinafter sometimes referred to as the "Play").

SECOND: The parties agree, as soon as possible, to form a Limited Partnership under the laws of the State of New York (hereinafter sometimes referred to as the "Limited Partnership") to produce the said Play. The said Limited Partnership will be known as

(a) The parties hereto will be the General Partners of the Limited Partnership, and the parties contributing to the capital thereof will be the Limited Partners of the Partnership.

(b) The capital of the Limited Partnership will be in an amount not more than   ($) and not less than ($), or such other amount as may mutually be agreed upon between the parties to this Agreement. The parties contemplate producing the Play in an (Off-Broadway, middle, Broadway) theatre.

(c) The Limited Partnership Agreement shall be based on a theatrical limited partnership agreement as prepared by Donald C. Farber, Esq., Tanner Gilbert Propp & Sterner, 99 Park Avenue, New York, New York 10016, the Attorney for the Joint Venture and the Limited Partnership.

(d) Each party agrees to use his best efforts to raise as much of the capital of the Limited Partnership as possible. In the event that the parties hereto cannot raise the complete capital necessary for the Limited Partnership and it is necessary to pay someone any money or share of the General Partners' profits, for the raising of any part of said capital, if the parties hereto are in agreement with respect to such an arrangement, then the amount so paid to said party(s) shall be contributed equally by the parties hereto.

(e) The Limited Partners shall receive Fifty Percent (50%) of the net profits of the Limited Partnership, and the General Partners shall receive the remaining Fifty Percent (50%) of the net profits. The net profits shall first be used to repay the Limited Partners to the extent of their investment in the Limited Partnership before the profits are shared with the General Partners.

If any star(s) or other person(s) are entitled to receive any part of the gross receipts or net profits, the same shall be deemed to be an expense and deducted before computing the net profits to be divided between the General and Limited Partners.

(f) Regardless of the amount of capital raised or contributed by each party to this Agreement, the producers' share of any net profits shall be divided equally between them, that is   percent (%) to
            and   percent (%) to

(g) Any net losses of the Limited Partnership over and above the capital thereof shall be borne by the parties hereto in the same proportion as they share in the General Partners' share of the profits; that is, equally.

(h) The parties agree to assign to the Limited Partnership, at their original cost, all rights in and to the option to produce the play which they have heretofore acquired and any other agreement entered into for the purpose of producing the Play.

(i) The producers' fee payable by the Limited Partnership shall be in the amount of   Percent (%) of the gross weekly box office receipts until the production budget is recouped and will, thereafter, be in the amount of   Percent (%) of the gross weekly box office receipts. The cash office charge shall be   ($) each week for each company and shall commence three weeks prior to rehearsals and shall terminate one week after the close of each production. Both the producers' fee and the cash office charge will be shared by the parties equally.

THIRD: Any and all obligations of any kind or nature for the Joint Venture and for the Limited Partnership shall be incurred only upon the consent of both parties to this Agreement.

FOURTH: All contracts and all checks on behalf of the Joint Venture and on behalf of the Limited Partnership may be signed by either party to this Agreement, or someone delegated to so sign by both parties to this Agreement.

FIFTH: Wherever producers' credits are given, the credits shall be as mutually agreed to by the parties to this Agreement.

SIXTH: Each party shall devote as much time as is reasonably necessary for the production and presentation of the Play, it being recognized and agreed that each party may be engaged in other activities, whether or not of a competing nature, so long as he devotes sufficient time to the Joint Venture and to the Limited Partnership, and to the proper running of the business of producing and presenting the Play.

SEVENTH: The Joint Venture shall terminate upon the happening of the first of the following:

(a) The formation of the Limited Partnership;

(b) Such date as the parties hereto may mutually agree upon;

(c) The withdrawal of any of the parties hereto.

EIGHTH: It is agreed that the pre-production money, that is the front money, shall be furnished equally by the parties to this Agreement, and in the event that it is necessary to assign any share of the producers' profits to someone else in exchange for front money, then the assignment shall be made equally by the parties to this Agreement.

All front monies so advanced, by the parties to this Agreement, as well as other budgeted expenditures on behalf of the Joint Venture, by either party, approved by the other party, shall be repaid to the party expending such sum immediately upon full capitalization of the Limited Partnership.

NINTH: It is agreed that the following parties will be engaged by the Joint Venture and the Limited Partnership in the following capacities:

(a) Donald C. Farber, Esq., Tanner Gilbert Propp & Sterner, 99 Park Avenue, New York, New York 10016.

TENTH: It is agreed that all decisions, artistic and business, will be made by the parties jointly. In the event that there is a dispute of an artistic nature which cannot be resolved, then the final decision will be made by   , and his decision shall be final and binding. In the event of a dispute of a business nature which cannot be resolved, then the final decision will be made by   , and his decision shall become final and binding.

ELEVENTH: Other than those decisions specifically covered in

Paragraph TENTH of this Agreement, any and all disputes or differences in connection with this Agreement, or the breach or alleged breach thereof, shall be submitted to arbitration to be held in New York City, by one arbitrator, under the rules and regulations of the American Arbitration Association then obtaining, and each of the parties hereto agrees to be bound by the determination of the arbitrator. Judgment on the award rendered may be entered in the highest court of the forum having jurisdiction.

TWELFTH: If any party(s) wish to terminate the run of the Play and the other party(s) wish to continue it, the party(s) wishing to continue (the "continuing party(s)") shall assume complete control of the production and presentation of the Play commencing immediately upon giving written notice to such effect after the party(s) seeking to terminate the run (the "retiring party(s)") shall have given notice thereof, and the continuing party(s) shall thereafter bear all the expenses and liabilities of the production of the Play and be entitled to receive all of the net profits in connection therewith as well as the management fee and office charge. The continuing party(s) shall indemnify the retiring party(s) from any liability incurred after the takeover and shall evidence such indemnity by appropriate instruments. The retiring party(s) shall forfeit all rights, title and interest in and to the production of the Play and the proceeds therefrom commencing with such takeover, but this shall not affect proceeds accrued prior thereto but not received, including proceeds from subsidiary rights in the Play.

THIRTEENTH: The provisions of this Agreement shall survive the termination of the Joint Venture and shall continue to bind the parties hereto. This Agreement shall be binding and shall inure to the benefit of the parties, their respective successors and assigns. This Agreement sets forth the entire Agreement of the parties and may not be changed except by an instrument in writing signed by each of the parties. The validity, construction, interpretation and effect of this Agreement shall be determined by and in accordance with the laws of the State of New York.

IN WITNESS WHEREOF, the parties hereto have set their hands and seals to this Agreement as of the day and year first above written.

_____

_____

APPENDIX D

Approved Production Contract For Plays

THIS CONTRACT, made and entered into as of the   day of   , 19   (*"Effective Date"*) by and between

whose address is

hereinafter referred to jointly and severally as *"Producer"*, and

whose address is

hereinafter referred to as *"Author"*.

WITNESSETH:

WHEREAS, The Dramatists Guild, Inc. has promulgated this form of agreement known as the Approved Production Contract (*"APC"*) which it has recommended to its members as being fair and reasonable to both authors and producers; and

WHEREAS, Author, a member of The Dramatists Guild, Inc. (*"Guild"*) has been or will be writing a certain play or other dramatic property, now entitled

hereinafter referred to as the *"Play"*; and

WHEREAS, Producer is or will be in the business of producing plays and desires to acquire the sole and exclusive rights to produce the Play in the United States, its territories and possessions, including Puerto Rico, and Canada (the *"Territory"*) and to acquire Author's services in connection therewith;

NOW, THEREFORE, in consideration of the mutual covenants herein contained and other good and valuable consideration, the parties hereto agree as follows:

ARTICLE I
INITIAL GRANT OF RIGHTS

SECTION 1.01 **Initial Grant of Rights to Produce Play.** Author hereby grants to Producer the sole and exclusive rights, subject to the terms of this Contract, to present the Play for one or more First Class Performances. For the purposes of this Contract, the term *"First Class Performances"* shall mean live stage productions of the Play on the speaking stage, within the Territory, under Producer's own management, in a regular evening bill in a first class theatre in a first class manner, with a first class cast and a first class director. The terms *"produce"* and *"present"* (and their derivatives) shall be used interchangeably.

SECTION 1.02 **Grant of Author's Services.** Author hereby agrees to:

(a) perform such services as may be reasonably necessary in making revisions in the Play;

(b) assist in the selection of the cast and consult with, assist and advise the Producer, director, scenic, lighting and costume designers and the choreographer and/or dance director, conductor and sound designer, if any, regarding any problem arising out of the production of the Play;

(c) attend rehearsals of the Play as well as out-of-town performances prior to the Official Press Opening (as defined in *SECTION 2.05* herein) of the Play in New York City, *provided, however,* that Author may be excused from such attendance on showing reasonable cause.

SECTION 1.03 **Termination of Rights if No Production.** Although nothing herein shall be deemed to obligate Producer to produce the Play, nevertheless, unless Producer presents the first paid public First Class Performance of the Play within the applicable Option Period described in *ARTICLE II* herein for which the prescribed payment has been made, Producer's rights to produce the Play and to the services of Author shall then automatically and without notice terminate.

SECTION 1.04 **Continuous Production Rights.** If the first paid public First Class Performance of the Play hereunder is presented within one of the Option Periods (including the extensions, if any, set forth in SECTIONS 2.03 and 2.04 herein), the rights granted to present the Play shall continue subject to the reopening provisions of ARTICLE X herein.

SECTION 1.05 **Definition of Author.** For the purposes of this Contract, the term *"Author"* shall mean each dramatist, collaborator, adaptor, bookwriter, composer, lyricist, novelist and owner of underlying rights whose literary or musical material is used in the Play. The term "Author" shall include any person who is involved in the initial stages of a collaborative process *and* who is deserving of billing credit as an Author *and* whose literary or musical contribution will be an integral part of the Play as presented in subsequent productions by other producers. It shall not include a person whose services are only those of a literal translator.

SECTION 1.06 **Reservation of Rights.** Author shall retain sole and complete title, both legal and equitable, in and to the Play and all rights and uses of every kind except as otherwise specifically herein provided. Author reserves all rights and uses now in existence or which may hereafter come into existence, except as specifically herein provided. Any rights reserved shall not be deemed competitive with any of Producer's rights and may be exercised by Author at any time except as otherwise specifically provided herein.

ARTICLE II
OPTION PERIODS AND PAYMENTS

SECTION 2.01 **Option Periods/Option Payments** In consideration of the foregoing grant of rights and of Author's services in writing the Play and Author's agreement to perform services in connection with the production of the Play as hereinabove provided, Producer agrees to pay Author the following sums (*"Option Payments"*) in order to maintain Producer's rights to present the Play, provided that the first paid public First Class Performance of the Play occurs prior to the expiration of the applicable *"Option Period"* described below:

(a) *"First Option Period"*—$5,000 for the period of 6 months following the Effective Date of this Contract, payable upon the execution of this Contract by Author and Producer.

(b) *"Second Option Period"*—$2,500 for a second consecutive 6-month period, payable on or before the last day of the First Option Period.

(c) *"Third Option Period"*—$5,500 for an additional period of up to 12 consecutive months, payable in the following manner: $2,500 for the first 6 months of such period, payable on or before the last day of the Second Option Period and $500 per month thereafter, for up to 6 months, payable on or before the last day of the preceding month. In order to exercise this right to extend for a Third Option Period, Producer must give Author written notice, on or before the last day of the Second Option Period, of the intended date of the first paid public First Class Performance together with copies of commitments representing actual or proposed contributions of Equity Capital (as defined in SECTION 3.03(b)(i) herein) which, in the aggregate, equal at least 50% of Production Costs (as defined in SECTION 3.03 herein); plus copies of documents representing one of the following:

(i) a commitment for the licensing of a first class theatre, with occupancy to occur before the end of the Third Option Period; or

(ii) a contract for the engagement of a star, featured actor or director pursuant to which such person agrees to render services before the end of the Third Option Period; or

(iii) if Producer and Author mutually agree in ARTICLE XXII herein that Producer shall have the rights, in the Territory, to present Developmental Productions (as defined in SECTION 4.01(f) herein), then a contract with a theatre or organization for the presentation of a Developmental Production of the Play, the first performance of which is to be presented before the end of the Third Option Period.

The extension of Producer's rights and option for the Third Option Period shall not be prevented or affected by the fact that any of these commitments or contracts may be made subject to conditions, including, but not limited to, the availability of a person or theatre, the attainment of full capitalization of the production, further negotiations regarding material terms, or the execution of a formal agreement, or the fact that any of these commitments or contracts may later be breached or held to be unenforceable.

SECTION 2.02 **Option Payments Non-Returnable.** Each of the foregoing Option Payments made by Producer shall be non-returnable (except to the extent described in *ARTICLE XVI* herein) but shall be deductible, to the extent permitted by the terms of *ARTICLE VI* herein, from the Advance Payments and Royalties (as defined respectively in *SECTIONS 3.01* and *4.02* herein) otherwise payable to Author.

SECTION 2.03 **Extension of Option Until Delivery of Completed Play.** If this Contract provides in *ARTICLE XXII* that the Play has not been completed at the Effective Date of this Contract, the payment for the First Option Period shall be made at the time and in the manner set forth in *ARTICLE XXII* herein, but the expiration of the Option Periods and the due dates for the subsequent Option Payments otherwise specified in this ARTICLE shall be extended and measured from the date on which the Completed Play is delivered to Producer. Producer shall maintain the sole and exclusive rights and option to present the Play while Producer awaits delivery of the Completed Play. Unless otherwise defined in *ARTICLE XXII* herein, a *"Completed Play"* shall mean the Play consisting of a script of at least 110 single spaced pages. If the Completed Play is not delivered within 6 months after the Effective Date of this Contract, Producer may, at any time thereafter, terminate this Contract upon written notice to Author. Author agrees that time is of the essence with respect to such delivery date.

SECTION 2.04 **Extension of Option for Try-Out Performances.** If, during one of the Option Periods, Producer presents Second Class Performances (as defined in *SECTION 9.01* herein) or Developmental Productions of the Play, the expiration of the Option Periods and due dates for subsequent Option Payments shall be extended for a period equal to the number of days on which performances of the Play were so presented (up to a maximum of 8 weeks) plus an additional 60 days.

SECTION 2.05 **Definition of "Official Press Opening".** For the purposes of this Contract, the term *"Official Press Opening"* shall mean the performance of the Play which Producer has publicly announced as the opening and to which the press is invited.

ARTICLE III

ADVANCE PAYMENTS

SECTION 3.01 **Calculation and Due Dates of Advance Payments.** (a) Producer shall pay Author the following *"Advance Payments"*, at the stated times, subject to the provisions of *SECTIONS 3.04* and *6.01* herein:

(i) On the first day of rehearsal at which Producer requires the attendance of all cast members of the Principal Company (as defined in *SECTION 3.01(b)* herein), but in no event later than 5 business days before the initial First Class Performance of the Play, Producer shall pay Author a sum equal to 3% of the amounts constituting Capitalization (as defined in *SECTION 3.03* herein) at such date.

(ii) Thereafter, at such times as additional amounts are contributed towards Capitalization, Producer shall pay Author, within 10 business days after Producer's receipt thereof, a sum equal to 3% of such additional contributions.

(iii) The sums otherwise payable by Producer pursuant to the foregoing calculation in this SECTION shall be reduced by an amount equal to 3% of such sums. The net amounts paid to Author shall constitute the Advance Payments.

(b) For the purposes of this Contract, a *"Company"* shall mean each unit of actors assembled to present the Play hereunder. *"Principal Company"* shall mean the first Company funded in an amount sufficient to present First Class Performances of the Play.

SECTION 3.02 **Maximum Advance.** The aggregate amount of Advance Payments payable by Producer pursuant to *SECTION 3.01* herein shall not exceed $35,000, regardless of the amount of Capitalization.

SECTION 3.03 **Definition of "Production Costs", "Capitalization" and "Equity Capital".** (a) For the purposes of this Contract, *"Production Costs"* shall mean the estimated costs of producing the Principal Company (including any contingency reserves), as described in the documents used in connection with the financing of such Company, including costs that may be paid, if permitted by the terms of such documents, by an overcall demand on investors, but not including any weekly operating expenses.

(b) For the purposes of this Contract, *"Capitalization"* shall mean:

(i) the aggregate of the following sums actually received by Producer (after all necessary bank clearances) for the purpose of paying Production Costs:

(A) all amounts contributed as Equity Capital. For the purposes of this Contract, *"Equity Capital"* shall mean the amounts contributed by investors in order to pay Production Costs and obtain an ownership interest in the venture producing the Principal Company, including all amounts received by Producer pursuant to an overcall made on the investors who previously contributed Equity Capital to such venture, but only to the extent such sums exceed 10% of the total Equity Capital contributions received by Producer from all investors immediately prior to the date on which the demand for such overcall is issued and only to the extent such sums are used by Producer to pay Production Costs; and

(B) Should Producer find it necessary to obtain loans to pay Production Costs, then the amount of such loan proceeds shall also be included to the extent such proceeds are in excess of 20% of the estimated Production Costs (or if the documents used in connection with the financing of the Principal Company set forth an amount representing minimum estimated Production Costs, then such amount); however, if Producer receives no Equity Capital pursuant to an overcall (whether or not an overcall demand is made), then the amount of such loan proceeds shall be included to the extent such proceeds are in excess of 30% of such estimated Production Costs;

(ii) but not including the foregoing sums to the extent allocated to pay the following items of Production Costs:

(A) all security bonds, deposits and other guarantees to be provided to any union or other collective bargaining organization, theatre or other entity;

(B) all Option Payments to Author;

(C) advertising, promotional and press related costs in excess of 10% of the minimum estimated Production Costs; and

(D) all sums described in *SECTION 6.01(b)* herein which are included as Production Costs and paid to a third party who presented the Play in the Territory as a Developmental Production or as other non-First Class Performances.

(c) All sums received by Producer to pay the operating costs of paid public performances of the Play (rather than Production Costs) shall be excluded in determining the amount of Capitalization, regardless of the source of any such sums or the manner in which such sums may be contributed.

SECTION 3.04 **Advance Payments Non-Returnable.** All Advance Payments made by Producer shall be non-returnable but shall be deductible, to the extent permitted by the terms of *ARTICLE VI* herein, from Royalties otherwise payable to Author.

ARTICLE IV

ROYALTIES

SECTION 4.01 **Definitions.** For the purposes of this Contract, the following terms shall have the indicated meanings:

(a) *"Out-of-Town Performances"*—First Class Performances of the Play outside of New York City prior to presentation of Preview or Regular Performances.

(b) *"Preview Performances"*—First Class Performances of the Play in New York City prior to the Official Press Opening in New York City. For the purposes of calculating Royalties under this Contract, the Official Press Opening in New York City shall be deemed a Preview Performance.

(c) *"Regular Performances"*—First Class Performances of the Play in New York City commencing with the first performance of the Play following the Official Press Opening of the Play in New York City.

(d) *"Touring Performances"*—First Class Performances of the Play hereunder outside of New York City, presented by a Company simultaneously with or subsequent to Out-of-Town, Preview or Regular Performances.

(e) *"Fixed-Fee Performances"*—All performances of the Play hereunder (other than Preview and Regular Performances) produced by or pursuant to a grant of rights from Producer, in return for which Producer receives compensation based in whole or in part on a fixed (i.e., guaranteed) fee.

(f) *"Developmental Productions"*—Productions of the Play presented pursuant to Actors' Equity Workshop Agreements.

(g) *"Backers' Auditions"*—Performances of the Play presented pursuant to the Actors' Equity Association Backers' Audition Code or, if the performances are outside the United States then pursuant to any other similar code, contract or agreement in effect in such location.

(h) *"Performance Week"*—The 6- or 7-day period, beginning on either Monday or, if there is no scheduled performance on Monday, then on Tuesday and continuing through Sunday, during which one or more performances of the Play are presented hereunder.

(i) *"Full Performance Week"*—Any Performance Week during which no fewer than 8 performances of the Play are presented.

(j) *"New York City"*—The theatrical district of the Borough of Manhattan of the City of New York unless the parties modify the definition, in *ARTICLE XXII* herein, to include any other location in the Borough of Manhattan.

SECTION 4.02 **Description of Royalties.** Author shall earn the following aggregate *"Royalties"* for each week of performances, described below, during which the Play is presented hereunder:

(a) **Out-of-Town Performances and Preview Performances**—5% of the Gross Weekly Box Office Receipts (as defined in *SECTION 4.03* herein) from Out-of-Town and Preview Performances up to and including the Performance Week in which the costs of presenting such Company have been Recouped (as defined in *SECTION 4.04* herein) and 10% thereafter. This Royalty is not subject to the Royalty Adjustment provisions of *ARTICLE V* herein until and unless such Company has attained Recoupment.

(b) **Regular Performances**—5% of the Gross Weekly Box Office Receipts from Regular Performances up to and including the Performance Week in which the costs of presenting such Company have been Recouped and 10% thereafter. This Royalty is subject to the Royalty Adjustment provisions of *ARTICLE V* herein.

(c) **Touring Performances**—5% of the Gross Weekly Box Office Receipts earned from Touring Performances up to and including the Performance Week in which the costs of presenting such Company have been Recouped and 10% thereafter. This Royalty is subject to the Royalty Adjustment provisions of *ARTICLE V* herein.

(d) **Fixed-Fee Performances**—For the purposes of this *SECTION 4.02(d)*, the term "Producer" shall mean Producer's grantee in those cases where Fixed-Fee Performances are produced by such grantee.

(i) Except as provided in *SECTION 4.02(d)(ii)* herein, Author's Royalty for Fixed-Fee Performances of the Play shall be calculated in the following manner:

(A) 10% of any fixed fee paid to Producer by such local promoter or sponsor for such Performances; plus

(B) 10% of Producer's share of box office receipts and any profits for such Performances (including box office receipts and profits paid as a salary, fee, royalty or other type of compensation for Producer's services), paid to Producer by such local promoter or sponsor.

(ii) With respect to first class theatres which have, after January 1, 1977, presented First Class Performances of plays pursuant to which the authors of such plays have customarily received royalties for such performances based on a percentage of gross weekly box office receipts (rather than on fixed fees), Author's Royalty for Fixed-Fee Performances of the Play presented in such theatres shall be calculated in the following manner:

(A) 10% of any fixed fee paid to Producer by the so-called "local promoter" or "local sponsor" for such Performances; plus

(B) if the local promoter or sponsor pays Producer a percentage of box office receipts and any profits for such Performances (including box office receipts and profits paid as a salary, fee, royalty or other type of compensation for Producer's services), then Author shall be paid, from up to 50% of Producer's share of such box office receipts and profits, a sum equal to 25% of the amounts paid to Author in (A); plus

(C) 10% of the balance of Producer's share of box office receipts and profits set forth in (B) above (after deduction of the sum paid to Author in (B) above);

(iii) The calculations set forth above may be made on a weekly basis or on a theatre-by-theatre basis at Producer's option.

(iv) If there is any dispute between Author and Producer as to whether a particular theatre should be classified under *SECTION 4.02(d)(i)* or *(ii)*, the parties shall submit the matter for resolution to the Theatrical Conciliation Council. The decision of the Council shall be final and binding on the parties.

(v) If Producer licenses the Play to an entity in which Producer has any financial or other interest, or if the Play is presented in a theatre in which Producer has a similar interest, the arrangements made between Producer and such entity or theatre shall not be materially different from the arrangements made in the industry between unrelated parties under similar circumstances. Furthermore, irrespective of whether there is any financial or other interest between Producer and such entity or theatre, the weekly operating expenses of such Fixed-Fee Performances which are customarily paid by the producer (e.g. compensation to actors), rather than by the local promoter or sponsor, shall be reflected in the amount of the fixed fee for the purpose of computing and paying Author's Royalties under this *SECTION 4.02(d)*. If Author or the Guild believes that any such arrangements made by Producer are materially different, or that the fixed fee does not reflect the weekly operating expenses customarily paid by the producer rather than the local promoter or sponsor then, in either case, Author, or the Guild, on behalf of Author, shall submit such matter to the Theatrical Conciliation Council which shall determine whether the arrangements are appropriate under the circumstances or whether the fixed fee reflects the weekly operating expenses customarily paid by producers, as the case may be. The decision of the Council shall be final and binding on the parties.

(e) ***Developmental Productions***—If the rights to present Developmental Productions of the Play are granted in *ARTICLE XXII* herein, Author shall earn a Royalty equal to the minimum compensation paid to an actor for such Developmental Production, excluding any per diem, travel and other allowances, if any, paid to the actor. Author and Producer shall not modify any provision of this Contract as a condition to the granting of rights to present Developmental Productions.

(f) ***Backers' Auditions***—No Royalties to Author.

SECTION 4.03 **Definition of "Gross Weekly Box Office Receipts".** (a) Where Author's Royalties, as provided herein, are based upon *"Gross Weekly Box Office Receipts",* the Royalties for such Performance Week shall be computed upon all sums received by Producer from all ticket sales to the Play, allocable to performances given in such week, less the following deductions:

(i) federal or other admission taxes;

(ii) customary commissions and fees, as may be prevailing from time to time, paid to or retained by third parties in connection with theatre parties, benefits, American Express or other similar credit card plans, telephone sales, automated ticket distribution or remote box offices, e.g., Ticketron and Ticket World (but not ticket brokers), and commissions or fees for group sales;

(iii) commissions and fees paid to or retained by credit card companies for sales of tickets;

(iv) those sums equivalent to the former 5% New York City Amusement Tax, the proceeds of which are now paid to the pension and/or welfare funds of various theatrical unions;

(v) subscription fees;

(vi) receipts from Actors' Fund Benefit performances provided the customary payments are made by the Actors' Fund to The Dramatists Guild Fund, Inc.;

(vii) receipts from two performances of the Play in each calendar year to the extent such receipts are contributed for theatre-related eleemosynary purposes; and

(viii) if applicable, library discounts, value added taxes and entertainment taxes, if any.

(b) Producer may also deduct from Gross Weekly Box Office Receipts allocable to any Performance Week any sums included as Gross Weekly Box Office Receipts in a prior Performance Week and which were included in Author's Royalty calculation but which sums subsequently are refunded or uncollectible due to dishonored checks, invalidated credit card receipts or for any other reason.

(c) If the Play is presented simultaneously by more than one Company, Gross Weekly Box Office Receipts received by each such Company shall be computed and paid separately.

SECTION 4.04 **Definition of "Recouped" and "Recoupment".** (a) For the purposes of this Contract, the terms *"Recouped"* or *"Recoupment"* shall mean, with respect to each Company presenting the Play, the recovery of all costs incurred in presenting such Company after payment or accrual (but not prepayment) of all operating expenses for such Company.

(b) For the purposes of determining Recoupment, the costs incurred in presenting a Company shall include the following *"Production Expenses":* fees of designers, directors, general and company managers; cost of sets, curtains, drapes and costumes; cost or payments on account of properties, furnishings, lighting and electrical equipment; premiums for bonds and insurance; unrecouped option and advance payments to persons other than Author; rehearsal charges, transportation charges, reasonable legal and accounting expenses, advance advertising, publicity and press expenses and other expenses and losses actually incurred in connection with the production and presentation of the Play up to and including the Official Press Opening of such Company and all sums described in *SECTION 6.01(b)* herein to be paid, as Production Costs, to a third party who presented the Play in the Territory as a Developmental Production or as other non-First Class Performances; but there shall not be included any compensation paid to Producer or to any person rendering the services of a producer other than a cash office charge not to exceed $500 per week (regardless of the amount actually paid) commencing 4 weeks before the opening of rehearsals and continuing until the Official Press Opening of the Company and other than Producer's Royalty (as defined in *SECTION 5.12* herein). No amounts charged as Production Expenses shall be charged again as operating expenses, or vice versa.

(c) Recoupment shall be calculated separately for each Company presenting the Play so that the profits or losses attributable to one Company shall not affect the calculation of Recoupment for any other Company. Recoupment shall be determined by the accountant engaged by Producer and, subject to *SECTION 5.08* herein, the determination made by such accountant shall be final and binding as among the parties hereto. Promptly upon the making of such determination by the accountant, Producer shall send Author written notice that Recoupment has occurred.

(d) In calculating Recoupment for the purposes of this Contract, the amounts of bonds, deposits or other items which, by their terms, are returnable to the Company shall not be included as costs to be recovered. Recoupment of the amounts incurred in presenting any Company shall be deemed final so that, once Recoupment has been attained, subsequent expenses that may be incurred by such Company will not alter the fact that such Company has Recouped within the meaning of this Contract.

(e) All expenses incurred by any Company to finance Touring or Off-Broadway Performances by that same Company must be Recouped before Author shall be entitled to post-Recoupment Royalties with respect to such Touring or Off-Broadway Performances. It is understood that the incurring of such expenses shall not affect or otherwise alter the payment of post-Recoupment Royalties, if any, by such Company for performances which precede such Touring or Off-Broadway Performances.

ARTICLE V
ROYALTY ADJUSTMENTS

SECTION 5.01 **Definition of "Weekly Breakeven".** (a) For the purposes of this Contract, the term *"Weekly Breakeven"* shall mean, for each Company presenting the Play hereunder, the operating expenses of such Company for each Performance Week as set forth in the accounting reports as customarily prepared by the accountant engaged by Producer. For the purpose of determining Weekly Breakeven, operating expenses shall consist of the following: $1,000 of Author's Royalty (regardless of the total Royalty actually paid to Author), compensation paid to the cast, director, stage manager, general and company managers, press agents, orchestra, and miscellaneous stage personnel, transportation charges, weekly cash office charge not to exceed $500 (regardless of the total cash office charge actually paid to Producer), advertising, press and publicity costs, legal and accounting expenses, the costs of exhibiting television commercials, theatre guaranty and expenses, rentals, miscellaneous supplies and all other reasonable expenses of whatever kind actually incurred in connection with the weekly operation of the Play, as distinguished from Production Expenses, but not including any compensation to Producer or a person rendering services of a producer, other than $250 of Producer's Royalty, or any money paid to Producer by way of a percentage of the Gross Weekly Box Office Receipts or otherwise for the making of any loan or the posting of any bond, or any cost incurred in producing the first television commercial (or any other type of audio-visual promotion), or any sum paid by Producer to any trade association of producers and/or theatre owners.

(b) Notwithstanding the foregoing, the costs incurred in producing any subsequent television commercials or any other type of audio-visual promotions shall be included in determining Weekly Breakeven, but shall be amortized over a period of no fewer than 13 weeks.

SECTION 5.02 **Definition of "Weekly Profits".** For the purposes of this Contract, the term *"Weekly Profits"* shall mean the amount by which Gross Weekly Box Office Receipts for a particular Performance Week exceed the Weekly Breakeven for such week.

SECTION 5.03 **Definition of "Losing Week" and "Weekly Losses".** For the purposes of this Contract, the term *"Losing Week"* shall mean any Performance Week for which the Gross Weekly Box Office Receipts do not exceed the Weekly Breakeven for such week, and the term *"Weekly Losses"* shall mean the amount by which Weekly Breakeven for a particular Performance Week exceeds the Gross Weekly Box Office Receipts for such week.

SECTION 5.04 **Adjustments for Out-of-Town and Preview Performances.** With respect to each Performance Week of Out-of-Town and Preview Performances, commencing with the week after the costs of presenting such Company have been Recouped, the Royalties payable to Author for such Out-of-Town and Preview Performances shall be subject to adjustment in the same manner as is applicable to Regular Performances as described in *SECTION 5.05(b)* herein.

SECTION 5.05 **Adjustments for Regular Performances.** With respect to each Company presenting Regular Performances, the Royalties payable to Author for such Regular Performances shall be subject to adjustment in the following manner:

(a) *Pre-Recoupment*—(i) If the Gross Weekly Box Office Receipts for any Performance Week of Regular Performances (except for the first 3 consecutive 7-day periods following the Official Press Opening of the Play in New York City and the Split Week, if any, as defined in *SECTION 5.05(a)(ii)* herein), up to and including the Performance Week in which the costs of presenting such Company have been Recouped, do not exceed 110% of Weekly Breakeven, Author's Royalty for such week, in lieu of the Royalties otherwise payable, shall be comprised of a fixed Royalty of $1,000 per Full Performance Week, plus a percentage Royalty equal to 25% of the Weekly Profits, if any, for such week; *provided, however*, in no event shall Author's fixed and percentage Royalty exceed a sum equal to 5% of the Gross Weekly Box Office Receipts for such week.

(ii) The Royalties payable to Author for each consecutive 7-day period of performances, commencing with the day following the Official Press Opening in New York City, shall be (in lieu of the Royalties otherwise payable) $1,000 for each such 7-day period, pro-rated based on the number of performances, fewer than 8, presented in any such period. This Royalty shall apply for no more than 3 consecutive 7-day periods unless the day following the third such period (i.e., the 22nd day following the Official Press Opening in New York City) is not the first day of a Performance Week, in which case the Royalty for the number of performances of the Play presented for the partial week as measured from such 22nd day up to the beginning of the next Performance Week (*"Split Week"*) shall continue to be at the rate of $1,000 per 7-day period, pro-rated as described in the preceding sentence; however, if the Gross Weekly Box Office Receipts for the Performance Week in which the Split Week occurs exceed 110% of Weekly Breakeven for such week, Author's Royalty for such Split Week shall be 5% of the Gross Weekly Box Office Receipts for the performances presented in such Split Week. The Royalty adjustment described in this *SECTION 5.05(a)(ii)* shall be applicable only to the extent that the three 7-day periods and Split Week, if any, occur prior to or during the Performance Week in which the costs of presenting such Company have been Recouped.

(b) *Post-Recoupment*—If the Gross Weekly Box Office Receipts for any Performance Week of Regular Performances, occurring after the Performance Week in which the costs of presenting such Company have been Recouped, do not exceed 120% of Weekly Breakeven, Author's Royalty for such week, in lieu of Royalties otherwise payable, shall be comprised of a fixed Royalty of $1,000 per Full Performance Week, plus a percentage Royalty equal to 35% of Weekly Profits, if any, for such week; *provided, however*, in no event shall Author's fixed and percentage Royalty exceed a sum equal to 10% of the Gross Weekly Box Office Receipts for such week. Notwithstanding the foregoing sentence, if the Director of the Play receives for any such week a royalty which is less than the full royalties payable pursuant to the Director's agreement with Producer, then Author's percentage Royalty described in the preceding calculation shall, for such week, be reduced, on a pro-rata basis, from 35% of such Weekly Profits (but in no event to less than 25% of Weekly Profits), with the other provisions of such calculation remaining unchanged.

SECTION 5.06 **Adjustments for Touring Performances.** With respect to each Company presenting Touring Performances of the Play, the Royalties payable to Author for such Touring Performances shall be subject to adjustment in the following manner:

(a) *Pre-Recoupment*—If the Gross Weekly Box Office Receipts for any Performance Week of Touring Performances, up to and including the Performance Week in which the costs of presenting the Touring Company have been Recouped, do not exceed 110% of Weekly Breakeven for such Touring Company, Author's Royalty for such week, in lieu of the Royalties otherwise payable, shall be comprised of a fixed Royalty of $1,000 per Full Performance Week, plus a percentage Royalty equal to 25% of the Weekly Profits, if any, for such week; *provided, however*, in no event shall Author's fixed and percentage Royalty exceed a sum equal to 5% of the Gross Weekly Box Office Receipts for such week.

(b) *Post-Recoupment*—If the Gross Weekly Box Office Receipts for any Performance Week of Touring Performances, occurring after the Performance Week in which the costs of presenting the Touring Company have been Recouped, do not exceed 120% of Weekly Breakeven for such Touring Company, Author's Royalty for such week, in lieu of Royalties otherwise payable, shall be comprised of a fixed Royalty of $1,000 per Full Performance Week, plus a percentage Royalty equal to 35% of the Weekly Profits, if any, for such week; *provided, however*, in no event shall Author's fixed and percentage Royalty exceed a sum equal to 10% of the Gross Weekly Box Office Receipts for such week. Notwithstanding the foregoing sentence, if the Director of the Play receives for any such week a royalty which is less than the full royalties payable pursuant to the Director's agreement with Producer, then Author's percentage Royalty described in the preceding calculation shall, for such week, be reduced, on a pro-rata basis, from 35% of such Weekly Profits (but in no event to less than 25% of Weekly Profits), with the other provisions of such calculation remaining unchanged.

SECTION 5.07 **Adjustments for Losing Weeks.** If any Company has Weekly Losses in any week of Regular or Touring Performances, Author's Royalty for performances by such Company for such Losing Week shall, in lieu of Royalties otherwise payable, be $1,000 per Full Performance Week.

SECTION 5.08 **Review of Weekly Breakeven and Recoupment Calculation.** Should either Author or Producer wish to challenge the accountant's determination of Weekly Breakeven or Recoupment, the challenging party, upon notice to the other party, shall, in lieu of commencing an arbitration proceeding, present the matter, in writing, for resolution to the Theatrical Conciliation Council, whose decision shall be advisory in nature. After receiving such decision, either party may bring the matter to arbitration as provided in *ARTICLE XX* herein.

SECTION 5.09 **Yearly Royalty Adjustment.** For a period of 4 consecutive Performance Weeks occurring during the months of December and/or January wherein one such Performance Week is the week in which Christmas occurs (*"Christmas Period"*), Producer may, provided he gives written notice to Author on or before December 1 of each such year, specifying which 4 consecutive Performance Weeks will constitute the Christmas Period for that year, adjust Author's Royalties otherwise payable in the following manner:

(a) *Pre-Recoupment*—The aggregate Weekly Losses incurred in up to 3 Losing Weeks, if any, occurring during such Christmas Period may be deducted from the Gross Weekly Box Office Receipts earned during any one Performance Week during such Christmas Period.

(b) *Post-Recoupment*—Author's Royalty for all 4 Performance Weeks during such Christmas Period may be calculated by separately aggregating the Gross Weekly Box Office Receipts for such weeks and the Weekly Breakeven for such weeks and then dividing each of those two sums by 4. The resulting amounts shall be treated as if they were the Gross Weekly Box Office Receipts and Weekly Breakeven for a single week. The Author's applicable post-Recoupment Royalty (which would otherwise be payable, without reference to this SECTION, after taking into account any other appropriate Royalty Adjustments set forth in this ARTICLE) shall be calculated based on such amounts and then multiplied by 4 to determine the Author's Royalty for the entire Christmas Period.

(c) The foregoing calculations shall be made and adjusted Royalties for such Christmas Period shall be paid within 7 days following the end of the last Performance Week during the Christmas Period. During the Christmas Period, Producer shall pay Author $1,000 for each Full Performance Week as an advance against the adjusted Royalties payable for such Christmas Period.

(d) The provisions of this SECTION may be applied by Producer in one or more years and to any or all (or none) of the Companies presenting the Play and Producer may choose a different Christmas Period for each Company; *provided, however,* that if Producer chooses to apply this Royalty Adjustment provision to a Company presenting Touring Performances, all performances by such Company during the applicable Christmas Period must be presented in one theatre.

(e) If any Company attains Recoupment during a Christmas Period, then Producer must, with respect to such Company, calculate Author's Royalties for the entire Period either on the basis of *SECTION 5.09(b)* or without reference to this SECTION, as Producer, in his sole discretion, may decide.

(f) The provisions of this SECTION shall not apply to Fixed-Fee Performances.

SECTION 5.10 **Pro-rata Adjustment for Fixed Royalties.** In any instance in which this Contract provides that Royalties payable to Author for a given Full Performance Week of a Company are to be, in whole or in part, a fixed-dollar amount, and if fewer than 8 performances of the Play are presented by such Company during such week, then the fixed-dollar Royalties otherwise payable to Author hereunder shall be reduced by an amount equal to one-eighth of such fixed-dollar dollar Royalties for each performance of the Play, fewer than 8, given in any such Performance Week.

SECTION 5.11 **Pro-rata Adjustment for Repertoire Performances.** If the Play is to be presented in repertoire with one or more other plays, Author and Producer shall agree on the method in which Author's Royalties shall be prorated and such method shall be set forth in *ARTICLE XXII* herein.

SECTION 5.12 **Proportionate Adjustment in Producer's Royalty.** (a) Regardless of the amount of royalties received by Producer for any week of performances, for the purposes of calculating Recoupment and Weekly Breakeven, *"Producer's Royalty"* shall be deemed to be limited to the following amounts but may not be deemed to be less than $250:

Producer's Royalty shall be calculated in the following manner:

(i) divide the amount of Royalties earned by Author for such week by an amount equal to 10% of the Gross Weekly Box Office Receipts for such week, then

(ii) multiply that number by an amount equal to the lesser of:

(A) 2.5% of the Gross Weekly Box Office Receipts for such week or

(B) the amount of royalties (but not the cash office charge) payable to Producer for such week as set forth in the documents used in connection with the financing of the Play.

(b) For the purposes of the calculation described in *SECTION 5.12(a)* herein, the amount of Royalties earned by Author shall be the full amount of Royalties otherwise payable to Author prior to the deduction of any Advance or Option Payments as permitted by this Contract.

(c) If Producer presents Off-Broadway Performances of the Play pursuant to the terms of *SECTION 9.02* herein, then in making this adjustment for such performances, Author's 10% Royalty referred to in *SECTION 5.12(a)(i)* shall be Author's post-Recoupment Off-Broadway Royalty set forth in *ARTICLE XXII* herein.

SECTION 5.13 **Pro-rata Adjustment of Weekly Breakeven.** If more than one Royalty calculation is applicable for performances presented in any Performance Week and one such calculation is to be made based on Weekly Profits or Weekly Losses (for example, if there are both Touring Performances and Fixed-Fee Performances presented in one Performance Week), the determination of the amount of such profits or losses to be allocated to such performances shall be made in the following manner: the amount of Weekly Breakeven applicable to such calculation shall be the actual Weekly Breakeven for the entire Performance Week, prorated, based on the ratio that the number of performances to which the Weekly Profits or Losses calculation is to be applied bears to the total number of performances presented during such Performance Week; and the amount of Gross Weekly Box Office Receipts used in calculating the profits or losses shall be only those receipts earned for the performances as to which the Weekly Profits or Losses calculation applies.

ARTICLE VI
DEDUCTIONS FROM ADVANCE AND ROYALTY PAYMENTS

SECTION 6.01 Deductions from Advances. (a) Option Payments made for the Third Option Period, if any, shall be deducted from the Advance Payments otherwise payable to Author. Option Payments for the First and Second Option Periods shall not be deducted from Advance Payments.

(b) If a third party has previously produced the Play in the Territory as a Developmental Production or as other non-First Class Performances and if Producer is required to make any payment to such third party in order to acquire all of the rights in the Play contemplated by this APC then, to the extent that such sums are included as Production Costs, Producer shall deduct from the Advance Payments otherwise payable to Author so much of such sums as equal the aggregate of all monies directly or indirectly paid to Author for such prior production (less customary per-diem and transportation expenses), but in no event more than the sums paid by Producer to such third party. Author and such third party shall give Producer a complete and accurate statement, signed by both Author and such third party, setting forth all monies paid to Author in connection with such prior production. The total sums payable by Producer to such third party and deductible from Author's Advance Payments shall be set forth in ARTICLE XXII herein.

SECTION 6.02 Deductions from Royalties. (a) All Option and Advance Payments received by Author may be deducted from Royalties earned by Author from any or all Companies presenting the Play, at the rate of up to 50% of such Royalties per Performance Week, commencing for the Performance Week in which such Company has reached Recoupment.

(b) The foregoing deductions shall be permitted only in such amounts as will not cause Author to earn, for any week in which such deductions are made, Royalties of less than $1,000 per Full Performance Week.

ARTICLE VII
GENERAL PAYMENT PROVISIONS

SECTION 7.01 Royalty Due Dates/Box Office Statements. (a) The portion of any Gross Weekly Box Office Receipts or Weekly Profits due to Author shall belong to Author and shall be held in trust by Producer as Author's property until payment. The trust nature of such funds shall not be questioned, whether the monies are physically segregated or not. In the event of breach of trust hereunder, Author may, at his option, pursue his remedies at law or in equity in lieu of the arbitration procedure established by this Contract.

(b) Within 7 days after the end of each Performance Week, Producer shall send to the Guild for Author's account, the amount due as Author's Royalties for such week, together with the daily box-office statements (for each person comprising Author) of each performance of the Play during such week, signed by the treasurer or treasurers of the theatre in which the performances are given and signed by Producer or Producer's duly authorized representative.

(c) Box-office statements and payments due for performances, in the United States, presented more than 500 miles from New York City shall be sent within 14 days after the end of each Performance Week, and for performances presented in Canada or in any location outside the Territory, within 21 days after the end of each such week, unless such payments are delayed or blocked due to the action or inaction of government authorities, in which case the payments shall be made as soon thereafter as possible.

(d) In cases where Author's compensation depends on the calculation of Weekly Breakeven or Weekly Profits, weekly operating statements shall be sent to the Guild (for each person comprising Author), at the same time Author's check is due.

(e) Producer shall also send to the Guild the actual production expense statements provided to investors as well as the periodic accounting reports as prepared by the accountant for the production.

(f) All reports and statements sent to the Guild pursuant to this ARTICLE shall be held confidential by Author, the Guild, and any Author's representative.

(g) Notwithstanding the provisions of *SECTION 7.01(c)* herein, Royalties for performances of the Play given in repertoire with one or more other plays shall be sent no later than 4 days after the end of every 4 Performance Weeks during which the Play is so performed, regardless of the number of performances presented.

SECTION 7.02 **Method of Payment.** All checks shall be sent to the Guild. Checks for payments due under *ARTICLES II* and *IX* herein shall be drawn to the order of the Guild. All other checks shall be drawn to the order of Author or, where Author indicates in writing to Producer and the Guild that Author is represented by an agent who is a member in good standing of the Society of Author's Representatives, Inc., then to the agent.

SECTION 7.03 **Separate Calculations.** If the Play is presented simultaneously by more than one Company, Royalties accruing from each Company shall be computed and paid separately.

SECTION 7.04 **Author's Division of Payments.** If Author is comprised of more than one person, all sums set forth herein as being payable to Author represent the aggregate of all amounts payable to all persons comprising Author. Such aggregate sums shall be divided equally unless otherwise provided in *ARTICLE XXII* herein.

SECTION 7.05 **Adaptor's Compensation.** If the Play is an English language adaptation made from a foreign language play or from other literary property, the adaptor shall receive at least ⅓rd of the compensation otherwise payable to Author pursuant to the terms of the APC with the amounts to be paid to be set forth in *ARTICLE XXII* herein.

SECTION 7.06 **Deductions.** No deductions shall be made from compensation due by Producer to Author on account of a debt due by Author to Producer unless an agreement in writing providing therefor shall have been made between Author and Producer and filed with the Guild; except, however, that such deduction may be made if it is less than $200 and a memorandum, signed or initialed by Author acknowledging his indebtedness, and receipted by Producer or his representative, accompanies the statement for the week in which the deduction is made.

ARTICLE VIII

GENERAL PRODUCTION PROVISIONS

SECTION 8.01 **Producer's Undertaking.** Producer, recognizing that the Play is the artistic creation of Author and that as such Author is entitled to protect the type and nature of the production of Author's creation, hereby agrees:

(a) Under his own management to rehearse, present and continue to present the Play, with a cast, director, scenic, lighting, costume and, where appropriate, sound designer, conductor, choreographer and/or dance director mutually agreeable to Producer and to Author, and to announce the name of Author as sole Author of the Play upon all programs and in all advertising matter in accordance with the terms of *SECTION 8.10* herein. Any change in the cast or any replacement of a director, conductor, choreographer and/or dance director shall likewise be subject to the mutual consent of the parties.

Author may designate another person to act on his behalf with respect to such approvals and appointments. If Author is not available for consultation in the United States (or wherever else the Play is being produced), the provisions of this SECTION shall not apply unless Author shall have designated another person to act on his behalf who is available for consultation where the Play is being produced.

(b) To rehearse, produce, present and continue to present the Play, including Touring Performances thereof, with neither Author nor Producer making or causing to be made any addition, omission or alteration in the manuscript or title of the Play as contracted for production without the consent of the other. Producer warrants that any change of any kind whatsoever in the manuscript, title, stage business or performance of the Play made by Producer or any third party and which is acceptable to Author shall be the property of Author. Producer shall cause to be prepared, executed and delivered to Author, not later than the Official Press Opening in New York City, such documents as may be necessary to transfer to Author all rights in any such changes in the manuscript or title of the Play; however, Producer shall not be responsible to deliver documents to Author for any materials or changes solicited by Author from any third party. Author shall not be obligated to make payment to any person suggesting or making any such changes unless Author has entered into a bona fide written agreement to do so; similarly, Producer shall not be required to make payment to any person solicited by Author to suggest or make changes unless Producer has entered into a bona fide written agreement to do so. Subject to *SECTION 8.16* herein, Author shall, without any obligation to Producer, be entitled to use any parts of the Play omitted.

(c) Producer may complain to the Guild that Author is unreasonable in refusing to make changes or additions. In such event the Guild shall appoint a representative or representatives and, if they so advise, shall lend its best efforts to prevail upon Author to make the suggested changes, it being understood, however, that the Guild shall have no power to compel Author to agree to such changes.

SECTION 8.02 **Author's Right to Attend Rehearsals/Author's Availability.** (a) Author shall have the right to attend all rehearsals and performances of the Play prior to the Official Press Opening in New York City.

(b) Author shall use all best efforts to be available one month ahead of scheduled rehearsal dates to perform the services required pursuant to the terms of this Contract.

SECTION 8.03 **Author's Exercise of Approval Rights.** If more than one person constitutes Author, then, where the approval or consent of Author is required anywhere in this Contract, and such persons cannot agree, the President of the Guild shall, upon the request of Producer or any person comprising Author, appoint a single arbitrator to pass on such unresolved disagreements.

SECTION 8.04 **Expenses.** (a) Producer shall reimburse Author for such hotel and travel expenses as Author may incur in making trips to attend rehearsals and up to 12 weeks of Out-of-Town Performances and the Official Press Opening in New York City, and at any other time when the presence of Author is required by Producer.

(b) In addition to the expenses to be reimbursed pursuant to *SECTION 8.04(a)* herein, if Author is a resident of the City of New York, Producer shall reimburse Author for such local travel expenses as Author may incur during the time when the Play is in rehearsal in New York City or being presented for Preview Performances, and shall also reimburse hotel expenses for an Author who resides in the City of New York but outside of the Borough of Manhattan, if such expenses are reasonably necessary due to Producer's rehearsal or production schedule.

(c) Unless specific dollar amounts are provided in *ARTICLE XXII* herein, the amounts reimbursable by Producer under this SECTION shall be the cost of reasonable hotel and travel accommodations. In any event, Author's hotel and travel accommodations shall be of a class equal to the greater of the class charged to the Company by Producer or Director.

(d) If Author is unavailable and designates another person to act on his behalf in connection with the consultations set forth in *SECTION 8.01(a)* herein, Author and Producer may agree in *ARTICLE XXII* to specify the extent to which such designee's expenses may be reimbursed, if at all.

SECTION **8.05 Copying Expenses.** Producer shall pay all costs incurred in making copies of the Play and any revisions thereof prior to the Official Press Opening in New York City and shall use best efforts to provide facilities, in or near any theatre in which the Play is presented, for the purpose of copying Author's revisions of the Play.

SECTION **8.06 Designs.** Pursuant to the rules and regulations of the United Scenic Artists Local 829, Author undertakes and agrees that Author will not sell, lease, license or authorize the use of any of the original designs of scenery, lighting or costumes created by the designers, without the written consent of the owner of such designs.

SECTION **8.07 Artwork.** If Producer owns the artwork and/or logo for the production of the Play, Producer grants to Author the right to use such artwork and logo in connection with Author's exploitation of the Play (but not for the purpose of creating Commercial Use Products as defined in *SECTION 11.01* herein), subject to all restrictions which may exist in connection with such uses and subject to all payments which must be made to any third party, which payments shall not be the responsibility of Producer. Author shall not use or grant to others the right to use such artwork and logo without first giving Producer 60 days prior written notice. Author shall indemnify Producer for any liability which may arise in connection with any such use.

SECTION **8.08 Production Script.** Prior to the last performance of the Play under this Contract or prior to one month after the Official Press Opening in New York City, whichever is earlier, Producer shall deliver to Author or Author's representative, as Author's property, a neat and legible script of the Play, as currently presented.

SECTION **8.09 Rights to Promote.** Author hereby grants to Producer and Producer's licensees and permitted assigns, the right to use Author's name, biography, photographs, likeness or recorded voice (referred to in this SECTION as "materials"), and the title of and excerpts from the Play for advertising, press and promotional purposes by any means or medium. Producer shall submit to Author, for approval, all materials which Producer intends to use. If Author does not advise Producer, within 72 hours of receipt of the materials, of desired changes therein, the materials shall be deemed approved as submitted by Producer. Producer shall include Author's biography in all programs used by Producer in which any other biography appears.

SECTION **8.10 Author's Billing.** (a) Author shall receive billing credit whenever Producer or Director is accorded billing credit; *provided, however,* with respect to ABC listings and "teaser" advertisements, radio and television advertisements and marquees, billing credit may be accorded to any one or more of Producer, Author or Director without according billing credit to the other(s), if such person(s) has achieved a level of prominence greater than those not receiving billing credit and such that the use of the name(s) of the person(s) excluded would not enhance the commercial value of the Play. If Producer and Author are unable to agree, then, upon the written request of Producer, the determination of whether such level of prominence has been achieved shall be made by a theatrical press agent designated by the Theatrical Conciliation Council. Such determination must be made prior to the publication of such credits. The designation of the press agent and such agent's determination shall be final and binding on the parties hereto.

(b) Author's billing shall be on a separate line beneath the title of the Play. It shall be in a type size no less than 40% of the type size used for the title of the Play (other than logo titles); *provided, however,* if the title of the Play appears more than once in any one advertisement, the placement and size of Author's billing shall be in relation to the title where used in closest proximity to the billing accorded to others involved in the Play. In no event shall Author's billing be smaller than the type size used for the billing accorded to Director and/or Producer (except where Producer's name appears as part of the name of the theatre).

(c) Author and Producer may supplement the provisions of *SECTION 8.10(b)* in *ARTICLE XXII* herein but shall not modify or supplement in any way the provisions of *SECTION 8.10(a)* herein.

SECTION 8.11 **Radio and Television Publicizing.** Producer shall have the right to authorize one or more radio and/or television excerpts of the Play, not exceeding 7 minutes each, for the purpose of exploiting and publicizing the theatre industry, performances of the Play, any person performing in the Play and for use on awards programs, without any additional approval by or payment to Author, provided Producer receives no compensation therefrom other than reimbursement of out-of-pocket expenses; however, Author shall have approval of any change in the script made in an excerpt produced under the control of Producer.

SECTION 8.12 **Producer's Credit.** (a) If Producer has presented the Play for its Official Press Opening, Author shall use all best efforts to require that Producer receive conspicuously placed billing credit in the following circumstances:

(i) if all or any portion of the Play is published, the credit shall appear on a page preceding the first page of the text of the Play;

(ii) if a motion picture or television production is produced based on the Play, the credit shall appear on the screen separately with no other credit; and

(iii) in the case of any Revival, Stock, Amateur or Ancillary Performances, as those terms are defined in SECTION 11.01 herein, the credit shall appear on the first page of credits in all programs used therefor.

(b) The credit referred to above shall contain the name(s) of Producer and co-producers, if any, and shall state that the Play was originally produced by them. The order, title and relative size and spacing of the names of Producer (and co-producers, if any) shall be identical to the billing contained in the program for the Play at the time of the Official Press Opening.

(c) No casual or inadvertent failure to comply with the provisions of this SECTION shall be deemed a breach of this Contract unless such failure can, but shall not, be rectified as soon as practicable.

SECTION 8.13 **Approval of Use of Producers' Names.** Producer shall not use the name of any other person, firm or corporation as a producer of the Play unless Author has consented in writing.

SECTION 8.14 **House Seat Records.** If Author receives an allocation of house seats pursuant to ARTICLE XXII herein, Author agrees to maintain a true, complete and accurate record, in accordance with the requirements of the Arts and Cultural Affairs Law of the State of New York and the regulations promulgated thereunder, of Author's disposition of such house seats. Author agrees not to dispose of such house seats at a price above the regular box-office prices for such tickets.

SECTION 8.15 **Debt by Author.** If Author is indebted to the Guild or to Producer, the Guild may file with the Negotiator (as described in ARTICLE XII herein) a memorandum to that effect, and the Negotiator shall thereupon withhold from Author's share of income held by the Negotiator, the amount of such indebtedness and shall pay the same over to the Guild and/or Producer as their interests may appear. The foregoing shall not limit Producer's rights to pursue other remedies in connection with the collection of any indebtedness.

SECTION 8.16 **Revue Sketches.** (a) Any sketch or number of a revue and any song or musical number in the Play which shall not have been used on the Official Press Opening in New York or within 3 weeks thereafter, or having been so used shall be omitted from the Play for 3 successive consecutive Performance Weeks, may be withdrawn by Author and used by him for any purpose, free of any claim by Producer, subject only to such financial interest in additional uses as Producer may theretofore have acquired.

(b) If a sketch, song or other contribution of one or more persons constituting Author is omitted from a condensed or tabloid version of the Play, then such person whose work is so omitted shall nevertheless share in the proceeds from such version, provided his contribution shall have been included in at least one-half of the then prior performances of the Play. In such case, each such person shall sha in the proceeds of the condensed or tabloid version in the same proportion that his original compensation hereunder bears to the total compensation due hereunder to all persons constituting Author.

ARTICLE IX
ADDITIONAL PRODUCTION RIGHTS

SECTION 9.01 Grant of Second Class Performance Rights. (a) Author hereby grants Producer the sole and exclusive rights to produce one or more Second Class Performances of the Play on the speaking stage in the Territory during the time that Producer continues to have rights to present the Play hereunder. For the purposes of this Contract, the term *"Second Class Performances"* shall mean all performances of the Play other than Stock, Amateur and Ancillary Performances (as those terms are defined in *SECTION 11.01* herein), Off-Broadway Performances (as defined in *SECTION 9.02* herein), and First Class Performances and Developmental (i.e., "workshop") Productions.

(b) Author's Royalties for Second Class Performances shall be calculated and paid in the manner set forth in *SECTION 4.02(d)* herein with respect to Touring Performances, unless Author's Royalty is calculated in whole or in part on the basis of a fixed fee payable to Producer, in which case the Royalty shall be calculated and paid in the manner set forth for Fixed-Fee Performances.

SECTION 9.02 Grant of Off-Broadway Performance Rights. (a) Author hereby grants Producer the sole and exclusive rights to produce one or more Off-Broadway Performances of the Play during the time that Producer continues to have rights to present the Play hereunder. The foregoing grant is subject to the conditions precedent that Producer has Vested (as defined in *SECTION 11.02* herein) in the Territory and that Producer is not simultaneously presenting any other performances of the Play in New York City. For the purposes of this Contract, the term *"Off-Broadway Performances"* shall mean performances of the Play in theatres which are classified as Off-Broadway pursuant to the Actors' Equity Association Agreement Governing Employment Off-Broadway, as that agreement may be amended from time to time.

(b) Author's Royalties for Off-Broadway Performances shall be calculated and paid in the manner set forth in *ARTICLES IV* and *V* herein with respect to Touring Performances except that Author's post-Recoupment Royalties shall be such amount as may be agreed upon by Author and Producer and set forth in *ARTICLE XXII* herein, but in no event more than 10% of the Gross Weekly Box Office Receipts.

SECTION 9.03 Grant of Rights in the British Isles, Australia and New Zealand. (a) Author hereby grants to Producer the sole and exclusive rights to produce one or more productions of the Play for a consecutive run, as theatrically understood, in a regular evening bill, in a first class manner, in a first class theatre, on the speaking stage in one or more of the following *"Additional Territories"*:

(i) The United Kingdom of Great Britain (i.e., England, Northern Ireland, Scotland and Wales) and in Ireland (collectively the *"British Isles"*)

(ii) Australia

(iii) New Zealand

(b) The foregoing grant is subject to the conditions precedent that Producer has Vested in the Territory and is not in breach of any provision of this Contract.

(c) Producer's rights to present the Play in the Additional Territories shall include the right to present "tryout" performances prior to the presentation of the Play in the Additional Territory equivalent of first class theatres.

(d) The terms of this Contract applicable to First Class Performances in the Territory shall apply to performances of the Play in the British Isles except as may be provided to the contrary herein.

(e) If Producer chooses to produce the Play pursuant to a lease or license to a third party in Australia or New Zealand, Producer's rights shall be subject to the following procedure: Producer shall give Author written notice of the terms of any third party offer for the production of the Play in such Additional Territory. Producer may accept the offer unless Author shall, within 5 business days after receipt of Producer's notice, give Producer written notice, delivered either in person or by wire communication, that the offer is unacceptable, stating Author's reasons therefor, together with a definite offer from a third party, on terms at least as favorable to Producer as those contained in the offer which Producer is willing to accept. If within the prescribed period of time Author submits such an offer, Author may accept such offer. If within the prescribed period of time Author fails to submit such an offer, then Producer may accept the original offer. If the offer presented by Author is from a producer or other entity or person in which Author has any financial or other interest, or if a dispute arises as to whether such offer is at least as favorable to Producer as the offer which Producer obtained, or if any other dispute arises under this *SECTION 9.03(e)*, the parties shall submit the matter to the Theatrical Conciliation Council for the purposes of (i) determining whether or not such offer is the result of good-faith arm's length negotiations, or (ii) determining whether the offer presented by Author is at least as favorable to Producer or (iii) resolving any other dispute, as the case may be. If the Council determines that the offer is the result of good-faith arm's length negotiations or is at least as favorable to Producer, as the case may be, then Author may accept such offer; however, if the Council determines that such offer is not the result of such negotiations, or is not at least as favorable to Producer, as the case may be, the offer presented by Producer shall be accepted. The decision of the Council in connection with any matter presented under this *SECTION 9.03(e)* shall be final and binding on the parties hereto.

SECTION 9.04 **Payments Required to Extend Rights in the Additional Territories.** The following provisions of this SECTION shall apply separately to each Additional Territory:

(a) Unless Producer presents the first paid public performance of the Play in an Additional Territory within 6 months after the date on which Producer has Vested in the Territory, Producer's rights to present the Play in such Additional Territory shall automatically terminate unless such rights are extended as provided in this SECTION.

(b) Producer shall be entitled to three consecutive 6-month extensions of such rights upon payment of $1,000 for the first extension, $1,500 for the second extension and $2,000 for the third extension, which payment must be made prior to the expiration of the rights period then in effect, *provided, however,* that for the third extension, Producer must give Author, simultaneously with the payment of $2,000, written notice of the intended date of the first paid public performance together with copies of documents representing one of the following:

(i) a commitment for the licensing of the Additional Territory equivalent of a first class theatre, with occupancy to occur before the end of the third extension period or

(ii) contracts for the engagement of the principal members of the cast or the director, pursuant to which such person(s) agrees to render services before the end of the third extension period.

The last paragraph of *SECTION 2.01(c)* shall also apply to the extension of Producer's rights under this SECTION.

SECTION 9.05 **Royalty Payments in the Additional Territories.** (a) Author's Royalties for performances of the Play in the British Isles, shall be calculated and paid in accordance with the provision of *ARTICLES IV and V* applicable to Touring and Fixed-Fee Performances, except that all references to fixed dollar amounts in such ARTICLES shall be reduced to one-third of the stated amounts. Author's Royalties for performances in Australia and New Zealand shall be 10% of the Gross Weekly Box Office Receipts.

(b) The payments made pursuant to *SECTION 9.04* herein for an Additional Territory may be deducted from the Royalties earned by Author from any Company presenting the Play in such Additional Territory at the rate of up to 50% of such Royalties per Performance Week commencing for the Performance Week in which such Company has reached Recoupment. Such deductions shall be permitted only in such amounts as will not cause Author to earn, for any week in which such deductions are made, Royalties of less than the foreign currency equivalent (at the time of payment) of $300 per Full Performance Week.

(c) Sums payable to Author in connection with performances of the Play in any Additional Territory shall be paid after deduction of all withholding and other taxes due thereon pursuant to the laws of the applicable Additional Territory, all conversion and remittance costs applicable to such payments and all payments required to be made to any author's society or similar organizations. Producer shall not be liable for losses incurred due to fluctuations in the exchange rate.

(d) In addition to the Royalties payable pursuant to this SECTION, if Author earns in any Performance Week Royalties equal to less than 10% of the Gross Weekly Box Office Receipts for such week from productions in Australia or New Zealand, Producer shall, simultaneously with the payment of Author's Royalties for such week, pay to the Guild, on Author's behalf (for the benefit of Author's representatives), a sum equal to 10% of the difference between the amount of Author's Royalties and a sum equal to 10% of the Gross Weekly Box Office Receipts.

SECTION 9.06 **Transfer of Rights to an Additional Territory Producer.** Provided Producer has complied with the provisions of *SECTION 9.03(b)* herein, Producer may produce the Play alone or in association with or under lease or license to an Additional Territory producer or manager, subject to Author's written consent. In such case, Producer's obligations to make the payments herein provided shall remain unimpaired. The contract between Producer and the Additional Territory producer or manager shall require the Play to be produced in the manner and on the terms provided herein with respect to productions in the Additional Territory.

SECTION 9.07 **Advances for Performances in the Additional Territories.** If the Play is produced in any Additional Territory in association with or under lease or license to an Additional Territory producer or manager pursuant to the provisions of this ARTICLE, and if, in connection therewith, Producer receives an advance payment applicable against royalties payable to Producer, or a lump sum in lieu of a portion of such royalties, Author shall receive 50% of such advance or lump sum as an advance against Royalties payable for such production. Author's share of the advance or lump sum received by Producer with respect to an Additional Territory may be deducted from the payments due pursuant to *SECTION 9.05* herein with respect to such Additional Territory.

SECTION 9.08 **Author's Presence in the Additional Territories.** If the Play is presented in any Additional Territory by or under grant of rights from Producer, Author shall have the right to be present for up to 3 weeks in order to attend rehearsals, tryouts and the opening of the first production of the Play in such Additional Territory. Producer shall reimburse Author for hotel and travel expenses during such period and at any other time when the presence of Author is required by Producer. Unless specific dollar amounts are provided in *ARTICLE XXII* herein, the amounts reimbursable by Producer under this SECTION shall be the cost of reasonable hotel and travel accommodations. In any event, Author's hotel and travel accommodations shall be of a class equal to the greater of the class charged to the Company by Producer or Director.

SECTION 9.09 **Producer's Financial Participation in Additional Territory Uses.** (a) If the Play is not presented in any Additional Territory by or under grant of rights from Producer within the period set forth in *SECTION 9.04* herein, then Author shall thereafter have the sole right to produce or authorize the production of the Play in any such Additional Territory in which Producer's rights have lapsed and, provided that Producer has Vested in the Territory and is not in breach of any provision of this Contract, Author shall pay Producer the following amounts:

(i) with respect to the British Isles, 25% of the compensation earned by Author (after deduction of agents' commissions, if any) regardless of when paid, in connection with each contract for the production of the Play (including any contracts for British Isles Subsidiary Rights, other than Media Productions in which Producer will have previously acquired a worldwide interest) entered into on or after the Effective Date of this Contract but prior to the expiration of 7 years from the date on which Producer has Vested in the Territory; *provided, however,* that with respect to each contract for the presentation of the British Isles equivalents of First or Second Class Performances, Author shall pay Producer 10% of the compensation earned by Author (after deduction of agents' commissions, if any) regardless of when paid, in connection with each such contract entered into after said 7-year period or after the close of the first First Class Performance in the British Isles, whichever first occurs, but before the expiration of 40 years from the date on which Producer Vested in the Territory; and

(ii) with respect to Australia and New Zealand, 35% of the compensation earned by Author (after deduction of agents' commissions, if any) regardless of when paid, in connection with each contract for the production of the Play (including any contracts for Australian or New Zealand Subsidiary Rights, other than Media Productions in which Producer will have previously acquired a worldwide interest) entered into on or after the Effective Date of this Contract but prior to the expiration of 6 years from the date on which Producer has Vested in the Territory;

(b) If the Play has been presented in any Additional Territory by or under a grant of rights from Producer in accordance with the provisions of this ARTICLE and Producer has Vested in such Additional Territory and is not in breach of any provision of this Contract, Producer's financial interest in Author's compensation derived from the disposition of Subsidiary Rights (as defined in *SECTION 11.01* herein) in such Additional Territory (other than Media Productions in which Producer will have previously acquired a worldwide interest), will be as follows:

(i) with respect to the British Isles, Producer will have the same financial interest in British Isles Subsidiary Rights as Producer has with respect to such Subsidiary Rights in the Territory, and the time periods described in the applicable Producer's Alternative (as defined in *SECTION 11.03(c)* herein) shall be measured from the last performance of the Play in the British Isles; and

(ii) with respect to Australia and New Zealand, Producer's financial interest in Australian and New Zealand Subsidiary Rights shall be equal to 40% of the compensation earned by Author (after deduction of agents' commissions, if any) regardless of when paid, in connection with each contract for the disposition of such Subsidiary Rights entered into on or after the Effective Date of this Contract but prior to the expiration of 7 years from the date on which Producer Vested in such Additional Territory or 4 years from the last performance of the Play in the Additional Territory, whichever is later.

SECTION 9.10 **Additional Rights to Present Backers' Auditions.** While Producer has the rights to present the Play hereunder, Producer shall also have the rights to present Backers' Auditions of the Play.

ARTICLE X

REOPENING RIGHTS

SECTION 10.01 **Reopenings in the Territory.** (a) Provided Producer has Vested in the Territory, Producer may, within 4 months after the last performance of the Play in the Territory, notify Author in writing of Producer's intention to reopen the Play in the Territory. In such case Producer may so reopen the Play within 12 months following such last performance; *provided, however,* that if the Play is not reopened within 4 months from such last performance, Producer must, in order to retain his right to reopen the Play, pay Author the following sums (as non-returnable advances against the Royalties payable): $500 per month for up to 4 months, commencing with the fourth month following the last performance, and $1,000 per month for up to an additional 4 months.

(b) If Producer presents the Play in the Territory but closes the Play prior to having Vested Producer may reopen the Play provided he gives the Author written notice, within 30 days after such closing, of Producer's intention to reopen the Play, pays Author $500 per month (as non-returnable advances against the Royalties payable), commencing one month following the closing until the Play has reopened, and commences rehearsals for such production no later than 3 months after the closing.

(c) All the provisions of this SECTION shall apply to each reopening in the Territory. Such reopenings may be First Class, Second Class or Off-Broadway Performances.

SECTION 10.02 **Reopenings in the Additional Territories.** (a) Provided Producer has Vested in the British Isles, Producer may, within 4 months after the close of the last performance in the British Isles, notify Author in writing of Producer's intention to reopen the Play in the British Isles. In such case Producer may reopen the Play in the British Isles, within 12 months following such last performance, in accordance with the provisions of *SECTION 10.01(a)* herein.

(b) If Producer presents the Play in the British Isles but closes the Play prior to having Vested in the British Isles, Producer may reopen the Play in the British Isles in accordance with the provisions of *SECTION 10.01(b)* herein.

(c) Provided Producer has Vested in Australia or New Zealand, Producer may retain the rights to reopen the Play in such Additional Territory upon paying Author (as non-returnable advances against the Royalties payable) $500 per month, for up to 6 months, commencing one month following the last performance in such Additional Territory. In no event may Producer reopen the Play after 7 years from the date on which Producer Vested in such Additional Territory.

(d) If Producer presents the Play in Australia or New Zealand but closes the Play prior to having Vested in such Additional Territory, Producer may reopen the Play in such Additional Territory in accordance with the provisions of *SECTION 10.01(b)* herein.

(e) All the provisions of this SECTION shall apply to each reopening of the Play in the applicable Additional Territory. Such reopenings must be the Additional Territory equivalent of First Class Performances.

SECTION 10.03 **Closing.** Producer shall in each instance, immediately upon determining to close a run of the Play, give written notice thereof to Author.

ARTICLE XI

SUBSIDIARY RIGHTS

SECTION 11.01 **Definitions Relating to Subsidiary Rights.** For the purposes of this Contract, the term *"Subsidiary Rights"* shall mean those rights in the Play relating to the following methods of exploitation:

(a) *"Media Productions"*—shall mean Audio-Visual Productions (as defined below), audio-only recordings and radio uses.

(b) *"Audio-Visual Productions"*—shall mean motion picture, television, video cassette, video disc and all other kinds of visual and audio-visual productions in connection with the Play, whether now existing or developed in the future. All of the foregoing shall be considered Audio-Visual Productions, regardless of the method or mode of reproduction, projection, transmission, exhibition or delivery used. However, Audio-Visual Productions shall not include Foreign Local Television Productions. For the purpose of this Contract, the term *"Foreign Local Television Productions"* shall mean all television productions of the Play in a foreign language produced and distributed exclusively for television exhibition outside the Territory and the Additional Territories.

(c) *"Commercial Use Products"*—shall mean wearing apparel; toys; games; figures; dolls; novelties; books; souvenir programs; and any other physical property representing a character in the Play or using the name, character or the title of the Play or otherwise connected with the Play or its title.

(d) *"Stock Performances"*—shall mean all performances of the Play presented in the English language pursuant to one of the Actors' Equity Association agreements governing employment of actors in productions classified, pursuant to the terms of such agreements, as "stock", "resident theatre", "university resident theatre", "dinner theatre", or "guest artist contract" productions (and the equivalents of such performances outside the United States).

(e) *"Amateur Performances"*—shall mean all performances of the Play presented in the English language and using only non-professional actors (i.e., an actor who is not a member of a performing arts union or guild in the Territory or outside the Territory, as the case may be).

(f) *"Ancillary Performances"*—shall mean all performances of the Play presented in the English language as condensed and tabloid versions, so-called concert tour versions and musical comedy, operetta and grand opera versions based on the Play as well as foreign language performances of all kinds in the Territory or each Additional Territory, as the case may be, and performances of the Play pursuant to one of the Actors' Equity Association agreements governing employment of actors in productions classified pursuant to the terms of such agreements as: "theatre for young audiences", "small professional theatre", and "non-profit theatre code" productions (and their equivalents outside the United States).

(g) *"Revival Performances"*—

(i) *In the City of New York*—all First Class, Second Class and Off-Broadway Performances of the Play in the City of New York and all performances at Lincoln Center (regardless of how classified), presented after the expiration of Producer's rights to present the Play in the Territory; and

(ii) *Outside the City of New York*—all First and Second Class Performances of the Play in the Territory, presented after the expiration of Producer's rights to present the Play in the Territory and presented outside the City of New York, provided that, with respect to each contract entered into for such production, the Play is presented in at least 3 cities throughout the Territory. Notwithstanding the foregoing, if any of such cities is the City of New York, the 3-city minimum shall automatically be waived. Until the Play is presented in the third city or in the City of New York, whichever first occurs, Author shall pay all sums due to Producer from such Revival Performances to the Guild, which shall hold such sums until the first presentation of the Play in the third city or the City of New York, whichever first occurs, and then pay such sums to Producer. No interest shall accrue to Producer's benefit on such sums held by the Guild.

(iii) *In the Additional Territories*—all performances of the Play in any of the Additional Territories (which are the Additional Territory equivalents of First or Second Class Performances in the Territory), presented after the expiration of Producer's rights to present the Play in such Additional Territory.

SECTION 11.02 **Definition of Vested.** For the purposes of this Contract, the term *"Vested"* shall mean that Producer has presented the Play in one of the manners described below:

(a) With respect to the Territory, for the following number of consecutive (as customarily defined in the theatre industry) paid public First Class Performances:

(i) 10 Preview Performances plus the Official Press Opening of the Play in New York City, or

(ii) 5 Preview Performances plus the Official Press Opening in New York City plus 5 Regular Performances, or

(iii) 5 Out-of-Town and 5 Preview Performances plus the Official Press Opening in New York City, provided there are no more than 28 days between the last Out-of-Town Performance and the first Preview Performance, or

(iv) 5 Preview Performances plus the Official Press Opening in New York City if the Play has been presented previously by someone other than Producer and is presented by Producer hereunder with substantially the same cast and scenic designs as existed in the prior presentation.

Each Preview Performance given in New York City within 10 days of the Official Press Opening in New York City (even though not consecutive) shall be considered a "consecutive" performance for the purpose of this paragraph, provided that the scale of box-office prices of each such Preview Performance is at least 65% of the scale of box-office prices announced for the Regular Performances and that each such Preview Performance is publicized in advance in the paid "ABC" listings of The New York Times and a similar listing in any other newspaper, magazine or other periodical of general circulation in the City of New York. Any Preview Performance given more than 10 days before the Official Press Opening shall not be considered a "consecutive" performance for the purpose of this paragraph.

(b) With respect to the Territory, for 64 consecutive paid public Out-of-Town Performances, whether or not the Play has its Official Press Opening in New York City, provided that breaks may be made in performances outside of New York City because of the necessities of travel so long as the 64 performances shall have been given within 80 days of the first performance.

(c) With respect to the Territory, for 64 consecutive Out-of-Town Performances in arenas or auditoriums if, because of the nature of the Play or the size or complexity of its contemplated production, the performance of the Play in a traditional first class theatre would not be feasible or desirable. The same provisions of *SECTION 11.02(b)* shall apply in connection with breaks for travel.

(d) With respect to the British Isles, for the following number of first class performances:

(i) if the Play is first produced in London, then for 21 consecutive performances in London, or

(ii) if the Play is first produced outside of London, for 64 performances within 80 days after the first performance, presented either outside of London, or partly in London and partly outside of London.

(e) With respect to Australia, for 21 consecutive performances, including an Official Press Opening, provided such performances are the Australian equivalent of First Class Performances in the Territory.

(f) With respect to New Zealand, for 21 consecutive performances, including an Official Press Opening, provided such performances are the New Zealand equivalent of First Class Performances in the Territory.

SECTION 11.03 **Participation in Subsidiary Rights.** Although Producer is acquiring rights in the Play and Author's services solely in connection with the production of the Play, Author recognizes that by a successful production Producer makes a contribution to the value of other rights in the Play. Therefore, although the relationship between the parties is limited to play production as herein provided, and Author alone owns and controls the Play with respect to all other uses, nevertheless, if Producer has Vested in the Territory and Producer is not in breach of any provision of this Contract, Author hereby agrees that:

(a) *No Outright Sale*—Author will not authorize or permit any outright sale of the right to use said Play for any of the Subsidiary Rights purposes during the period therein specified without Producer's prior consent. In no event shall there be any outright sale of any such rights prior to the first paid public First Class Performance of the Play, except that an outright sale of rights for Audio-Visual Productions may be permitted if made subject to the provisions of *SECTION 13.07* herein.

(b) *Best Efforts*—Author will use best efforts to exploit the Play for Subsidiary Rights purposes.

(c) *"Producer's Alternatives"*—

(i) Producer shall have the right to choose one of the 4 Producer's Alternatives set forth in this SECTION and shall give Author and the Guild written notice of such choice on or before 12 o'clock midnight on the first day of rehearsal at which Producer requires all cast members of the Principal Company. If Producer fails to give such notice in a timely manner, Author may choose which Producer's Alternative will apply upon giving Producer and the Guild written notice of such choice on or before 12 o'clock midnight on the next business day following said rehearsal date. If both Producer and Author fail to choose a Producer's Alternative in a timely manner, Producer's Alternative III will apply.

(ii) *Participation in Territory*—With respect to the exploitation of Subsidiary Rights in the Territory, Author shall promptly pay to Producer, based on the applicable Producer's Alternative, the designated percentage of Author's compensation directly or indirectly earned (after deduction of agents' commissions, if any), from the disposition of the specified Subsidiary Rights anywhere in the Territory, pursuant to each contract entered into on or after the Effective Date of this Contract but prior to the expiration of the periods described in the applicable Producer's Alternative (regardless of when such compensation is paid); *provided, however,* that with respect to Media Productions, Producer's participation shall be in Author's compensation earned from exploitations anywhere in the world:

Under _Producer's Alternative_ #	If any of the following Subsidiary Rights are disposed of	Author will promptly pay Producer, based on the following percentages of Author's compensation directly or indirectly earned (after deduction of agent's commissions, if any), from such dispositions pursuant to each contract entered into on or after the Effective Date of this Contract but prior to the expiration of the specified periods of time after the last performance of the Play hereunder (regardless of when such compensation is paid):
I	Media Productions	50% in perpetuity
	Stock Performances	50% for the first 5 years then 25% for the next 3 years
	Amateur and Ancillary Performances	0%
	Revival Performances	20% for 40 years
	Commercial Use Products	See _SECTION 11.05_
II	Media Productions	50% in perpetuity
	Stock and Ancillary Performances	0%
	Amateur Performances	50% for the first 5 years then 25% for the next 3 years
	Revival Performances	20% for 40 years
	Commercial Use Products	See _SECTION 11.05_
III	Media Productions	50% in perpetuity
	Stock, Amateur and Ancillary Performances	10% for the first 5 years then 25% for the next 5 years
	Revival Performances	20% for 40 years
	Commercial Use Products	See _SECTION 11.05_
IV	Media Productions	30% in perpetuity
	Stock, Amateur and Ancillary Performances	30% for the first 20 years then 25% for the next 10 years and 20% for the next 10 years (total of 40 years)
	Revival Performances	20% for 40 years
	Commercial Use Products	See _SECTION 11.05_

provided, however, that if this Alternative IV is chosen, Producer hereby assigns to Author the first $100,000 otherwise payable to Producer pursuant to this Alternative.

(d) *Revival Participation*—In paying Producer's financial participation in Revival Performances, Author shall secure the payment of one-half of such sum (i.e., 10%) from the producer of the Revival Performances.

(e) *Foreign Participation*—Author shall have the exclusive right to negotiate and contract for all performances of the Play and for other Subsidiary Rights purposes described in this ARTICLE outside the Territory and outside the Additional Territories, and Author shall promptly pay Producer 25% of the compensation earned by Author (after deduction of agents' commissions, if any), regardless of when paid, in connection with each such contract (other than contracts for Media Productions in which Producer will have previously acquired a worldwide interest) entered into on or after the Effective Date of this Contract but prior to 7 years from the date on which Producer Vested in the Territory. With respect to contracts for Foreign Local Television Productions, Author shall pay Producer 50% of such compensation earned by Author (after deduction of agents' commissions, if any) for such contracts entered into on or after the Effective Date of this Contract but prior to 15 years from the date on which Producer Vested in the Territory.

(f) *Participation in Audio-Visual Sequels*—If the producer of the Audio-Visual Production, in the original contract for Audio-Visual Production rights, is granted the right to make one or more Audio-Visual Production remakes, prequels, sequels or spin-offs upon the payment of additional compensation, then, if and when such additional compensation is paid, Producer's share of such compensation shall be one-half of the Media Productions percentage set forth in the applicable Producer's Alternative.

SECTION 11.04 **Author's Share of Subsidiary Rights.** No person who is not an Author (as specifically defined in *SECTION 1.05* herein) may participate in Author's share of any Subsidiary Rights proceeds.

SECTION 11.05 **Producer's Rights Regarding Commercial Use Products.** (a) Anything to the contrary herein notwithstanding, Author hereby grants to Producer the sole and exclusive rights to create, manufacture and sell (or have created, manufactured and sold) Commercial Use Products, during the time that Producer retains any rights to present the Play hereunder, except that if on the last day of such period, a contract exists with a third party for the creation, manufacture or sale of Commercial Use Products, then such contract will continue in full force and effect until the expiration of its term, but in no event for more than 5 years from the date of such contract (or the last extension thereof). This grant of rights shall be for the Territory and for each Additional Territory in which Producer presents or licenses the rights to present the Play. Producer shall pay Author the following amounts, regardless of when paid, in connection with each contract entered into for the exploitation of Commercial Use Products:

(i) with respect to sales of such products on the premises of theatres in which Producer presents the Play, a sum equal to 10% of the gross retail sales (after deduction of taxes);

(ii) with respect to sales of such products in other locations, a sum equal to 50% of Producer's net receipts from such sales (i.e., the gross amounts paid to Producer less all customary third party costs actually incurred in the creation, manufacture and sale of such Commercial Use Products).

(b) After the expiration of Producer's rights to exploit Commercial Use Products in the Territory or any Additional Territory, Author may exploit or enter into contracts for the exploitation of Commercial Use Products in such locations in which Producer's rights have expired, subject to any contracts which may continue in effect as described in *SECTION 11.05(a)* herein. Author will pay Producer the following amounts (after deduction of agents' commissions, if any) regardless of when paid, in connection with each such contract entered into before the expiration of 40 years after the last performance of the Play in the Territory or such Additional Territory, as the case may be, provided Producer has Vested in such location:

(i) with respect to sales of such products on the premises of theatres in which Author's Play is presented, a sum equal to 10% of the gross retail sales (after deduction of taxes);

(ii) with respect to sales of such products in other locations, a sum equal to 50% of Author's net receipts from such sales (i.e., the gross amounts paid to Author less all customary third party costs actually incurred in the creation, manufacture and sale of such Commercial Use Products).

(c) In addition to Producer's rights and financial interest described in *SECTIONS 11.05(a)* and *(b)* herein, provided Producer has Vested in the Territory, Producer shall also have such rights and financial interest on a worldwide basis in those cases where the rights to exploit Commercial Use Products are disposed of together with Author's dispositions of rights to exploit any or all Media Productions.

(d) If there are Revival Performances in the Territory or any Additional Territory, Producer's right to share in Commercial Use Products income, from contracts entered into simultaneously with or subsequent to those Performances in such location (other than contracts which are related to the disposition of rights to Media Productions), shall revert to Author; *provided, however,* that Producer shall have the right to make arrangements with the producers of Revival Performances with respect to the exploitation of Commercial Use Products created or manufactured by Producer, and to retain all sums derived therefrom.

(e) None of the sums described in this SECTION, paid to or retained by Producer in connection with the exploitation of Commercial Use Products, shall be included in the calculation of Recoupment hereunder.

SECTION 11.06 **Producer's Rights to Consult in Dispositions of Subsidiary Rights.** If Producer shall be entitled to share in Author's Subsidiary Rights income with respect to the Territory, or with respect to any of the Additional Territories, Author will not undertake to grant any Subsidiary Rights in the Territory and the applicable Additional Territories, during the periods in which Producer is entitled to share in such income, without giving Producer the reasonable opportunity to consult fully with Author in connection with the exploitation of all such rights.

SECTION 11.07 **Restrictions on Dispositions by Author.** (a) In addition to Producer's rights as set forth in *SECTION 11.06* herein, Author represents that, except to the extent set forth in *ARTICLE XXII* herein, Author has not authorized or permitted, and covenants that Author shall not authorize or permit, unless Producer first consents in writing, the exploitation (or publicity regarding future exploitations) of any of the rights hereinbelow described, prior to the dates specified below:

Rights	Specified Date
(i) Worldwide Media Productions (other than radio) and Foreign Local Television Productions:	the Effective Date of this Contract, subject to the provisions of *ARTICLE XIII* herein.
(ii) Separately with respect to the Territory and each Additional Territory: First and Second Class, Stock, Amateur and Ancillary Performances, Off-Broadway and Revival Performances (and their equivalents outside the Territory); and radio:	the date on which all of Producer's rights to produce the Play have expired in the Territory or such Additional Territory, as the case may be, or the date on which Producer has in writing declared that he will not reopen the Play.
(iii) Separately with respect to the Territory and each Additional Territory: Commercial Use Products:	the date on which all of Producer's rights to produce the Play have expired in the Territory or such Additional Territory, as the case may be, subject to any contracts which may continue in effect as described in *SECTION 11.05* herein.

(b) If Author has disposed of any rights in the Play outside the Territory prior to the Effective Date of this Contract then, provided Producer Vests in the Territory, Producer will receive a sum equal to one half the amount Producer would have been entitled to receive hereunder had Producer Vested in the Territory prior to the disposition of such rights. Except to the extent that such sums have been previously paid by Author, such sums shall be paid to Producer from Author's share of the first monies, if any, received by Author on or after the Effective Date of this Contract from all Subsidiary Rights exploitations.

SECTION 11.08 **Reservation of Audio-Visual Production Rights Outside the Territory.** If Author disposes of any rights outside the Territory, other than Audio-Visual Production rights, Author shall reserve in Author's contract therefor, and for Author's own use, all Audio-Visual Production rights in such foreign area (including the Additional Territories) and such contract shall provide that the exercise of such reserved rights in such foreign area, by Author or any person authorized by Author, shall not be deemed restricted in any way by the terms of such contract or competitive with any rights so disposed of.

ARTICLE XII

THE NEGOTIATOR

SECTION 12.01 **Choice of Negotiator.** Edward E. Colton is appointed as Negotiator.

SECTION 12.02 **Alternate Negotiator.** Franklin R. Weissberg is appointed as Alternate Negotiator. The Alternate Negotiator shall have all the rights and duties of the Negotiator and shall have the power to act in the Negotiator's absence.

SECTION 12.03 **Disqualification of Negotiator.** If it appears that the Negotiator and/or the Alternate Negotiator by reason of his relations with any Producer who has received motion picture financing, directly or indirectly, or his representation of any Author or Producer of the Play or for any other reason whatsoever, might, in the disposition of the Audio-Visual Production rights in the Play, act in a dual capacity or occupy a position possibly conflicting with complete representation of Author, the Dramatists Guild Council may, upon the request of Author or Producer involved, replace the Negotiator and/or the Alternate Negotiator with a Temporary Negotiator, for the purposes of disposing of the Audio-Visual Production rights in connection with the Play.

SECTION 12.04 **Selection of New Negotiator.** The Negotiator and Alternate Negotiator shall each serve until he resigns, is removed by action of the Theatrical Conciliation Council or otherwise becomes unable to perform his services. Any new Negotiator and any new Alternate Negotiator (other than a Temporary Negotiator) shall be appointed by action of the Theatrical Conciliation Council.

SECTION 12.05 **Duties of Negotiator.** (a) The Negotiator shall act as the representative of the Author in connection with the disposition of Audio-Visual Production rights in the Play, and shall have the right generally to conduct negotiations therefor subject to such written instructions as may be issued to him by the Theatrical Conciliation Council. Whenever Author and Producer are represented by an agent in connection with the disposition of such rights, the Negotiator shall cooperate with and work in conjunction with said agent. The Negotiator shall have the right to consummate such sale or lease after consultation with Producer and subject to the approval of Author and after according Producer all the rights to which Producer is entitled pursuant to the terms of this Contract. The Negotiator shall also receive and distribute the monies resulting therefrom as provided herein. All contracts shall be signed by the Negotiator or, in his absence, the Alternate Negotiator and countersigned by a person designated by the Guild. In order to aid Author and Producer in obtaining the best possible terms, the Negotiator shall keep Producer apprised of current practices in the sale of Audio-Visual Production rights.

(b) If such rights are disposed of prior to the production of the Play, the Audio-Visual Production rights contract must be signed before the beginning of rehearsals. In such a case the contract shall be on the basis of a minimum guaranteed payment or an advance, plus or on account of percentage payments based on the receipts of the Audio-Visual Production or the box-office receipts of the Play, or both, and shall be subject to the approval of the Guild and Producer.

SECTION 12.06 **Disposition of Proceeds.** All monies received from the disposition of Audio-Visual Production rights in the Play shall be forthwith deposited by the Negotiator in a special account entitled "The Dramatists Guild Negotiator's Account" in a bank located in New York City as may be designated from time to time by the Guild. All withdrawals therefrom shall be made by check signed by the Negotiator or, in his absence, the Alternate Negotiator or, if appointed, the Temporary Negotiator, and countersigned by a person designated by the Guild.

SECTION 12.07 **Compensation of Negotiator.** Prior to making any withdrawals from the proceeds deposited in the Dramatists Guild Negotiator Account in connection with the Play, there shall first be deducted 1¼% of such sums so deposited. Said 1¼% shall be deducted from the amounts payable to the agents in respect of the agents' commission or, if there are no agents, then from the total sums on deposit prior to making any payments to Author or Producer. Said 1¼% shall be divided 85% to the Negotiator and 15% to the Guild as full and complete compensation for their services in connection with the disposition of the Audio-Visual Production rights in the Play.

SECTION 12.08 **Instructions to Negotiator.** The Negotiator shall, in connection with the disposition of Audio-Visual Production rights in the Play, follow the procedures set forth in EXHIBIT B attached hereto and made a part of this Contract.

ARTICLE XIII

GENERAL PROVISIONS REGARDING
AUDIO-VISUAL PRODUCTIONS

SECTION 13.01 **Cooperation by Author.** Author agrees to cooperate and shall cause his agent to cooperate with the Negotiator and shall promptly transmit to the Negotiator all offers for Audio-Visual Production rights received directly by or on behalf of Author and shall disclose to the Negotiator any arrangements, actual or contemplated, between Author and any third party with whom negotiations may be pending for the disposal of the Audio-Visual Production rights. Moreover, Author agrees that unless Producer shall consent thereto, Author will not insist on any commitment or agreement with any such third party for Author's personal services as author, actor, director, or in any other capacity, as a condition of disposition of the Audio-Visual Production rights to such third party.

SECTION 13.02 **Conflicts.** The release date of the Audio-Visual Production rights production shall not interfere with either the Regular or Touring Performances of the Play. Such release date shall be fixed by Author, and Producer shall be given written notice thereof. If Producer files no objection with the Negotiator within 3 business days after such notice is sent, the release date will be deemed to be satisfactory to Producer. If within such 3-day period, Producer states in writing his reasons for objecting, the Negotiator shall give due consideration to Producer's objections and shall then fix a release date which shall be binding and conclusive on the parties.

SECTION 13.03 **Rights of Producer.** If Producer deems himself aggrieved by any disposition of Audio-Visual Production rights, his sole recourse shall be against Author and then only for fraud or willful misconduct; Author's refusal to grant the right to make a motion picture or other Audio-Visual Production remake, prequel, sequel or spin-off of the Play or of the picture or other Audio-Visual Production made therefrom shall not be a basis for Producer deeming himself aggrieved; and in no event shall Producer have any recourse, in law or in equity, against any purchaser or lessee of such right or against anyone claiming thereunder, or against the Negotiator, the Guild, or others who voted for the selection of the Negotiator.

SECTION 13.04 **Revues.** A separate song or sketch from a revue may be disposed of for Audio-Visual Production rights purposes only at the expiration of 18 months after the end of Producer's right to present the Play hereunder. Author shall give Producer notice of such proposed disposition. If Producer, within 5 days after notice to him thereof, objects thereto, then the approval of the Theatrical Conciliation Council hereof shall first be obtained before such disposition can be made. Unless otherwise agreed among those constituting Author, Author's share of the proceeds (after deduction of Producer's share, if any is owing) shall be participated in only by the authors of the song or sketch so disposed of.

SECTION 13.05 **Rights in Case of New Producer.** (a) If the Audio-Visual Production rights have not been disposed of within 5 years after the date on which Producer has Vested in the Territory, and if a third party presents Revival Performances commencing after said 5-year period, then the compensation which Producer shall be entitled to receive from Author's disposition of rights in Audio-Visual Productions as provided in *SECTION 11.03(c)* herein shall be reduced in the following manner provided that Author pays the amount of such reduction to the producer of the Revival Performances: if the producer of such Revival Performances presents at least the same number of First Class Performances and at least the same number of Second Class Performances (counted separately) as Producer, Producer's share of Audio-Visual Production rights proceeds earned after the date on which such performances are equalled shall be reduced by 25%; if the number of First Class and the number of Second Class Performances (counted separately) presented by the producer of the Revival Performances exceeds by more than 150% the number of each such class of Performances presented by Producer, Producer's share of Audio-Visual Production rights proceeds earned after the date on which the number of Producer's Performances (of both classes) are so exceeded, shall be reduced by 50%; if neither of the foregoing occurs, then Producer's share of such proceeds shall remain unchanged.

(b) The foregoing reduction in Producer's share of Audio-Visual Production rights proceeds may occur only once, regardless of the number of producers presenting Revival Performances.

SECTION 13.06 **Defaults by Producer.** (a) If Producer is in default to a member of the Guild in the payment of compensation or other monies accruing from the production of the Play, the Guild may file with Producer and the Negotiator a memorandum to that effect, and the Negotiator shall thereupon withhold from Producer's share of Audio-Visual Production rights proceeds, the amount stated in such memorandum and shall forthwith notify Producer in writing thereof. Unless Producer demands arbitration thereon within 10 days after Producer's receipt of such notice, the Negotiator shall make payment to Author of the amount shown to be due in such memorandum.

(b) If Producer shall have furnished a bond, and the Guild shall have drawn on such bond because of Producer's defaulted obligations on the Play, and Producer shall have failed to replenish the bond after notice and demand according to its terms, the Guild may file with Producer and the Negotiator a memorandum to that effect, stating the amount so to be replenished, and the Negotiator shall thereupon withhold from Producer's share the amount stated in such memorandum, and shall forthwith notify Producer in writing thereof. Unless Producer demands arbitration thereon within 10 days after Producer's receipt of such notice, the Negotiator shall make payment to Author of the amount shown to be due in such memorandum.

(c) In either case, if arbitration is demanded, the Negotiator will hold the amount in question until the arbitration award is rendered and final and shall then pay such amount in accordance with the final award.

SECTION 13.07 **Prior Disposition of Audio-Visual Production Rights.** If Author shall have sold any of the Audio-Visual Production rights in the Play to Producer prior to entering into this Contract, then Author and Producer may not enter into this Contract until one year following the date of the agreement for the disposition of such Audio-Visual Production rights.

ARTICLE XIV
AGENTS

SECTION 14.01 **Employment of Agent/Commissions.** Author may employ an agent for the disposition of rights in the Play. The commission of such agent shall not exceed 10% of the amount received from such dispositions except for Amateur Performances, for which the commission shall no exceed 20%. The commissions paid to such agents may be deducted from the proceeds of any disposition in which Producer shares before payment is made to Producer (except for cast album proceeds payable hereunder to Producer from which no commission shall be deducted and except in relation to motion picture uses from which the commissions may be deducted only if Producer has consented to the agent's representation of Producer as provided in *SECTION 14.02* herein).

SECTION 14.02 **Producer's Consent to Agent for Sale of Motion Picture Rights.** I Producer has not consented to the agent's also representing Producer with respect to motion picture uses, the agent's commission with respect thereto shall not exceed 10% of the proceeds of such disposition to which Author is entitled after payment of Producer's share, and shall be deducted only from Author's share of such proceeds. If Producer shall consent to the agent's also representing him, then the agent's commission shall not exceed 10% of the proceeds of such disposition and shall be deducted from all such proceeds before payment is made to Producer. In either case, the agent's commission for motio picture uses shall be reduced in accordance with the provisions of *SECTION 12.07* herein.

SECTION 14.03 **Restrictions in Appointments.** In no event shall Author appoint Producer, o any corporation in which Producer has an interest, or any employee of Producer, or the attorney fo Producer, or a member of a firm of attorneys representing Producer, as Author's agent or representative No Author's agent or officer, directing head or employee of an agent shall, with respect to the Play, ac in the dual capacity of agent and producer (the word "producer" as used in this SECTION shall includ any person having executive direction or any stock interest in Producer, if a corporation, or who is one o the general partners of any partnership, general or limited) in connection with this Contract; and if h does so act, his agency shall be abandoned insofar as the Play is concerned, and he shall not be entitle to collect or receive any monies or commissions in connection with this Contract.

SECTION 14.04 **Payments.** All monies derived from the disposal of rights in the Play shall b paid to Author's agent, but only if the agent is the Dramatists Play Service, Inc., or is a member in goo standing of the Society of Author's Representatives, Inc. Otherwise such monies shall be paid to th Guild which shall pay such monies directly to Author, agent and Producer as their respective interest shall appear.

SECTION 14.05 **No Deductions Other Than Agent's Commissions.** Neither Author no Producer shall make any claim for commissions in connection with any disposition of the Play for an purpose; nor shall Producer be reimbursed by Author for any expenses or disbursements claimed b Producer unless Author, prior to the expenditure thereof, shall have agreed upon the repayment of suc disbursements in writing and such agreement has completed the Certification Procedure described i *ARTICLE XVI* herein.

ARTICLE XV
THEATRICAL CONCILIATION COUNCIL

SECTION 15.01 **Theatrical Conciliation Council.** The Theatrical Conciliation Counc (*"Council"*), an association of professionals in the theatre industry, shall meet for the purposes and at th times set forth in this Contract and at any other time, at the request of Author or Producer, to conside questions and problems that may arise from time to time during the term of this Contract (includin without limitation any issue which may arise under *SECTIONS 4.02(d), 5.08, 8.10* and *9.03(e)* herein

Each submission to the Council shall be made in a writing describing the matter to be considered with a copy thereof sent to the other party to this Contract.

SECTION 15.02 **Membership of Council.** The Council shall be comprised of two groups of members, i.e. Author Members and Producer Members. Author Members shall consist of playwrights, who have had First Class Performances of at least one of their plays produced in New York City, and the executive director of the Guild. Producer Members shall consist of theatrical producers and/or theatre owners or operators, who have produced or presented First Class Performances of at least one play in New York City, or executive directors (or other persons holding similar positions) of theatrical producer/owner-operator organizations.

SECTION 15.03 **Members of Council.** The members of the Council shall be those persons listed in *EXHIBIT A* attached hereto.

SECTION 15.04 **Replacement of Members.** If a member of either group resigns, is removed in accordance with the by-laws of the Council, or otherwise becomes unable to perform his services, a new member, meeting the qualifications set forth in *SECTION 15.02* herein, shall be chosen by a majority of the remaining members of such group.

SECTION 15.05 **Action by Council.** Any decision or other action by the Council, as contemplated by this Contract, shall require a majority vote of all members voting in person at a meeting at which no less than and no more than 5 members of each group are in attendance. If this Contract provides, or if the parties have agreed in writing, that the decision of the Council shall be binding on the parties, then if the 10 members referred to above cannot be assembled within 7 days after the Council has received written notice of the matter to be considered, the matter may be submitted to arbitration by either Author or Producer in accordance with the provisions of *ARTICLE XX* herein. If the 10 members of the Council are assembled in a timely manner but cannot reach a decision within 7 days after all parties have presented their arguments in support of their positions, then, prior to adjourning the meeting, the Council shall select, by majority vote of those members present, a disinterested third party to resolve the dispute. If a majority of such Council members cannot agree on such third party, then the matter may be submitted to arbitration by either Author or Producer in accordance with the provisions of *ARTICLE XX* herein.

SECTION 15.06 **Binding Nature of Council Decisions.** If this Contract provides, or if the parties have agreed, in *ARTICLE XXII* or elsewhere in writing, that the decision or other action of the Council on a particular matter shall be binding on the parties, then once such matter is decided or action taken by the members constituting the Council on the date of such decision or action, neither of the parties hereto may resubmit the same matter to the Council at a later date for any reason including, without limitation, that the membership of the Council has changed.

SECTION 15.07 **Members of Council Held Harmless.** Producer and Author each represents and covenants (a) that neither of them will directly or indirectly undertake or threaten to undertake any claim, action or proceeding of any kind against any Council member in connection with the action or inaction of any such person in his capacity as a member of the Council or the Joint Review Board (as defined in *SECTION 16.06* herein) and (b) that Producer and Author will hold each Council member harmless from any liability in connection with such actions or inactions.

ARTICLE XVI

CERTIFICATION PROCEDURE

SECTION 16.01 **Submission of Contract to the Guild.** For the purposes of this ARTICLE, the term "Contract" shall include this Contract and any written amendment thereto. On the first business day following the full execution of this Contract, Author shall commence the *"Certification Procedure"* described in this ARTICLE by submitting two copies of the Contract to the Guild in order to obtain the

Guild's opinion as to whether this Contract, as signed, conforms with or is reasonably equivalent to (as described below) the form of Approved Production Contract.

SECTION 16.02   Standards for Certification.   If this Contract, as signed, does not modify any of the provisions of the APC, the Guild shall certify that this Contract conforms therewith. If, however, this Contract, as signed, does modify any of the provisions of the APC, the Guild shall certify that this Contract is reasonably equivalent to the APC only if the modifications are reasonably necessary to counterbalance or neutralize special circumstances relating to or arising from the nature of the Play or its contemplated production, which circumstances could reasonably be expected to affect materially Producer's ability to (a) finance the Play, or (b) return to investors their capital contributions within a period then prevailing for other productions of similar size and type, or (c) obtain all the benefits to be accorded to Producer as contemplated by the APC.

SECTION 16.03   Response from Guild.   Within 10 business days following the full execution of this Contract, the Guild shall notify both Author and Producer of its opinion by sending each of them either:

(a) one copy of this Contract bearing the Guild's signature thereby certifying that, in the opinion of the Guild, this Contract conforms with or is reasonably equivalent to the APC; or

(b) a letter advising that it is the Guild's opinion that this Contract neither conforms with nor is reasonably equivalent to the APC. Such letter must specify the reasons for the Guild's opinion and shall contain suggested revisions, which shall be set forth in detail and which would, in the Guild's opinion, make this Contract reasonably equivalent to the APC. This Contract shall automatically terminate 10 business days following the receipt by Producer of the Guild's letter unless, prior to the expiration of such 10-business-day period, one of the following events occurs:

(i) Producer sends the Guild a copy of this Contract to which is affixed a copy of the Guild's letter signed by both Author and Producer, thereby indicating their agreement with the suggested revisions, in which case this Contract as so revised shall thereupon be deemed to have been certified by the Guild as being reasonably equivalent to the APC; or

(ii) Producer submits this Contract and the Guild's letter to the Joint Review Board (as defined in *SECTION 16.06* herein) in which case this Contract shall continue in full force and effect, as signed, and the provisions of *SECTION 16.05* herein shall be applicable; or

(iii) Producer sends the Guild a letter signed by both Author and Producer amending this Contract to eliminate the automatic termination provisions contained in this *SECTION 16.03(b)*, in which case this Contract shall continue in full force and effect, as signed, notwithstanding the lack of certification. The signing of such letter by Author will be considered by the Guild as the tendering of Author's resignation from the Guild, which the Guild may accept.

If this Contract shall automatically terminate due to the operation of this *SECTION 16.03(b)*, Author shall immediately return all Option Payments received from Producer, less a sum equal to the pro-rata portion of the Option Payment allocable to that portion of the Option Period measured from the Effective Date of this Contract through the date of termination, which sum may be retained by Author.

SECTION 16.04   Guild's Failure to Respond.   If the Guild fails to send Author and Producer one of the foregoing responses within the applicable 10-business-day period, the Guild shall be deemed to have certified that this Contract is in conformity with or reasonably equivalent to the APC.

SECTION 16.05   Submission of Contract to Joint Review Board.   If Producer or Author does not agree either with the Guild's suggested revisions or with the Guild's opinion that this Contract neither conforms with nor is reasonably equivalent to the APC, and if Producer and Author do not send the Guild the letter referred to in *SECTION 16.03 (b) (iii)* herein, then, in order to prevent the termination of this Contract pursuant to the terms of *SECTION 16.03 (b)* herein, Producer shall submit this Contract and the Guild's letter to the Joint Review Board (as described in *SECTION 16.06* herein) within the applicable 10-business-day period. The Joint Review Board, in making its determination as to whether this Contract conforms with or is reasonably equivalent to the APC, will apply the Standards for Certification set forth in *SECTION 16.02* herein. Within 10 business days after its receipt of such documents, the Joint Review Board will send to Author, Producer and the Guild a written decision either:

(a) that this Contract, as signed, conforms with or is reasonably equivalent to the APC in which case this Contract shall be deemed to have been certified by the Guild; or

(b) that specific revisions, which shall be set forth in detail by the Joint Review Board in its decision, are required to make this Contract reasonably equivalent to the APC. This Contract shall automatically terminate 10 business days following the receipt by Producer of such decision unless, prior to the expiration of such 10-business-day period, one of the following events occurs:

(i) Producer sends the Guild a copy of this Contract to which is affixed a copy of the decision of the Joint Review Board signed by both Author and Producer, thereby indicating their agreement with the suggested revisions, in which case this Contract as so revised shall thereupon be deemed to have been certified by the Guild as being reasonably equivalent to the APC; or

(ii) producer sends the Guild a letter signed by both Author and Producer amending this Contract to eliminate the automatic termination provision of this *SECTION 16.05(b)*, in which case this Contract shall continue in full force and effect as signed, notwithstanding the lack of certification. The signing of such letter by Author will be considered by the Guild as the tendering of Author's resignation from the Guild, which the Guild may accept.

If this Contract shall automatically terminate due to the operation of this *SECTION 16.05(b)*, Author shall immediately return all Option Payments received from Producer, less a sum equal to the pro-rata portion of the Option Payment allocable to that portion of the Option Period measured from the Effective Date of this Contract through the date of termination, which sum may be retained by Author; or

(c) that the Joint Review Board cannot reach agreement in which case Author shall have 5 business days, following receipt of the decision, to send Producer written notice that Author rescinds this Contract. If Author does not send Producer notice of rescission within said 5-business-day period, this Contract shall continue in full force and effect, as signed, notwithstanding the lack of certification.

SECTION 16.06 **Joint Review Board.** (a) The *"Joint Review Board"* shall consist of two persons (and two alternates) chosen from the then current membership of the Theatrical Conciliation Council. Promptly upon the submission of this Contract to the Joint Review Board, the Author Members shall choose one person and one alternate from their group, and the Producer Members will choose one person and one alternate from their group. The alternates may attend meetings of the Joint Review Board, but shall not cast a vote unless the designated member is unavailable to do so. All decisions of the Joint Review Board shall be made by agreement between the Author Member and Producer Member.

(b) The decision of the Board, pursuant to *SECTION 16.05 (a)*, *(b)* or *(c)* herein, shall be final and binding on the Author, Producer and the Guild, subject to the right of Author and Producer to amend this Contract to eliminate the termination provision of *SECTION 16.05(b)*.

SECTION 16.07 **Expedited Review Procedure.** If Producer and Author agree that the review of this Contract contemplated by the foregoing provisions must be accelerated, they may jointly petition the Guild and, if necessary, the Joint Review Board, in writing, to render its opinion as promptly as possible, but in no event later than 5 business days after its receipt of the documents specified above.

SECTION 16.08 **Notices.** All notices and other communications to be given pursuant to the provisions of this *ARTICLE XVI* shall be in writing, addressed to the party receiving the notice at the address indicated at the beginning of this Contract (or such other address as shall have been designated by written notice), and shall be sent only by (a) personal delivery with receipt acknowledged in writing or (b) registered or certified mail, return receipt requested. Notices shall be deemed given on the day received (at anytime prior to 5 p.m. on such day) at the address specified for the delivery of notices.

ARTICLE XVII
WARRANTIES, REPRESENTATIONS AND COVENANTS

SECTION 17.01 Scope of Warranties, Representations and Covenants. Author hereby makes the following warranties, representations, and covenants with respect to the Play.

(a) Author is the sole and exclusive Author, owner and the copyright proprietor of the Play and of all rights of every kind or nature therein, and Author has the right and authority to enter into this Contract and to grant the rights granted herein.

(b) Author makes such additional warranties, representations, covenants and indemnities, if any, as may be set forth in *ARTICLE XXII* herein.

ARTICLE XVIII
CLAIMS FOR INFRINGEMENT

SECTION 18.01 Conduct of Defense. If any infringement or interference with the rights of any third party is claimed because of the production of the Play, then Producer and Author shall jointly conduct the defense of any action arising therefrom unless either of them choose to engage separate counsel. In no event shall Author be responsible for any material in the Play supplied by Producer. Upon any suit being brought against Author or Producer alone, such person shall promptly inform the other of such fact.

SECTION 18.02 Expenses of Defense. If Producer and Author conduct a joint defense of any such third party action, they shall share equally the expenses thereof; however, if Producer or Author engage separate counsel, they shall each bear their own expenses. When Author writes the Play at the request of Producer from material supplied him by Producer and an action is brought on the grounds of plagiarism, then Producer shall defend the action at his own expense and pay all damages that may be found as the result of the plagiarism and pay any judgment rendered against Author on account thereof. If the act or omission upon which any claim is based shall be found to have been caused by either Author or Producer alone, then no part of the expenses shall be paid by the party not at fault, who shall be entitled to all legal remedies that may be available against the party at fault.

ARTICLE XIX
TERMINATION

SECTION 19.01 Failure to Pay Royalties. If Producer at any time fails to make any Royalty payment when due (time being of the essence of this Contract) Author may, at Author's option, send Producer written notice to correct such failure or breach within 5 business days after the receipt of such notice. Producer shall either correct such breach within said 5 days or, if Producer disagrees with Author's allegations, Producer shall send Author written notice thereof within said 5 days and either party, or the Guild on behalf of Author, shall immediately submit the dispute to arbitration as provided in *ARTICLE XX* herein. The award of the arbitrator shall require the party losing such dispute to pay the costs of the arbitration plus the prevailing party's reasonable legal fees. If Producer does not, within said 5-day period, correct such breach or send Author the above mentioned notice, or if Producer does send the notice and the arbitrator determines that all or part of such Royalties should be paid and Producer does not make the payments due as required by the award within 10 business days after Producer's receipt of a copy of such award, then all of Producer's rights granted pursuant to this Contract shall cease, terminate and revert to Author upon the expiration of said 5-day or 10-day period, as the case may be, unless the Guild agrees in writing to extend Producer's time to make such payment. If Producer's office or place of business shall be more than 100 miles from the place from which the notice is sent, then the notices set forth in this SECTION shall be sent by wire communication.

SECTION 19.02 **Failure to Produce Play/Improper Assignment.** All rights granted to Producer under this Contract shall terminate automatically and without notice if Producer: fails to produce the Play within the time and in the manner provided in *SECTION 1.03* herein; or fails to Vest prior to the expiration of Producer's production rights hereunder; or fails to make any Option Payment or Advance Payment when it becomes due; or if Producer assigns the rights herein except as permitted in *SECTION 21.01.*

SECTION 19.03 **Effects of Termination.** If the rights of Producer to present the Play shall cease and terminate in the manner provided in this ARTICLE, Producer shall immediately cease dealing with the Play in any manner and shall forthwith return to Author all literary materials relating to the Play which are in Producer's possession or control, except that Producer may retain one copy of such materials, but not for commercial use or sale. To the extent that termination occurs due to Producer's failure to make any Advance Payments to Author, Author shall return to Producer all Advance Payments theretofore made.

ARTICLE XX

ARBITRATION

SECTION 20.01 **Obligation to Arbitrate.** (a) Any claim, dispute, or controversy arising between Producer and Author under or in connection with or out of this Contract, or the breach thereof, shall be submitted to arbitration pursuant to the terms of this ARTICLE unless Author selects other remedies as permitted by *SECTION 7.01* herein or unless otherwise specifically provided in the APC. The Guild shall receive notice of such arbitration and shall have the right to be party to the same. Failure by Producer to pay any amount claimed to be due by Author or by the Guild is evidence of a dispute entitling the claimant to an arbitration. Judgment upon the award rendered may be entered in the highest Court of the forum, State or Federal, having jurisdiction.

(b) All arbitrations shall be conducted in the City of New York before arbitrators selected from the Theatrical Production Arbitration Board herein created and in accordance with the procedures herein set forth except where Author and Producer agree to hold the arbitration outside New York. In such event, the arbitrators shall be selected from the panel of the American Arbitration Association and the arbitration shall be held in accordance with the rules of said Association.

SECTION 20.02 **Theatrical Production Arbitration Board.** The Theatrical Production Arbitration Board (*"Board"*) shall consist of 24 permanent members. 8 shall be chosen by the Guild Council (to be known as the *"Author's Slate"*) and 8 by a majority of the Producer Members of the Theatrical Conciliation Council (to be known as the *"Producer's Slate"*). Within 20 days thereafter, a majority of the 16 persons so chosen shall appoint 8 additional persons as public members (to be known as the *"Public Slate"*), provided such persons have never been a member of the Guild or produced a play or owned or operated a theatre. All such persons shall serve until replacement is required as set forth in *SECTION 20.03* herein.

SECTION 20.03 **Replacements.** In the event of the death, resignation, illness, incapacity or unavailability of any member, or if a member of the Public Slate shall produce or have a play produced or become a theatre owner or operator, such member shall be replaced by a temporary or permanent successor to be appointed in the following manner: by the Council of the Guild, if the vacancy is in the Author's Slate; by the Producer Members of the Theatrical Conciliation Council if it is in the Producer's Slate; by a majority of the members of the Author's and Producer's Slates, jointly, if it is in the Public Slate.

SECTION 20.04 **Rules.** The Board, by a majority vote of all members, shall have full power to establish such rules and procedures as it may deem necessary, not inconsistent herewith. In the absence of such rules, the procedure under this ARTICLE shall be in accordance with the commercial arbitration rules then obtaining of the American Arbitration Association, except as hereinbelow otherwise provided.

SECTION 20.05 **The Complaint.** The party aggrieved, whether Author, Producer or Guild (hereinafter referred to as the *"Complainant"*) shall file with the American Arbitration Association 5 copies of a written complaint setting forth the claim, dispute, difficulty, misunderstanding, charge or controversy to be arbitrated and the relief which the Complainant requests. A copy of the complaint shall be mailed by the American Arbitration Association to the party complained against (hereinafter referred to as the *"Respondent"*) and another to the Guild, if the Guild is not the Complainant.

SECTION 20.06 **The Answer.** The Respondent shall, within 8 days of the mailing to him of the complaint, file 5 copies of a written answer with the American Arbitration Association and the American Arbitration Association shall mail one copy to the Complainant and another to the Guild, if the Guild is not the Complainant. Where the copy of the complaint is mailed to a Respondent at an address more than 500 miles from New York, he shall have 3 additional days to file his answer. If no written answer is filed within such period, the Respondent nevertheless will be deemed to have entered a general denial of the allegations of the complaint.

SECTION 20.07 **Participation by the Guild.** The Guild may file a complaint and demand arbitration, with or without Author's consent; and Author, in such event, shall be a party to the arbitration, and shall not discontinue the arbitration without the consent of the Guild.

SECTION 20.08 **Selection of Arbitrators.** (a) Author, or the Guild, if it has initiated the arbitration, shall appoint one arbitrator from the Author's Slate and Producer shall appoint one arbitrator from the Producer's Slate. These two arbitrators shall be appointed within 10 days from the date of the mailing of the complaint to the Respondent.

(b) If either the Author or the Producer fails to appoint an arbitrator within 10 days after the mailing of the complaint as aforesaid, then such appointment shall be made promptly from the Author's Slate by the Guild and from the Producer's Slate by the American Arbitration Association. If the Guild initiated the arbitration and fails to appoint an arbitrator within said 10-day period, then such appointment shall be made from the Author's Slate by the American Arbitration Association.

(c) Immediately after the appointment of the aforesaid 2 arbitrators, the third arbitrator shall be appointed within 5 days by the 2 arbitrators to be chosen from among the persons on the Public Slate. The American Arbitration Association shall appoint from members of its panels any arbitrator or arbitrators required where for any reason appointment has not been made from the Slates herein provided for.

SECTION 20.09 **Power of Arbitrators.** The arbitrators are empowered to award damages against any party to the controversy in such sums as they shall deem fair and reasonable under the circumstances, to require specific performance of a contract, to grant any other remedy or relief, injunctive or otherwise, which they deem just and equitable. The arbitrators are also empowered to render a partial award before making a final award and grant such relief, injunctive or otherwise, in such partial award as they deem just and equitable. Subject to the provisions of *SECTION 19.01* herein, the arbitrators shall determine and indicate in their written award by whom and in what proportion the cost of arbitration shall be borne.

SECTION 20.10 **Special Arbitration.** If the Author or Producer demands an immediate arbitration upon a complaint by either alleging violation of *SECTION 1.02(c)* or *SECTION 8.01(a)* or *(b)* and 5 copies of the complaint are filed with the Guild at any time after 10 days before the date for which rehearsals have been scheduled, the arbitration procedure outlined in this ARTICLE shall be accelerated as follows:

(a) The arbitration hearing shall be held within 3 days after the filing of the complaint.

(b) The complaint shall be delivered or telegraphed to the Respondent by the American Arbitration Association. The Respondent must file 5 copies of his answer with the American Arbitration Association within 24 hours thereafter.

(c) The name of the arbitrator appointed by the Complainant shall be set forth in the complaint and the name of the arbitrator appointed by the Respondent shall be set forth in the answer. If either person so named shall be unavailable a substitute shall be forthwith named by Author or Producer, as the case may be. The third arbitrator shall be appointed by the persons so selected within 24 hours after the receipt of the answer by the American Arbitration Association. The American Arbitration Association shall appoint from members of its panels any arbitrator or arbitrators required where for any reason appointment has not been made from the Slates herein provided for.

ARTICLE XXI
MISCELLANEOUS PROVISIONS

SECTION 21.01 **Assignability of Rights.** Except as provided below, neither this Contract nor the rights granted herein to Producer shall be licensed or assigned by Producer without his first having obtained the consent in writing of the Author. Notwithstanding the foregoing, Producer may, without Author's consent, license or assign this Contract or any of the rights contained herein to a corporation, partnership or other entity of which any person comprising Producer is a controlling party or controlling shareholder or has a controlling interest, provided that any licensee or assignee shall assume all of the obligations of this Contract and that Producer shall remain personally liable for the fulfillment thereof in the same manner as though no such license or assignment had been made. A copy of any such license or assignment shall be filed with the Guild.

SECTION 21.02 **Obligations to Not-for-Profit Theatre Organizations.** Notwithstanding the provisions of *SECTION 11.04* herein, with respect to amounts owed to a not-for-profit theatre organization which has presented the Play prior to Producer's production hereunder, where such amounts are measured as a percentage of Subsidiary Rights income or Gross Weekly Box Office Receipts (or both), Producer and Author shall share such payments in the following manner:

(a) Subsidiary Rights income payments of up to 5% of 100% of such income shall be shared by Producer and Author in the same percentages as they share in such income;

(b) Gross Weekly Box Office Receipts payments of up to 1½% shall be shared equally by Producer and Author.

SECTION 21.03 **Inspection of Contracts.** Author and Producer shall each have the right to inspect contracts entered into by the other if such contracts would affect the inspecting party's financial interest hereunder.

SECTION 21.04 **Equal Employment Opportunity.** Author and Producer agree, that in connection with the presentation of the Play, they will promote equal employment opportunities in consonance with the artistic integrity of the Play.

SECTION 21.05 **Non-Applicability of APC.** The APC shall not apply to any agreement relating to the purchase of rights in the Play made on the basis such that no part of the consideration is contingent upon the production of the Play upon the speaking stage in the Territory.

SECTION 21.06 **Notices.** All notices given pursuant to this Contract shall be in writing and delivered either in person, by wire communication or by registered or certified mail, return receipt requested, to the party being notified, at the address first above written (or such other address as may be designated by written notice). A copy of each notice shall be sent (at the same time and in the same manner as the original notice is sent) to the Guild and to the persons, if any, specified in *ARTICLE XXI* herein. Unless specified to the contrary herein, notices shall be deemed given on the day received (at any time prior to 5 p.m. on such day) at the address specified for delivery of such notices.

SECTION 21.07 **Proof of Execution.** In making proof of the execution of this Contract or of any of the terms hereof, for any purpose, the use of a copy of this Contract filed with the Guild shall be sufficient provided that at any time after 2 years from the Effective Date, there may be produced from the files of the Guild, in lieu of the copy of this Contract originally deposited therein, a microfilm of said copy.

SECTION 21.08 **Counting of Business Days.** Whenever this Contract provides for the measurement of time by the passage of *"business days"*, Saturdays, Sundays and legal holidays in the Territory and if applicable in any Additional Territory, shall not be counted. If such measurement is made in *"days"*, then only such legal holidays shall not be counted.

SECTION 21.09 **Binding Nature of Contract.** This Contract shall be binding upon and inure to the benefit of the respective parties hereto and their respective successors in interest and permitted assigns, but shall be effective only after having completed the Certification Procedure set forth in *ARTICLE XVI* herein.

SECTION 21.10 **Changes in Writing.** This Contract may not be amended and no amendment will be effective unless and until the amendment is reduced to writing, signed by the parties hereto and has completed the Certification Procedure set forth in *ARTICLE XVI* herein. This Contract may not be amended orally under any circumstances. Any attempted oral amendment of this Contract shall be null and void and of no legal effect.

SECTION 21.11 **Permissible Variation in Certification Procedure.** (a) If the following two conditions exist at the time this Contract is presented to the Guild for Certification, the Guild reserves the right to certify this Contract regardless of the terms contained herein:

(i) this Contract is entered into with a producer who has, after the date of the promulgation of the APCs, entered into a contract (or amendment of such a contract) for the presentation in New York City of First Class Performances of a play written by an author who, at the date of signing such contract (or amendment) was a member of the Guild, and

(ii) on the date of signing this Contract, such prior contract (or amendment) has not been determined by either the Guild or the Joint Review Board to conform with or to be reasonably equivalent to the APC (other than by reason of the Guild's failure to respond timely, as provided in *SECTION 16.04* herein, or the Joint Review Board's inability to reach a decision).

In such case, the Guild's decision to certify under the foregoing circumstances shall be final and unreviewable by the Joint Review Board, and the provisions of *SECTION 16.05* herein shall not apply to that certification.

(b) The foregoing provisions of this SECTION shall not apply if the prior contract (or amendment) was not in conformity with or reasonably equivalent to the APC due to, in whole or in part, the existence of provisions which were less favorable to the producer than those contained in the APC.

SECTION 21.12 **Severability.** Should any part, term or provision of this Contract be decided by the courts to be in conflict with any law of the state where made or of the United States, the validity of the remaining parts, terms or provisions shall not be affected thereby.

SECTION 21.13 **Applicable Law.** Unless the parties specify to the contrary in *ARTICLE XXI* herein, this Contract shall be governed by and construed in accordance with the substantive laws of the State of New York without reference to rules regarding the conflict of laws.

SECTION 21.14 **Counterparts.** This Contract may be executed in several counterparts and all counterparts so executed by all the parties hereto and affixed to this Contract shall constitute a valid and binding agreement, even though all of the parties have not signed the same counterpart. The Guild's certification of this Contract, pursuant to the Certification Procedure described in *ARTICLE XVI* herein, shall be affixed to any one of the counterparts signed by Producer.

SECTION 21.15 **Headings and Captions.** The headings and captions of the ARTICLES and SECTIONS of this Contract are inserted for convenience only and shall not be used to define, limit, extend or describe the scope or intent of any provision herein.

SECTION 21.16 **Pronouns.** Whenever the context may require, any pronoun used herein shall include the corresponding masculine, feminine or neuter forms.

ARTICLE XXII
ADDITIONAL PRODUCTION TERMS

(Producer and Author may add to this Contract certain additional terms provided that such terms do not conflict with or modify any of the provisions of this APC unless such provisions of the APC expressly permit modification in this ARTICLE. Examples of acceptable additional terms are the following: Rights to Present Developmental Productions; Revised Definition of Completed Play; Author's Billing Credits; Author's Travel Expenses; House Seats; Special Arrangements Among Persons Comprising Author; Merger of Rights with Underlying Rights; Royalty Adjustments for Repertoire Performances; Persons to Whom Copies of Notices Should be Sent and Agency Clause. Modifications in the terms of the APC may also be made in order to counterbalance or neutralize special circumstances as described in *SECTION 16.02* herein.)

SECTION 22.01

Signature Page For Approved Production Contract For Plays
For the Play Entitled

_____

IN WITNESS WHEREOF, each of the parties has signed this Contract as of the Effective Date of this Contract.

Producer(s)*	Date of Signing	Author(s)	Date of Signing
_____	_____	_____	_____
_____	_____	_____	_____

This Contract is Certified by the Guild in accordance with the provisions of *ARTICLE XVI* herein.

THE DRAMATISTS GUILD, INC.

By _____

Date of Signing _____

(If Producer is a corporation, the following must be signed by the person or persons in control thereof, i.e., the person or persons (a) owning or controlling a majority of its stock or a majority of its voting stock; or (b) using their name as part of the corporate title; or (c) rendering services in connection with the Play as Producer or (d) whose name is included in publicity advertising or programs as Producer or co-Producer of the Play.)

In consideration of the execution of this Contract by Author, the undersigned (if more than one, then the undersigned jointly and severally) hereby agrees to jointly be liable with Producer for the full performance of each and every covenant and provision of this Contract on Producer's part to be performed, including but not limited to the payment of all monies due Author hereunder.

_____

_____

_____

* Where the Contract is signed by a corporate Producer, the officer signing should state his office and the corporate seal should be affixed. Where the officer signing for the corporation is other than the President, a certified copy of a resolution should be furnished showing the authority of said person so to sign.

Where this Contract is signed by a partnership, all the general partners must sign and the partnership name should also be stated.

EXHIBIT A

MEMBERS OF THE
THEATRICAL CONCILIATION COUNCIL

Author Members

James Goldman
Garson Kanin
Arthur Kopit
David E. LeVine
Peter Stone
Stephen Sondheim
Terrence McNally

Producer Members

Richard Barr
Bernard B. Jacobs
Norman Kean
James M. Nederlander
Robert E. Nederlander
Harvey Sabinson
Gerald Schoenfeld

EXHIBIT B

Instructions to the Negotiator

Procedure to Be Followed in the Sale or Lease of Plays for Audio-Visual Production

It is recognized that with regard to the procedure to be followed in the disposition of motion picture rights to plays, theatrical productions are divided into two groups, those completely or substantially financed by motion picture producers and those not so financed (herein referred to as "financed independently of the motion picture industry"). The distinction takes on significance where the disposition of motion picture rights is concerned. The significance lies in the fact that the producer who has motion picture backing (by reason of financial, employment or other contractual relations) occupies a dual position. He is both buyer and seller. As a result of this dual role, it is impossible for him, however strict and unexceptionable his conduct, to escape criticism. This duality does not exist, however, for the producer whose production is financed independently of the motion picture industry. You should bear this distinction in mind in carrying out your duties. It is suggested that you request every producer to make a voluntary disclosure to you of any relationship that he may have which conflicts with the basic relationship of being jointly interested with Author in the proceeds of motion picture monies.

The same possibility of conflict of interests may exist with respect to the disposition of any other Audio Visual Production rights the proceeds of which are shared by the producer of the stage production. The principles set forth in this Exhibit shall apply as well, to the extent practicable, to the disposition of such rights and all references contained herein to the term "motion pictures" shall also be deemed to refer to Audio-Visual Productions where the context and industry practices appear to the Negotiator to warrant it.

I Plays Produced by Producers Independently of Motion Picture Backing

You will offer Producer full opportunity to satisfy you that he is certain of his own knowledge that neither all nor any substantial part of his financial backing is directly or indirectly derived from any motion picture producer. You will not, in this connection, be required to exact any onerous legal proof of Producer, but will rely on your own best judgment, remembering, however, that the burden of proof is on Producer. In the event of Producer's electing to take advantage of this opportunity and of his satisfying you that no substantial part of the financing of the Play was derived from the motion picture industry, it is recognized that his interest in securing the highest price, or the best conditions of sale, or both, is identical with that of Author and that it is to Author's advantage to have the constant benefit of Producer's advice and experience throughout the negotiations of the motion picture rights to the Play.

In the event of Producer's refusal or failure to satisfy you as above, you will decide all questions of his participation in negotiations according to your own best judgment. As provided in *SECTION 13.03* of the APC, you are not to be in any way liable for the exercise of discretion.

The Producer having Vested in the Territory, you shall, upon request of either Author (or his agent) or Producer, call a conference between Author (or his agent), Producer and yourself to the end of fixing a price at which the Play may be offered for sale for motion picture purposes; and shall thereafter offer the Play for such sale at the price established.

If at any time during the negotiations for the sale or lease of the Play it is, in your opinion or in the opinion of either Author (or his agent) or Producer, advisable either to reduce or to raise the price at which the Play is to be held for sale, you will again call for a conference for the establishment of a new price. At no time shall the holding price of the Play be changed in either direction without affording Author and Producer full opportunity to confer. Any offer received by you must be forthwith communicated to Author, or his agent, and Producer.

It is desirable that the sales price shall be mutually satisfactory to both Author and Producer. In the event Author decides to accept a definite offer which is unsatisfactory to Producer then, except in the event of the contingency provided for in the second succeeding paragraph, the following procedure shall be followed: You shall forthwith advise Producer by telegram of the price, method of payment and release date. This offer may be accepted by you unless Producer shall, within 2 business days after receipt of the notice, advise you by telegram that the offer is rejected, giving his reasons therefor. If Producer rejects the offer he shall have a period not to exceed 5 business days from the date of the notification from Producer above referred to in which to submit to you a definite "better offer" which shall mean an offer (a) from a party of financial standing capable of making the payments set forth in the offer at the respective times therein provided for, (b) for a price in excess of that contained in the offer which Author is willing to accept and (c) on other terms at least as favorable to Author as those contained in the offer which Author is willing to accept.

If within the prescribed period of time Producer brings in a "better offer" such offer shall be accepted. If, however, the "better offer" is from Producer or an entity in which Producer has any financial or other interest, Producer shall so notify the Author of such offer specifying the price, method of payment and release date. The Author shall then have 10 business days from receipt of Producer's notice to try to obtain a "better offer" by offering the Play in the open market with the Producer's offer as a minimum. If within the prescribed period of time the Author brings in a "better offer", such offer shall be accepted, unless the Producer gives notice within one business day after receipt of Author's notice of an intention to make a higher bid, which shall be made within 2 business days after receipt of Author's notice. This bidding procedure may continue indefinitely until the highest acceptable offer is received. In the event Author and Producer do not agree as to whether or not the offer brought in by Producer is (a) from a party of financial standing capable of making the payments set forth in the offer at the respective times therein provided for, (b) for a price in excess of that contained in the offer which Author is willing to accept, (c) on terms at least as favorable to Author as those contained in the offer which Author is willing to accept and (d) from an entity in which Producer has no financial or other interest, then it is agreed as follows:

You shall have the right in your sole discretion (i) to determine said issue or (ii) to request the American Arbitration Association to appoint two persons who, together with you will constitute the arbitrators to determine said issue. If you by reason of your relationship with either Author or Producer or for any other reason whatsoever, occupy a position as a result of which you may not be able unbiasedly to determine said issue then, if requested by either Author or Producer or on your own volition, you shall request the American Arbitration Association to appoint three persons who, without you, will constitute the arbitrators to determine said issue, which determination shall hereafter also be referred to as a determination under (ii) hereof. The determination by you under the contingency provided for in (i) or the determination of the majority of the three persons referred to in (ii) shall be binding and conclusive upon Author and Producer. In the event alternative (ii) is adopted, the arbitration shall take place on two days' notice, Sundays and holidays excluded, and the cost of said arbitration shall be borne by Author and Producer in equal proportion. Except as hereinbefore provided for, the rules and regulations of the American Arbitration Association shall apply to any determination made under alternative (ii) but any determination made under (i) shall be made by you without any formal hearing. You shall have the right to make the decision under alternative (i) except in such situations where, in your uncontrolled determination the question involved is a close one.

The exception referred to in the second preceding paragraph is as follows: In the event Producer is associated with or employed by a motion picture producer or has been financed wholly or in substantial part by a motion picture producer or an officer thereof, then you shall not be obligated to offer Producer any period in which to bring in a definite offer in excess of that acceptable to Author, but except as aforesaid, the provisions of the foregoing paragraph shall apply.

If at any time during the negotiations for the sale or even after the consummation of the sale you or Author find any reasonable grounds for doubting the veracity of Producer's statement of his financial backing, you or Author shall forthwith report said doubts to the Council of the Guild and either Author or the Guild may then demand an arbitration under the terms of *ARTICLE XX* of the APC to establish the fact of misrepresentation, if any.

II Plays Financed by Motion Picture Producers in Whole or in Part

The phrase *"motion picture backer"* as hereinafter employed is construed as describing any film or television producer, subsidiary or affiliate or officer or employee thereof, contributing, in whole or in part, to the financing of the stage production of the Play. The phrase *"motion picture backed producer"* as hereinafter employed is construed as describing any producer whose production is financed in whole or in substantial part by a motion picture backer or a producer who has had a past or present executive employment relationship or other significant contractual or business relationship with a motion picture backer.

Such productions fall into three classifications, as follows:

(1) That in which Producer has in writing disclosed to Author, upon signing the APC for the Play, the fact that he is, or desires to be, motion picture financed;

(2) That in which Producer does not make such disclosure upon signing the APC, but makes it before the date of the Play's first full cast rehearsal;

(3) That in which Producer has made no such disclosure at any time but is not, at the time of negotiations for the Play's sale to motion pictures, able to satisfy the Negotiator of his complete independence of motion picture financing.

The object of such classification is to protect the interests of all three parties and to avoid the complications which result from motion picture financing of which Author is not aware.

III Procedure in Case Production Falls Under Above Classification (1)

It is desirable from all points of view that Producer whose production is to be financed by motion picture capital should, prior to the signing of the APC, disclose in writing to Author either the fact of such financing, or his desire or intention, to obtain such financing. When such disclosure is made and Author signs the APC, it shall be assumed that Author is satisfied with such financing and you will accord the motion picture backers the protection provided in the following procedure.

The Producer having Vested in the Territory, you shall decide when, in your judgment, acting as Author's representative, a holding price at which the motion picture rights to the Play are to be offered for sale or lease should be fixed and after full consultation with both Producer and Author you will arrange with Author to fix that price.

If the fixing of this price gives you any reason to suspect collusion between the motion picture producer and Author which might operate against the spirit and content of the APC or the interest of Producer, or Author's best financial interest, you will forthwith report your suspicions to the Theatrical Conciliation Council as a violation of the APC.

The price being fixed to your satisfaction, however, you will

(a) Immediately offer the rights at this price to the motion picture backer, with the stipulation that he shall have 2 days in which to accept or reject the price named.

(b) If at the end of said 2 days the motion picture backer, does not accept the Play at the price named, then the Play may be offered in the open market with the rejected price as a minimum, and no further opportunity will be given to, or bids received from the motion picture producer to meet or better any other bids from any other motion picture corporation in excess of the price rejected by him.

(c) If the Play is not sold in the open market at the price named, or better, you and Author may by agreement reduce the holding price one or more times. If you do so, however, the procedure hereinbefore outlined must be repeated.

If at any time following a rejection by the motion picture backer, Author and Negotiator elect to demand of the motion picture backer an offer as evidence of its interest in the property and the motion picture backer does not submit any such offer within one week after receipt of the Negotiator's request to do so, then the Play shall be considered free and clear of any obligation to the motion picture backer which financed it and shall be offered in the open market and no further opportunity will be given to, or bids received from the motion picture backer to meet or better any other bids from any other motion picture producer in excess of the price rejected by him.

If the motion picture backer does so manifest its interest by making an offer, this offer must be submitted as a fixed sum, or a fixed sum plus a percentage of receipts, together with a summary of the terms of the proposed contract which shall be acceptable to the Negotiator. Author shall by the terms of such offer have one week after receipt in which to give notice as to whether Author accepts or rejects it. If Author rejects it, however, he may still use it as a minimum holding price at which to offer the property on the open market but no bid will be received from the motion picture backer in excess of such holding price. If, however, no offers are received in excess of this holding price, Author may, if he wishes, offer the Play in the open market at a sum at or below the price set by the motion picture backer and rejected by Author. In this instance, however, the motion picture backer will be free to file offers with you in competition with any other motion picture company and no bid from such backer shall be received in such competition in excess of such minimum holding price. But if Author receives a bid from any other motion picture company at the same price as that offered by the backer, the backer's bid (if kept open) shall receive preference, provided that the other terms of the contract offered by the backer are as favorable as those offered by the other motion picture company.

In all cases of such motion picture financed productions, you will at all times keep Author fully informed of all facts relating to sale or lease, including (but not by way of limitation) offers received, steps in negotiation, execution of the contract and consummation of the sale, but you will not reveal any such facts to anyone other than Author, and the Guild; and you will particularly caution Author against disclosing any such information to the motion picture backed producer.

IV Procedure Under Classification (2)

When Producer has made no written disclosure of motion picture financing upon signing the APC, but has made it between that date and the date of the first rehearsal of the Play, then Author shall have the right to choose between instructing the Negotiator either to follow the above procedure or instructing him to proceed as in the ensuing paragraph.

V Procedure Under Classification (3)

Where Producer has not at any time in writing disclosed to Author the fact of any motion picture financing, or cannot, at the time of the negotiations for the Play's sale or lease to pictures, satisfy the Negotiator of his independence of motion picture financing, or has received motion picture backing at some time after the date of the first rehearsal and prior to the offering for sale or lease, whether such backing is disclosed or not, then the Negotiator shall use his utmost efforts to secure a competitive open market for the picture rights to the Play without any of the advantages to the motion picture backer as set forth in the above machinery. In such cases Author, of course, will be doubly cautioned against disclosing any offers to Producer.

APPENDIX E

Approved Production Contract For Musical Plays

APPROVED PRODUCTION CONTRACT FOR MUSICAL PLAYS

THIS CONTRACT, made and entered into as of the   day of   , 19   ("*Effective Date*") by and between

whose address is

hereinafter referred to jointly and severally as "*Producer*", and the following persons residing at the indicated addresses:

"*Bookwriter*":

"*Composer*":

"*Lyricist*":

hereinafter referred to jointly as "*Author*".

© 1985 The Dramatists Guild, Inc.

WITNESSETH:

WHEREAS, The Dramatists Guild, Inc. has promulgated this form of agreement known as the Approved Production Contract (*"APC"*) which it has recommended to its members as being fair and reasonable to both authors and producers; and

WHEREAS, Author, a member of The Dramatists Guild, Inc. (*"Guild"*) has been or will be writing the book, music and lyrics of a certain musical play or other dramatic property, now entitled

hereinafter referred to as the *"Play"*; and

WHEREAS, Producer is or will be in the business of producing plays and desires to acquire the sole and exclusive rights to produce the Play in the United States, its territories and possessions, including Puerto Rico, and Canada (the *"Territory"*) and to acquire Author's services in connection therewith;

NOW, THEREFORE, in consideration of the mutual covenants herein contained and other good and valuable consideration, the parties hereto agree as follows:

ARTICLE I
INITIAL GRANT OF RIGHTS

SECTION 1.01 **Initial Grant of Rights to Produce Play.** Author hereby grants to Producer the sole and exclusive rights, subject to the terms of this Contract, to present the Play for one or more First Class Performances. For the purposes of this Contract, the term *"First Class Performances"* shall mean live stage productions of the Play on the speaking stage, within the Territory, under Producer's own management, in a regular evening bill in a first class theatre in a first class manner, with a first class cast and a first class director. The terms *"produce"* and *"present"* (and their derivatives) shall be used interchangeably.

SECTION 1.02 **Grant of Author's Services.** Author hereby agrees to:

(a) perform such services as may be reasonably necessary in making revisions in the Play;

(b) assist in the selection of the cast and consult with, assist and advise the Producer, director, scenic, lighting and costume designers and the choreographer and/or dance director, conductor and sound designer, if any, regarding any problem arising out of the production of the Play;

(c) attend rehearsals of the Play as well as out-of-town performances prior to the Official Press Opening (as defined in *SECTION 2.05* herein) of the Play in New York City, *provided, however,* that Author may be excused from such attendance on showing reasonable cause.

SECTION 1.03 **Termination of Rights if No Production.** Although nothing herein shall be deemed to obligate Producer to produce the Play, nevertheless, unless Producer presents the first paid public First Class Performance of the Play within the applicable Option Period described in *ARTICLE II* herein for which the prescribed payment has been made, Producer's rights to produce the Play and to the services of Author shall then automatically and without notice terminate.

SECTION 1.04 **Continuous Production Rights.** If the first paid public First Class Performance of the Play hereunder is presented within one of the Option Periods (including the extensions, if any, set forth in *SECTIONS 2.03* and *2.04* herein), the rights granted to present the Play shall continue subject to the reopening provisions of *ARTICLE X* herein.

SECTION 1.05 **Definition of Author.** For the purposes of this Contract, the term *"Author"* shall mean each dramatist, adaptor, bookwriter, composer and lyricist whose literary or musical material is used in the Play. The term "Author" shall include any person who is involved in the initial stages of a collaborative process *and* who is deserving of billing credit as an Author *and* whose literary or musical contribution will be an integral part of the Play as presented in subsequent productions by other producers. It shall not include a person whose services are only those of a literal translator.

SECTION 1.06 **Reservation of Rights.** Author shall retain sole and complete title, both legal and equitable, in and to the Play and all rights and uses of every kind except as otherwise specifically herein provided. Author reserves all rights and uses now in existence or which may hereafter come into existence, except as specifically herein provided. Any rights reserved shall not be deemed competitive with any of Producer's rights and may be exercised by Author at any time except as otherwise specifically provided herein. All contracts for the publication of the music and lyrics of the Play shall provide that the copyright be in the names of the Composer and Lyricist.

ARTICLE II

OPTION PERIODS AND PAYMENTS

SECTION 2.01 **Option Periods/Option Payments.** In consideration of the foregoing grant of rights and of Author's services in writing the Play and Author's agreement to perform services in connection with the production of the Play as hereinabove provided, Producer agrees to pay Author the following sums (*"Option Payments"*) in order to maintain Producer's rights to present the Play, provided that the first paid public First Class Performance of the Play occurs prior to the expiration of the applicable *"Option Period"* described below:

(a) *"First Option Period"*—$18,000 for the period of 12 months following the Effective Date of this Contract, payable upon the execution of this Contract by Author and Producer.

(b) *"Second Option Period"*—$9,000 for a second consecutive 12-month period, payable on or before the last day of the First Option Period.

(c) *"Third Option Period"*—$900 per month for a maximum of 12 consecutive months. Payment for the first such month shall be made on or before the last day of the Second Option Period; thereafter, payment for each additional month of such extension shall be made on or before the last day prior to the commencement of such month.

SECTION 2.02 **Option Payments Non-Returnable.** Each of the foregoing Option Payments made by Producer shall be non-returnable (except to the extent described in *ARTICLE XVI* herein) but shall be deductible, to the extent permitted by the terms of *ARTICLE VI* herein, from the Advance Payments and Royalties (as defined respectively in *SECTIONS 3.01* and *4.02* herein) otherwise payable to Author.

SECTION 2.03 **Extension of Option Until Delivery of Completed Play.** If this Contract provides in *ARTICLE XXII* that the Play has not been completed at the Effective Date of this Contract, the payment for the First Option Period shall be made at the time and in the manner set forth in *ARTICLE XXII* herein, but the expiration of the Option Periods and the due dates for the subsequent Option Payments otherwise specified in this ARTICLE shall be extended and measured from the date on which the Completed Play is delivered to Producer. Producer shall maintain the sole and exclusive rights and option to present the Play while Producer awaits delivery of the Completed Play. Unless otherwise defined in *ARTICLE XXII* herein, a *"Completed Play"* shall mean the Play consisting of a book of at least 80 single-spaced pages plus a score consisting of music and lyrics for at least 12 songs. If the Completed Play is not delivered within 6 months after the Effective Date of this Contract, Producer may, at any time thereafter, terminate this Contract upon written notice to Author. Author agrees that time is of the essence with respect to such delivery date.

SECTION 2.04 **Extension of Option for Try-Out Performances.** If, during one of the Option Periods, Producer presents Second Class Performances (as defined in *SECTION 9.01* herein) or Developmental Productions of the Play, the expiration of the Option Periods and due dates for subsequent Option Payments shall be extended for a period equal to the number of days on which performances of the Play were so presented (up to a maximum of 8 weeks) plus an additional 60 days.

SECTION 2.05 **Definition of "Official Press Opening".** For the purposes of this Contract, the term *"Official Press Opening"* shall mean the performance of the Play which Producer has publicly announced as the opening and to which the press is invited.

ARTICLE III

ADVANCE PAYMENTS

SECTION 3.01 **Calculation and Due Dates of Advance Payments.** (a) Producer shall pay Author the following *"Advance Payments"*, at the stated times, subject to the provisions of *SECTIONS 3.04* and *6.01* herein:

(i) On the first day of rehearsal at which Producer requires the attendance of all cast members of the Principal Company (as defined in *SECTION 3.01(b)* herein), but in no event later than 5 business days before the initial First Class Performance of the Play, Producer shall pay Author a sum equal to 2% of the amounts constituting Capitalization (as defined in *SECTION 3.03* herein) at such date.

(ii) Thereafter, at such times as additional amounts are contributed towards Capitalization, Producer shall pay Author, within 10 business days after Producer's receipt thereof, a sum equal to 2% of such additional contributions.

(iii) The sums otherwise payable by Producer pursuant to the foregoing calculation in this SECTION shall be reduced by an amount equal to 2% of such sums. The net amounts paid to Author shall constitute the Advance Payments.

(b) For the purposes of this Contract, a *"Company"* shall mean each unit of actors assembled to present the Play hereunder. *"Principal Company"* shall mean the first Company funded in an amount sufficient to present First Class Performances of the Play.

SECTION 3.02 **Maximum Advance.** The aggregate amount of Advance Payments payable by Producer pursuant to *SECTION 3.01* herein shall not exceed $60,000, regardless of the amount of Capitalization.

SECTION 3.03 **Definition of "Production Costs", "Capitalization" and "Equity Capital".** (a) For the purposes of this Contract, *"Production Costs"* shall mean the estimated costs of producing the Principal Company (including any contingency reserves), as described in the documents used in connection with the financing of such Company, including costs that may be paid, if permitted by the terms of such documents, by an overcall demand on investors, but not including any weekly operating expenses.

(b) For the purposes of this Contract, *"Capitalization"* shall mean:

(i) the aggregate of the following sums actually received by Producer (after all necessary bank clearances) for the purpose of paying Production Costs:

(A) all amounts contributed as Equity Capital. For the purposes of this Contract, *"Equity Capital"* shall mean the amounts contributed by investors in order to pay Production Costs and obtain an ownership interest in the venture producing the Principal Company, including all amounts received by Producer pursuant to an overcall demand made on the investors who previously contributed Equity Capital to such venture, but only to the extent such sums exceed 10% of the total Equity Capital contributions received by Producer from all investors immediately prior to the date on which the demand for such overcall is issued and only to the extent such sums are used by Producer to pay Production Costs; and

(B) should Producer find it necessary to obtain loans to pay Production Costs, then the amount of such loan proceeds shall also be included to the extent such proceeds are in excess of 20% of the estimated Production Costs (or if the documents used in connection with the financing of the Principal Company set forth an amount representing minimum estimated

Production Costs, then such amount); however, if Producer receives no Equity Capital pursuant to an overcall (whether or not an overcall demand is made), then the amount of such loan proceeds shall be included to the extent such proceeds are in excess of 30% of such estimated Production Costs;

(ii) but not including the foregoing sums to the extent allocated to pay the following items of Production Costs:

(A) all security bonds, deposits and other guarantees to be provided to any union or other collective bargaining organization, theatre or other entity;

(B) all Option Payments to Author;

(C) advertising, promotional and press related costs in excess of 10% of the minimum estimated Production Costs; and

(D) all sums described in *SECTION 6.01(b)* herein which are included as Production Costs and paid to a third party who presented the Play in the Territory as a Developmental Production or as other non-First Class Performances.

(c) All sums received by Producer to pay the operating costs of paid public performances of the Play (rather than Production Costs) shall be excluded in determining the amount of Capitalization, regardless of the source of any such sums or the manner in which such sums may be contributed.

SECTION 3.04 Advance Payments Non-Returnable. All Advance Payments made by Producer shall be non-returnable but shall be deductible, to the extent permitted by the terms of *ARTICLE VI* herein, from Royalties otherwise payable to Author.

ARTICLE IV
ROYALTIES

SECTION 4.01 Definitions. For the purposes of this Contract, the following terms shall have the indicated meanings:

(a) *"Out-of-Town Performances"*—First Class Performances of the Play outside of New York City prior to presentation of Preview or Regular Performances.

(b) *"Preview Performances"*—First Class Performances of the Play in New York City prior to the Official Press Opening in New York City. For purposes of calculating Royalties under this Contract, the Official Press Opening in New York City shall be deemed a Preview Performance.

(c) *"Regular Performances"*—First Class Performances of the Play in New York City commencing with the first performance of the Play following the Official Press Opening of the Play in New York City.

(d) *"Touring Performances"*—First Class Performances of the Play hereunder outside of New York City, presented by a Company simultaneously with or subsequent to Out-of-Town, Preview or Regular Performances.

(e) *"Fixed-Fee Performances"*—All performances of the Play hereunder (other than Preview and Regular Performances) produced by or pursuant to a grant of rights from Producer, in return for which Producer receives compensation based in whole or in part on a fixed (i.e., guaranteed) fee.

(f) *"Developmental Productions"*—Productions of the Play presented pursuant to Actors' Equity Workshop Agreements.

(g) *"Backers' Auditions"*—Performances of the Play presented pursuant to the Actors' Equity Association Backers' Audition Code or, if the performances are outside the United States then pursuant to any other similar code, contract or agreement in effect in such location.

(h) *"Performance Week"*—The 6- or 7-day period, beginning on either Monday or, if there is no scheduled performance on Monday, then on Tuesday and continuing through Sunday, during which one or more performances of the Play are presented hereunder.

(i) *"Full Performance Week"*—Any Performance Week during which no fewer than 8 performances of the Play are presented.

(j) *"New York City"*—The theatrical district of the Borough of Manhattan of the City of New York unless the parties modify the definition, in *ARTICLE XXII* herein, to include any other location in the Borough of Manhattan.

SECTION 4.02 **Description of Royalties.** Author shall earn the following aggregate *"Royalties"* for each week of performances, described below, during which the Play is presented hereunder:

(a) *Out-of-Town Performances and Preview Performances—*

(i) *Pre-Recoupment*—(A) $4,500 per Full Performance Week for the first 12 Performance Weeks of Out-of-Town Performances and for each week of Preview Performances. This Royalty is subject to the Royalty Adjustment provisions of *ARTICLE V* herein.

(B) 4.5% of the Gross Weekly Box Office Receipts (as defined in *SECTION 4.03* herein) for each Performance Week of Out-of-Town Performances commencing for the 13th such week, if any, and for each subsequent Performance Week of Preview Performances continuing until the earlier of the Official Press Opening in New York City or the end of the Performance Week in which the costs of presenting such Company have been Recouped. This Royalty is subject to the Royalty Adjustment provisions of *ARTICLE V* herein.

(ii) *Post-Recoupment*—6% of the Gross Weekly Box Office Receipts from Out-of-Town and Preview Performances commencing for the first Performance Week after the week in which the costs of presenting such Company have been Recouped. This Royalty is subject to the Royalty Adjustment provisions of *ARTICLE V* herein.

(b) *Regular Performances*—4.5% of the Gross Weekly Box Office Receipts from Regular Performances up to and including the Performance Week in which the costs of presenting such Company have been Recouped and 6% thereafter. This Royalty is subject to the Royalty Adjustment provisions of *ARTICLE V* herein.

(c) *Touring Performances*—4.5% of the Gross Weekly Box Office Receipts from Touring Performances up to and including the Performance Week in which the costs of presenting such Company have been Recouped and 6% thereafter. This Royalty is subject to the Royalty Adjustment provisions of *ARTICLE V* herein.

(d) *Fixed-Fee Performances*—For the purposes of this *SECTION 4.02(d)*, the term "Producer" shall mean Producer's grantee in those cases where Fixed-Fee Performances are produced by such grantee.

(i) Except as provided in *SECTION 4.02(d)(ii)* herein, Author's Royalty for Fixed-Fee Performances of the Play shall be calculated in the following manner:

(A) 6% of any fixed fee paid to Producer by such local promoter or sponsor for such Performances; plus

(B) 6% of Producer's share of box office receipts and any profits for such Performances (including box office receipts and profits paid as a salary, fee, royalty or other type of compensation for Producer's services), paid to Producer by such local promoter or sponsor.

(ii) With respect to first class theatres which have, after January 1, 1977, presented First Class Performances of plays pursuant to which the authors of such plays have customarily received royalties for such performances based on a percentage of gross weekly box office receipts (rather than on fixed fees), Author's Royalty for Fixed-Fee Performances of the Play presented in such theatres shall be calculated in the following manner:

(A) 6% of any fixed fee paid to Producer by the so-called "local promoter" or "local sponsor" for such Performances; plus

(B) if the local promoter or sponsor pays Producer a percentage of box office receipts and any profits for such Performances (including box office receipts and profits paid as a salary, fee, royalty or other type of compensation for Producer's services), then Author shall be paid, from up to 50% of Producer's share of such box office receipts and profits, a sum equal to 25% of the amounts paid to Author in (A); plus

(C) 6% of the balance of Producer's share of box office receipts and profits set forth in (B) above (after deduction of the sum paid to Author in (B) above);

(iii) The calculations set forth above may be made on a weekly basis or on a theatre-by-theatre basis at Producer's option.

(iv) If Producer cannot, in good faith, arrange for the presentation of Fixed-Fee Performances because the royalty participants connected with the Play, including Author and Producer, are entitled to receive, by the terms of their contracts, royalties which, in the aggregate, exceed 15% of the sums payable to Producer by such local promoter or sponsor (without reference to *SECTION 4.02(d)(ii)(B)* above), Author hereby agrees to accept the following Royalty in lieu of Author's Royalty described above: Author's Royalty for such Fixed-Fee Performances shall be calculated by multiplying 15% by Author's pro-rata share of the total royalties all the royalty participants were otherwise entitled to receive. (For purposes of example only, if all royalty participants were entitled to receive aggregate royalties of 18% of the sums payable to Producer and Author's 6% royalty represents one-third of such amount, then Author will receive a Royalty equal to one-third of 15% i.e., 5%.) *Provided, however,* that if Producer elects this Royalty calculation, Author shall accrue the amount of the difference between the amount of Royalties paid pursuant to such calculation and the amount of Royalties which would have been paid for such Performances if such calculation were not used, and Producer shall pay Author the amount of such unpaid Royalties from 50% of the sums, if any, set forth in *SECTIONS 4.02(d)(ii)(C)* and *4.02(d)(i)(B)* above (remaining after payment of Author's Royalty referred to in such SECTIONS), payable *pari passu* with the other royalty participants similarly sharing in such sums, but only to the extent such sums are earned from the Performances as to which this Royalty calculation is used.

(v) If there is any dispute between Author and Producer as to whether a particular theatre should be classified under *SECTION 4.02(d)(i)* or *(ii)*, the parties shall submit the matter for resolution to the Theatrical Conciliation Council. The decision of the Council shall be final and binding on the parties.

(vi) If Producer licenses the Play to an entity in which Producer has any financial or other interest, or if the Play is presented in a theatre in which Producer has a similar interest, the arrangements made between Producer and such entity or theatre shall not be materially different from the arrangements made in the industry between unrelated parties under similar circumstances. Furthermore, irrespective of whether there is any financial or other interest between Producer and such entity or theatre, the weekly operating expenses of such Fixed-Fee Performances which are customarily paid by the producer (e.g. compensation to actors) rather than by the local promoter or sponsor, shall be reflected in the amount of the fixed fee for the purpose of computing and paying Author's Royalties under this *SECTION 4.02(d)*. If Author or the Guild believes that any such arrangements made by Producer are materially different, or that the fixed fee does not reflect the weekly operating expenses customarily paid by the producer rather than the local promoter or sponsor then, in either case, Author, or the Guild, on behalf of Author, shall submit such matter to the Theatrical Conciliation Council which shall determine whether the arrangements are appropriate under the circumstances or whether the fixed fee reflects the weekly operating expenses customarily paid by producers, as the case may be. The decision of the Council shall be final and binding on the parties.

(e) *Developmental Productions*—If the rights to present Developmental Productions of the Play are granted in *ARTICLE XXII* herein, Author shall earn a Royalty equal to the minimum compensation paid to an actor for such Developmental Production, excluding any per diem, travel and other allowances, if any, paid to the actor. Author and Producer shall not modify any provision of this Contract as a condition to the granting of rights to present Developmental Productions.

(f) *Backers' Auditions*—No Royalties to Author.

SECTION 4.03 **Definition of "Gross Weekly Box Office Receipts".** (a) Where Author's Royalties, as provided herein, are based upon *"Gross Weekly Box Office Receipts"*, the Royalties for such Performance Week shall be computed upon all sums received by Producer from all ticket sales to the Play, allocable to performances given in such week, less the following deductions:

(i) federal or other admission taxes;

(ii) customary commissions and fees, as may be prevailing from time to time, paid to or retained by third parties in connection with theatre parties, benefits, American Express or other similar credit card plans, telephone sales, automated ticket distribution or remote box offices, e.g., Ticketron and Ticket World (but not ticket brokers), and commissions or fees for group sales;

(iii) commissions and fees paid to or retained by credit card companies for sales of tickets;

(iv) those sums equivalent to the former 5% New York City Amusement Tax, the proceeds of which are now paid to the pension and/or welfare funds of various theatrical unions;

(v) subscription fees;

(vi) receipts from Actors' Fund Benefit performances provided the customary payments are made by the Actors' Fund to The Dramatists Guild Fund, Inc.;

(vii) receipts from two performances of the Play in each calendar year to the extent such receipts are contributed for theatre-related eleemosynary purposes; and

(viii) if applicable, library discounts, value added taxes and entertainment taxes, if any.

(b) Producer may also deduct from Gross Weekly Box Office Receipts allocable to any Performance Week any sums included as Gross Weekly Box Office Receipts in a prior Performance Week and which were included in Author's Royalty calculation but which sums subsequently are refunded or uncollectible due to dishonored checks, invalidated credit card receipts or for any other reason.

(c) If the Play is presented simultaneously by more than one Company, Gross Weekly Box Office Receipts received by each such Company shall be computed and paid separately.

SECTION 4.04 **Definition of "Recouped" and "Recoupment".** (a) For the purposes of this Contract, the terms *"Recouped"* or *"Recoupment"* shall mean, with respect to each Company presenting the Play, the recovery of all costs incurred in presenting such Company after payment or accrual (but not prepayment) of all operating expenses for such Company.

(b) For the purposes of determining Recoupment, the costs incurred in presenting a Company shall include the following *"Production Expenses"*: fees of designers, directors, general and company managers; cost of sets, curtains, drapes and costumes; cost or payments on account of properties, furnishings, lighting and electrical equipment; premiums for bonds and insurance; unrecouped option and advance payments to persons other than Author; rehearsal charges, transportation charges, reasonable legal and accounting expenses, advance advertising, publicity and press expenses and other expenses and losses actually incurred in connection with the production and presentation of the Play up to and including the Official Press Opening of such Company and all sums described in *SECTION 6.01(b)* herein to be paid, as Production Costs, to a third party who presented the Play in the Territory as a Developmental Production or as other non-First Class Performances; but there shall not be included any compensation paid to Producer or to any person rendering the services of a producer other than a cash office charge not to exceed $1,500 per week (regardless of the amount actually paid) commencing 4 weeks before the opening of rehearsals and continuing until the Official Press Opening of the Company and other than Producer's Royalty (as defined in *SECTION 5.13* herein). No amounts charged as Production Expenses shall be charged again as operating expenses, or vice versa.

(c) Recoupment shall be calculated separately for each Company presenting the Play so that the profits or losses attributable to one Company shall not affect the calculation of Recoupment for any other Company. Recoupment shall be determined by the accountant engaged by Producer and, subject to *SECTION 5.09* herein, the determination made by such accountant shall be final and binding as among the parties hereto. Promptly upon the making of such determination by the accountant, Producer shall send Author written notice that Recoupment has occurred.

(d) In calculating Recoupment for the purposes of this Contract, the amounts of bonds, deposits or other items which, by their terms, are returnable to the Company shall not be included as costs to be recovered. Recoupment of the amounts incurred in presenting any Company shall be deemed final so that, once Recoupment has been attained, subsequent expenses that may be incurred by such Company will not alter the fact that such Company has Recouped within the meaning of this Contract.

(e) All expenses incurred by any Company to finance Touring or Off-Broadway Performances by that same Company must be Recouped before Author shall be entitled to post-Recoupment Royalties with respect to such Touring or Off-Broadway Performances. It is understood that the incurring of such expenses shall not affect or otherwise alter the payment of post-Recoupment Royalties, if any, by such Company for performances which precede such Touring or Off-Broadway Performances.

ARTICLE V
ROYALTY ADJUSTMENTS

SECTION 5.01 **Definition of "Weekly Breakeven".** (a) For the purposes of this Contract, the term *"Weekly Breakeven"* shall mean, for each Company presenting the Play hereunder, the operating expenses of such Company for each Performance Week as set forth in the accounting reports as customarily prepared by the accountant engaged by Producer. For the purpose of determining Weekly Breakeven, operating expenses shall consist of the following: $3,000 of Author's Royalty (regardless of the total Royalty actually paid to Author), compensation paid to the cast, director, stage manager, general and company managers, press agents, orchestra, and miscellaneous stage personnel, transportation charges, weekly cash office charge not to exceed $1,500 (regardless of the total cash office charge actually paid to Producer), advertising, press and publicity costs, legal and accounting expenses, the costs of exhibiting television commercials, theatre guaranty and expenses, rentals, miscellaneous supplies and all other reasonable expenses of whatever kind actually incurred in connection with the weekly operation of the Play, as distinguished from Production Expenses, but not including any compensation to Producer or a person rendering services of a producer, other than $1,500 of Producer's Royalty, or any money paid to Producer by way of a percentage of the Gross Weekly Box Office Receipts or otherwise for the making of any loan or the posting of any bond, or any sum paid by Producer to any trade association of producers and/or theatre owners.

(b) The costs incurred in producing television commercials and any other type of audio-visual promotions shall be included in determining Weekly Breakeven, but the costs of each such commercial or audio-visual promotion shall be amortized at the rate of $3,000 per Performance Week.

SECTION 5.02 **Definition of "Weekly Profits".** For the purposes of this Contract, the term *"Weekly Profits"* shall mean the amount by which Gross Weekly Box Office Receipts for a particular Performance Week exceed the Weekly Breakeven for such week.

SECTION 5.03 Definition of "Losing Week" and "Weekly Losses". For the purposes of this Contract, the term *"Losing Week"* shall mean any Performance Week for which the Gross Weekly Box Office Receipts do not exceed the Weekly Breakeven for such week, and the term *"Weekly Losses"* shall mean the amount by which Weekly Breakeven for a particular Performance Week exceeds the Gross Weekly Box Office Receipts for such week.

SECTION 5.04 Definition of "Potential and Actual Gross Ticket Sales". For the purposes of this Contract, the term *"Potential Gross Ticket Sales"* shall mean the dollar amount of total ticket sales that would be earned, without discounts or deductions of any kind, if every seat in the theatre, available for purchase as specified in the applicable ticket manifest, were sold for each performance during a given Full Performance Week. *"Actual Gross Ticket Sales"* shall mean the aggregate amounts received by Producer from total tickets sold in a given Performance Week.

SECTION 5.05 Adjustments for Out-of-Town and Preview Performances. (a) Author may earn additional Royalties for the first 12 Performance Weeks of Out-of-Town Performances and any number of Performance Weeks of Preview Performances (other than the performance constituting the Official Press Opening in New York City) under the following circumstances:

(i) provided Producer has presented Out-of-Town Performances of the Play and, *provided further,* that after adding the aggregate Weekly Profits, if any, earned for each Performance Week of Out-of-Town Performances (up to the first 12 such weeks) and Preview Performances, and subtracting therefrom the aggregate losses, if any, theretofor incurred for each Losing Week of Out-of-Town Performances (up to the first 12 such weeks) and Preview Performances, there exists a cumulative net operating profit for such Performances, then Author shall earn additional Royalties equal to the amount by which the Royalties which Author would have earned if they were calculated pursuant to *SECTION 4.02(c)* herein (after taking into account the applicable Royalty Adjustments set forth in this ARTICLE), exceed the amount of Royalties actually earned by Author for such Performances. Such additional Royalties shall be payable only from and shall not exceed 50% of the cumulative net operating profits of such Out-of-Town and Preview Performances. If Producer is required to pay to one or more third parties any portion of such cumulative net operating profits, then the 50% of cumulative net operating profits, otherwise available to pay additional Royalties, shall be reduced by one-half of such third-party payments, with such reduction not to exceed an amount equal to 5% of 100% of such cumulative net operating profits. In no event shall the total Royalties payable to Author pursuant to this SECTION for such Out-of-Town and Preview Performances exceed 4.5% of the Gross Weekly Box Office Receipts of such Performances.

(ii) The calculation described in this SECTION shall be made by the accountant engaged by Producer. In making this calculation, such accountant shall not include any income or expense attributable to the performance constituting the Official Press Opening in New York City. The additional Royalties, if any, which may be due shall be paid to Author no later than 60 days following the Official Press Opening of the Play in New York City and shall be accompanied by a statement from such accountant describing the calculation of such additional Royalties.

(b) With respect to each Performance Week of Out-of-Town and Preview Performances commencing with the 13th week of Out-of-Town Performances, if any, the Royalties payable to Author for such Out-of-Town Performances and all subsequent Preview Performances shall be subject to adjustment in the same manner as is applicable to Regular Performances as described in *SECTION 5.06(a)(i)* and, if the costs of presenting such Company have been Recouped, then as described in *SECTION 5.06(b)* herein.

SECTION 5.06 **Adjustments for Regular Performances.** With respect to each Company
esenting Regular Performances, the Royalties payable to Author for such Regular Performances shall
: subject to adjustment in the following manner:

(a) *Pre-Recoupment—*

(i) If the Gross Weekly Box Office Receipts for any Performance Week of Regular
Performances up to and including the Performance Week in which the costs of presenting such
Company have been Recouped, do not exceed 110% of Weekly Breakeven, Author's Royalty for
such week, in lieu of the Royalties otherwise payable, shall be comprised of a fixed Royalty of
$3,000 per Full Performance Week, plus a percentage Royalty equal to 25% of the Weekly Profits, if
any, for such week; *provided, however,* in no event shall Author's fixed and percentage Royalty
exceed a sum equal to 4.5% of the Gross Weekly Box Office Receipts for such week.

(ii) With respect to Regular Performances in New York City only, if, in the first 21
Performance Weeks of Regular Performances, commencing with the first Performance Week fol-
lowing the Official Press Opening of the Play in New York City, Producer has received Actual
Gross Ticket Sales in 17 of 21 such weeks equal to at least 87% of Potential Gross Ticket Sales,
then, commencing for the Performance Week following such 17th Performance Week, Author's
Royalty shall increase from 4.5% to 6% of the Gross Weekly Box Office Receipts, subject to the
adjustments specified in the preceding *SECTION 5.06(a)(i).* However, if at any time thereafter,
Actual Gross Ticket Sales for any 3 consecutive Performance Weeks of Regular Performances fall
below 87% of Potential Gross Ticket Sales for each of such weeks, then, commencing for the first
Performance Week thereafter, Author's Royalty will revert to 4.5% of the Gross Weekly Box Office
Receipts until the Play has subsequently earned Actual Gross Ticket Sales during 17 of any consecutive 21 Performance Weeks of Regular Performances, equal to 87% of Potential Gross Ticket
Sales for each of such weeks, at which point, Author's Royalties shall increase again to 6% subject
to the same calculation above described (the *"87% Formula"*). The 87% Formula shall continue to
apply up to and including the Performance Week in which the costs of presenting the Principal
Company have been Recouped, at which point, the 87% Formula shall cease and be of no further
force or effect regardless of the number of weeks that may have accrued to the benefit of either
Producer or Author at such date.

(b) *Post-Recoupment—*If the Gross Weekly Box Office Receipts for any Performance Week of
[egular Performances, occurring after the Performance Week in which the costs of presenting such
]ompany have been Recouped, do not exceed 115% of Weekly Breakeven, Author's Royalty for such
yeek, in lieu of Royalties otherwise payable, shall be comprised of a fixed Royalty of $3,000 per Full
'erformance Week, plus a percentage Royalty equal to 35% of Weekly Profits, if any, for such week;
rovided, however, in no event shall Author's fixed and percentage Royalty exceed a sum equal to 6% of
he Gross Weekly Box Office Receipts for such week. Notwithstanding the foregoing sentence, if the
)irector of the Play receives for any such week a royalty which is less than the full royalties payable
ursuant to the Director's agreement with Producer, then Author's percentage Royalty described in the
receding calculation shall, for such week, be reduced, on a pro-rata basis, from 35% of such Weekly
'rofits (but in no event to less than 25% of Weekly Profits), with the other provisions of such calculation
emaining unchanged.

SECTION 5.07 **Adjustments for Touring Performances.** With respect to each Company
presenting Touring Performances of the Play, the Royalties payable to Author for such Touring
'erformances shall be subject to adjustment in the following manner:

(a) *Pre-Recoupment—*If the Gross Weekly Box Office Receipts for any Performance Week of
[ouring Performances, occurring at any time prior to and including the Performance Week in which the
osts of presenting the Touring Company have been Recouped, do not exceed 110% of Weekly
3reakeven for such Touring Company, Author's Royalty for such week, in lieu of the Royalties otherwise
>ayable, shall be comprised of a fixed Royalty of $3,000 per Full Performance Week, plus a percentage
Royalty equal to 25% of the Weekly Profits, if any, for such week; *provided, however,* in no event shall

Author's fixed and percentage Royalty exceed a sum equal to 4.5% of the Gross Weekly Box Off Receipts for such week.

(b) *Post-Recoupment*—If the Gross Weekly Box Office Receipts for any Peformance Week Touring Performances, occurring after the Performance Week in which the costs of presenting Touring Company have been Recouped, do not exceed 115% of Weekly Breakeven for such Tour Company, Author's Royalty for such week, in lieu of Royalties otherwise payable, shall be comprised a fixed Royalty of $3,000 per Full Performance Week, plus a percentage Royalty equal to 35% of Weekly Profits, if any, for such week; *provided, however,* in no event shall Author's fixed and percenta Royalty exceed a sum equal to 6% of the Gross Weekly Box Office Receipts for such week. Notwi standing the foregoing sentence, if the Director of the Play receives for any such week a royalty whicl less than the full royalties payable pursuant to the Director's agreement with Producer, then Auth percentage Royalty described in the preceding calculation shall, for such week, be reduced, on a pro-r basis, from 35% of such Weekly Profits (but in no event to less than 25% of Weekly Profits), with other provisions of such calculation remaining unchanged.

SECTION 5.08 **Adjustments for Losing Weeks.** If any Company has Weekly Losses in a week of Regular or Touring Performances, Author's Royalty for performances by such Company such Losing Week shall, in lieu of Royalties otherwise payable, be $3,000 per Full Performance Wee

SECTION 5.09 **Review of Weekly Breakeven and Recoupment Calculation.** Should eitl Author or Producer wish to challenge the accountant's determination of Weekly Breakeven or Reco ment, the challenging party, upon notice to the other party, shall, in lieu of commencing an arbitrati proceeding, present the matter, in writing, for resolution to the Theatrical Conciliation Council, wh decision shall be advisory in nature. After receiving such decision, either party may bring the matter arbitration as provided in *ARTICLE XX* herein.

SECTION 5.10 **Yearly Royalty Adjustment.** For a period of 4 consecutive Performance Wee occurring during the months of December and/or January wherein one such Performance Week is t week in which Christmas occurs (*"Christmas Period"*), Producer may, provided he gives written not to Author on or before December 1 of each such year, specifying which 4 consecutive Performar Weeks will constitute the Christmas Period for that year, adjust Author's Royalties otherwise payable the following manner:

(a) *Pre-Recoupment*—The aggregate Weekly Losses incurred in up to 3 Losing Weeks, if a occurring during such Christmas Period may be deducted from the Gross Weekly Box Office Recei earned during any one Performance Week during such Christmas Period.

(b) *Post-Recoupment*—Author's Royalty for all 4 Performance Weeks during such Christmas Peri may be calculated by separately aggregating the Gross Weekly Box Office Receipts for such weeks a the Weekly Breakeven for such weeks and then dividing each of those two sums by 4. The resulti amounts shall be treated as if they were the Gross Weekly Box Office Receipts and Weekly Breakev for a single week. The Author's applicable post-Recoupment Royalty (which would otherwise be p able, without reference to this SECTION, after taking into account any other appropriate Roya Adjustments set forth in this ARTICLE) shall be calculated based on such amounts and then multipl by 4 to determine the Author's Royalty for the entire Christmas Period.

(c) The foregoing calculations shall be made and adjusted Royalties for such Christmas Period sh be paid within 7 days following the end of the last Performance Week during the Christmas Peric During the Christmas Period, Producer shall pay Author $3,000 for each Full Performance Week as advance against the adjusted Royalties payable for such Christmas Period.

(d) The provisions of this SECTION may be applied by Producer in one or more years and to a or all (or none) of the Companies presenting the Play and Producer may choose a different Christm Period for each Company; *provided, however,* that if Producer chooses to apply this Royalty Adjustme provision to a Company presenting Touring Performances, all performances by such Company during the applicable Christmas Period must be presented in one theatre.

(e) If any Company attains Recoupment during a Christmas Period, then Producer must, with respect to such Company, calculate Author's Royalties for the entire period either on the basis of *SECTION 5.10(b)* or without reference to this SECTION, as Producer in his sole discretion may decide.

(f) The provisions of this SECTION shall not apply to Fixed-Fee Performances.

SECTION 5.11 **Pro-rata Adjustment for Fixed Royalties.** In any instance in which this Contract provides that Royalties payable to Author for a given Full Performance Week of a Company are to be, in whole or in part, a fixed-dollar amount, and if fewer than 8 performances of the Play are presented by such Company during such week, then the fixed-dollar Royalties otherwise payable to Author hereunder shall be reduced by an amount equal to one-eighth of such fixed-dollar Royalties for each performance of the Play, fewer than 8, given in any such Performance Week.

SECTION 5.12 **Pro-rata Adjustment for Repertoire Performances.** If the Play is to be presented in repertoire with one or more other plays, Author and Producer shall agree on the method in which Author's Royalties shall be prorated and such method shall be set forth in *ARTICLE XXII* herein.

SECTION 5.13 **Proportionate Adjustment in Producer's Royalty.** (a) Regardless of the amount of royalties received by Producer for any week of performances, for the purposes of calculating Recoupment and Weekly Breakeven, *"Producer's Royalty"* shall be deemed to be limited to the following amounts but may not be deemed to be less than $1,500:

Producer's Royalty shall be calculated in the following manner:

(i) divide the amount of Royalties earned by Author for such week by an amount equal to 6% of the Gross Weekly Box Office Receipts for such week, then

(ii) multiply that amount by an amount equal to the lesser of:

(A) 3% of the Gross Weekly Box Office Receipts for such week or

(B) the amount of royalties (but not the cash office charge) payable to Producer for such week as set forth in the documents used in connection with the financing of the Play.

(b) For the purposes of the calculation described in *SECTION 5.13(a)* herein, the amount of Royalties earned by Author shall be the full amount of Royalties otherwise payable to Author prior to the deduction of any Advance or Option Payments as permitted by this Contract.

(c) If Producer presents Off-Broadway Performances of the Play pursuant to the terms of *SECTION 3.02* herein, then in making this adjustment for such performances, Author's 6% Royalty referred to in *SECTION 5.13(a)(i)* shall be Author's post-Recoupment Off-Broadway Royalty set forth in *ARTICLE XXII* herein.

SECTION 5.14 **Pro-rata Adjustment of Weekly Breakeven.** If more than one Royalty calculation is applicable for performances presented in any Performance Week and one such calculation is to be made based on Weekly Profits or Weekly Losses (for example, if there are both Touring Performances and Fixed-Fee Performances presented in one Performance Week), the determination of the amount of such profits or losses to be allocated to such performances shall be made in the following manner: the amount of Weekly Breakeven applicable to such calculation shall be the actual Weekly Breakeven for the entire Performance Week, prorated, based on the ratio that the number of performances to which the Weekly Profits or Losses calculation is to be applied bears to the total number of performances presented during such Performance Week; and the amount of Gross Weekly Box Office Receipts used in calculating the profits or losses shall be only those receipts earned for the performances as to which the Weekly Profits or Losses calculation applies.

ARTICLE VI
DEDUCTIONS FROM ADVANCE AND ROYALTY PAYMENTS

SECTION 6.01 **Deductions from Advances.** (a) Option Payments made for all but the First Option Period shall be deducted from the Advance Payments otherwise payable to Author.

(b) If a third party has previously produced the Play in the Territory as a Developmental Production or as other non-First Class Performances and if Producer is required to make any payment to such third party in order to acquire all of the rights in the Play contemplated by this APC then, to the extent that such sums are included as Production Costs, Producer shall deduct from the Advance Payments otherwise payable to Author so much of such sums as equal the aggregate of all monies directly or indirectly paid to Author for such prior production (less customary per-diem and transportation expenses), but in no event more than the sums paid by Producer to such third party. Author and such third party shall give Producer a complete and accurate statement, signed by both Author and such third party, setting forth all monies paid to Author in connection with such prior production. The total sums payable by Producer to such third party and deductible from Author's Advance Payments shall be set forth in *ARTICLE XXII* herein.

SECTION 6.02 **Deductions from Royalties.** (a) All Option and Advance payments received by Author may be deducted from Royalties earned by Author from any or all Companies presenting the Play, at the rate of up to 50% of such Royalties per Performance Week, commencing for the Performance Week in which such Company has reached Recoupment.

(b) The foregoing deductions shall be permitted only in such amounts as will not cause Author to earn, for any week in which such deductions are made, Royalties of less than $3,000 per Full Performance Week.

ARTICLE VII
GENERAL PAYMENT PROVISIONS

SECTION 7.01 **Royalty Due Dates/Box Office Statements.** (a) The portion of any Gross Weekly Box Office Receipts or Weekly Profits due to Author shall belong to Author and shall be held in trust by Producer as Author's property until payment. The trust nature of such funds shall not be questioned, whether the monies are physically segregated or not. In the event of breach of trust hereunder, Author may, at his option, pursue his remedies at law or in equity in lieu of the arbitration procedure established by this Contract.

(b) Within 7 days after the end of each Performance Week, Producer shall send to the Guild for Author's account, the amount due as Author's Royalties for such week, together with the daily box-office statements (for each person comprising Author) of each performance of the Play during such week signed by the treasurer or treasurers of the theatre in which the performances are given and signed Producer or Producer's duly authorized representative.

(c) Box-office statements and payments due for performances, in the United States, presented more than 500 miles from New York City shall be sent within 14 days after the end of each Performance Week, and for performances presented in Canada or in any location outside the Territory, within 21 days after the end of each such week, unless such payments are delayed or blocked due to the action inaction of government authorities, in which case the payments shall be made as soon thereafter possible.

(d) In cases where Author's compensation depends on the calculation of Weekly Breakeven Weekly Profits, weekly operating statements shall be sent to the Guild (for each person comprising Author), at the same time Author's check is due.

(e) Producer shall also send to the Guild the actual production expense statements provided investors as well as the periodic accounting reports as prepared by the accountant for the production

(f) All reports and statements sent to the Guild pursuant to this ARTICLE shall be held confidential by Author, the Guild, and any Author's representative.

(g) Notwithstanding the provisions of *SECTION 7.01(c)* herein, Royalties for performances of the Play given in repertoire with one or more other plays shall be sent no later than 4 days after the end of every 4 Performance Weeks during which the Play is so performed, regardless of the number of performances presented.

SECTION 7.02 **Method of Payment.** All checks shall be sent to the Guild. Checks for payments due under *ARTICLES II* and *IX* herein shall be drawn to the order of the Guild. All other checks shall be drawn to the order of Author or, where Author indicates in writing to Producer and the Guild that Author is represented by an agent who is a member in good standing of the Society of Author's Representatives, Inc., then to the agent.

SECTION 7.03 **Separate Calculations.** If the Play is presented simultaneously by more than one Company, Royalties accruing from each Company shall be computed and paid separately.

SECTION 7.04 **Author's Division of Payments.** If Author is comprised of more than one person, all sums set forth herein as being payable to Author represent the aggregate of all amounts payable to all persons comprising Author. Subject to the provisions of *SECTION 8.20* herein, such aggregate sums shall be divided equally unless otherwise provided in *ARTICLE XXII* herein.

SECTION 7.05 **Adaptor's Compensation.** If the Play is an English language adaptation made from a foreign language play or from other literary property, and if the adaptor is not the English language Bookwriter, then notwithstanding the provisions of *SECTION 1.05* herein, the adaptor shall not be deemed to be one of the persons comprising Author and neither the adaptor nor the author of the foreign language play or other literary property shall receive any portion of Author's Royalty hereunder.

SECTION 7.06 **Deductions.** No deductions shall be made from compensation due by Producer to Author on account of a debt due by Author to Producer unless an agreement in writing providing therefor shall have been made between Author and Producer and filed with the Guild; except, however, that such deduction may be made if it is less than $200 and a memorandum, signed or initialed by Author acknowledging his indebtedness, and receipted by Producer or his representative, accompanies the statement for the week in which the deduction is made.

ARTICLE VIII

GENERAL PRODUCTION PROVISIONS

SECTION 8.01 **Producer's Undertaking.** Producer, recognizing that the Play is the artistic creation of Author and that as such Author is entitled to protect the type and nature of the production of Author's creation, hereby agrees:

(a) Under his own management to rehearse, present and continue to present the Play, with a cast, director, scenic, lighting, costume and, where appropriate, sound designer, conductor, choreographer and/or dance director mutually agreeable to Producer and to Author, and to announce the name of Author as sole Author of the book, music and lyrics of the Play upon all programs and in all advertising matter in accordance with the terms of *SECTION 8.10* herein. Any change in the cast or any replacement of a director, conductor, choreographer and/or dance director shall likewise be subject to the mutual consent of the parties. Author may designate another person to act on his behalf with respect to such approvals and appointments. If Author is not available for consultation in the United States (or wherever else the Play is being produced), the provisions of this SECTION shall not apply unless Author shall have designated another person to act on his behalf who is available for consultation where the Play is being produced.

(b) To rehearse, produce, present and continue to present the Play, including Touring Performances thereof, with neither Author nor Producer making or causing to be made any addition, omission or alteration in the book, music, lyrics or title of the Play as contracted for production without the consent of both Producer and only the author of the affected portion of the Play (i.e. Bookwriter, Composer or Lyricist), with any change in the title requiring approval of a majority of Bookwriter, Composer and Lyricist. Producer warrants that any change of any kind whatsoever in the manuscript, title, stage business or performance of the Play made by Producer or any third party and which is acceptable to Author shall be the property of the Bookwriter, Composer or Lyricist, as the case may be. Producer shall cause to be prepared, executed and delivered to Author, not later than the Official Press Opening in New York City such documents as may be necessary to transfer to Author all rights in any such changes in the manuscript or title of the Play; however, Producer shall not be responsible to deliver documents to Author for any materials or changes solicited by Bookwriter, Composer or Lyricist from any third party. Neither Bookwriter, Composer nor Lyricist shall be obligated to make payment to any person suggesting or making any such changes unless he has entered into a bona fide written agreement to do so; similarly Producer shall not be required to make payment to any person solicited by Bookwriter, Composer or Lyricist to suggest or make changes unless Producer has entered into a bona fide written agreement to do so. Subject to *SECTION 8.16* herein, Author shall, without any obligation to Producer, be entitled to use any parts of the Play omitted.

(c) Producer may complain to the Guild that Author is unreasonable in refusing to make changes or additions. In such event the Guild shall appoint a representative or representatives and, if they so advise, shall lend its best efforts to prevail upon Author to make the suggested changes, it being understood, however, that the Guild shall have no power to compel Author to agree to such changes.

SECTION 8.02 **Author's Right to Attend Rehearsals/Author's Availability.** (a) Author shall have the right to attend all rehearsals and performances of the Play prior to the Official Press Opening in New York City.

(b) Author shall use all best efforts to be available one month ahead of scheduled rehearsal dates to perform the services required pursuant to the terms of this Contract.

SECTION 8.03 **Author's Exercise of Approval Rights.** (a) Where the approval or consent of Author is required, the Bookwriter, Composer and Lyricist of the Play shall vote as 3 separate units (regardless of the number of persons constituting each such unit), with each unit having one vote and with a majority of such votes controlling, unless otherwise provided in *ARTICLE XXII* herein. Where the approval or consent of Author is required anywhere in this Contract, and such persons cannot agree, the President of the Guild shall, upon the request of Producer or any person comprising Author, appoint single arbitrator to pass on such unresolved disagreements.

(b) If, after the Play has been presented for at least 3 weeks in New York City, Producer, because of some emergency, requests the approval of Author to make changes or replacements as provided i *SECTION 8.01* herein and Producer is unable to obtain any response from Bookwriter, Composer or Lyricist, within 72 hours after requesting same, then the right to vote of such person failing to timely respond shall be forfeit and the votes of the others shall control.

SECTION 8.04 **Expenses.** (a) Producer shall reimburse Author for such hotel and travel expense as Author may incur in making trips to attend rehearsals and up to 12 weeks of Out-of-Town Performances and the Official Press Opening in New York City, and at any other time when the presence of Author is required by Producer.

(b) In addition to the expenses to be reimbursed pursuant to *SECTION 8.04(a)* herein, if Book writer, Composer or Lyricist is a resident of the City of New York, Producer shall reimburse such person for such local travel expenses as such person may incur during the time when the Play is in rehearsal in New York City or being presented for Preview Performances, and shall also reimburse hotel expenses for such persons who reside in the City of New York but outside of the Borough of Manhattan, if such expenses are reasonably necessary due to Producer's rehearsal or production schedule.

(c) Unless specific dollar amounts are provided in *ARTICLE XXII* herein, the amounts reimbursable by Producer under this SECTION shall be the cost of reasonable hotel and travel accommodations. In any event, Author's hotel and travel accommodations shall be of a class equal to the greater of the class charged to the Company by Producer or Director.

(d) If Author is unavailable and designates another person to act on his behalf in connection with the consultations set forth in *SECTION 8.01(a)* herein, Author and Producer may agree in *ARTICLE XXII* to specify the extent to which such designee's expenses may be reimbursed, if at all.

SECTION 8.05 **Copying Expenses.** Producer shall pay all costs incurred in making copies of the Play and any revisions thereof prior to the Official Press Opening in New York City and shall use best efforts to provide facilities, in or near any theatre in which the Play is presented, for the purpose of copying Author's revisions of the Play.

SECTION 8.06 **Designs.** Pursuant to the rules and regulations of the United Scenic Artists Local 829, Author undertakes and agrees that Author will not sell, lease, license or authorize the use of any of the original designs of scenery, lighting or costumes created by the designers, without the written consent of the owner of such designs.

SECTION 8.07 **Artwork.** If Producer owns the artwork and/or logo for the production of the Play, Producer grants to Author the right to use such artwork and logo in connection with Author's exploitation of the Play (but not for the purpose of creating Commercial Use Products as defined in *SECTION 11.01* herein), subject to all restrictions which may exist in connection with such uses and subject to all payments which must be made to any third party, which payments shall not be the responsibility of Producer. Author shall not use or grant to others the right to use such artwork and logo without first giving Producer 60 days prior written notice. Author shall indemnify Producer for any liability which may arise in connection with any such use.

SECTION 8.08 **Production Script.** Prior to the last performance of the Play under this Contract or prior to one month after the Official Press Opening in New York City, whichever is earlier, Producer shall deliver to Author or Author's representative, as Author's property, a neat and legible script of the Play, as currently presented.

SECTION 8.09 **Rights to Promote.** Author hereby grants to Producer and Producer's licensees and permitted assigns, the right to use the names of Bookwriter, Composer and Lyricist and each of their biographies, photographs, likeness or recorded voice (referred to in this SECTION as "materials"), and the title of and excerpts from the Play for advertising, press and promotional purposes by any means or medium. Producer shall submit to the Bookwriter, Composer and Lyricist, for approval, all materials which Producer intends to use. If the Bookwriter, Composer or Lyricist does not advise Producer, within 72 hours of receipt of the materials of desired changes therein, the materials shall be deemed approved as submitted by Producer. Producer shall include Author's biography in all programs used by Producer in which any other biography appears.

SECTION 8.10 **Author's Billing.** (a) Author shall receive billing credit whenever Producer or Director is accorded billing credit; *provided, however,* with respect to ABC listings and "teaser" advertisements, radio and television advertisements and marquees, billing credit may be accorded to any one or more of Producer, Author or Director without according billing credit to the other(s), if such person(s) has achieved a level of prominence greater than those not receiving billing credit and such that the use of the name(s) of the person(s) excluded would not enhance the commercial value of the Play. If Producer and Author are unable to agree, then, upon the written request of Producer, the determination of whether such level of prominence has been achieved shall be made by a theatrical press agent designated by the Theatrical Conciliation Council. Such determination must be made prior to the publication of such credits. The designation of the press agent and such agent's determination shall be final and binding on the parties hereto.

(b) Author's billing shall be on one or more separate lines beneath the title of the Play. It shall be in a type size no less than 40% of the type size used for the title of the Play (other than logo titles); *provided, however,* if the title of the Play appears more than once in any one advertisement, the placement and size of Author's billing shall be in relation to the title where used in closest proximity to the billing accorded to others involved in the Play. In no event shall Author's billing be smaller than the type size used for the billing accorded to Director and/or Producer (except where Producer's name appears as part of the name of the theatre).

(c) Author and Producer may supplement the provisions of *SECTION 8.10(b)* in *ARTICLE XXII* herein but shall not modify or supplement in any way the provisions of *SECTION 8.10(a)* herein.

SECTION 8.11 **Radio and Television Publicizing.** Producer shall have the right to authorize one or more radio and/or television excerpts of or based on the Play, not exceeding 12 minutes each, for the purpose of exploiting and publicizing the theatre industry, performances of the Play, any person performing in the Play and for use on awards programs, without any additional approval by or payment to Author, provided Producer receives no compensation therefrom other than reimbursement of out-of-pocket expenses; however, Author shall have approval of any change in the book, music or lyrics made in an excerpt produced under the control of Producer.

SECTION 8.12 **Producer's Credit.** (a) If Producer has presented the Play for its Official Press Opening, Author shall use all best efforts to require that Producer receive conspicuously placed billing credit in the following circumstances:

(i) if all or any portion of the Play is published, the credit shall appear on a page preceding the first page of the text of the Play;

(ii) if a motion picture or television production is produced based on the Play, the credit shall appear on the screen separately with no other credit; and

(iii) in the case of any Revival, Stock, Amateur or Ancillary Performances, as those terms are defined in *SECTION 11.01* herein, the credit shall appear on the first page of credits in all programs used therefor.

(b) The credit referred to above shall contain the name(s) of Producer and co-producers, if any, and shall state that the Play was originally produced by them. The order, title and relative size and spacing of the names of Producer (and co-producers, if any) shall be identical to the billing contained in the program for the Play at the time of the Official Press Opening.

(c) No casual or inadvertent failure to comply with the provisions of this SECTION shall be deemed a breach of this Contract unless such failure can, but shall not, be rectified as soon as practicable.

SECTION 8.13 **Approval of Use of Producers' Names.** Producer shall not use the name of any other person, firm or corporation as producer of the Play unless Author has consented in writing.

SECTION 8.14 **House Seat Records.** If Author receives an allocation of house seats pursuant to *ARTICLE XXII* herein, Author agrees to maintain a true, complete and accurate record, in accordance with the requirements of the Arts and Cultural Affairs Law of the State of New York and the regulations promulgated thereunder, of Author's disposition of such house seats. Author agrees not to dispose of such house seats at a price above the regular box-office prices for such tickets.

Section 8.15 **Debt by Author.** If Author is indebted to the Guild or to Producer, the Guild may file with the Negotiator (as described in *ARTICLE XII* herein) a memorandum to that effect, and the Negotiator shall thereupon withhold from Author's share of income held by the Negotiator, the amount of such indebtedness and shall pay the same over to the Guild and/or Producer as their interests may appear. The foregoing shall not limit Producer's rights to pursue other remedies in connection with the collection of any indebtedness.

Section 8.16 **Revue Sketches.** (a) Any sketch or number of a revue and any song or musical number in the Play which shall not have been used on the Official Press Opening in New York or within 3 weeks thereafter, or having been so used shall be omitted from the Play for 3 successive consecutive Performance Weeks, may be withdrawn by Author and used by him for any purpose, free of any claim by Producer, subject only to such financial interest in additional uses as Producer may theretofore have acquired.

(b) If a sketch, song or other contribution of one or more persons constituting Author is omitted from a condensed or tabloid version of the Play, then such person whose work is so omitted shall nevertheless share in the proceeds from such version, provided his contribution shall have been included in at least one-half of the then prior performances of the Play. In such case, each such person shall share in the proceeds of the condensed or tabloid version in the same proportion that his original compensation hereunder bears to the total compensation due hereunder to all persons constituting Author.

Section 8.17 **Cast Albums.** (a) Producer and Author may agree, in *ARTICLE XXII* herein, on the terms regarding the creation of Cast Albums. For the purposes of this Contract, the term *"Cast Albums"* shall mean all audio recordings of the Play (or any portion thereof) performed by the cast of any production that is presented by or under lease or license from Producer. Author and Producer shall calculate and share, in perpetuity, the proceeds (other than amounts advanced by record companies for the creation of the album or for investment in the Play) received from the worldwide exploitation of such Cast Albums in the manner set forth in *ARTICLE XXII* herein, but in no event shall Author receive less than 60% and Producer less than 40% of such proceeds and in no event shall Producer's share of such proceeds be included in the calculation of Recoupment hereunder.

(b) If Producer in *ARTICLE XXII* acquires the rights to create Cast Albums but does not produce or license a production of the Play in the British Isles, Australia or New Zealand pursuant to the provisions of *ARTICLE IX* herein, then Author, without any financial obligation to Producer, shall be free to authorize a record company, other than the record company designated for the original cast album, to record the cast album in such area except that prior to entering into such an agreement, Author will give the record company that records the original cast album, written notice of the terms of the proposed agreement and such record company shall have 30 days within which to match the monetary terms of such other offer.

Section 8.18 **Music Publishing Rights.** Author and Producer may agree, in *ARTICLE XXII* herein, on certain terms regarding the disposition of the various music publishing rights in the music and lyrics of the Play.

Section 8.19 **Musical Scores.** Producer shall in the first instance furnish all necessary orchestral scores, conductor's scores, orchestra parts and vocal parts (*"Scores"*) at Producer's own expense. Subject to the provisions of the following sentence, Producer shall be the sole and exclusive owner of the physical Scores (as distinguished from the copyrights therein) and Producer may, subject to Author's copyrights in such Scores, sell, license, assign, rent or otherwise dispose of such Scores and retain any sums received therefrom, which sums shall not be counted in the calculation of Recoupment. Notwithstanding the foregoing, if Author elects to own the Scores, then such election shall be set forth in *ARTICLE XXII* herein and the following provisions shall apply:

(a) The Scores shall belong jointly to the Lyricist and Composer of the Play immediately upon delivery thereof to Producer. Such Scores may be used by the Lyricist and Composer at any time after the close of the First Class Performances in the Territory, whether or not the deductions or payments referred to in this SECTION have been completed.

(b) The Composer and Lyricist alone shall have the right to contract for the publication of the music and lyrics of the Play or any part thereof, without prejudice to the right of Producer to arrange for separate payment to Producer by the music publisher. The Composer and Lyricist alone may permit the reproduction of the music and lyrics or any part thereof by discs or any other means or devices.

(c) Producer shall, at the request of the Composer and Lyricist, or the Guild, make available to the Guild as soon as feasible after the Official Press Opening in New York City, said Scores for the purpose of making a copy thereof. Upon the close of the run of each Company, Producer shall deliver to the Composer and Lyricist the complete Scores and prompt book; *provided, however,* that the Producer may make and retain a copy of such Scores and prompt book but not for use or sale.

(d) Producer may deduct from the Royalties otherwise payable to each of the Composer and Lyricist $500 in the aggregate in each Performance Week in which such deduction would not reduce the Royalties payable to Author to less than $4,500 for Out-of-Town and Preview Performances or less than $3,000 for all other performances hereunder, until a sum equal to 50% of the Producer's actual expenditure for the Scores shall have been recovered by Producer. Producer shall pay to the Guild the monies so deducted until there shall have been presented to the Guild evidence of Producer's actual expenditures for such Scores, whereupon the Guild shall pay Producer the monies held by it to the extent of 50% of such actual expenditures. The deduction so made, unless otherwise agreed upon, shall be borne by the Composer and Lyricist according to their respective percentages of compensation.

(e) The Composer and Lyricist may at their option pay outright to the Producer at any time a sum equal to 50% of Producer's expenditures for such Scores or such remaining balance thereof as may then be unpaid.

SECTION 8.20 **Additional Collaboration.** This SECTION shall apply only in the case of a musical adapted from a book, play, motion picture or other underlying copyrighted work written by someone other than Producer and in which Producer, prior to the engagement of the Bookwriter, Composer and Lyricist, acquires an option on or owns the rights to adapt such underlying work for the musical stage.

(a) *Replacement Before First Rehearsal*—After delivery of any draft of the Play, but prior to the first full cast rehearsal, Producer may reject any component, i.e., book, music or lyrics or, if the author of such component is comprised of more than one person, then all or any part of the component written by such person(s) (the *"rejected component"*). The rejection of any such component is subject to the approval of any remaining authors. Upon such rejection:

(i) the author of the rejected component shall be entitled to retain the amount of the Option paid or payable to him hereunder as of the date of rejection, but will not be entitled to any additional Option Payments which might otherwise become payable after the date of rejection. All rights and material contributed by such author shall revert to him, except that he may not use any such material in a manner that would infringe upon or otherwise violate the rights of Producer or of the authors of the underlying work or of the other components of the Play, and he shall not receive billing credit, Royalties or Subsidiary Rights income in connection with any presentation of the Play.

(ii) Producer may not use any part of the rejected component but may enter into an APC with a replacement author, acceptable to the remaining authors, if any, to write new material for the component.

(iii) Should a dispute arise as to whether Producer is using any part of the rejected component, such dispute shall be submitted for resolution to the Theatrical Conciliation Council whose decision shall be final and binding.

(b) ***Replacement During Rehearsal but Before First Paid Public Performance***—From the first day of full cast rehearsal until the day prior to the first paid public First Class Performance of the Play hereunder, Producer may reject a component and enter into an APC with a replacement author for such rejected component, subject to the approval of all the remaining authors. Such approval will be deemed granted by any remaining author who fails to communicate with Producer regarding such approvals within 3 days after receiving written notice from Producer of the proposed change. If an APC is entered into with a new author, Producer shall retain all rights under this Contract to use any part of the rejected component and the following shall apply:

(i) The replaced author shall retain all Option and Advance Payments paid or owing at the date of rejection but shall not be entitled to any additional Advance Payments which might otherwise become payable after the date of rejection. The replaced author shall also receive ½ of such author's share of the Royalties and Subsidiary Rights income and all other sums otherwise payable under this Contract. Such author shall retain his ownership interest in the Play and in all copyrights and other rights therein and thereto, except that he shall not be entitled to exercise any control over, nor to participate in any decisions with respect to, their exploitation.

(ii) Any Royalty, share of Subsidiary Rights income or other sums payable to the new author shall not reduce the amounts payable to the remaining co-authors, if any.

(iii) The new author shall receive billing credit if he chooses to accept it. Any dispute regarding the substance or existence of billing for the replaced author shall be submitted to arbitration as provided in *ARTICLE XX* herein.

(c) ***Replacement From the First Paid Public First Class Performance Until the Day Prior to the Official Press Opening in New York City***—From and after the first paid public First Class Performance of the Play hereunder until the day prior to the Official Press Opening in New York City, Producer may reject a component and enter into an APC with a replacement author for such rejected component, subject to the approval of all of the remaining authors. Such approval will be deemed granted by any remaining author who fails to communicate with Producer regarding such approvals within one day after receiving written notice from Producer of the proposed change. If an APC is entered into with a new author, Producer shall retain all rights under this Contract to use any part of the rejected component and the following shall apply:

(i) The replaced author shall receive his full share of the Option and Advance Payments, Royalties and Subsidiary Rights income otherwise payable under this Contract, subject to *SECTION 8.20 (c)(iii)* herein. Such author also shall retain his ownership interest in the Play and in all copyrights and other rights therein and thereto, without the restrictions described in *SECTION 8.20 (b)(i)* herein.

(ii) Subject to *SECTION 8.20(c)(iii)* herein, any Royalty or other sum payable to the new author shall not reduce the amounts payable to the remaining co-authors, if any.

(iii) The new author's share of Subsidiary Rights income, to the extent it does not exceed one-sixth of Author's total Subsidiary Rights compensation, shall be borne by the original Author (including the replaced author) and by Producer in the same ratio as Author and Producer share such compensation hereunder. Any amount by which the new author's share of Subsidiary Rights compensation exceeds one-sixth of the Author's total Subsidiary Rights compensation shall be borne by Producer.

(iv) The replaced author shall receive his contracted-for billing credit if he chooses to accept it. The new author shall be entitled to such billing credit as he and Producer shall agree, subject to the replaced author's contractual rights.

(d) ***Author of Multiple Components/Multiple Authors of One Component.***

(i) If the author of a rejected component is also the author of any other non-rejected component the provisions of this SECTION shall apply to the author as if he were not the author of the non-rejected component, and all Option, Advance, and Royalty Payments, Subsidiary Rights and all other sums otherwise payable to author for all components written by him shall be deemed to be allocated equally between or among such components in making the calculations referred to in this SECTION.

(ii) If there are multiple authors of a component and Producer rejects one such author (with the approval of the other authors), the provisions of this SECTION shall apply only to the rejected author of such part and all of the Option, Advance, and Royalty Payments, Subsidiary Rights and all other sums payable to the authors of such component, as a whole, shall be deemed to be allocated equally between or among such authors, unless otherwise provided in *ARTICLE XXII* herein, in making the calculations referred to in this SECTION.

(e) *Royalty Payments to New Author*—The rejection and subsequent addition of any new author shall neither reduce the aggregate Royalties payable pursuant to *ARTICLES IV* and *V* herein nor increase that portion of such Royalties payable to the new author beyond the amount of such Royalties which were payable to the replaced author.

SECTION 8.21 Deleted Music and Lyrics. Unless otherwise specified in *ARTICLE XXII* herein, all rights in and to any music and lyrics which shall be deleted from the Play prior to the Official Press Opening in New York City shall revert to the Composer and Lyricist, respectively, for their use, free from any claim by the Producer provided, however, that the Composer and Lyricist shall not have any right to use or authorize the use of any such lyrics which (a) refer to any character in the Play by the same name as the character in the Play if the name is sufficiently distinctive to identify with the Play or (b) depict or portray an important situation which is contained in the Play or (c) contain any of the distinctive dialogue or distinctive phrases from the Play or (d) have as their title the name of any character in, or the title of the Play if such name is sufficiently distinctive to identify with the Play. If any such compositions are included in any agreement for an Audio-Visual Production of the Play, the Composer and Lyricist shall not be entitled to any larger additional compensation by reason thereof and the Producer's share of the income therefrom shall not be diminished.

ARTICLE IX

ADDITIONAL PRODUCTION RIGHTS

SECTION 9.01 Grant of Second Class Performance Rights. (a) Author hereby grants Producer the sole and exclusive rights to produce one or more Second Class Performances of the Play on the speaking stage in the Territory during the time that Producer continues to have rights to present the Play hereunder. For the purposes of this Contract, the term *"Second Class Performances"* shall mean all performances of the Play other than Stock, Amateur and Ancillary Performances (as those terms are defined in *SECTION 11.01* herein), Off-Broadway Performances (as defined in *SECTION 9.02* herein), and First Class Performances and Developmental (i.e. "workshop") Productions.

(b) Author's Royalties for Second Class Performances shall be calculated and paid in the manner set forth in *SECTION 4.02(d)* herein with respect to Touring Performances, unless Author's Royalty is calculated in whole or in part on the basis of a fixed fee payable to Producer, in which case the Royalty shall be calculated and paid in the manner set forth for Fixed-Fee Performances.

SECTION 9.02 Grant of Off-Broadway Performance Rights. (a) Author hereby grants Producer the sole and exclusive rights to produce one or more Off-Broadway Performances of the Play during the time that Producer continues to have rights to present the Play hereunder. The foregoing grant is subject to the conditions precedent that Producer has Vested (as defined in *SECTION 11.02* herein) in the Territory and that Producer is not simultaneously presenting any other performances of the Play in New York City. For the purposes of this Contract, the term *"Off-Broadway Performances"* shall mean performances of the Play in theatres which are classified as Off-Broadway pursuant to the Actors' Equity Association Agreement Governing Employment Off-Broadway, as that agreement may be amended from time to time.

(b) Author's Royalties for Off-Broadway Performances shall be calculated and paid in the manner set forth in *ARTICLES IV* and *V* herein with respect to Touring Performances except that Author's post-Recoupment Royalties shall be such amount as may be agreed upon by Author and Producer and set forth in *ARTICLE XXII* herein, but in no event more than 7% of the Gross Weekly Box Office Receipts.

SECTION 9.03 Grant of Rights in the British Isles, Australia and New Zealand. (a) Author hereby grants to Producer the sole and exclusive rights to produce one or more productions of the Play for a consecutive run, as theatrically understood, in a regular evening bill, in a first class manner, in a first class theatre, on the speaking stage in one or more of the following *"Additional Territories"*:

(i) The United Kingdom of Great Britain (i.e., England, Northern Ireland, Scotland and Wales) and in Ireland (collectively the *"British Isles"*)

(ii) Australia

(iii) New Zealand

(b) The foregoing grant is subject to the conditions precedent that Producer has Vested in the Territory and is not in breach of any provision of this Contract.

(c) Producer's rights to present the Play in the Additional Territories shall include the right to present "tryout" performances prior to the presentation of the Play in the Additional Territory equivalent of first-class theatres.

(d) The terms of this Contract applicable to First Class Performances in the Territory shall apply to performances of the Play in the British Isles except as may be provided to the contrary herein.

(e) If Producer chooses to produce the Play pursuant to a lease or license to a third party in Australia or New Zealand, Producer's rights shall be subject to the following procedure: Producer shall give Author written notice of the terms of any third party offer for the production of the Play in such Additional Territory. Producer may accept the offer unless Author shall, within 5 business days after receipt of Producer's notice, give Producer written notice, delivered either in person or by wire communication, that the offer is unacceptable, stating Author's reasons therefor, together with a definite offer from a third party, on terms at least as favorable to Producer as those contained in the offer which Producer is willing to accept. If within the prescribed period of time Author submits such an offer, Author may accept such offer. If within the prescribed period of time Author fails to submit such an offer, then Producer may accept the original offer. If the offer presented by Author is from a producer or other entity or person in which Author has any financial or other interest, or if a dispute arises as to whether such offer is at least as favorable to Producer as the offer which Producer obtained, or if any other dispute arises under this *SECTION 9.03(e)*, the parties shall submit the matter to the Theatrical Conciliation Council for the purposes of (i) determining whether or not such offer is the result of good-faith arm's length negotiations, or (ii) determining whether the offer presented by Author is at least as favorable to Producer or (iii) resolving any other dispute, as the case may be. If the Council determines that the offer is the result of good-faith arm's length negotiations or is at least as favorable to Producer, as the case may be, then Author may accept such offer; however, if the Council determines that such offer is not the result of such negotiations, or is not at least as favorable to Producer, as the case may be, the offer presented by Producer shall be accepted. The decision of the Council in connection with any matter presented under this *SECTION 9.03(e)* shall be final and binding on the parties hereto.

SECTION 9.04 Payments Required to Extend Rights in the Additional Territories. The following provisions of this SECTION shall apply separately to each Additional Territory:

(a) Unless Producer presents the first paid public performance of the Play in an Additional Territory within 6 months after the close of First Class Performances in New York City, Producer's rights to present the Play in such Additional Territory shall automatically terminate unless such rights are extended as provided in this SECTION.

(b) Producer shall be entitled to three consecutive 6-month extensions of such rights upon paymen of $1,000 for the first extension, $1,500 for the second extension and $2,000 for the third extension, whic payment must be made prior to the expiration of the rights period then in effect, *provided, however, tha* for the third extension, Producer must give Author, simultaneously with the payment of $2,000, writte notice of the intended date of the first paid public performance together with copies of document representing one of the following:

(i) a commitment for the licensing of the Additional Territory equivalent of a first clas theatre, with occupancy to occur before the end of the third extension period or

(ii) contracts for the engagement of the principal members of the cast or the director, pu suant to which such person(s) agrees to render services before the end of the third extension perio

The extension of Producer's rights and option for the third extension period shall not be prevented c affected by the fact that any of these commitments or contracts may be made subject to conditions, suc as the availability of a person or theatre, the attainment of full capitalization of the production, furthe negotiations regarding material terms, the execution of a formal agreement, or any other condition, c the fact that any of these commitments or contracts may later be breached or unenforceable.

SECTION **9.05 Royalty Payments in the Additional Territories.** (a) Author's Royalties fo performances of the Play in the British Isles, shall be calculated and paid in accordance with th provision of *ARTICLES IV* and *V* applicable to Touring and Fixed-Fee Performances, except that a references to fixed dollar amounts in such ARTICLES shall be reduced to one-third of the state amounts. Author's Royalties for performances in Australia and New Zealand shall be 6% of the Gros Weekly Box Office Receipts.

(b) The payments made pursuant to *SECTION 9.04* herein for an Additional Territory may b deducted from the Royalties earned by Author from any Company presenting the Play in such Add tional Territory at the rate of up to 50% of such Royalties per Performance Week commencing for th Performance Week in which such Company has reached Recoupment. Such deductions shall be permit ted only in such amounts as will not cause Author to earn, for any week in which such deductions a made, Royalties of less than the foreign currency equivalent (at the time of payment) of $900 per Fu Performance Week.

(c) Sums payable to Author in connection with performances of the Play in any Additional Ter ritory shall be paid after deduction of all withholding and other taxes due thereon pursuant to the laws c the applicable Additional Territory, all conversion and remittance costs applicable to such payments an all payments required to be made to any author's society or similar organizations. Producer shall not b liable for losses incurred due to fluctuations in the exchange rate.

(d) In addition to the Royalties payable pursuant to this SECTION, if Author earns in an Performance Week Royalties equal to less than 6% of the Gross Weekly Box Office Receipts for suc week from productions in Australia or New Zealand, Producer shall, simultaneously with the payment o Author's Royalties for such week, pay to the Guild, on Author's behalf (for the benefit of Author' representatives), a sum equal to 10% of the difference between the amount of Author's Royalties and sum equal to 6% of the Gross Weekly Box Office Receipts.

SECTION **9.06 Transfer of Rights to an Additional Territory Producer.** Provided Produce has complied with the provisions of *SECTION 9.03(b)* herein, Producer may produce the Play alone or i association with or under lease or license to an Additional Territory producer or manager, subject t Author's written consent. In such case, Producer's obligations to make the payments herein provide shall remain unimpaired. The contract between Producer and the Additional Territory producer c manager shall require the Play to be produced in the manner and on the terms provided herein wit respect to productions in the Additional Territory.

SECTION **9.07 Advances for Performances in the Additional Territories.** If the Play produced in any Additional Territory in association with or under lease or license to an Additiona

Territory producer or manager pursuant to the provisions of this ARTICLE, and if, in connection therewith, Producer receives an advance payment applicable against royalties payable to Producer, or a lump sum in lieu of a portion of such royalties, Author shall receive 50% of such advance or lump sum as an advance against Royalties payable for such production. Author's share of the advance or lump sum received by Producer with respect to an Additional Territory may be deducted from the payments due pursuant to *SECTION 9.05* herein with respect to such Additional Territory.

SECTION 9.08 **Author's Presence in the Additional Territories.** If the Play is presented in any Additional Territory by or under grant of rights from Producer, Author shall have the right to be present for up to 3 weeks in order to attend rehearsals, tryouts and the opening of the first production of the Play in such Additional Territory. Producer shall reimburse Author for hotel and travel expenses during such period and at any other time when the presence of Author is required by Producer. Unless specific dollar amounts are provided in *ARTICLE XXII* herein, the amounts reimbursable by Producer under this SECTION shall be the cost of reasonable hotel and travel accommodations. In any event, Author's hotel and travel accommodations shall be of a class equal to the greater of the class charged to the Company by Producer or Director.

SECTION 9.09 **Producer's Financial Participation in Additional Territory Uses.** (a) If the Play is not presented in any Additional Territory by or under grant of rights from Producer within the period set forth in *SECTION 9.04* herein, then Author shall thereafter have the sole right to produce or authorize the production of the Play in any such Additional Territory in which Producer's rights have lapsed and, provided that Producer has Vested in the Territory and is not in breach of any provision of this Contract, Author shall pay Producer the following amounts:

(i) with respect to the British Isles, 25% of the compensation earned by Author (after deduction of agents' commissions, if any) regardless of when paid, in connection with each contract for the production of the Play (including any contracts for British Isles Subsidiary Rights, other than Media Productions in which Producer will have previously acquired a worldwide interest) entered into on or after the Effective Date of this Contract but prior to the expiration of 7 years from the date on which Producer has Vested in the Territory; *provided, however,* that with respect to each contract for the presentation of the British Isles equivalents of First or Second Class Performances, Author shall pay Producer 10% of the compensation earned by Author (after deduction of agents' commissions, if any) regardless of when paid, in connection with each such contract entered into after said 7-year period or after the close of the first First Class Performance in the British Isles, whichever first occurs, but before the expiration of 40 years from the date on which Producer Vested in the Territory; and

(ii) with respect to Australia and New Zealand, 35% of the compensation earned by Author (after deduction of agents' commissions, if any) regardless of when paid, in connection with each contract for the production of the Play (including any contracts for Australian or New Zealand Subsidiary Rights, other than Media Productions in which Producer will have previously acquired a worldwide interest) entered into on or after the Effective Date of this Contract but prior to the expiration of 6 years from the date on which Producer has Vested in the Territory;

(b) If the Play has been presented in any Additional Territory by or under a grant of rights from Producer in accordance with the provisions of this ARTICLE and Producer has Vested in such Additional Territory and is not in breach of any provision of this Contract, Producer's financial interest in Author's compensation derived from the disposition of Subsidiary Rights in such Additional Territory (other than Media Productions in which Producer will have previously acquired a worldwide interest), will be as follows:

(i) with respect to the British Isles, Producer will have the same financial interest in British Isles Subsidiary Rights as Producer has with respect to such Subsidiary Rights in the Territory, and the time periods described in the applicable Producer's Alternative (as defined in *SECTION 11.03(c)* herein) shall be measured from the last performance of the Play in the British Isles; and

(ii) with respect to Australia and New Zealand, Producer's financial interest in Australian and New Zealand Subsidiary Rights shall be equal to 40% of the compensation earned by Author (after deduction of agents' commissions, if any) regardless of when paid, in connection with each contract for the disposition of such Subsidiary Rights entered into on or after the Effective Date of this Contract but prior to the expiration of 7 years from the date on which Producer Vested in such Additional Territory or 4 years from the last performance of the Play in the Additional Territory, whichever is later.

SECTION 9.10 Additional Rights to Present Backers' Auditions. While Producer has the rights to present the Play hereunder, Producer shall also have the rights to present Backers' Auditions of the Play.

ARTICLE X
REOPENING RIGHTS

SECTION 10.01 Reopenings in the Territory. (a) Provided Producer has Vested in the Territory, Producer may, within 4 months after the last performance of the Play in the Territory, notify Author in writing of Producer's intention to reopen the Play in the Territory. In such case Producer may so reopen the Play within 12 months following such last performance; *provided, however,* that if the Play is not reopened within 4 months from such last performance, Producer must, in order to retain his rights to reopen the Play, pay Author the following sums (as non-returnable advances against the Royalties payable): $500 per month for up to 4 months, commencing with the fourth month following the last performance, and $1,000 per month for up to an additional 4 months.

(b) If Producer presents the Play in the Territory but closes the Play prior to having Vested, Producer may reopen the Play provided he gives the Author written notice, within 30 days after such closing, of Producer's intention to reopen the Play, pays Author $500 per month (as non-returnable advances against the Royalties payable), commencing one month following the closing until the Play has reopened, and commences rehearsals for such production no later than 3 months after the closing.

(c) All the provisions of this SECTION shall apply to each reopening in the Territory. Such reopenings may be First Class, Second Class or Off-Broadway Performances.

SECTION 10.02 Reopenings in the Additional Territories. (a) Provided Producer has Vested in the British Isles, Producer may, within 4 months after the close of the last performance in the British Isles, notify Author in writing of Producer's intention to reopen the Play in the British Isles. In such case Producer may reopen the Play in the British Isles, within 12 months following such last performance, in accordance with the provisions of *SECTION 10.01(a)* herein.

(b) If Producer presents the Play in the British Isles but closes the Play prior to having Vested in the British Isles, Producer may reopen the Play in the British Isles in accordance with the provisions of *SECTION 10.01(b)* herein.

(c) Provided Producer has Vested in Australia or New Zealand, Producer may retain the rights to reopen the Play in such Additional Territory upon paying Author (as non-returnable advances against the Royalties payable) $900 per month, for up to 6 months, commencing one month following the last performance in such Additional Territory. In no event may Producer reopen the Play after 7 years from the date on which Producer Vested in such Additional Territory.

(d) If Producer presents the Play in Australia or New Zealand but closes the Play prior to having Vested in such Additional Territory, Producer may reopen the Play in such Additional Territory in accordance with the provisions of *SECTION 10.01(b)* herein.

(e) All the provisions of this SECTION shall apply to each reopening of the Play in the applicable Additional Territory. Such reopenings must be the Additional Territory equivalent of First Class Performances.

SECTION 10.03 Closing. Producer shall in each instance, immediately upon determining to close a run of the Play, give written notice thereof to Author.

ARTICLE XI

SUBSIDIARY RIGHTS

SECTION 11.01 **Definitions Relating to Subsidiary Rights.** For the purposes of this Contract, the term *"Subsidiary Rights"* shall mean those rights in the Play relating to the following methods of exploitation:

(a) *"Media Productions"*—shall mean Audio-Visual Productions (as defined below) and radio uses.

(b) *"Audio-Visual Productions"*—shall mean motion picture, television, video cassette and video disc productions; soundtrack albums, tapes and discs for all of the foregoing; and all other kinds of visual and audio-visual productions in connection with the Play, whether now existing or developed in the future. All of the foregoing shall be considered Audio-Visual Productions, regardless of the method or mode of reproduction, projection, transmission, exhibition, or delivery used. However, Audio-Visual Productions shall not include Foreign Local Television Productions. For the purposes of this Contract, the term *"Foreign Local Television Productions"* shall mean all television productions of the Play in a foreign language produced and distributed exclusively for television exhibition outside the Territory and the Additional Territories.

(c) *"Commercial Use Products"*—shall mean wearing apparel; toys; games; figures; dolls; novelties; books; souvenir programs; and any other physical property representing a character in the Play or using the name, character or the title of the Play or otherwise connected with the Play or its title.

(d) *"Stock Performances"*—shall mean all performances of the Play presented in the English language pursuant to one of the Actors' Equity Association agreements governing employment of actors in productions classified, pursuant to the terms of such agreements, as "stock", "resident theatre", "university resident theatre", "dinner theatre", or "guest artist contract" productions (and the equivalents of such performances outside the United States).

(e) *"Amateur Performances"*—shall mean all performances of the Play presented in the English language and using only non-professional actors (i.e., an actor who is not a member of a performing arts union or guild in the Territory or outside the Territory, as the case may be).

(f) *"Ancillary Performances"*—shall mean all performances of the Play presented in the English language as condensed and tabloid versions, so-called concert tour versions and opera versions based on the Play as well as foreign language performances of all kinds in the Territory or each Additional Territory, as the case may be, and performances of the Play pursuant to one of the Actors' Equity Association agreements governing employment of actors in productions classified pursuant to the terms of such agreements as: "theatre for young audiences", "small professional theatre" and "non-profit theatre code" productions (and their equivalents outside the United States).

(g) *"Revival Performances"*—

(*i*) *In the City of New York*—all First Class, Second Class and Off-Broadway Performances of the Play in the City of New York and all performances at Lincoln Center (regardless of how classified), presented after the expiration of Producer's rights to present the Play in the Territory; and

(*ii*) *Outside the City of New York*—all First and Second Class Performances of the Play in the Territory, presented after the expiration of Producer's rights to present the Play in the Territory and presented outside the City of New York, provided that, with respect to each contract entered into for such production, the Play is presented in at least 3 cities throughout the Territory. Notwithstanding the foregoing, if any of such cities is the City of New York, the 3-city minimum shall automatically be waived. Until the Play is presented in the third city or in the City of New York, whichever first occurs, Author shall pay all sums due to Producer from such Revival Performances to the Guild, which shall hold such sums until the first presentation of the Play in the third city or the City of New York, whichever first occurs, and then pay such sums to Producer. No interest shall accrue to Producer's benefit on such sums held by the Guild.

(iii) In the Additional Territories—all performances of the Play in any of the Additional Territories (which are the Additional Territory equivalents of First or Second Class Performances in the Territory), presented after the expiration of Producer's rights to present the Play in such Additional Territory.

(iv) Remakes, Prequels, Sequels and Spin-Offs—Revival Performances shall also include performances of all "remakes", "prequels" (i.e. stories which occur at an earlier point in time than the story in the Play), "sequels" and "spin-offs" of the Play produced in the manner described in *SECTIONS 11.01(g)(i),(ii)* and *(iii)* above.

SECTION 11.02 **Definition of Vested.** For the purposes of this Contract, the term *"Vested"* shall mean that Producer has presented the Play in one of the manners described below:

(a) With respect to the Territory, for the following number of consecutive (as customarily defined in the theatre industry) paid public First Class Performances:

(i) 10 Preview Performances plus the Official Press Opening of the Play in New York City, or

(ii) 5 Preview Performances plus the Official Press Opening in New York City plus 5 Regular Performances, or

(iii) 5 Out-of-Town and 5 Preview Performances plus the Official Press Opening in New York City, provided there are no more than 42 days between the last Out-of-Town Performance and the first Preview Performance, or

(iv) 5 Preview Performances plus the Official Press Opening in New York City if the Play has been presented previously by someone other than Producer and is presented by Producer hereunder with substantially the same cast and scenic designs as existed in the prior presentation.

Each Preview Performance given in New York City within 10 days of the Official Press Opening in New York City (even though not consecutive) shall be considered a "consecutive" performance for the purpose of this paragraph, provided that the scale of box-office prices of each such Preview Performance is at least 65% of the scale of box-office prices announced for the Regular Performances and that each such Preview Performance is publicized in advance in the paid "ABC" listings of The New York Times and a similar listing in any other newspaper, magazine or other periodical of general circulation in the City of New York. Any Preview Performance given more than 10 days before the Official Press Opening shall not be considered a "consecutive" performance for the purpose of this paragraph.

(b) With respect to the Territory, for 64 consecutive paid public Out-of-Town Performances, whether or not the Play has its Official Press Opening in New York City, provided that breaks may be made in performances outside of New York City because of the necessities of travel so long as the 64 performances shall have been given within 80 days of the first performance.

(c) With respect to the Territory, for 64 consecutive Out-of-Town Performances in arenas or auditoriums if, because of the nature of the Play or the size or complexity of its contemplated production, the performance of the Play in a traditional first class theatre would not be feasible or desirable. The same provisions of *SECTION 11.02(b)* shall apply in connection with breaks for travel.

(d) With respect to the British Isles, for the following number of first class performances:

(i) if the Play is first produced in London, then for 21 consecutive performances in London, or

(ii) if the Play is first produced outside of London, for 64 performances within 80 days after the first performance, presented either outside of London, or partly in London and partly outside of London.

(e) With respect to Australia, for 21 consecutive performances, including an Official Press Opening, provided such performances are the Australian equivalent of First Class Performances in the Territory.

(f) With respect to New Zealand, for 21 consecutive performances, including an Official Press Opening, provided such performances are the New Zealand equivalent of First Class Performances in the Territory.

SECTION 11.03 **Participation in Subsidiary Rights.** Although Producer is acquiring rights in the Play and Author's services solely in connection with the production of the Play, Author recognizes that by a successful production Producer makes a contribution to the value of other rights in the Play. Therefore, although the relationship between the parties is limited to play production as herein provided, and Author alone owns and controls the Play with respect to all other uses, nevertheless, if Producer has Vested in the Territory and Producer is not in breach of any provision of this Contract, Author hereby agrees that:

(a) *No Outright Sale*—Author will not authorize or permit any outright sale of the right to use said Play for any of the Subsidiary Rights purposes during the period therein specified without Producer's prior consent. In no event shall there be any outright sale of any such rights prior to the first paid public First Class Performance of the Play, except that an outright sale of rights for Audio-Visual Productions may be permitted if made subject to the provisions of *SECTION 13.07* herein.

(b) *Best Efforts*—Author will use best efforts to exploit the Play for Subsidiary Rights purposes.

(c) *"Producer's Alternatives"*—

(i) Producer shall have the right to choose Alternative I or II of the 3 Producer's Alternatives set forth in this SECTION. The choice of Alternative III must be specified by Author and Producer in ARTICLE XXII upon the signing of this Contract. The choice of Alternative I or II must be made by giving Author and the Guild written notice of such choice on or before 12 o'clock midnight on the first day of rehearsal at which Producer requires all cast members of the Principal Company. If Producer fails to give such notice in a timely manner, Author may choose which Producer's Alternative will apply upon giving Producer and the Guild written notice of such choice on or before 12 o'clock midnight on the next business day following said rehearsal date. If both Producer and Author fail to choose a Producer's Alternative in a timely manner, Producer's Alternative III will apply.

(ii) *Participation in Territory*—With respect to the exploitation of Subsidiary Rights in the Territory, Author shall promptly pay to Producer, based on the applicable Producer's Alternative, the designated percentage of Author's compensation directly or indirectly earned (after deduction of agents' commissions, if any), from the disposition of the specified Subsidiary Rights anywhere in the Territory, pursuant to each contract entered into on or after the Effective Date of this Contract but prior to the expiration of the periods described in the applicable Producer's Alternative (regardless of when such compensation is paid); *provided, however,* that with respect to Media Productions, Producer's participation shall be in Author's compensation earned from exploitations anywhere in the world:

Under *Producer's* *Alternative* #	If any of the following Subsidiary Rights are disposed of	Author will promptly pay Producer, based on the following percentages of Author's compensation directly or indirectly earned (after deduction of agent's commissions, if any), from such dispositions pursuant to each contract entered into on or after the Effective Date of this Contract but prior to the expiration of the specified periods of time after the last performance of the Play hereunder (regardless of when such compensation is paid):
I	Media Productions	50% in perpetuity
	Stock and Ancillary Performances	50% for the first 5 years then 25% for the next 5 years
	Amateur Performances	25% for 5 years
	Revival Performances	20% for 40 years
	Commercial Use Products	See *SECTION 11.05*
II	Media Productions	50% in perpetuity
	Stock and Ancillary Performances	30% for 36 years
	Amateur Performances	0%
	Revival Performances	20% for 40 years
	Commercial Use Products	See *SECTION 11.05*
III	Media Productions	30% in perpetuity
	Stock, Amateur and Ancillary Performances	30% for the first 20 years then 25% for the next 10 years and 20% for the next 10 years (total of 40 years)
	Revival Performances	20% for 40 years
	Commercial Use Products	See *SECTION 11.05*

(d) *Revival Participation—*

(i) In paying Producer's financial participation in Revival Performances, Author shall secure the payment of one-half of such sum (i.e., 10%) from the producer of the Revival Performances.

(ii) Notwithstanding the provisions of *SECTION 11.03(c)*, Producer's financial participation in remake, prequel, sequel and spin-off Revival Performances shall be 10% rather than 20%.

(e) *Foreign Participation—*Author shall have the exclusive right to negotiate and contract for all performances of the Play and for other Subsidiary Rights purposes described in this ARTICLE outside the Territory and outside the Additional Territories, and Author shall promptly pay Producer 25% of the compensation earned by Author (after deduction of agents' commissions, if any), regardless of when paid, in connection with each such contract (other than contracts for Media Productions in which Producer will have previously acquired a worldwide interest) entered into on or after the Effective Date of this Contract but prior to 7 years from the date on which Producer Vested in the Territory. With respect to contracts for Foreign Local Television Productions, Author shall pay Producer 50% of such compensation earned by Author (after deduction of agents' commissions, if any) for such contracts entered into on or after the Effective Date of this Contract but prior to 15 years from the date on which Producer Vested in the Territory.

(f) *Participation in Audio-Visual Sequels—*If the producer of the Audio-Visual Production, in the original contract for Audio-Visual Production rights, is granted the right to make one or more Audio-

Visual Production remakes, prequels, sequels or spin-offs upon the payment of additional compensation, then, if and when such additional compensation is paid, Producer's share of such compensation shall be one-half of the Media Productions percentage set forth in the applicable Producer's Alternative.

SECTION 11.04 **Author's Share of Subsidiary Rights.** No person who is not an Author (as specifically defined in *SECTION 1.05* herein) may participate in Author's share of any Subsidiary Rights proceeds; *provided, however,* that for the purposes of this SECTION only, the term "Author" shall include each collaborator, adaptor, novelist and owner of underlying rights whose material is used in the Play.

SECTION 11.05 **Producer's Rights Regarding Commercial Use Products.** (a) Anything to the contrary herein notwithstanding, Author hereby grants to Producer the sole and exclusive rights to create, manufacture and sell (or have created, manufactured and sold) Commercial Use Products, during the time that Producer retains any rights to present the Play hereunder, except that if on the last day of such period, a contract exists with a third party for the creation, manufacture or sale of Commercial Use Products, then such contract will continue in full force and effect until the expiration of its term, but in no event for more than 5 years from the date of such contract (or the last extension thereof). This grant of rights shall be for the Territory and for each Additional Territory in which Producer presents or licenses the rights to present the Play. Producer shall pay Author the following amounts, regardless of when paid, in connection with each contract entered into for the exploitation of Commercial Use Products:

(i) with respect to sales of such products on the premises of theatres in which Producer presents the Play, a sum equal to 10% of the gross retail sales (after deduction of taxes);

(ii) with respect to sales of such products in other locations, a sum equal to 50% of Producer's net receipts from such sales (i.e., the gross amounts paid to Producer less all customary third party costs actually incurred in the creation, manufacture and sale of such Commercial Use Products).

(b) After the expiration of Producer's rights to exploit Commercial Use Products in the Territory or any Additional Territory, Author may exploit or enter into contracts for the exploitation of Commercial Use Products in such location in which Producer's rights have expired, subject to any contracts which may continue in effect as described in *SECTION 11.05(a)* herein. Author will pay Producer the following amounts (after deduction of agents' commissions, if any) regardless of when paid, in connection with each such contract entered into before the expiration of 40 years after the last performance of the Play in the Territory or such Additional Territory, as the case may be, provided Producer has Vested in such location:

(i) with respect to sales of such products on the premises of theatres in which Author's Play is presented, a sum equal to 10% of the gross retail sales (after deduction of taxes);

(ii) with respect to sales of such products in other locations, a sum equal to 50% of Author's net receipts from such sales (i.e., the gross amounts paid to Author less all customary third party costs actually incurred in the creation, manufacture and sale of such Commercial Use Products).

(c) In addition to Producer's rights and financial interest described in *SECTIONS 11.05(a)* and *(b)* herein, provided Producer has Vested in the Territory, Producer shall also have such rights and financial interest on a worldwide basis in those cases where the rights to exploit Commercial Use Products are disposed of together with Author's dispositions of rights to exploit any or all Media Productions.

(d) If there are Revival Performances in the Territory or any Additional Territory, Producer's right to share in Commercial Use Products income, from contracts entered into simultaneously with or subsequent to those Performances in such location (other than contracts which are related to the disposition of rights to Media Productions), shall revert to Author; *provided, however,* that Producer shall have the right to make arrangements with producers of the Revival Performances with respect to the exploitation of Commercial Use Products created or manufactured by Producer, and to retain all sums derived therefrom.

(e) None of the sums described in this SECTION, paid to or retained by Producer in connection with the exploitation of Commercial Use Products, shall be included in the calculation of Recoupment hereunder.

SECTION 11.06 **Producer's Rights to Consult in Dispositions of Subsidiary Rights.** If Producer shall be entitled to share in Author's Subsidiary Rights income with respect to the Territory, or with respect to any of the Additional Territories, Author will not undertake to grant any Subsidiary Rights in the Territory and the applicable Additional Territories, during the periods in which Producer is entitled to share in such income, without giving Producer the reasonable opportunity to consult fully with Author in connection with the exploitation of all such rights.

SECTION 11.07 **Restrictions on Dispositions by Author.** (a) In addition to Producer's rights as set forth in *SECTION 11.06* herein, Author represents that, except to the extent set forth in *ARTICLE XXII* herein, Author has not authorized or permitted, and covenants that Author shall not authorize or permit, unless Producer first consents in writing, the exploitation (or publicity regarding future exploitations) of any of the rights hereinbelow described, prior to the dates specified below:

Rights	Specified Date
(i) Worldwide Media Productions (other than radio) and Foreign Local Television Productions:	the Effective Date of this Contract, subject to the provisions of *ARTICLE XIII* herein.
(ii) Separately with respect to the Territory and each Additional Territory: First and Second Class, Stock, Amateur, Ancillary, Off-Broadway and Revival Performances (and their equivalents outside the Territory); and radio:	the date on which all of Producer's rights to produce the Play have expired in the Territory or such Additional Territory, as the case may be, or the date on which Producer has in writing declared that he will not reopen the Play, except that selected songs may be released for radio use at anytime.
(iii) Separately with respect to the Territory and each Additional Territory: Commercial Use Products:	the date on which all of Producer's rights to produce the Play have expired in the Territory and each Additional Territory, as the case may be, subject to any contracts which may continue in effect as described in *SECTION 11.05* herein.
(iv) Worldwide music publishing and mechanical reproduction rights including, without limitation, cast album rights:	the date of the Official Press Opening of the Play in New York City, subject to *SECTION 8.18* herein.

(b) If Author has disposed of any rights in the Play outside the Territory prior to the Effective Date of this Contract then, provided Producer Vests in the Territory, Producer will receive a sum equal to one-half the amount Producer would have been entitled to receive hereunder had Producer Vested in the Territory prior to the disposition of such rights. Except to the extent that such sums have been previously paid by Author, such sums shall be paid to Producer from Author's share of the first monies, if any, received by Author on or after the Effective Date of this Contract from all Subsidiary Rights exploitations.

SECTION 11.08 **Reservation of Audio-Visual Production Rights Outside the Territory.** If Author disposes of any rights outside the Territory, other than Audio-Visual Production rights, Author shall reserve in Author's contract therefor, and for Author's own use, all Audio-Visual Production rights in such foreign area (including the Additional Territories) and such contract shall provide that the exercise of such reserved rights in such foreign area, by Author or any person authorized by Author, shall not be deemed restricted in any way by the terms of such contract or competitive with any rights so disposed of.

ARTICLE XII

THE NEGOTIATOR

SECTION 12.01 Choice of Negotiator. Edward E. Colton is appointed as Negotiator.

SECTION 12.02 Alternate Negotiator. Franklin R. Weissberg is appointed as Alternate Negotiator. The Alternate Negotiator shall have all the rights and duties of the Negotiator and shall have the power to act in the Negotiator's absence.

SECTION 12.03 Disqualification of Negotiator. If it appears that the Negotiator and/or the Alternate Negotiator by reason of his relations with any Producer who has received motion picture financing, directly or indirectly, or his representation of any Author or Producer of the Play or for any other reason whatsoever, might, in the disposition of the Audio-Visual Production rights in the Play, act in a dual capacity or occupy a position possibly conflicting with complete representation of Author, the Dramatists Guild Council may, upon the request of Author or Producer involved, replace the Negotiator and/or the Alternate Negotiator with a Temporary Negotiator, for the purposes of disposing of the Audio-Visual Production rights in connection with the Play.

SECTION 12.04 Selection of New Negotiator. The Negotiator and Alternate Negotiator shall each serve until he resigns, is removed by action of the Theatrical Conciliation Council or otherwise becomes unable to perform his services. Any new Negotiator and any new Alternate Negotiator (other than a Temporary Negotiator) shall be appointed by action of the Theatrical Conciliation Council.

SECTION 12.05 Duties of Negotiator. (a) The Negotiator shall act as the representative of the Author in connection with the disposition of Audio-Visual Production rights in the Play, and shall have the right generally to conduct negotiations therefor subject to such written instructions as may be issued to him by the Theatrical Conciliation Council. Whenever Author and Producer are represented by an agent in connection with the disposition of such rights, the Negotiator shall cooperate with and work in conjunction with said agent. The Negotiator shall have the right to consummate such sale or lease after consultation with Producer and subject to the approval of Author and after according Producer all the rights to which Producer is entitled pursuant to the terms of this Contract. The Negotiator shall also receive and distribute the monies resulting therefrom as provided herein. All contracts shall be signed by the Negotiator or, in his absence, the Alternate Negotiator and countersigned by a person designated by the Guild. In order to aid Author and Producer in obtaining the best possible terms, the Negotiator shall keep Producer apprised of current practices in the sale of Audio-Visual Production rights.

(b) If such rights are disposed of prior to the production of the Play, the Audio-Visual Production rights contract must be signed before the beginning of rehearsals. In such a case the contract shall be on the basis of a minimum guaranteed payment or an advance, plus or on acccount of percentage payments based on the receipts of the Audio-Visual Production or the box office receipts of the Play, or both, and shall be subject to the approval of the Guild and Producer.

SECTION 12.06 Disposition of Proceeds. All monies received from the disposition of Audio-Visual Production rights in the Play shall be forthwith deposited by the Negotiator in a special account entitled "The Dramatists Guild Negotiator's Account" in a bank located in New York City as may be designated from time to time by the Guild. All withdrawals therefrom shall be made by check signed by the Negotiator or, in his absence, the Alternate Negotiator or, if appointed, the Temporary Negotiator, and countersigned by a person designated by the Guild.

SECTION 12.07 Compensation of Negotiator. Prior to making any withdrawals from the proceeds deposited in the Dramatists Guild Negotiator Account in connection with the Play, there shall first be deducted 1¼% of such sums so deposited. Said 1¼% shall be deducted from the amounts payable to the agents in respect of the agents' commission or, if there are no agents, then from the total sums on deposit prior to making any payments to Author or Producer. Said 1¼% shall be divided 85% to the

Negotiator and 15% to the Guild as full and complete compensation for their services in connection with the disposition of the Audio-Visual Production rights in the Play.

SECTION 12.08 **Instructions to Negotiator.** The Negotiator shall, in connection with the disposition of Audio-Visual Production rights in the Play, follow the procedures set forth in *EXHIBIT B* attached hereto and made a part of this Contract.

ARTICLE XIII
GENERAL PROVISIONS REGARDING
AUDIO-VISUAL PRODUCTIONS

SECTION 13.01 **Cooperation by Author.** Author agrees to cooperate and shall cause his agent to cooperate with the Negotiator and shall promptly transmit to the Negotiator all offers for Audio-Visual Production rights received directly by or on behalf of Author and shall disclose to the Negotiator any arrangements, actual or contemplated, between Author and any third party with whom negotiations may be pending for the disposal of the Audio-Visual Production rights. Moreover, Author agrees that unless Producer shall consent thereto, Author will not insist on any commitment or agreement with any such third party for Author's personal services as author, actor, director, or in any other capacity, as a condition of disposition of the Audio-Visual Production rights to such third party.

SECTION 13.02 **Conflicts.** The release date of the Audio-Visual Production rights production shall not interfere with either the Regular or Touring Performances of the Play. Such release date shall be fixed by Author, and Producer shall be given written notice thereof. If Producer files no objection with the Negotiator within 3 business days after such notice is sent, the release date will be deemed to be satisfactory to Producer. If within such 3-day period, Producer states in writing his reasons for objecting, the Negotiator shall give due consideration to Producer's objections and shall then fix a release date which shall be binding and conclusive on the parties.

SECTION 13.03 **Rights of Producer.** If Producer deems himself aggrieved by any disposition of Audio-Visual Production rights, his sole recourse shall be against Author and then only for fraud or willful misconduct; Author's refusal to grant the right to make a motion picture or other Audio-Visual Production remake, prequel, sequel or spin-off of the Play or of the picture or other Audio-Visual Production made therefrom shall not be a basis for Producer deeming himself aggrieved; and in no event shall Producer have any recourse, in law or in equity, against any purchaser or lessee of such rights, or against anyone claiming thereunder, or against the Negotiator, the Guild, or others who voted for the selection of the Negotiator.

SECTION 13.04 **Revues.** A separate song or sketch from a revue may be disposed of for Audio-Visual Production rights purposes only at the expiration of 18 months after the end of Producer's rights to present the Play hereunder. Author shall give Producer notice of such proposed disposition. If Producer, within 5 days after notice to him thereof, objects thereto, then the approval of the Theatrical Conciliation Council hereof shall first be obtained before such disposition can be made. Unless otherwise agreed among those constituting Author, Author's share of the proceeds (after deduction of Producer's share, if any is owing) shall be participated in only by the authors of the song or sketch so disposed of.

SECTION 13.05 **Rights in Case of New Producer.** (a) If the Audio-Visual Production rights have not been disposed of within 5 years after the date on which Producer has Vested in the Territory, and if a third party presents Revival Performances commencing after said 5-year period, then the compensation which Producer shall be entitled to receive from Author's disposition of rights in Audio-Visual Productions as provided in *SECTION 11.03(c)* herein shall be reduced in the following manner provided that Author pays the amount of such reduction to the producer of the Revival Performances: if the producer of such Revival Performances presents at least the same number of First Class Performances and at least the same number of Second Class Performances (counted separately) as Producer, Producer's share of Audio-Visual Production rights proceeds earned after the date on which such performances are equalled shall be reduced by 25%; if the number of First Class and the number of Second Class Performances (counted separately) presented by the producer of the Revival Performances exceeds by more than 150% the number of each such class of Performances presented by Producer, Producer's share of Audio-Visual Production rights proceeds earned after the date on which the number of Producer's Performances (of both classes) are so exceeded, shall be reduced by 50%; if neither of the foregoing occurs, then Producer's share of such proceeds shall remain unchanged.

(b) The foregoing reduction in Producer's share of Audio-Visual Production rights proceeds may occur only once, regardless of the number of producers presenting Revival Performances.

SECTION 13.06 **Defaults by Producer.** (a) If Producer is in default to a member of the Guild in the payment of compensation or other monies accruing from the production of the Play, the Guild may file with Producer and the Negotiator a memorandum to that effect, and the Negotiator shall thereupon withhold from Producer's share of Audio-Visual Production proceeds, the amount stated in such memorandum and shall forthwith notify Producer in writing thereof. Unless Producer demands arbitration thereon within 10 days after Producer's receipt of such notice, the Negotiator shall make payment to Author of the amount shown to be due in such memorandum.

(b) If Producer shall have furnished a bond, and the Guild shall have drawn on such bond because of Producer's defaulted obligations on the Play, and Producer shall have failed to replenish the bond after notice and demand according to its terms, the Guild may file with Producer and the Negotiator a memorandum to that effect, stating the amount so to be replenished, and the Negotiator shall thereupon withhold from Producer's share the amount stated in such memorandum, and shall forthwith notify Producer in writing thereof. Unless Producer demands arbitration thereon within 10 days after Producer's receipt of such notice, the Negotiator shall make payment to Author of the amount shown to be due in such memorandum.

(c) In either case, if arbitration is demanded, the Negotiator will hold the amount in question until the arbitration award is rendered and final and shall then pay such amount in accordance with the final award.

SECTION 13.07 **Prior Disposition of Audio-Visual Production Rights.** If Author shall have sold any of the Audio-Visual Production rights in the Play to Producer prior to entering into this Contract, then Author and Producer may not enter into this Contract until one year following the date of the agreement for the disposition of such Audio-Visual Production rights.

ARTICLE XIV
AGENTS

SECTION 14.01 **Employment of Agent/Commissions.** Author may employ an agent for the disposition of rights in the Play. The commission of such agent shall not exceed 10% of the amounts received from such dispositions except for Amateur Performances, for which the commission shall not exceed 20%. The commissions paid to such agents may be deducted from the proceeds of any disposition in which Producer shares before payment is made to Producer (except for Cast Album proceeds payable hereunder to Producer from which no commission shall be deducted and except in relation to motion picture uses from which the commissions may be deducted only if Producer has consented to the agent's representation of Producer as provided in *SECTION 14.02* herein).

SECTION 14.02 **Producer's Consent to Agent for Sale of Motion Picture Rights.** If Producer has not consented to the agent's also representing Producer with respect to motion picture uses, the agent's commission with respect thereto shall not exceed 10% of the proceeds of such disposition to which Author is entitled after payment of Producer's share, and shall be deducted only from Author's share of such proceeds. If Producer shall consent to the agent's also representing him, then the agent's commission shall not exceed 10% of the proceeds of such disposition and shall be deducted from such proceeds before payment is made to Producer. In either case, the agent's commission for motion picture uses shall be reduced in accordance with the provisions of *SECTION 12.07* herein.

SECTION 14.03 **Restrictions in Appointments.** In no event shall Author appoint Producer, or any corporation in which Producer has an interest, or any employee of Producer, or the attorney for Producer, or a member of a firm of attorneys representing Producer, as Author's agent or representative. No Author's agent or officer, directing head or employee of an agent shall, with respect to the Play, act in the dual capacity of agent and producer (the word "producer" as used in this SECTION shall include any person having executive direction or any stock interest in Producer, if a corporation, or who is one of the general partners of any partnership, general or limited) in connection with this Contract; and if he does so act, his agency shall be abandoned insofar as the Play is concerned, and he shall not be entitled to collect or receive any monies or commissions in connection with this Contract.

SECTION 14.04 **Payments.** All monies derived from the disposal of rights in the Play shall be paid to Author's agent, but only if the agent is the Dramatists Play Service, Inc., or is a member in good standing of the Society of Author's Representatives, Inc. Otherwise such monies shall be paid to the Guild which shall pay such monies directly to Author, agent and Producer as their respective interests shall appear.

SECTION 14.05 **No Deductions Other Than Agent's Commissions.** Neither Author nor Producer shall make any claim for commissions in connection with any disposition of the Play for any purpose; nor shall Producer be reimbursed by Author for any expenses or disbursements claimed by Producer unless Author, prior to the expenditure thereof, shall have agreed upon the repayment of such disbursements in writing and such agreement has completed the Certification Procedure described in *ARTICLE XVI* herein.

ARTICLE XV
THEATRICAL CONCILIATION COUNCIL

SECTION 15.01 **Theatrical Conciliation Council.** The Theatrical Conciliation Council (*"Council"*), an association of professionals in the theatre industry, shall meet for the purposes and at the times set forth in this Contract and at any other time, at the request of Author or Producer, to consider questions and problems that may arise from time to time during the term of this Contract (including without limitation any issue which may arise under *SECTIONS 4.02(d), 5.07, 8.10* and *9.03(e)* herein). Each submission to the Council shall be made in a writing describing the matter to be considered with a copy thereof sent to the other party to this Contract.

SECTION 15.02 **Membership of Council.** The Council shall be comprised of two groups of members, i.e. Author Members and Producer Members. Author Members shall consist of playwrights, who have had First Class Performances of at least one of their plays produced in New York City, and the executive director of the Guild. Producer Members shall consist of theatrical producers and/or theatre owners or operators, who have produced or presented First Class Performances of at least one play in New York City, or executive directors (or other persons holding similar positions) of theatrical producer/owner-operator organizations.

SECTION 15.03 **Members of Council.** The members of the Council shall be those persons listed in *EXHIBIT A* attached hereto.

SECTION 15.04 **Replacement of Members.** If a member of either group resigns, is removed in accordance with the by-laws of the Council, or otherwise becomes unable to perform his services, a new member, meeting the qualifications set forth in *SECTION 15.02* herein, shall be chosen by a majority of the remaining members of such group.

SECTION 15.05 **Action by Council.** Any decision or other action by the Council, as contemplated by this Contract, shall require a majority vote of all members voting in person at a meeting at which no less than and no more than 5 members of each group are in attendance. If this Contract provides, or if the parties have agreed in writing, that the decision of the Council shall be binding on the parties, then if the 10 members referred to above cannot be assembled within 7 days after the Council has received written notice of the matter to be considered, the matter may be submitted to arbitration by either Author or Producer in accordance with the provisions of *ARTICLE XX* herein. If the 10 members of the Council are assembled in a timely manner but cannot reach a decision within 7 days after all parties have presented their arguments in support of their positions, then, prior to adjourning the meeting, the Council shall select, by majority vote of those members present, a disinterested third party to resolve the dispute. If a majority of such Council members cannot agree on such third party, then the matter may be submitted to arbitration by either Author or Producer in accordance with the provisions of *ARTICLE XX* herein.

SECTION 15.06 **Binding Nature of Council Decisions.** If this Contract provides, or if the parties have agreed, in *ARTICLE XXII* or elsewhere in writing, that the decision or other action of the Council on a particular matter shall be binding on the parties, then once such matter is decided or action taken by the members constituting the Council on the date of such decision or action, neither of the parties hereto may resubmit the same matter to the Council at a later date for any reason including, without limitation, that the membership of the Council has changed.

SECTION 15.07 **Members of Council Held Harmless.** Producer and Author each represents and covenants (a) that neither of them will directly or indirectly undertake or threaten to undertake any claim, action or proceeding of any kind against any Council member in connection with the action or inaction of any such person in his capacity as a member of the Council or the Joint Review Board (as defined in *SECTION 16.06* herein) and (b) that Producer and Author will hold each Council member harmless from any liability in connection with such actions or inactions.

ARTICLE XVI
CERTIFICATION PROCEDURE

SECTION 16.01 **Submission of Contract to the Guild.** For the purposes of this ARTICLE, the term "Contract" shall include this Contract and any written amendment thereto. On the first business day following the full execution of this Contract, Author shall commence the *"Certification Procedure"* described in this ARTICLE by submitting two copies of the Contract to the Guild in order to obtain the Guild's opinion as to whether this Contract, as signed, conforms with or is reasonably equivalent to (as described below) the form of Approved Production Contract.

SECTION 16.02 **Standards for Certification.** If this Contract, as signed, does not modify any of the provisions of the APC, the Guild shall certify that this Contract conforms therewith. If, however, this Contract, as signed, does modify any of the provisions of the APC, the Guild shall certify that this Contract is reasonably equivalent to the APC only if:

(a) the modifications are reasonably necessary to counterbalance or neutralize special circumstances relating to or arising from the nature of the Play or its contemplated production, which circumstances could reasonably be expected to affect materially Producer's ability to (i) finance the Play, or (ii) return to investors their capital contributions within a period then prevailing for other productions of similar size and type, or (iii) obtain all the benefits to be accorded to Producer as contemplated by the APC; or

(b) the modifications consist of an increase in the 6% Post-Recoupment Royalty otherwise payable to Author under the APC, in exchange for

(i) a reasonably equivalent reduction or elimination of the Advance otherwise payable to Author under the APC and

(ii) an increase in the Post-Recoupment Royalty adjustment factor from 115% to 120% of Weekly Breakeven.

SECTION 16.03   **Response from Guild.**   Within 10 business days following the full execution of this Contract, the Guild shall notify both Author and Producer of its opinion by sending each of them either:

(a) one copy of this Contract bearing the Guild's signature thereby certifying that, in the opinion of the Guild, this Contract conforms with or is reasonably equivalent to the APC; or

(b) a letter advising that it is the Guild's opinion that this Contract neither conforms with nor is reasonably equivalent to the APC. Such letter must specify the reasons for the Guild's opinion and shall contain suggested revisions, which shall be set forth in detail and which would, in the Guild's opinion, make this Contract reasonably equivalent to the APC. This Contract shall automatically terminate 10 business days following the receipt by Producer of the Guild's letter unless, prior to the expiration of such 10-business-day period, one of the following events occurs:

(i) Producer sends the Guild a copy of this Contract to which is affixed a copy of the Guild's letter signed by both Author and Producer, thereby indicating their agreement with the suggested revisions, in which case this Contract as so revised shall thereupon be deemed to have been certified by the Guild as being reasonably equivalent to the APC; or

(ii) Producer submits this Contract and the Guild's letter to the Joint Review Board (as defined in *SECTION 16.06* herein) in which case this Contract shall continue in full force and effect, as signed, and the provisions of *SECTION 16.05* herein shall be applicable; or

(iii) Producer sends the Guild a letter signed by both Author and Producer amending this Contract to eliminate the automatic termination provisions contained in this *SECTION 16.03(b)*, in which case this Contract shall continue in full force and effect, as signed, notwithstanding the lack of certification. The signing of such letter by Author will be considered by the Guild as the tendering of Author's resignation from the Guild, which the Guild may accept.

If this Contract shall automatically terminate due to the operation of this *SECTION 16.03 (b)*, Author shall immediately return all Option Payments received from Producer, less a sum equal to the pro-rata portion of the Option Payment allocable to that portion of the Option Period measured from the Effective Date of this Contract through the date of termination, which sum may be retained by Author.

SECTION 16.04   **Guild's Failure to Respond.**   If the Guild fails to send Author and Producer one of the foregoing responses within the applicable 10-business-day period, the Guild shall be deemed to have certified that this Contract is in conformity with or reasonably equivalent to the APC.

SECTION 16.05   **Submission of Contract to Joint Review Board.**   If Producer or Author does not agree either with the Guild's suggested revisions or with the Guild's opinion that this Contract neither conforms with nor is reasonably equivalent to the APC, and if Producer and Author do not send the Guild the letter referred to in *SECTION 16.03 (b) (iii)* herein, then, in order to prevent the termination of this Contract pursuant to the terms of *SECTION 16.03 (b)* herein, Producer shall submit this Contract and the Guild's letter to the Joint Review Board (as described in *SECTION 16.06* herein) within the applicable 10-business-day period. The Joint Review Board, in making its determination as to whether this Contract conforms with or is reasonably equivalent to the APC, will apply the Standards for Certification set forth in *SECTION 16.02* herein.   Within 10 business days after its receipt of such documents, the Joint Review Board will send to Author, Producer and the Guild a written decision either:

(a) that this Contract, as signed, conforms with or is reasonably equivalent to the APC in which case this Contract shall be deemed to have been certified by the Guild; or

(b) that specific revisions, which shall be set forth in detail by the Joint Review Board in its decision, are required to make this Contract reasonably equivalent to the APC. This Contract shall automatically terminate 10 business days following the receipt by Producer of such decision unless, prior to the expiration of such 10-business-day period, one of the following events occurs:

(i) Producer sends the Guild a copy of this Contract to which is affixed a copy of the decision of the Joint Review Board signed by both Author and Producer, thereby indicating their agreement with the suggested revisions, in which case this Contract as so revised shall thereupon be deemed to have been certified by the Guild as being reasonably equivalent to the APC; or

(ii) Producer sends the Guild a letter signed by both Author and Producer amending this Contract to eliminate the automatic termination provision of this *SECTION 16.05(b)*, in which case this Contract shall continue in full force and effect as signed, notwithstanding the lack of certification. The signing of such letter by Author will be considered by the Guild as the tendering of Author's resignation from the Guild, which the Guild may accept.

If this Contract shall automatically terminate due to the operation of this *SECTION 16.05(b)*, Author shall immediately return all Option Payments received from Producer, less a sum equal to the pro-rata portion of the Option Payment allocable to that portion of the Option Period measured from the Effective Date of this Contract through the date of termination, which sum may be retained by Author; or

(c) that the Joint Review Board cannot reach agreement in which case Author shall have 5 business days, following receipt of the decision, to send Producer written notice that Author rescinds this Contract. If Author does not send Producer notice of rescission within said 5-business-day period, this Contract shall continue in full force and effect, as signed, notwithstanding the lack of certification.

SECTION 16.06 **Joint Review Board.** (a) The *"Joint Review Board"* shall consist of two persons (and two alternates) chosen from the then current membership of the Theatrical Conciliation Council. Promptly upon the submission of this Contract to the Joint Review Board, the Author Members shall choose one person and one alternate from their group, and the Producer Members will choose one person and one alternate from their group. The alternates may attend meetings of the Joint Review Board, but shall not cast a vote unless the designated member is unavailable to do so. All decisions of the Joint Review Board shall be made by agreement between the Author Member and Producer Member.

(b) The decision of the Board, pursuant to *SECTION 16.05 (a), (b) or (c)* herein, shall be final and binding on the Author, Producer and the Guild, subject to the right of Author and Producer to amend this Contract to eliminate the termination provision of *SECTION 16.05(b)*.

SECTION 16.07 **Expedited Review Procedure.** If Producer and Author agree that the review of this Contract contemplated by the foregoing provisions must be accelerated, they may jointly petition the Guild and, if necessary, the Joint Review Board, in writing, to render its opinion as promptly as possible, but in no event later than 5 business days after its receipt of the documents specified above.

SECTION 16.08 **Notices.** All notices and other communications to be given pursuant to the provisions of this *ARTICLE XVI* shall be in writing, addressed to the party receiving the notice at the address indicated at the beginning of this Contract (or such other address as shall have been designated by written notice), and shall be sent only by (a) personal delivery with receipt acknowledged in writing or (b) registered or certified mail, return receipt requested. Notices shall be deemed given on the day received (at anytime prior to 5 p.m. on such day) at the address specified for the delivery of notices.

ARTICLE XVII
Warranties, Representations and Covenants

Section 17.01 Scope of Warranties, Representations and Covenants. Author hereby makes the following warranties, representations, and covenants with respect to the Play.

(a) Author is the sole and exclusive Author, owner and the copyright proprietor of the Play and of all rights of every kind or nature therein, and Author has the right and authority to enter into this Contract and to grant the rights granted herein.

(b) Author makes such additional warranties, representations, covenants and indemnities, if any, as may be set forth in *ARTICLE XXII* herein.

ARTICLE XVIII
Claims for Infringement

Section 18.01 Conduct of Defense. If any infringement or interference with the rights of any third party is claimed because of the production of the Play, then Producer and Author shall jointly conduct the defense of any action arising therefrom unless either of them choose to engage separate counsel. In no event shall Author be responsible for any material in the Play supplied by Producer. Upon any suit being brought against Author or Producer alone, such person shall promptly inform the other of such fact.

Section 18.02 Expenses of Defense. If Producer and Author conduct a joint defense of any such third party action, they shall share equally the expenses thereof; however, if Producer or Author engage separate counsel, they shall each bear their own expenses. When Author writes the Play at the request of Producer from material supplied him by Producer and an action is brought on the grounds of plagiarism, then Producer shall defend the action at his own expense and pay all damages that may be found as the result of the plagiarism and pay any judgment rendered against Author on account thereof. If the act or omission upon which any claim is based shall be found to have been caused by either Author or Producer alone, then no part of the expenses shall be paid by the party not at fault, who shall be entitled to all legal remedies that may be available against the party at fault.

ARTICLE XIX
Termination

Section 19.01 Failure to Pay Royalties. If Producer at any time fails to make any Royalty payment when due (time being of the essence of this Contract) Author may, at Author's option, send Producer written notice to correct such failure or breach within 5 business days after the receipt of such notice. Producer shall either correct such breach within said 5 days or, if Producer disagrees with Author's allegations, Producer shall send Author written notice thereof within said 5 days and either party, or the Guild on behalf of Author, shall immediately submit the dispute to arbitration as provided in *ARTICLE XX* herein. The award of the arbitrator shall require the party losing such dispute to pay the costs of the arbitration plus the prevailing party's reasonable legal fees. If Producer does not, within said 5-day period, correct such breach or send Author the above mentioned notice, or if Producer does send the notice and the arbitrator determines that all or part of such Royalties should be paid and Producer does not make the payments due as required by the award within 10 business days after Producer's receipt of a copy of such award, then all of Producer's rights granted pursuant to this Contract shall cease, terminate and revert to Author upon the expiration of said 5-day or 10-day period, as the case may be, unless the Guild agrees to extend Producer's time to make such payment. If Producer's office or place of business shall be more than 100 miles from the place from which the notice is sent, then the notices set forth in this SECTION shall be sent by wire communication.

SECTION 19.02 **Failure to Produce Play/Improper Assignment.** All rights granted to Producer under this Contract shall terminate automatically and without notice if Producer: fails to produce the Play within the time and in the manner provided in *SECTION 1.03* herein; or fails to Vest prior to the expiration of Producer's production rights hereunder; or fails to make any Option or Advance Payment when it becomes due; or if Producer assigns the rights herein except as permitted in *SECTION 21.01.*

SECTION 19.03 **Effects of Termination.** If the rights of Producer to present the Play shall cease and terminate in the manner provided in this ARTICLE, Producer shall immediately cease dealing with the Play in any manner and shall forthwith return to Author all literary materials relating to the Play which are in Producer's possession or control, except that Producer may retain one copy of such materials, but not for commercial use or sale. To the extent that termination occurs due to Producer's failure to make any Advance Payment to Author, Author shall return to Producer all Advance Payments theretofore made.

ARTICLE XX

ARBITRATION

SECTION 20.01 **Obligation to Arbitrate.** (a) Any claim, dispute, or controversy arising between Producer and Author under or in connection with or out of this Contract, or the breach thereof, shall be submitted to arbitration pursuant to the terms of this ARTICLE unless Author selects other remedies as permitted by *SECTION 7.01* herein or unless otherwise specifically provided in the APC. The Guild shall receive notice of such arbitration and shall have the right to be party to the same. Failure by Producer to pay any amount claimed to be due by Author or by the Guild is evidence of a dispute entitling the claimant to an arbitration. Judgment upon the award rendered may be entered in the highest Court of the forum, State or Federal, having jurisdiction.

(b) All arbitrations shall be conducted in the City of New York before arbitrators selected from the Theatrical Production Arbitration Board herein created and in accordance with the procedures herein set forth except where Author and Producer agree to hold the arbitration outside New York. In such event, the arbitrators shall be selected from the panel of the American Arbitration Association and the arbitration shall be held in accordance with the rules of said Association.

SECTION 20.02 **Theatrical Production Arbitration Board.** The Theatrical Production Arbitration Board (*"Board"*) shall consist of 24 permanent members. 8 shall be chosen by the Guild Council (to be known as the *"Author's Slate"*) and 8 by a majority of the Producer Members of the Theatrical Conciliation Council (to be known as the *"Producer's Slate"*). Within 20 days thereafter, a majority of the 16 persons so chosen shall appoint 8 additional persons as public members (to be known as the *"Public Slate"*), provided such persons have never been a member of the Guild or produced a play or owned or operated a theatre. All such persons shall serve until replacement is required as set forth in *SECTION 20.03* herein.

SECTION 20.03 **Replacements.** In the event of the death, resignation, illness, incapacity or unavailability of any member, or if a member of the Public Slate shall produce or have a play produced or become a theatre owner or operator, such member shall be replaced by a temporary or permanent successor to be appointed in the following manner: by the Council of the Guild, if the vacancy is in the Author's Slate; by the Producer Members of the Theatrical Conciliation Council if it is in the Producer's Slate; by a majority of the members of the Author's and Producer's Slates, jointly, if it is in the Public Slate.

SECTION 20.04 **Rules.** The Board, by a majority vote of all members, shall have full power to establish such rules and procedures as it may deem necessary, not inconsistent herewith. In the absence of such rules, the procedure under this ARTICLE shall be in accordance with the commercial arbitration rules then obtaining of the American Arbitration Association, except as hereinbelow otherwise provided.

SECTION 20.05 **The Complaint.** The party aggrieved, whether Author, Producer or Guild (here-inafter referred to as the *"Complainant"*) shall file with the American Arbitration Association 5 copies of a written complaint setting forth the claim, dispute, difficulty, misunderstanding, charge or controversy to be arbitrated and the relief which the Complainant requests. A copy of the complaint shall be mailed by the American Arbitration Association to the party complained against (hereinafter referred to as the *"Respondent"*) and another to the Guild, if the Guild is not the Complainant.

SECTION 20.06 **The Answer.** The Respondent shall, within 8 days of the mailing to him of the complaint, file 5 copies of a written answer with the American Arbitration Association and the American Arbitration Association shall mail one copy to the Complainant and another to the Guild, if the Guild is not the Complainant. Where the copy of the complaint is mailed to a Respondent at an address more than 500 miles from New York, he shall have 3 additional days to file his answer. If no written answer is filed within such period, the Respondent nevertheless will be deemed to have entered a general denial of the allegations of the complaint.

SECTION 20.07 **Participation by the Guild.** The Guild may file a complaint and demand arbitration, with or without Author's consent; and Author, in such event, shall be a party to the arbitration, and shall not discontinue the arbitration without the consent of the Guild.

SECTION 20.08 **Selection of Arbitrators.** (a) Author, or the Guild, if it has initiated the arbitration, shall appoint one arbitrator from the Author's Slate and Producer shall appoint one arbitrator from the Producer's Slate. These two arbitrators shall be appointed within 10 days from the date of the mailing of the complaint to the Respondent.

(b) If either the Author or the Producer fails to appoint an arbitrator within 10 days after the mailing of the complaint as aforesaid, then such appointment shall be made promptly from the Author's Slate by the Guild and from the Producer's Slate by the American Arbitration Association. If the Guild initiated the arbitration and fails to appoint an arbitrator within said 10-day period, then such appointment shall be made from the Author's Slate by the American Arbitration Association.

(c) Immediately after the appointment of the aforesaid 2 arbitrators, the third arbitrator shall be appointed within 5 days by the 2 arbitrators to be chosen from among the persons on the Public Slate. The American Arbitration Association shall appoint from members of its panels any arbitrator or arbitrators required where for any reason appointment has not been made from the Slates herein provided for.

SECTION 20.09 **Power of Arbitrators.** The arbitrators are empowered to award damages against any party to the controversy in such sums as they shall deem fair and reasonable under the circumstances, to require specific performance of a contract, to grant any other remedy or relief, injunctive or otherwise, which they deem just and equitable. The arbitrators are also empowered to render a partial award before making a final award and grant such relief, injunctive or otherwise, in such partial award as they deem just and equitable. Subject to the provisions of *SECTION 19.01* herein, the arbitrators shall determine and indicate in their written award by whom and in what proportion the cost of arbitration shall be borne.

SECTION 20.10 **Special Arbitration.** If the Author or Producer demands an immediate arbitration upon a complaint by either alleging violation of *SECTION 1.02(c)* or *SECTION 8.01(a) or (b)* and 5 copies of the complaint are filed with the Guild at any time after 10 days before the date for which rehearsals have been scheduled, the arbitration procedure outlined in this ARTICLE shall be accelerated as follows:

(a) The arbitration hearing shall be held within 3 days after the filing of the complaint.

(b) The complaint shall be delivered or telegraphed to the Respondent by the American Arbitration Association. The Respondent must file 5 copies of his answer with the American Arbitration Association within 24 hours thereafter.

(c) The name of the arbitrator appointed by the Complainant shall be set forth in the complaint and the name of the arbitrator appointed by the Respondent shall be set forth in the answer. If either person so named shall be unavailable a substitute shall be forthwith named by Author or Producer, as the case may be. The third arbitrator shall be appointed by the persons so selected within 24 hours after the receipt of the answer by the American Arbitration Association. The American Arbitration Association shall appoint from members of its panels any arbitrator or arbitrators required where for any reason appointment has not been made from the Slates herein provided for.

ARTICLE XXI
Miscellaneous Provisions

Section 21.01 **Assignability of Rights.** Except as provided below, neither this Contract nor the rights granted herein to Producer shall be licensed or assigned by Producer without his first having obtained the consent in writing of the Author. Notwithstanding the foregoing, Producer may, without Author's consent, license or assign this Contract or any of the rights contained herein to a corporation, partnership or other entity of which any person comprising Producer is a controlling party or controlling shareholder or has a controlling interest, provided that any licensee or assignee shall assume all of the obligations of this Contract and that Producer shall remain personally liable for the fulfillment thereof in the same manner as though no such license or assignment had been made. A copy of any such license or assignment shall be filed with the Guild.

Section 21.02 **Obligations to Not-for-Profit Theatre Organizations.** Notwithstanding the provisions of *SECTION 11.04* herein, with respect to amounts owed to a not-for-profit theatre organization which has presented the Play prior to Producer's production hereunder, where such amounts are measured as a percentage of Subsidiary Rights income or Gross Weekly Box Office Receipts (or both), Producer and Author shall share such payments in the following manner:

(a) Subsidiary Rights income payments of up to 5% of 100% of such income shall be shared by Producer and Author in the same percentages as they share in such income;

(b) Gross Weekly Box Office Receipts payments of up to 1½% shall be shared equally by Producer and Author.

Section 21.03 **Inspection of Contracts.** Author and Producer shall each have the right to inspect contracts entered into by the other if such contracts would affect the inspecting party's financial interest hereunder.

Section 21.04 **Equal Employment Opportunity.** Author and Producer agree, that in connection with the presentation of the Play, they will promote equal employment opportunities in consonance with the artistic integrity of the Play.

Section 21.05 **Non-Applicability of APC.** The APC shall not apply to any agreement relating to the purchase of rights in the Play made on the basis such that no part of the consideration is contingent upon the production of the Play upon the speaking stage in the Territory.

Section 21.06 **Notices.** All notices given pursuant to this Contract shall be in writing and delivered either in person, by wire communication or by registered or certified mail, return receipt requested, to the party being notified, at the address first above written (or such other address as may be designated by written notice). A copy of all notices shall be sent (at the same time and in the same manner as the original notice is sent) to the Guild and to the persons, if any, specified in *ARTICLE XXII* herein. Unless specified to the contrary herein, notices shall be deemed given on the day received (at any time prior to 5 p.m. on such day) at the address specified for delivery of such notices.

Section 21.07 **Proof of Execution.** In making proof of the execution of this Contract or of any of the terms hereof, for any purpose, the use of a copy of this Contract filed with the Guild shall be sufficient provided that at any time after 2 years from the Effective Date, there may be produced from the files of the Guild, in lieu of the copy of this Contract originally deposited therein, a microfilm of said copy.

SECTION 21.08 **Counting of Business Days.** Whenever this Contract provides for the measurement of time by the passage of *"business days"*, Saturdays, Sundays and legal holidays in the Territory, and if applicable in any Additional Territory, shall not be counted. If such measurement is made in *"days"*, then only such legal holidays shall not be counted.

SECTION 21.09 **Binding Nature of Contract.** This Contract shall be binding upon and inure to the benefit of the respective parties hereto and their respective successors in interest and permitted assigns, but shall be effective only after having completed the Certification Procedure set forth in *ARTICLE XVI* herein.

SECTION 21.10 **Changes in Writing.** This Contract may not be amended and no amendment will be effective unless and until the amendment is reduced to writing, signed by the parties hereto and has completed the Certification Procedure set forth in *ARTICLE XVI* herein. This Contract may not be amended orally under any circumstances. Any attempted oral amendment of this Contract shall be null and void and of no legal effect.

SECTION 21.11 **Permissible Variation in Certification Procedure.** (a) If the following two conditions exist at the time this Contract is presented to the Guild for Certification, the Guild reserves the right to certify this Contract regardless of the terms contained herein:

(i) this Contract is entered into with a producer who has, after the date of the promulgation of the APCs, entered into a contract (or amendment of such a contract) for the presentation in New York City of First Class Performances of a play written by an author who, at the date of signing such contract (or amendment) was a member of the Guild, and

(ii) on the date of signing this Contract, such prior contract (or amendment) has not been determined by either the Guild or the Joint Review Board to conform with or to be reasonably equivalent to the APC (other than by reason of the Guild's failure to respond timely, as provided in *SECTION 16.04* herein, or the Joint Review Board's inability to reach a decision).

In such case, the Guild's decision to certify under the foregoing circumstances shall be final and unreviewable by the Joint Review Board, and the provisions of *SECTION 16.05* herein shall not apply to that certification.

(b) The foregoing provisions of this SECTION shall not apply if the prior contract (or amendment) was not in conformity with or reasonably equivalent to the APC due to, in whole or in part, the existence of provisions which were less favorable to the producer than those contained in the APC.

SECTION 21.12 **Severability.** Should any part, term or provision of this Contract be decided by the courts to be in conflict with any law of the state where made or of the United States, the validity of the remaining parts, terms or provisions shall not be affected thereby.

SECTION 21.13 **Applicable Law.** Unless the parties specify to the contrary in *ARTICLE XXII* herein, this Contract shall be governed by and construed in accordance with the substantive laws of the State of New York without reference to rules regarding the conflict of laws.

SECTION 21.14 **Counterparts.** This Contract may be executed in several counterparts and all counterparts so executed by all the parties hereto and affixed to this Contract shall constitute a valid and binding agreement, even though all of the parties have not signed the same counterpart. The Guild's certification of this Contract, pursuant to the Certification Procedure described in *ARTICLE XVI* herein, shall be affixed to any one of the counterparts signed by Producer.

SECTION 21.15 **Headings and Captions.** The headings and captions of the ARTICLES and SECTIONS of this Contract are inserted for convenience only and shall not be used to define, limit, extend or describe the scope or intent of any provision herein.

SECTION 21.16 **Pronouns.** Whenever the context may require, any pronoun used herein shall include the corresponding masculine, feminine or neuter forms.

ARTICLE XXII
ADDITIONAL PRODUCTION TERMS

(Producer and Author may add to this Contract certain additional terms provided that such terms do not conflict with or modify any of the provisions of this APC unless such provisions of the APC expressly permit modification in this ARTICLE. Examples of acceptable additional terms are the following: Rights to Present Developmental Productions; Revised Definition of Completed Play; Author's Billing Credits; Cast Album Provisions; Music Publication Provisions; Orchestral Score Ownership; Choice of Producer's Alternative III; Author's Travel Expenses; House Seats; Special Arrangements Among Persons Comprising Author; Merger of Rights; Royalty Adjustments for Repertoire Performances; Persons to Whom Copies of Notices Should be Sent; and Agency Clause. Modifications in the terms of the APC may also be made in order to counterbalance or neutralize special circumstances as described in *SECTION 16.02* herein.)

SECTION 22.01 **Division of Payments.** The division of payments hereunder among those persons comprising Author shall be as follows:

Author	Percentage Share
Bookwriter	%
Composer	%
Lyricist	____%
	100%

ACCEPTABLE ADDITIONAL CLAUSES FOR APPROVED PRODUCTION CONTRACT FOR
MUSICAL PLAYS

SECTION 22.02   **Additional Warranties, Representations and Covenants.**   (a) The Play is or will be duly
protected by copyright in the United States of America and Bookwriter with respect to the connecting dialogue,
Composer with respect to the music and Lyricist with respect to the lyrics have not done or omitted and will
not do or omit any act and, to the best of each respective Author's knowledge, no person has done or omitted
any act, the result of which could cause the Play to fall into the public domain in the United States or in any
country which is a signatory to the Universal Copyright Convention, the Buenos Aires Convention or the Berne
Convention. The warranties by Bookwriter, Composer, and Lyricist hereinabove set forth do not extend to the
Basic Work. Without limiting the generality of the foregoing, no publication will be authorized by the
Bookwriter, Composer, or Lyricist with respect to their respective contributions unless it be made a condition
thereof that the Play be duly protected by copyright in all countries that are members of the Universal Copyright
Convention, the Buenos Aires Convention and the Berne Convention;

(b) the Play will be written by the Author and is based on a story by   entitled

(c) the Play does not and will not libel, slander or defame or violate, infringe upon, conflict or interfere
with any rights of privacy or publicity or any other rights whatsoever of any third party;

(d) to the best of Author's knowledge there is not now and shall not be outstanding any grant, assignment,
encumbrance, claim, contract, license, commitment or other disposition of any right, title or interest in or to
the Play or any of the rights granted hereunder, adverse to or inconsistent with the rights granted hereunder
to Producer and the enjoyment and exercise thereof by Producer, or by which such rights, or their exercise by
Producer, or any third party pursuant to a grant of rights from Producer, might be diminished, encumbered,
impaired or invalidated in any way;

(e) except for material in the public domain, and the story   by   upon which the
Play is based there exists no literary, dramatic or musical material created by Author which is substantially similar
to the Play and as to which Producer has not acquired the rights hereunder;

(f) to the best of Author's knowledge there is no claim, action, suit or proceeding relating to the Play
pending or threatened before any court, administrative or governmental body;

(g) Bookwriter with respect to the connecting dialogue, Composer with respect to the music and Lyricist
with respect to the lyrics will indemnify and hold harmless the Producer and all others claiming by, through
or under Producer against any claims, demands, suits, losses, costs, expenses (including reasonable counsel fees),
damages or recoveries (including any amounts paid by Producer in settlement, but only if each respective Author
consents thereto in writing, which consent shall not be withheld unreasonably) by reason of that Author's breach
of any of the representations, warranties or covenants contained herein.

Producer will indemnify and hold harmless each of the parties comprising the Author and all others
claiming by, through or under each of the parties comprising the Author against any claims, demands, suits,
losses, costs, expenses (including reasonable counsel fees), damages or recoveries (including any amounts paid
by each of the parties comprising the Author in settlement, but only if Producer consents thereto in writing,
which consent shall not be withheld unreasonably) by reason of Producer's breach of any of the terms contained
herein.

SECTION 22.03   **Cast Album.**   Producer, with Author's consent (not to be withheld unreasonably), is
hereby granted the exclusive right to contract for the disposition of the rights to make Cast Albums of any
and all Companies presenting the Play hereunder. The proceeds received by Producer from the disposition of
such Cast Album rights, after deduction of such sums as are required to be paid by Producer (or advance by
the record company) such as the cost of the services of the cast and orchestra (including, but not limited to,
any percentages payable to performers and other elements reasonably required to be furnished by Producer for
said album) shall be divided 60% to Author and 40% to Producer. Author shall not be entitled to a share of
any investment made by the record company in the production. Author shall have the right to approve any
use of Author's name, likeness and biographical resume in connection with the said Cast Albums. Lyricist and

Composer shall arrange with the publisher of the music for a maximum limit for mechanical rights payments of 75% of the statutory rate for the Cast Album; however, the fee for mechanical rights shall be in an amount that is customary for such fees and will be in an amount satisfactory to both the Composer and the Lyricist.

(a) The record company will not in any way restrict the recording and release of an original cast motion picture or television production sound track album;

(b) Producer arranges for payment, accompanied by statements showing clearly and in detail the nature and sources of the royalties, to be sent directly to Author by the record company, and arranges that the contract with the record company shall grant to Author the right, at least semi-annually, to examine and make copies from the books and records of the record company relating to the Cast Album of the Play.

(c) The Composer and Lyricist have approval of the record producer and Author shall sign the Cast Album agreement.

(d) Composer and Lyricist shall own and control all small performing rights and publishing and recording rights in the music and lyrics.

SECTION 22.04   **Music Publication.**   (a) Composer and Lyricist shall jointly have the sole right to select and contract with the music publisher for the score and to retain all proceeds from the publication, mechanical reproduction, synchronization, small performing, and all other rights in the separate musical compositions in the score of the Play. The foregoing shall not be deemed to diminish Producer's interest, if any, in-proceeds from dramatic rights in the separate music and compositions. Producer and Bookwriter shall retain their proportionate percentage interests in dramatic productions utilizing the musical compositions regardless of whether the entire Play is used.

(b) The Composer with regard to the music and Lyricist with regard to the lyrics warrant, represent and covenant that the contract with the music publisher who publishes the respective music and the lyrics of the Play does contain or will contain provisions to the following effect:

(i) The music publisher has not made and will not make a contract that would interfere with the disposition of the Audio-Visual Production rights in the Play and that it shall execute, without additional compensation, such instruments and agreements as the Composer and Lyricist or the producer of the Audio-Visual production may reasonably request consistent with the contract or proposed contract that Author shall make or desire to make with such producer. The music publisher shall abide by any restrictions on music imposed in any agreement of the Composer and Lyricist regarding the disposition of Audio-Visual Production rights in the Play.

(ii) The music publisher shall grant to the cast album record company, video disc and/or video tape company contracted with by Producer of the Play, and/or Author and/or the purchaser of the Audio-Visual Production rights to the Play, such recording license as is usual and standard for such recordings upon terms and conditions satisfactory to Composer and Lyricist but without additional compensation therefor.

(iii) The music publisher shall make no disposition of the music and lyrics of the Play contrary to the restrictions set forth in the Approved Production Contract between the Composer and Lyricist and Producer.

(c) The Composer with regard to the music and Lyricist with regard to the lyrics agree that if Producer has Vested in the Territory, neither they nor their respective music publisher nor anyone claiming through them shall, without Producer's prior written consent, sell, license or otherwise dispose of the right to use any of the music or lyrics of the separate musical compositions of the Play (except in connection with the sale, license or disposition of rights in the Play as a whole), in connection or for synchronization with any Audio-Visual Production or commercial until the expiration of 5 years from the last performance in the United States or Canada of the Play hereunder, but after the expiration of said 5 years they shall be free to sell and license not more than one musical composition of the Play in connection with any Audio-Visual Production rights, production or commercial, *provided, however,* that no right shall be given to use any such composition as a "production number" or as a "grand use" (as those terms are commonly understood in the entertainment industry) nor shall any right be given to use the title of such composition as or in connection with an

Audio-Visual Production, and *provided, further* that if no Audio-Visual Production rights in the Play have been sold, licensed or otherwise disposed of by the end of said 5 year period, then the Composer and the Lyricist and their music publisher may deal in the separate musical compositions without limitation, subject to all Producer's rights to share in the proceeds therefrom as Producer is entitled to receive pursuant to this Contract. Anything herein to the contrary notwithstanding, the Composer and Lyricist also agree that they will not, before the end of said 5 year period, make any disposition of musical compositions which contain or involve the titled of the Play, the names of the characters of the Play or distinctive incidents, dialogue or phrases from the Play, except in connection with the sale, license or disposition of rights in and to the Play as a whole. Nothing herein contained shall be deemed to restrict rights customarily administered by the American Society of Composers, Authors and Publishers, Broadcast Music, Inc. or any similar organization, to license small performing rights throughout the world in the music and lyrics of the separate musical compositions in the Play. If at any time the Audio-Visual Production rights in the Play are sold, the restrictions on the use of the separate musical compositions and the titles thereof shall be superseded to the extent such restrictions are inconsistent with the contract between the producer of the Audio-Visual Production and the Composer and Lyricist (or their publisher).

SECTION 22.05 **Author's Billing.** (a) Author shall receive billing in all advertising and publicity issued by, authorized by, or under the control of Producer, excluding the theatre marquee, but only if no other name except the star's appearing above the title is on the marquee, so-called "ABC" and "teaser" ads and critic's quotations where only the title of the Play, the name of the theatre, and name of any star above the title appears. The name of the Author shall be at least fifty (50%) percent of the size of the type used for the largest letter in the title of the Play. Wherever the name of any person comprising the Author shall appear, all names of such persons will appear. The billing credit referred to herein shall be as follows:

"Book and lyrics by   , Music by

(b) Wherever, aside from theatre programs, credits are accorded in connection with the Play in so-called "billing box", and Author is entitled to credit, the size of both Author's and Producer's billing credits shall be determined by the size of the title of the Play.

(c) "Teaser" ads are any advertisements, including without limitation posters and billboards, which mention only the title of the Play, critical quotations and/or names of the theatre and/or any star billed above the title, and which do not mention any credits for Producer, Author, actors, director, designer and the like. It is understood, however, that Author will receive billing in the first run of window cards.

(d) No inadvertent failure to accord the billing credit herein provided shall be deemed a breach hereof, but such failure shall be remedied promptly upon written notice from the Author to Producer or any of the Authors.

(e) Bookwriter, Composer and Lyricist shall have approval of biographical materials issued by Producer as well as of the biography in the playbills.

SECTION 22.06 **Producers Acquired Rights to Musical Adaptation.** Producer has acquired the rights to do a musical adaptation of a story pursuant to   . Bookwriter, Composer and Lyricist each acknowledge he has seen and read the aforementioned agreements assigning the rights in the Basic Work (   ) by   and agree to such terms as they affect each of them.

SECTION 22.07 **Transportation and Living Expenses.** The reasonable hotel and travelling expenses to be paid by Producer to each person comprising the Author while away from their respective homes provided for in Section 8.04 and Section 9.08 shall be:

(i) One Hundred Fifty Dollars ($150.00) per day (if in England, the equivalent in English pounds; if in Australia, the equivalent in Australian currency, or if in New Zealand, the equivalent in New Zealand currency) for hotel and other living expenses during the rehearsal period and such other times as each is reasonably available and is required by Producer to be away from his home and

(ii) economy-class jet transportation expenses from his home and back and from place to place out of town when he is reasonably available and when such travel is required to attend rehearsals and tryouts.

The hotel and traveling expenses hereinabove set forth shall also apply to the San Francisco and Los Angeles productions of the Play.

SECTION 22.08 **House Seats.** For each performance of the Play under the management of Producer, Producer shall cause two (2) pair of tickets for adjoining house seats within the first ten (10) rows of the center orchestra section and five additional pairs of good orchestra seats, to be held at the box office for each person comprising the Author, which may be used by a designee of Author, to purchase at the regular box office price. The tickets will be held until twenty-four (24) hours prior to each performance, unless Producer's office or the box office of the theatre is informed prior to that time that Author guarantees payment thereof, in which case the tickets will continue to be held up to the time of performance. In addition, each person comprising the Author shall maintain and deliver to Producer at Producer's request such books and records as are required to enable Producer to comply with the house seat regulation of the Attorney General of the State of New York or other laws or regulation pertaining to allocation and distribution of house seats. Author acknowledges and agrees that the theatre tickets made available hereunder cannot, except in accordance with the regulations promulgated by the Office of the Attorney General, be resold at a premium or otherwise.

SECTION 22.09 **Developmental Productions.** (a) Producer shall have the sole and exclusive right to present Developmental Productions of the Play in the Territory on the terms provided in Section 4.02(e) above.

(b) Author shall have approval of the locations of such Developmental Productions, such approvals not to be unreasonably withheld.

(c) Author's consent to any financial terms that affect him shall be required.

(d) Author shall have the right to be present at the rehearsals and performances of such Developmental Productions, and to be reimbursed for his round-trip transportation and out-of-pocket expenses to said rehearsals and performances.

SECTION 22.10 **Force Majeure.** If Producer shall be prevented from producing the Play within an applicable Option Period, or if any production hereunder shall be interrupted, due to epidemic, fire, action of the elements, strikes, labor disputes, governmental order, court order, act of God, public enemy, wars, riots, civil commotion, illness of stars or any other cause beyond Producer's control, such as breakdown of the theatre's heating or air-conditioning systems, or any other cause, such prevention or interruption shall not be deemed a breach of this Agreement or a cause for forfeiture of Producer's rights hereunder, and the Option Period shall be extended for the actual number of days of such prevention; provided, however, that if any extension of the Option Period or any interruption of production due to any such cause shall continue for 3 months, then— Author shall have the right to terminate the applicable Option Period or Producer's right to resume production (as the case may be) by written notice received by Producer not later than 15 days prior to the effective date of the termination of Producer's rights, provided, however, that Producer shall have the right any time before such effective date of termination to extend the term of this Agreement for the Second and Third Option Periods (if it has not already done so), produce the Play, or recommence such production, in which case Producer's rights hereunder shall remain in full force and effect pursuant to the terms of this Agreement.

SECTION 22.11 **Notices.** Copies of all notices hereunder to Producer shall be sent to Tanner, Gilbert, Propp & Sterner, 99 Park Avenue, New York, New York 10016, Attention: Donald C. Farber, Esq.

SECTION 22.12 **Definition of Vested.** Section 11.02 above shall be deemed amended by the addition of Clause 11.02(a)(v), which shall read as follows: "Any combination of 10 Preview and Regular Performances, plus the Official Press Opening in New York City."

SECTION 22.13 **Agency Clause for Bookwriter and/or Lyricist.**   hereby appoints as his sole and exclusive agent with respect to the Play, and authorizes and directs the Producer to make all payments due or to become due to him hereunder, to and in the name of said agent, and to accept the receipt of said agent a full evidence and satisfaction of such payments. In consideration of the services rendered and to be rendered by such agent, said   hereby agrees that said agent is entitled to receive and retain as its compensation ten (10%) percent of all proceeds payable to him by the Producer hereunder, and said hereby agrees that his said agent is entitled to receive and retain ten (10%) percent of all other proceeds payable to him with respect to the Play (including but not limited to his share of proceeds derived from any and all subsidiary and additional rights, whether or not the Producer participates therein), except that with respect to proceeds derived from amateur performances said agent's commission shall be twenty (20%) percent. Producer hereby retains said agent and agrees that said agent is entitled to receive and retain as its commission ten (10%) percent of the Producer's share of all proceeds payable to the said   from the sale, lease, license or other disposition of subsidiary and additional rights in and to the Play, except that with respect to amateur performances, said agent's commission thereof shall be twenty (20%) percent. The foregoing shall not be construed to give the agent any commissions computed upon any share of monies or other proceeds from any first class production of the Play produced by the Producer in the United States or Canada or produced in the British Isles by the Producer alone or in association with a British producer, or produced by a British producer under a lease or rights from Producer hereunder. Any claim, controversy or difference between any of the persons constituting   and said agent, or the Producer and said agent, arising out of or relevant to this contract, or in connection with the Play, shall be settled by arbitration in New York, New York, in accordance with the rules then obtaining of the American Arbitration Association and any judgment may be entered in any court of any forum having jurisdiction thereof.

SECTION 22.14   **Agency Clause for Composer. (See 22.13.)**

SECTION 22.15   **Amendment of Section 4.04.**   Section 4.04 of the Contract is hereby amended so as to include the following in the definition of "recoupment":

(f) In determining whether the production costs have been recouped, there shall be taken into account as income to Producer all sums derived directly or indirectly from the production and presentation of the Play, including not only income from all performances and other activities controlled by Producer (such as souvenir programs and Commercial Use Products) but also, and without limiting the generality of the foregoing, any share of net receipts due to or to become due to Producer in connection with the exploitation or other disposition of any subsidiary rights in the Play in which Producer is entitled to participate pursuant to this Contract.

SECTION 22.16   **Amendment of Section 8.04.**   Section 8.04(a) of the Contract is hereby amended so as to include the term "designer" after the term "conductor" on the sixth line.

SECTION 22.17   **Amendment of Section 8.08.**   Section 8.08 is hereby amended so as to add the following provision:

The script referred to in Section 8.08 shall be a stage manager's script containing lighting, property plots and all other information usually contained in such scripts, provided that the delivery of such script does not constitute any statement of position by Producer with respect to the use of the script.

SECTION 22.18   **Amendment of Section 8.19.**   Section 8.19 is hereby amended so as to add the following provision:

Composer and Lyricist shall also (and they do hereby elect to) own the Scores, as that term is defined in Section 8.19 as well as the copyright therein, in the same manner and to the same extent as the music and lyrics.

SECTION 22.19   **Amendment of Section of 11.01.**   Section 11.01 is hereby amended so as to include the word "souvenir" prior to the word "books" on the second line.

SECTION 22.20   **Amendment of Section 11.05.**   Section 11.05 is hereby amended so as to add the following provision:

No deal will be made for a commercial use that will interfere with the disposition of the motion picture or television rights, and any disposition of the commercial uses will be subject to any motion picture or television deal.

SECTION 22.21   **Amendment of Article XII.**   Wherever the phrase "Audio-Visual Production rights" appears in Article XII, the following shall be deemed substituted in its place and stead: "Motion Picture rights".

SECTION 22.22   **Merger.**   (a) A "Merger" shall mean that circumstance in which all contributions of the Author shall combine and become a unified whole for the purpose of performance and disposition of subsidiary rights, and upon merger, no one element may be used or disposed of without all other elements (with the exception of publishing rights to the book, music and lyrics, "small performing rights" in the music and "grand rights". Merger shall occur when Producer has vested pursuant to Section 11.02 of this Contract.

(b) Notwithstanding anything herein to the contrary, it is specifically agreed and understood between the parties that, while it is intended that the provisions of this Contract with respect to merger shall control the exploitation of rights in the Play as herein provided, it is not the intention of the parties that the Play be deemed, nor is the Play, a "Joint Work" within the meaning of that term under the United States Copyright Act of 1976, and it is agreed and understood that for the purposes thereof, the book of the Play shall be deemed a separate work, the copyright of which shall be owned by the Bookwriter, and the music and lyrics of the Play shall be deemed a separate work, the copyright of which shall be owned by Composer and Lyricist, as their respective interests may appear.

SECTION 22.23 **Print Publication.** Notwithstanding anything contained in this Contract to the contrary, if the book of the Play shall be published in printed form separate and apart from the lyrics and music of the Play, the proceeds therefrom shall be retained solely by the Bookwriter. If the book of the Play shall be published in printed form with the lyrics of the Play but not the music of the Play, the proceeds therefrom shall be divided equally between the Bookwriter and Lyricist.

SECTION 22.24 **Reversion.** If the Play shall not be presented in accordance with the provisions of this Contract, subject to any further agreement among the individual Authors, all rights in the lyrics shall revert to Lyricist, free from any claim by Producer, Bookwriter or Composer; all rights in the music shall revert to Composer, free from any claim by Producer, Bookwriter or Lyricist; and all rights in the book shall revert to Bookwriter free of any claim by Producer, Lyricist or Composer.

SECTION 22.25 **Turnaround.** If the Producer's rights terminate or are abandoned prior to their expiration, Author shall have the option to bring a new producer to the project who will pay the underlying rights owner according to the terms of the present agreement with the Producer and the term of the option shall be extended for 12 months.

Signature Page For Approved Production Contract For Musical Plays
For the Play Entitled

_____

IN WITNESS WHEREOF, each of the parties has signed this Contract as of the Effective Date of this Contract.

Producer(s)*	Date of Signing	Author(s)	Date of Signing
_____	____	_____ Bookwriter	____
_____	____	_____ Composer	____
_____	____	_____ Lyricist	____

This Contract is Certified by the Guild in accordance with the provisions of *ARTICLE XVI* herein.

THE DRAMATISTS GUILD, INC.

By _____

Date of Signing _____

(If Producer is a corporation, the following must be signed by the person or persons in control thereof, i.e., the person or persons (a) owning or controlling a majority of its stock or a majority of its voting stock; or (b) using their name as part of the corporate title; or (c) rendering services in connection with the Play as Producer or (d) whose name is included in publicity advertising or programs as Producer or co-Producer of the Play.)

In consideration of the execution of this Contract by Author, the undersigned (if more than one, then the undersigned jointly and severally) hereby agrees to jointly be liable with Producer for the full performance of each and every covenant and provision of this Contract on Producer's part to be performed, including but not limited to the payment of all monies due Author hereunder.

_____

_____

_____

* Where the Contract is signed by a corporate Producer, the officer signing should state his office and the corporate seal should be affixed. Where the officer signing for the corporation is other than the President, a certified copy of a resolution should be furnished showing the authority of said person so to sign.

Where this Contract is signed by a partnership, all the general partners must sign and the partnership name should also be stated.

EXHIBIT A

**MEMBERS OF THE
THEATRICAL CONCILIATION COUNCIL**

Author Members	Producer Members
James Goldman	Richard Barr
Garson Kanin	Bernard B. Jacobs
Arthur Kopit	Norman Kean
David E. LeVine	James M. Nederlander
Peter Stone	Robert E. Nederlander
Stephen Sondheim	Harvey Sabinson
Terrence McNally	Gerald Schoenfeld

EXHIBIT B

Instructions to the Negotiator

Procedure to Be Followed in the Sale or Lease of Plays for
Audio-Visual Production

It is recognized that with regard to the procedure to be followed in the disposition of motion picture rights to plays, theatrical productions are divided into two groups, those completely or substantially financed by motion picture producers and those not so financed (herein referred to as "financed independently of the motion picture industry"). The distinction takes on significance where the disposition of motion picture rights is concerned. The significance lies in the fact that the producer who has motion picture backing (by reason of financial, employment or other contractual relations) occupies a dual position. He is both buyer and seller. As a result of this dual role, it is impossible for him, however strict and unexceptionable his conduct, to escape criticism. This duality does not exist, however, for the producer whose production is financed independently of the motion picture industry. You should bear this distinction in mind in carrying out your duties. It is suggested that you request every producer to make a voluntary disclosure to you of any relationship that he may have which conflicts with the basic relationship of being jointly interested with Author in the proceeds of motion picture monies.

The same possibility of conflict of interests may exist with respect to the disposition of any other Audio-Visual Production rights the proceeds of which are shared by the producer of the stage production. The principles set forth in this Exhibit shall apply as well, to the extent practicable, to the disposition of such rights and all references contained herein to the term "motion pictures" shall also be deemed to refer to Audio-Visual Productions where the context and industry practices appear to the Negotiator to warrant it.

I Plays Produced by Producers Independently
of Motion Picture Backing

You will offer Producer full opportunity to satisfy you that he is certain of his own knowledge that neither all nor any substantial part of his financial backing is directly or indirectly derived from any motion picture producer. You will not, in this connection, be required to exact any onerous legal proof of Producer, but will rely on your own best judgment, remembering, however, that the burden of proof is on Producer. In the event of Producer's electing to take advantage of this opportunity and of his satisfying you that no substantial part of the financing of the Play was derived from the motion picture industry, it is recognized that his interest in securing the highest price, or the best conditions of sale, or both, is identical with that of Author and that it is to Author's advantage to have the constant benefit of Producer's advice and experience throughout the negotiations of the motion picture rights to the Play.

In the event of Producer's refusal or failure to satisfy you as above, you will decide all questions of his participation in negotiations according to your own best judgment. As provided in *SECTION 13.03* of the APC, you are not to be in any way liable for the exercise of discretion.

The Producer having Vested in the Territory, you shall, upon request of either Author (or his agent) or Producer, call a conference between Author (or his agent), Producer and yourself to the end of fixing a price at which the Play may be offered for sale for motion picture purposes; and shall thereafter offer the Play for such sale at the price established.

If at any time during the negotiations for the sale or lease of the Play it is, in your opinion or in the opinion of either Author (or his agent) or Producer, advisable either to reduce or to raise the price at which the Play is to be held for sale, you will again call for a conference for the establishment of a new price. At no time shall the holding price of the Play be changed in either direction without affording Author and Producer full opportunity to confer. Any offer received by you must be forthwith communicated to Author, or his agent, and Producer.

It is desirable that the sales price shall be mutually satisfactory to both Author and Producer. In the event Author decides to accept a definite offer which is unsatisfactory to Producer then, except in the event of the contingency provided for in the second succeeding paragraph, the following procedure shall be followed: You shall forthwith advise Producer by telegram of the price, method of payment and release date. This offer may be accepted by you unless Producer shall, within 2 business days after receipt of the notice, advise you by telegram that the offer is rejected, giving his reasons therefor. If Producer rejects the offer he shall have a period not to exceed 5 business days from the date of the notification from Producer above referred to in which to submit to you a definite "better offer" which shall mean an offer (a) from a party of financial standing capable of making the payments set forth in the offer at the respective times therein provided for, (b) for a price in excess of that contained in the offer which Author is willing to accept and (c) on other terms at least as favorable to Author as those contained in the offer which Author is willing to accept.

If within the prescribed period of time Producer brings in a "better offer" such offer shall be accepted. If, however, the "better offer" is from Producer or an entity in which Producer has any financial or other interest, Producer shall so notify the Author of such offer specifying the price, method of payment and release date. The Author shall then have 10 business days from receipt of Producer's notice to try to obtain a "better offer" by offering the Play in the open market with the Producer's offer as a minimum. If within the prescribed period of time the Author brings in a "better offer", such offer shall be accepted, unless the Producer gives notice within one business day after receipt of Author's notice of an intention to make a higher bid, which shall be made within 2 business days after receipt of Author's notice. This bidding procedure may continue indefinitely until the highest acceptable offer is received. In the event Author and Producer do not agree as to whether or not the offer brought in by Producer is (a) from a party of financial standing capable of making the payments set forth in the offer at the respective times therein provided for, (b) for a price in excess of that contained in the offer which Author is willing to accept, (c) on terms at least as favorable to Author as those contained in the offer which Author is willing to accept and (d) from an entity in which Producer has no financial or other interest, then it is agreed as follows:

You shall have the right in your sole discretion (i) to determine said issue or (ii) to request the American Arbitration Association to appoint two persons who, together with you will constitute the arbitrators to determine said issue. If you by reason of your relationship with either Author or Producer or for any other reason whatsoever, occupy a position as a result of which you may not be able unbiasedly to determine said issue then, if requested by either Author or Producer or on your own volition, you shall request the American Arbitration Association to appoint three persons who, without you, will constitute the arbitrators to determine said issue, which determination shall hereafter also be referred to as a determination under (ii) hereof. The determination by you under the contingency provided for in (i) or the determination of the majority of the three persons referred to in (ii) shall be binding and conclusive upon Author and Producer. In the event alternative (ii) is adopted, the arbitration shall take place on two days' notice, Sundays and holidays excluded, and the cost of said arbitration shall be borne by Author and Producer in equal proportion. Except as hereinbefore provided for, the rules and regulations of the American Arbitration Association shall apply to any determination made under alternative (ii) but any determination made under (i) shall be made by you without any formal hearing. You shall have the right to make the decision under alternative (i) except in such situations where, in your uncontrolled determination the question involved is a close one.

The exception referred to in the second preceding paragraph is as follows: In the event Producer is associated with or employed by a motion picture producer or has been financed wholly or in substantial part by a motion picture producer or an officer thereof, then you shall not be obligated to offer Producer any period in which to bring in a definite offer in excess of that acceptable to Author, but except as aforesaid, the provisions of the foregoing paragraph shall apply.

If at any time during the negotiations for the sale or even after the consummation of the sale you or Author find any reasonable grounds for doubting the veracity of Producer's statement of his financial backing, you or Author shall forthwith report said doubts to the Council of the Guild and either Author or the Guild may then demand an arbitration under the terms of *ARTICLE XX* of the APC to establish the fact of misrepresentation, if any.

II Plays Financed by Motion Picture Producers in Whole or in Part

The phrase *"motion picture backer"* as hereinafter employed is construed as describing any film or television producer, subsidiary or affiliate or officer or employee thereof, contributing, in whole or in part to the financing of the stage production of the Play. The phrase *"motion picture backed producer"* as hereinafter employed is construed as describing any producer whose production is financed in whole or in substantial part by a motion picture backer, or a producer who has had a past or present executive employment relationship or other significant contractual or business relationship with a motion picture backer.

Such productions fall into three classifications, as follows:

(1) That in which Producer has in writing disclosed to Author, upon signing the APC for the Play, the fact that he is, or desires to be, motion picture financed;

(2) That in which Producer does not make such disclosure upon signing the APC, but makes it before the date of the Play's first full cast rehearsal;

(3) That in which Producer has made no such disclosure at any time but is not, at the time of negotiations for the Play's sale to motion pictures, able to satisfy the Negotiator of his complete independence of motion picture financing.

The object of such classification is to protect the interests of all three parties and to avoid the complications which result from motion picture financing of which Author is not aware.

III Procedure in Case Production Falls Under Above Classification (1)

It is desirable from all points of view that Producer whose production is to be financed by motion picture capital should, prior to the signing of the APC, disclose in writing to Author either the fact of such financing, or his desire or intention, to obtain such financing. When such disclosure is made and Author signs the APC, it shall be assumed that Author is satisfied with such financing and you will accord the motion picture backers the protection provided in the following procedure.

The Producer having Vested in the Territory, you shall decide when, in your judgment, acting as Author's representative, a holding price at which the motion picture rights to the Play are to be offered for sale or lease should be fixed and after full consultation with both Producer and Author you will arrange with Author to fix that price.

If the fixing of this price gives you any reason to suspect collusion between the motion picture producer and Author which might operate against the spirit and content of the APC or the interest of Producer, or Author's best financial interest, you will forthwith report your suspicions to the Theatrical Conciliation Council as a violation of the APC.

The price being fixed to your satisfaction, however, you will

(a) Immediately offer the rights at this price to the motion picture backer, with the stipulation that he shall have 2 days in which to accept or reject the price named.

(b) If at the end of said 2 days the motion picture backer, does not accept the Play at the price named, then the Play may be offered in the open market with the rejected price as a minimum, and no further opportunity will be given to, or bids received from the motion picture producer to meet or better any other bids from any other motion picture corporation in excess of the price rejected by him.

(c) If the Play is not sold in the open market at the price named, or better, you and Author may by agreement reduce the holding price one or more times. If you do so, however, the procedure hereinbefore outlined must be repeated.

If at any time following a rejection by the motion picture backer, Author and Negotiator elect to demand of the motion picture backer an offer as evidence of its interest in the property and the motion picture backer does not submit any such offer within one week after receipt of the Negotiator's request to do so, then the Play shall be considered free and clear of any obligation to the motion picture backer which financed it and shall be offered in the open market and no further opportunity will be given to, or bids received from, the motion picture backer to meet or better any other bids from any other motion picture producer in excess of the price rejected by him.

If the motion picture backer does so manifest its interest by making an offer, this offer must be submitted as a fixed sum, or a fixed sum plus a percentage of receipts, together with a summary of the terms of the proposed contract which shall be acceptable to the Negotiator. Author shall by the terms of such offer have one week after receipt in which to give notice as to whether Author accepts or rejects it. If Author rejects it, however, he may still use it as a minimum holding price at which to offer the property on the open market but no bid will be received from the motion picture backer in excess of such holding price. If, however, no offers are received in excess of this holding price, Author may, if he wishes, offer the Play in the open market at a sum at or below the price set by the motion picture backer and rejected by Author. In this instance, however, the motion picture backer will be free to file offers with you in competition with any other motion picture company and no bid from such backer shall be received in such competition in excess of such minimum holding price. But if Author receives a bid from any other motion picture company at the same price as that offered by the backer, the backer's bid (if kept open) shall receive preference, provided that the other terms of the contract offered by the backer are as favorable as those offered by the other motion picture company.

In all cases of such motion picture financed productions, you will at all times keep Author fully informed of all facts relating to sale or lease, including (but not by way of limitation) offers received, steps in negotiation, execution of the contract and consummation of the sale, but you will not reveal any such facts to anyone other than Author, and the Guild; and you will particularly caution Author against disclosing any such information to the motion picture backed producer.

IV Procedure Under Classification (2)

When Producer has made no written disclosure of motion picture financing upon signing the APC, but has made it between that date and the date of the first rehearsal of the Play, then Author shall have the right to choose between instructing the Negotiator either to follow the above procedure or instructing him to proceed as in the ensuing paragraph.

V Procedure Under Classification (3)

Where Producer has not at any time in writing disclosed to Author the fact of any motion picture financing, or cannot, at the time of the negotiations for the Play's sale or lease to pictures, satisfy the Negotiator of his independence of motion picture financing, or has received motion picture backing at some time after the date of the first rehearsal and prior to the offering for sale or lease, whether such backing is disclosed or not, then the Negotiator shall use his utmost efforts to secure a competitive open market for the picture rights to the Play without any of the advantages to the motion picture backer as set forth in the above machinery. In such cases Author, of course, will be doubly cautioned against disclosing any offers to Producer.

APPENDIX F

Collaboration Agreement

AGREEMENT made as of this   day of   , 19 , by and between   (sometimes hereinafter referred to as "   " or the "Bookwriter-Lyricist") and   (sometimes referred to as "   " or the "Composer").

WITNESSETH:

WHEREAS, the parties to this Agreement are collaborating on a Musical Play for which   will write the book and the lyrics and   will compose the music, which Play is at this time entitled

NOW, THEREFORE, the parties do agree as follows:

1. The parties agree that Bookwriter-Lyricist will write the book and lyrics and that Composer will write the music for the Play. The parties agree that they will jointly register and own the copyright in the music and lyrics. It is agreed that all receipts from all sources in connection with the Play shall be shared by the parties as follows: two-thirds (2/3) to   and one-third (1/3) to   . All rights in the individual musical compositions for the Play shall be held by   and   jointly and they (and their publishing companies) shall participate equally in the so-called "small performing rights" in the musical compositions contained in the Play as well as the publishing and recording contracts.

2. Each of the parties represents and warrants that the material written and/or hereafter written by such party for the Play shall be original with such party and shall not violate or infringe the copyright, common law copyright, right of privacy, or any other personal or property right whatsoever of any person or entity or constitute a libel or slander, and that such party fully owns and controls such material and all rights therein and has full right to enter into this Agreement and all production contracts and other contracts and consents to be entered into hereunder.

3. No contract for the production, presentation or publication of the Play, the music and lyrics, or any part thereof, or the disposition of any right therewith connected, shall be valid without the signature thereto of both of the parties to the Agreement. Both parties shall have approval of the Director of the Play. Bookwriter-Lyricist shall have all authors' approvals, except that Composer shall have approval of the Musical Director and Arranger thereof. Powers of Attorney may, however, be granted by one party to the other, by written instrument, setting forth specific conditions under which said Power of Attorney shall be valid. For services rendered under this Power of Attorney, whether in conducting negotiations or consummating a contract, no agency fee or extra compensation will be demanded.

4. Any contracts concerning the use of the Play for a first-class production shall be based on the Approved Production Contract of the Dramatists Guild, Inc., which is current and in use at that time, with any changes approved by Donald C. Farber, Esq.

5. Duplicate contracts concerning the Play, the music and the publishing and recording rights therein, including but not limited to the production thereof or the disposition of any rights in the Play, shall be given to each of the parties to this Agreement. Payments to each of the parties shall be made in accordance with the specific instructions from each such party.

6. In any contract for the production or presentation of the Play or for the disposition of any rights therein, the parties shall use their best efforts to secure the insertion in said contracts of clauses providing that on programs, billings, posters, advertisements or other printed matter used in connection with any production thereof or other use thereof in any manner, the names   , as Bookwriter-Lyricist, and   , as Composer, shall be in all billing credits, in that order, in equal size and prominence of type. It is further agreed that in no event shall either name appear as an author without the other name.

7. No change or alteration shall be made in the book or lyrics of the Play by either of the parties without the written consent of   . No change or alteration shall be made in the music of the Play without the written consent of

8. In the event that either of the parties to this Agreement wishes to sell, pledge, lease or assign, or otherwise dispose of or encumber his share of royalty interests, stock, or subsidiary interest, motion picture interests, foreign interest or the like, or any part or portion thereof (other than the small performing rights and publishing rights reserved to each), it is agreed that such party (called the "selling party") shall give to the other (called the "buying party") in a written notice with full particulars, sent by registered mail, an option for a period of fourteen (14) days during which the buying party may purchase such rights in said Play as may be offered, at a price and upon such terms as stated in said written notice. Should the buying party fail, within the said fourteen (14) days, to exercise said option in writing, or if the option is exercised, fail to complete the purchase upon the terms and conditions stated in the said notice, then the selling party may sell such rights to any other person, subject to the conditions set forth in the following paragraph.

Before the consummation of the sale to any other person the selling party must give the other party to this Agreement written notice containing the name and all conditions of the proposed sale to said third party and must give the other party to this Agreement ten (10) business days within which to match the said offer in all respects exclusive of any specific terms which would not be expedient for the other party to this Agreement to match such as the procuring of a particular star, director, etc. If said offer is not matched within the said ten (10) business days, then the selling party may complete said sale to said third party upon such terms and conditions, and a copy of the contract for the sale of such rights shall be sent to the other party hereto forthwith.

9. All expenses which may reasonably be incurred under this Agreement shall be mutually agreed upon in advance and shall be shared one-half (½) by   and one-half (½) by   . This also applies to any tax or assessment made by the Dramatists Guild, Inc., on the Play.

10. It is expressly understood that the parties hereto do not form, nor shall this Agreement be construed to constitute, a partnership between them.

11. Anything to the contrary hereinabove notwithstanding, the contributions of the respective parties hereto shall be owned by the con-

tributor thereof, and the written consent of both parties shall be required for any sale, license or other disposition of the Play, provided, however, that in the event the play becomes "vested" in accordance with the terms of the Dramatists Guild, Inc., Approved Production Contract (the "APC"), the respective contributions of the parties hereunder to the Play shall be deemed merged for all purposes in the sense that no party may deal with the Play or any parts thereof except as herein provided, and the term of this Agreement shall be co-extensive with the life of the copyright in and to the Play. In the event that the Play does not become "vested" in accordance with the terms of the APC, then this Agreement shall be deemed terminated and of no further effect and each of the parties hereto shall continue to own their respective contributions to the Play free and clear of any interest therein of the other party thereto. In the event of death of either of the parties hereto during the existence of this Agreement, then the survivor of the parties shall have the sole right to change the Play, negotiate and contract with regard to the disposition thereof, and act generally with regard thereto as though he were the sole author thereof, except, however, that the name of the decedent shall always appear as provided in Paragraph 6 of this Agreement, and the said survivor further shall cause to be paid to the heirs or legal representatives of the deceased party the agreed upon per centum of the net receipts of the said Play, and furnish true copies of all agreements to the personal representatives of the deceased.

12. Any controversy or claim arising out of or relating to this contract, or the breach thereof, shall be settled by arbitration by one arbitrator in accordance with the rules of the American Arbitration Association and judgment upon the award rendered by the arbitrator may be entered in any court having jurisdiction thereof.

13. The terms and conditions of this Agreement shall be binding upon and shall inure to the benefit of the executors, administrators and assigns of the parties hereto.

IN WITNESS WHEREOF, the parties hereto have hereunto set their hands and seals as of the day and year first above written.

_____
Bookwriter-Lyricist

_____
Composer

Option Agreement for Other Than a First—Class Production

This AGREEMENT is made and entered into as of the 1st day of June, 1987, by and between _____ , whose address is _____ York, New York, 10114 ("Producer"), and _____ , whose address is _____ ("Author").

WITNESSETH:

WHEREAS, Author has written a certain play presently entitled _____ (the "Play"); and

WHEREAS, Producer desires to produce the Play and to acquire Author's services in connection therewith; and

NOW, THEREFORE, in consideration of the mutual promises and covenants herein contained, and other good and valuable consideration, it is agreed:

1. <u>Representations and Warranties.</u>

Author represents, warrants and guarantees that:

(a) Author is the sole Author of the Play and that the same is original with such Author except to the extent that it contains material which is in the public domain and was not copied in whole or in part from any other work, nor will the uses contemplated herein violate, conflict with or infringe upon the copyright, right of publicity or any other right of any person, firm or corporation; and

(b) Author has not granted, assigned, encumbered or otherwise disposed of any right, title or interest in or to the Play or any of the rights granted hereunder. Author has the sole and exclusive right to enter into this Agreement and the full warrant and authority to grant the rights granted hereby.

(c) There is not now outstanding and there has not been any grant, assignment, encumbrance, claim, contract, license commitment or other disposition of any right, title, or interest in or to the Play or any of the rights granted hereunder to Producer or by which the exploitation of the rights granted to Producer and the enjoyment and exercise thereof by Producer might be diminished, encumbered, impaired, invalidated or affected in any way.

2. Indemnity

(a) Author will indemnify Producer against any and all losses, costs, expenses including reasonable attorneys fees, damages or recoveries (including payments made in settlement, but only if Author consents thereto in writing) caused by or arising out of the breach of the representations or warranties herein made by Author.

(b) Producer agrees that he shall be solely liable for all costs incurred in connection with any presentation of the Play and he shall indemnify and hold Author harmless from any claims arising therefrom.

3. Grant of Rights and Authors' Services

Author has delivered a complete draft of the Play to Producer and Author hereby agrees:

(a) In consideration of the sum of $500.00 as an advance against the royalty payments hereinafter provided, the Author hereby grants to the Producer the sole and exclusive right and license to produce the Play and to present it as a professional Off-Broadway or middle theatre production in the City of New York to open or before June 1, 1988. If before June 1, 1988 the Producer gives author notice together with payment of $350.00, the right and license herein granted shall be extended for the play to open on or before January 1, 1989.

(b) That he will perform such services as may be reasonably necessary in making revisions;

(c) That he will assist in the selection of the cast and consult with, assist and advise director, scenic, lighting and costume designers in the problems arising out of the production;

(d) That he will attend rehearsals of the Play as well as out of town performances (if any) prior to the New York Opening of the Play.

4. Outside Production Date

Although nothing herein shall be deemed to obligate Producer to produce the Play, Producer shall without limitation as to any other rights which may be granted hereunder, have the option to produce the Play as an off-off-Broadway or regional theatre production or a workshop or showcase presentation at any time prior to the Off-Broadway or middle theatre production. Unless on or before June 1, 1988 (or January 1, 1989 if the option is extended) Producer produces and presents the Play on the speaking stage in a regular evening bill as a paid public performance in an Off-Broadway or middle theatre in New York City, Producer's right to produce the Play and to the services of Author shall then terminate.

5. Exclusivity and Continuous Run

The rights granted to the Producer are the sole and exclusive rights to produce the Play (the Producer may acquire an option pursuant to the terms of this agreement as hereinafter set forth to produce the Play in the British Isles and in the U.S. and Canada and on tour), and the author agrees that he will not grant the rights to permit anyone to perform the said Play in any media (exclusive of movies) within the United States of America, Canada or the British Isles, during the term of the option herein granted and the run of the Play, or during the period that the Producer retains any rights or option to produce the Play anywhere in the United States, Canada or the British Isles, and further agrees that he will not grant the right to anyone to do a movie version of the Play which would be released during the term of the option or the run of the Play, or during the period that the Producer retains any right or option to produce the Play in the United States, Canada or the British Isles, without the written consent of the Producer, which consent will not be unreasonably withheld.

If the Play is produced within the option period herein granted, the exclusive right to produce the Play in New York City shall continue during its New York City continuous run. The Play shall be deemed closed (that is, the New York City continuous run shall have terminated) if no paid performances have been given in New York City for a period of 4 weeks. After the Play has closed and after all options to produce the Play shall revert to the Author subject to any other terms specifically herein set forth.

If the Play is produced outside the City of New York on tour or otherwise, the exclusive right to produce the Play after the option period herein stated shall continue during its outside New York City continuous run. Outside New York City continuous run as herein defined shall mean that there shall not be a lapse of more than eight (8) weeks between presentations of the Play before a paying audience outside New York City. If the option period has expired and if more than eight (8) weeks elapse between any such paid performances, then all rights shall revert to the author except those that may have been specifically herein vested.

6. Consideration

(a) In consideration of the foregoing, and of Author's services in writing and revising the Play and Author's agreement to perform services in connection with the production of the Play as herein provided, Producer agrees to pay Author such sums as may equal five percent (5%), (going to six and one half percent (6½%) on recoupment of the total production costs), of the gross weekly box office receipts of each production of the Play produced under Producer's management, license or control.

(b) Anything to the contrary herein notwithstanding if all other royalty participants, including the Producer with respect to the Producer's fee, agree to a waiver of one-half of his usual royalty, the Author agrees to waive one-half of his royalty, that is two and one-half percent of the gross weekly box office receipts, until recoupment of the total production costs of the production (less bonds, deposits and other recoverable items) on the express condition that: 1.) Each week's operating profits are paid directly to the investors as payment toward recoupment of such total production costs; and 2.) After recoupment of such total production costs the Author's royalty shall be in an amount equal to seven percent (7%) of the gross weekly box office receipts. Producer does hereby agree to such waiver of one-half of Producer's fee.

(c) If the Play is presented for a workshop or showcase production or in a regional or off-off-Broadway theatre Author will be paid a fee of $25.00 per performance.

The Author shall be entitled to inspect the books and records of the Producer for any production hereunder during regular business hours and upon reasonable notice, but not more often than once every six months.

7. Traveling Expenses and Per Diem

Author shall have the right to be present at any or all out of town performances of the Play up to the official New York Opening. The hotel and traveling expenses to be paid by Producer to Author in connection with such out of town performances of the Play, if any, shall be (i) $100 per day for hotel and/or other living expenses and (ii) economy air transportation expenses to and from Author's places of residence as indicated herein, and from place to place out of town.

8. Tours and Out of Town Productions

Producer's production rights hereunder shall be deemed to include "bus and truck" tours of the Play and other out of town (outside of New York City) production of the Play (whether first class or Off-Broadway type productions) provided Producer has presented the Play hereunder for not fewer than twenty-one paid public performances. For each out of town other than first class production, Author will receive notice within three months from the last paid public performance and a fee of five hundred dollars ($500) to be paid as an advance against royalties in the amount as set forth in paragraph 6(a) above. In connection with any such engagements, Author's royalties may be computed on the basis of Producer's receipts (including but not limited to fixed fees, guarantees, profits, rentals, and any Producer's share of box office receipts), but only if the following conditions exist in connection with such engagements or productions:

(i) that Producer's gross compensation, whether direct or indirect, for presenting the production is a fixed fee or a combination of a guarantee and a share of the box office receipts, payable to the Producer by a so-called "local promoter" or "local sponsor" or other third party acting in a similar capacity; and

(ii) that all other creative royalty participants' royalties and the Producer's management fee be computed on the same basis.

If the foregoing conditions in subdivisions (i) and (ii) hereof are not met, Author's royalties shall be computed on the gross box office receipts of any such engagements and productions.

It is understood that Producer shall have the right to present or license first class out of town productions whether or not Producer has exercised the Broadway option under paragraph 10 and that such performances shall be governed by the terms of the Approved Production Contract ("APC") as herein set forth in paragraph 10 of this Agreement provided, however, that the terms of this paragraph shall also be applicable.

9. Production in the United Kingdom and Ireland

If the Producer has produced the Play Off-Broadway or in a middle theatre in New York for not less than twenty-one paid public performances, Producer shall have the exclusive right to produce the Play on the speaking stage in the United Kingdom and in Ireland upon all the terms and conditions which apply to a New York production, to open at any time up to and including six (6) months after the close of the production in New York, upon sending Author written notice within two months from the close of the last paid public performance accompanied by a payment of one thousand dollars ($1,000) as a non-returnable advance against the royalties in an amount as set forth in paragraph 6(a) above. Producer may produce the Play in association with or under lease to a British or Irish producer. In such case Producer's obligation to make the royalty payments herein provided shall remain unimpaired. If it is to be produced on the West End in London, such contract between Producer and the British or Irish producer shall require the Play to be produced under the same terms as would apply if the original New York production had been produced under the Approved Production Contract for a first class production.

10. Broadway Production

Producer shall have the exclusive option, exercisable by written notice given to Author at any time prior to the later of, (i) the expiration of the Outside Production Date described in paragraph 4 hereof if there is no Off-Broadway or middle theatre production of the Play, or (ii) sixty (60) days after the last performance of the Play Off-Broadway or in a middle theatre, to acquire the right to present the Play as a first class production on Broadway in New York City. The time within which the foregoing option may be exercised shall be automatically extended if Producer acquires or exercises rights to produce and present the Play on tour or in the United Kingdom and Ireland under paragraphs 8 or 9 hereof, and Producer may then exercise such option at any time prior to sixty days (60) after the last performances of a British or Irish production, tour or other out of town performance under paragraphs 8 and 9 hereof.

In the event Producer elects to present the play on Broadway and exercise the option under paragraph 10(a) hereof, the minimum terms of the Approved Production Contract then in use shall become applicable and shall govern the relationship between Author and Producer with respect to the first class presentation in the United State and/or Canada, and the exploitation of other rights under the Contract.

If prior to the Broadway Opening, Producer has become entitled to a share of subsidiary rights in the Play pursuant to this Agreement, such Broadway production shall not affect, limit or reduce such Producer's share thereof and Producer shall continue to be entitled to receive such share irrespective of the number of Broadway performances of the Play and irrespective of anything contained in the Approved Production Contract to the contrary, provided that if Producer becomes entitled to a greater share of subsidiary rights pursuant to the Approved Production Contract, Producer shall receive such greater share, but not shares from both contracts.

In the event Producer shall elect to exercise the option in accordance with paragraph 10(a) hereof, then Author shall enter into and execute and deliver the Approved Production Contract within seven (7) days of Producer's submission thereof to Author. Notwithstanding the failure or omission of Author to execute and/or deliver the said Contract, it is agreed that upon exercise of such option, all rights in and to the Play which are granted and transferred to Producer by Author in accordance with the said Contract shall be deemed automatically vested in Producer effective as of the date of the exercise of the option, which rights shall be irrevocable under any and all circumstances except in accordance with the terms of the Approved Production Contract.

11. Force Majeure

If Producer shall be prevented from exercising any option hereunder, or if any production of the Play hereunder shall be prevented or interrupted, due to epidemic, fire, action of the elements, strikes, labor disputes, governmental order, court order, act of God, public enemy, wars, riots, civil commotion, illness or any other similar cause beyond the Producer's control, whether of a similar or dissimilar nature, such prevention or interruption shall not be deemed a breach of this agreement or a cause for forfeiture of Producer's rights hereunder, and the time for exercise of such option and/or the time by which the first paid public performance must take place shall be extended for the number of days during which the exercise of such option or presentation of such production was prevented; provided that if a failure to exercise any option or any prevention or interruption of production due to any such cause shall continue for sixty (60) days, then Author shall have the right to terminate Producer's production rights for the interrupted run or terminate Producer's right to exercise such option (as the case may be) by written notice to Producer.

12. Approvals and Changes

(a) No changes in the text of the Play shall be made without approval of Author. Such changes shall become the property of Author. Cast, director, scenery costume and lighting designers, and permanent replacements thereof of all productions of the Play hereunder shall be subject to Author's approval not to be unreasonably withheld. The Author does hereby specifically approve John Jones, the Producer, as the director of any productions of the Play in any media.

(b) In any case where Producer requests the approval of Author as provided above and the Producer is unable to obtain Author's response to such request forty-eight hours after having sent him a telegram requesting the same, or personally requesting the same, then Author's consent and/or approval shall be deemed to have been given. Author shall have the right to appoint in writing a representative to respond to requests for approval.

13. Subsidiary Rights

Although the Producer is acquiring the rights and services of the Author solely in connection with the production of the Play, the Author recognizes that by a successful production the Producer makes a contribution to the value of the uses of the Play in other media. Therefore, although the relationship between the parties is limited to play production as herein provided, and the Author owns and controls the

Play with respect to all other uses, nevertheless, if the Producer has produced the Play as provided herein the Author agrees that the Producer shall receive an amount equal to the percentage of net receipts (regardless of when paid) specified herein below received by Author if the Play has been produced for the number of consecutive performances set forth and if before the expiration of ten (10) years subsequent to the date of the last paid public performance of the Play in New York City, any of the following rights are disposed of anywhere throughout the world: motion picture, or with respect to the Continental United States and Canada, any of the following rights; radio, television, touring performances, stock performances, Broadway performances, Off-Broadway performances, amateur performances foreign language performances, condensed tabloid versions, so-called concert tour versions, commercial and merchandising uses, and audio and video cassettes and discs: Ten percent (10%) if the Play shall run for at least twenty-one (21) consecutive paid performances; twenty percent (20%) if the Play shall run for at least forty-two consecutive paid performances; thirty percent (30%) if the Play shall run for at least fifty-six (56) consecutive paid performances; forty percent (40%) if the Play shall run for sixty-five (65) consecutive paid performances or more. For the purposes of computing the number of performances, provided the Play officially opens in New York City, the first paid performance shall be deemed to be the first performance, however only seven paid previews will be counted in this computation.

14. Computation of Royalties

"Gross weekly box office receipts" shall be computed in the manner determined by the League of New York Theatres provided, however, that in making such computation there shall be deducted: (a) any Federal admission taxes, (b) any commissions paid in connection with theatre parties or benefits; (c) those sums equivalent to the former five (5%) percent New York City Amusement Tax, the net proceeds of which are set aside in Pension and Welfare Funds in the theatrical unions and ultimately paid to said funds; (d) commissions paid in connection with automated ticket distribution or remote box offices, e.g., Ticketron (but not ticket brokers) and any fees paid or discounts allowed in connection with credit card sales; (e) subscription fees; and (f) discounts provided to any discount ticket service (e.g. TDF).

15. Accounting

Within seven (7) days after the end of each calendar week Producer agrees to forward to Author the amounts due as compensation for such week and also, within such time, to furnish office statements of each performance of the Play during such week, signed by the treasurer or treasurers of the theatre in which performances are given, and countersigned by Producer or his duly authorized representative. Box office statements and payments due for productions presented more than 500 miles from New York City may be furnished and paid within fourteen (14) days after the end of each week, and for productions presented in the United Kingdom or Ireland, within forty-five (45) days. In cases where Author's compensation depends on operating profits or losses, weekly operating statements shall be sent to Author with payment.

16. Billing Credits

In all programs, houseboards, painted signs and paid advertising of the Play under the control of Producer, (except marquees, ABC and teaser ads and small ads where no credits are given other than to the title of the Play, the name(s) of the star(s) if any, the name of the theatre and/or one or more critics' quotes), credit shall be given to Author.

The name of Author shall be in type at least sixty percent (60%) of the size, boldness and prominence of the title of the Play or the size and prominence of the star(s) whichever shall be larger. No names except the title of the 16and star(s) or a director of prominence shall be more prominent than Author's name, and no names other than the star(s) or Producer shall appear above that of the Author.

Wherever credits are accorded in connection with the Play in a so-called "billing box" pursuant to which the Author is entitled to credit, the size of both the Author and Producer's credits shall be determined by the size of the title of the Play in such "billing box" and will appear only in the billing box.

No inadvertent failure to accord the billing herein provided shall be deemed a breach hereof, unless the same shall not be remedied promptly upon written notice from Author to Producer.

17. House Seats

Producer shall hold one (1) pair of adjoining house seats for Author or his designee, for all Off-Broadway or middle theatre performances of the Play in New York City, and two (2) pairs for each Broadway performances located in the first ten (10) rows in the center section of the orchestra. Additionally, Author shall have the right to purchase four (4) additional pairs of seats in good locations for Opening Night. Such house seats shall be held seventy-two hours (72) prior to the scheduled performance and shall be paid for at the regularly established box office prices. Author acknowledges and agrees that the theatre tickets made available hereunder cannot, except in accordance with the regulations promulgated by the office of the Attorney General of the State of New York, be resold at a premium or otherwise, and that complete and accurate records will be maintained by him, which may be inspected at reasonable times by a duly designated representative of Producer and/or the Attorney General of the State of New York, with respect to the disposition of all tickets made available hereunder.

18. Radio and Television Exploitation

Producer shall have the right to authorize one or more radio and/or television presentations of excerpts from Producer's production of the Play (each such presentation not to exceed fifteen (15) minutes) for the sole purpose of exploiting and publicizing the production of the Play, including presentation on the Antoinette Perry Award (Tony) television program and similar award programs, provided Producer receives no compensation or profits (other than reimbursement for out of pocket expenses), directly or indirectly, for authorizing such radio or television presentations.

19. Right of Assignment

Producer shall have the right to assign this Agreement to a partnership in which Producer or an entity controlled by Producer is a general partner; to a joint venture in which the Producer is one of the joint venturers; or to a corporation in which the Producer is one of the joint venturers; or to a corporation in which the Producer is one of the controlling principals. Any other assignments will require the Producers approval in writing.

20. Ownership of Copyright and Ideas Contributed by Third Parties

The Author shall control the uses and disposition of the Play except as otherwise provided hereunder. All rights in and to the Play not expressly granted to Producer hereunder are hereby reserved to Author and for Author's use and disposition. All ideas with respect to the Play, whether contributed by the director, or a third party, shall belong to Author. Any copyright of the Play, including any extensions or renewals thereof throughout the world, shall be in the name of the Author.

21. Limitations on Use of Costume and Scenery Designs

Pursuant to the rules and regulations of the United Scenic Artists, Designing Artists and Theatrical Costume Designers' Contract, Author undertakes and agrees that he will not sell, lease, license or authorize the use of any of the original designs of scenery and costumes created by the designers under the standard Scenic Designing Artists and Theatrical Costume Designing Contracts for the productions, without the designer's consent to Producer's consent.

22. Notices

Any notice to be given hereunder shall be sent by registered or certified mail, return receipt requested, or telegraph or cable addressed to the parties at their respective addresses given herein, or by delivering the same personally to the parties at the addresses first set forth herein. Any party may designate a different address by notice so given. Copies of all notices shall be sent to: Tanner Gilbert Propp & Sterner, 99 Park Avenue, New York, New York 10016, Attention: Donald C. Farber, Esq.

23. Arbitration

Any dispute or controversy arising under, out of, or in connection with this Agreement or the making or validity thereof, its interpretation or any breach thereof, shall be determined and settled by arbitration by one arbitrator who shall be selected by mutual agreement of the parties hereto, in New York City, pursuant to the Rules of the American Arbitration Association. The arbitrator is directed to award to the prevailing party reasonable attorneys' fees, costs and disbursements, including reimbursement for the cost of witnesses, travel and subsistence during the arbitration hearings. Any award rendered shall be final and conclusive upon the parties and a judgment thereon may be entered by the appropriate court of the forum having jurisdiction.

24. Applicable Law, Entire Agreement

This Agreement shall be deemed to have been made in New York, New York and shall be governed by New York law applicable to agreements duly executed and to be performed wholly within the State of New York. This Agreement shall be the complete and binding agreement between the parties and may not be amended except by an agreement in writing signed by the parties hereto.

25. Successors and Assigns

The terms and conditions of this Agreement shall be binding upon the respective executors, administrators, successors and assigns of the parties hereto, provided, however, that none of the parties hereto shall, except as otherwise herein provided, have the right, without the written consent of the parties, to assign his or her rights or obligations hereunder, except the right to receive the share of the proceeds, if any, from the Play, payable to such party hereunder.

IN WITNESS WHEREOF, the parties hereto have hereunto set their hands the day and year first above written.

_____

Producer

_____

Author

Appendix H

Limited Partnership Agreement

LIMITED PARTNERSHIP AGREEMENT*
OF
THE GRAND LIMITED PARTNERSHIP

BILL BOE

General Partner,

with a capitalization of $650,000

to finance, produce and present in an Off-Broadway
(including so-called "Middle") theatre a
musical play presently entitled

GRAND GRAND

---

*The dollar amounts, the time periods, and percentages set forth in this sample agreement are typical.

LIMITED PARTNERSHIP AGREEMENT
OF
THE GRAND LIMITED PARTNERSHIP

Agreement of Limited Partnership made this 1st day of June 1987, by and among Bill Boe residing at 321 Sailen Court New York, N.Y 12334 as general partner, and such parties who from time to time execute this Agreement as limited partners.

WITNESSETH:

WHEREAS, the parties hereto desire to form a limited partnership under and subject to the laws of the State of New York; and

WHEREAS, the parties desire to enter into an Agreement of Limited Partnership to express the terms and conditions of such limited partnership and their respective rights and obligations with respect thereto;

NOW, THEREFORE, in consideration of the foregoing and of the mutual covenants and conditions herein contained, and other good and valuable consideration, receipt of which is hereby acknowledged by each party to the others, the parties hereto, for themselves, their respective heirs, executors, administrators, successors and assigns, hereby agree as follows:

ONE: The following terms as used herein shall have the following meanings:

(a) "Additional Limited Partner" shall mean any person admitted to the Partnership subsequent to the formation thereof.

(b) "Agreement" shall mean the Agreement of Limited Partnership, as set forth herein and as amended from time to time, as the context requires. Words such as "herein," hereinafter," "hereof," "hereby," and "hereunder," when used with reference to this Agreement, refer to this Agreement as a whole, unless the context otherwise requires.

(c) "Author" shall mean the following persons, collectively: (i) the composer of the original music and the author of the libretto for the Play, Jack Jack and (ii) the lyricist for the Play, Helen Helen.

(d) "Bankruptcy" as to any Person shall mean the filing of a petition for relief as to any such Person as debtor or bankrupt under the Bankruptcy Act of 1898 or the Bankruptcy Code of 1978 or like provision of law (except if such petition is contested by such Person and has been dismissed within 90 days); insolvency of such Person as finally determined by a court proceeding; filing by such Person of a petition of application to accomplish the same or for the appointment of a receiver or a trustee for such Person or a substantial part of his assets; or commencement of any proceedings relating to such Person under any reorganization, arrangement, insolvency, adjustment of debt or liquidation law of any jurisdiction, whether now in existence or hereinafter in effect, either by such person or by another, provided that if such proceeding is commenced by another, such Person indicates his approval of such proceeding, consents thereby or acquiesces therein, or such proceeding is contested by such Person and has not been finally dismissed within 90 days.

(e) "Capital Contribution" shall mean the total amount of money contributed to the Partnership by a Limited Partner in return for a share of the Partnership's Net Profits as more fully described herein.

(f) "Expenses" shall mean contingent expenses and liabilities, as well as unmatured expenses and liabilities, and until the final determination thereof, the General Partner shall have the absolute right to establish, as the amount thereof, such sums as he, in his sole discretion, shall deem advisable.

(g) "General Partner" shall mean Bill Boe whose residence address is 321 Sailen Court New York 12334, or any person who, at the time of reference thereto, has been admitted as a successor to the interest of Bill Boe or as an additional General Partner, in each such Person's capacity as a General Partner.

(h) "Gross Receipts" shall mean all sums derived by the Partnership from any source whatsoever from the exploitation or turning to account of its rights in the Play (which shall be acquired from the General Partner upon formation of the Partnership), including all proceeds derived by the Partnership from the liquidation of the physical production of the Play at the conclusion of the run thereof, and from the return of bonds and other recoverable items included in the Production Expenses.

(i) "Interests" shall mean the securities offered hereunder, which in the aggregate shall entitle the owner or owners thereof to fifty percent (50%) of the Net Profits of the Partnership. A Limited Partner purchasing Interests shall be entitled to receive the ratio of fifty percent (50%) of the Net Profits which his Capital Contribution bears to the

Total Capitalization [eg. a Capital Contribution in the sum of $13,000 would give a Limited Partner an Interest entitling him to one percent (1%) of the Net Profits].

(j) "Limited Partner" shall mean any Person who is a limited partner of the Partnership at the time of reference thereto, in such person's capacity as a Limited Partner.

(k) "Net Profits" shall mean the excess of Gross Receipts over all Production Expenses, Running Expenses and Other Expenses. This shall include any Production Expenses incurred or paid out by the General Partner prior to the inception of the Partnership, for which the General Partner shall be reimbursed upon Total Capitalization.

(l) "Notice" shall mean a writing, containing the information required by this Agreement to be communicated to any Person, personally delivered to such Person or sent by registered or certified mail, postage prepaid, to such Person at the last known address of such Person. The date of personal delivery or the date of mailing thereof, as the case may be, shall be deemed the date of receipt of Notice.

(m) "Offering Circular" shall mean the offering circular required to be filed with the Securities and Exchange Commission ("SEC") together with Form 1A, and relevant exhibits, for a general exemption from registration of these Interests under the Securities Act of 1933, as same may be amended.

(n) "Option Period" shall mean the term commencing June 1, 1987 and ending one (1) year therefrom (June 1, 1988) unless extended by the General Partner for a period of six (6) months thereafter (until (December 1, 1988) pursuant to the terms of the Production Contract to be assigned to the Partnership upon its formation, a copy of which Production Contract may be examined at the offices of counsel for the Partnership, Tanner Gilbert Propp & Sterner, 99 Park Avenue, New York, New York 10016, (212) 986-7714 ("Legal Counsel").

(o) "Other Expenses" shall mean all expenses of whatsoever kind or nature other than Production Expenses and Running Expenses actually and reasonably incurred in connection with the operation of the business of the Partnership, including, but without limiting the foregoing, commissions paid to agents, and monies paid or payable in connection with claims for plagiarism, libel and negligence.

(p) "Partnership" shall mean the limited partnership formed pursuant to this Agreement as such limited partnership may from time to time be constituted.

(q) "Person" shall mean any individual, general partnership, limited partnership, corporation, joint venture, trust, business trust, cooperative or association and the heirs, executors, administrators, successors and assigns thereof, where the context so admits. All pronouns and any variations thereof used herein shall be deemed to refer to the masculine, feminine, neuter, singular or plural, as the identity of the Person referred to may require.

(r) "Play" shall mean a new musical play written by the Author and presently entitled GRAND GRAND.

(s) "Production Contract" shall mean the agreement dated May 1, 1986 between the General Partner (as "Producer") and Author, pursuant to which the General Partner has acquired and will assign to the Partnership upon its formation certain theatrical stage production rights in and to the Play, and certain other and subsidiary rights therein (see the definition of "Option Period" herein).

(t) "Production Expenses" shall mean fees of the director, choreographer, designers, orchestrator, cost of sets, curtains, drapes, costumes, properties, furnishings, electrical equipment, premiums for bonds and insurance, cash deposits with Actors' Equity Association or other similar organizations by which, according to custom or usual practices of the theatrical business, such deposits may be required to be made, advances to the Author, rehearsal charges and expenses, transportation charges, cash office charges, reasonable legal and auditing expenses, advance publicity, theatre costs and expenses, and all other expenses and losses of whatever kind (other than expenditures precluded hereunder) actually incurred in connection with the production of the Play preliminary to the official opening of the Play. The General Partner has heretofore incurred or paid, and, prior to the inception of the Partnership, may incur or pay further Production Expenses as herein set forth, and the amount thereof, and no more, shall be included in the Production Expenses of the Partnership, and upon Total Capitalization the General Partner shall be reimbursed for the expenses so paid by him.

(u) "Running Expenses" shall mean all expenses, charges and disbursements of whatever kind actually incurred in connection with the operation of the Play, including without limiting the generality of the foregoing, royalties and/or other compensation to or for the Author, business and general managers, director, choreographer, orchestrator, cast, stage help, transportation, cash office charge, reasonable legal and auditing expenses, theatre operating expenses, and all other expenses and losses of whatever kind actually incurred in connection with the operation of the Play, as well as taxes of whatever kind and nature other than taxes on the income of the respective Limited Partners and General Partner. Such Running Expenses shall include, without limitation, payments made in the form of Gross Receipts as well as participations in Net Profits to or for any of the aforementioned Persons, services or rights.

(v) "Total Capitalization" shall mean receipt by the Partnership of Capital Contributions totalling $650,000.

(w) "Unit" shall mean an Interest equal to a one percent (1%) share of the Net Profits of the Partnership sold to a subscriber in return for his Capital Contribution of $13,000. Fractional Units may be sold. The Partnership intends to offer for sale a total of fifty (50) Units.

TWO: (a) The parties hereto hereby form a limited partnership pursuant to the provisions of the New York Partnership Law. The Partnership shall conduct its business and promote the purposes stated herein under the name "The Grand Grand Limited Partnership," or such other name or names as the General Partner from time to time may select. The address of the principal office of the Partnership shall be c/o Sam Andersam 665 West 45th Street, New York, New York 10018; telephone number (212) 333-4444, or such other place or places as the General Partner may select. Notice of any change in the Partnership's principal office shall be given to the Limited Partners.

(b) Except as otherwise provided herein, the purpose of the Partnership shall be to produce and present the Play in an Off-Broadway or Middle theatre in New York City, to open on or about March 1, 1986 or before the expiration of the Option Period, as same may be extended, and otherwise to produce and present the Play and exploit and turn to account the rights at any time held by the Partnership in connection with the production and presentation of the Play pursuant to the Production contract.

THREE The Partnership shall commence on the date on which, pursuant to the New York Partnership Law, a duly executed Certificate of Limited Partnership is filed in the Office of the Clerk of New York County, which Certificate shall be filed after the execution of this Agreement by the General Partner and at least one Limited Partner. Amendments to the Certificate of Limited Partnership, if any, shall be filed expeditiously with the Office of the Clerk of New York County reflecting the identities of any Additional Limited Partners and their Capital Contributions as well as any other changes required to be reflected in such amended Certificate.

(b) The Partnership shall terminate upon the occurrence of any of the following: (i) the Bankruptcy, death, insanity or resignation of the individual General Partner and the dissolution, cessation of business or Bankruptcy of the corporate General Partner, if any; (ii) the expiration of all of the Partnership's right, title and interest in the Play; (iii) a date fixed by the General Partner after abandonment of all further Partnership activities; or (iv) any other event causing the dissolution of the Partnership under the laws of the State of New York. Notwithstanding the foregoing, the Partnership shall not be dissolved upon the occurrence of the Bankruptcy, death, dissolution or withdrawal or adjudication of incompetence of a General Partner if any of the remaining Persons constituting the General Partner elects within 30 days after such an event to continue the business of the Partnership.

(c) Dissolution of the Partnership shall be effective on the day on which the event occurs giving rise to the dissolution, but the Partnership shall not terminate until a Certificate of Dissolution shall be filed in the State of New York, County of New York and the assets of the Partnership shall have been distributed as provided herein. Notwithstanding the dissolution of the Partnership, prior to the termination of the Partnership the business of the Partnership shall continue to be governed by this Agreement.

FOUR: (a) The Total Capitalization has been established on the basis of the estimated production requirements for the production of the Play as described above, and is an amount which in the opinion of the General Partner shall be sufficient to mount the production of the Play in an Off-Broadway theatre containing approximately 499 seats. The partnership intends and hereby authorizes the General Partner to sell and issue a total of fifty (50) Units and to admit as Limited Partners and Additional Limited Partners those Persons whose Capital Contributions have been accepted by the General Partner in accordance with this Agreement. Each Limited Partner and Additional Limited Partner shall contribute to the capital of the Partnership the sum set forth as his contribution opposite his signature affixed to the Subscription Form annexed hereto. The Capital Contribution of each Limited Partner shall be payable at the time of his execution and delivery to the General Partner of the Agreement. Capital Contributions will be used for payment of all expenses incurred in connection with the production and presentation of the Play. All persons whose Capital Contributions and subscriptions are accepted by the General Partner shall be deemed to be Limited Partners.

(b) If fifty (50) Units are not sold prior to the expiration of the Option Period, the General Partner shall terminate the offering hereunder, and all Capital Contributions shall be returned to the subscribers thereof, with accrued interest, if any, except to the extent utilized by consent of individual subscribers who have waived their right of refund.

(c) No Limited Partner will be required to contribute any additional funds to the Partnership above his initial Capital Contribution.

(d) If the Expenses actually incurred shall exceed the Total Capitalization, the General Partner may, by making contributions himself, by obtaining additional funds from the Limited Partners, or by making loans to the Partnership, make available to the Partnership such sums as shall equal the excess, but such additional contributions or loans shall not have the effect of reducing the share of Net Profits payable to the Limited Partners. If, however, any such loans are made to the Partnership, such loans shall be entitled to be repaid in full, without interest, prior to the return of any Capital Contributions to the Limited Partners.

(e) Unless otherwise provided herein, the General Partner shall have sole discretion in establishing the conditions of the offering and sale of Units; and the General Partner is hereby authorized and directed to take whatever action he deems necessary, convenient, appropriate or desirable in connection therewith, including, but not limited to, the preparation and filing on behalf of the Partnership of an offering circular with the SEC and the securities commissions (or similar agencies) of those states and jurisdictions which the General Partner shall deem necessary.

FIVE: Subject to the provisions of Paragraphs NINETEEN, hereof, the General Partner will, upon the organization of the Partnership, assign to the Partnership all right, title and interest in all assets acquired by him for the presentation of the Play, for which he will be reimbursed by the Partnership upon Total Capitalization, for his actual expenditures in acquiring such assets, and the Partnership will assume all of the General Partner's obligations under any agreements respecting such assets.

SIX: After payment or reasonable provision for payment of all debts, liabilities, taxes and contingent liabilities of the Partnership, and after provision for a reserve in the amount of $100,000, all remaining cash shall be distributed at least annually to the Limited Partners together with the statement of operation herein provided for, pro-rata, until their Capital Contributions to the Partnership shall have been repaid. Thereafter, all cash in excess of such contingent liabilities shall be paid to the General Partner and Limited Partners in the same proportion in which they shall share in the Net Profits.

SEVEN: The Net Profits that may accrue from the business of the Partnership shall be distributed and divided among the General Partner and Limited Partners as follows:

(a) The Capital Contributions of the Limited Partners shall first be repaid as provided above.

(b) The Limited Partners shall each be entitled to receive that proportion of fifty percent (50%) of the Net Profits which his Capital Contribution bears to the Total Capitalization, excluding, however, from such Limited Partners all Persons who, pursuant to Paragraph FOUR hereof, may be entitled to compensation only from the General Partner's share of such Net Profits, and excluding the contributions so made by such Persons.

(c) The General Partner shall be entitled to receive fifty percent (50%) of the Net Profits.

(d) Until Net Profits shall have been earned, losses suffered and incurred by the Partnership, up to the Total Capitalization plus additional contributions referred to in Paragraph FOUR hereof, shall be borne entirely by the Limited Partners in proportion to, and only to the extent of, their respective Capital Contributions. After Net Profits shall have been earned, then, to the extent of such Net Profits, the General Partner and Limited Partners shall share any such losses pro-rata in the same proportion as they are entitled to share in Net Profits pursuant to the provisions of this paragraph SEVEN.

(e) It is understood and agreed that the Partnership will be entitled to use Net Profits for other productions of the Play and is not required to distribute any such amounts.

EIGHT: No Limited Partner shall be personally liable for any debts, obligations or losses of the Partnership beyond the amount of his Capital Contribution to the Partnership and his share of any undistributed Net Profits. A Limited Partner shall be liable only to make his Capital Contribution and shall not be required to lend any funds to the Partnership. If any sum by way of repayment of Capital Contribution or distribution of Net Profits shall have been paid prior or subsequent to the termination date of the Partnership, and at any time subsequent to such repayment there shall be any unpaid debts, taxes, liabilities or obligations of the Partnership, and the Partnership shall not have sufficient assets to meet them, then each Limited Partner and General Partner may be obligated to repay the Partnership, to the extent of his Capital Contribution so returned to him or any Net Profits so distributed to him, as the General Partner may need for such purpose and demand. In such event, the Limited Partners and General Partner shall first repay any Net Profits theretofore distributed to them, respectively, and if insufficient, the Limited Partners shall return Capital Contributions which may have been repaid to them, such return by the Limited Partners, respectively, to be made in proportion to the amounts of Capital Contributions which may have been so repaid to them, respectively. All such repayments by Limited Partners shall be repaid promptly after receipt by each Limited Partner from the General Partners of a written notice requesting such repayment.

NINE: Upon the termination of the Partnership, the assets of the Partnership shall be liquidated as promptly as possible and the cash proceeds shall be applied as follows in the following order of priority:

(a) To the payment of debts, taxes, obligations and liabilities of the Partnership and the necessary expenses of liquidation. Where there is a contingent debt, obligation or liability, a reserve shall be set up to meet it, and if and when such contingency shall cease to exist, the monies, if any, in such reserve shall be distributed as provided for in this Paragraph NINE.

(b) To the repayment of Capital Contributions of the Limited Partners, such Partners sharing such repayment proportionately to their respective Capital Contributions.

(c) The surplus, if any, of such assets then remaining shall be divided among the General Partner and Limited Partners in the proportion that they share in the Net Profits.

TEN: If a Limited Partner shall die, his executors or administrators, or, if he shall become insane or been dissolved if not a natural person, his committee or other representative, shall have the same rights that the Limited Partner would have had if he had not died or become insane, and the Interest of such Limited Partner shall, until the termination of the Partnership, be subject to all of the terms, provisions and conditions of this Agreement as if such Limited Partner had not died, become insane or been dissolved.

ELEVEN: (a) The General Partner shall:

(i) at all times from the inception of financial transactions during the continuance of the Partnership, keep or cause to be maintained full and faithful books of account in which shall be entered fully and accurately each transaction of the Partnership. All of such books of account shall be at all times open to the inspection and examination of the Limited Partners, or their representatives. The General Partner shall likewise have available for examination and inspection of the Limited Partners or their representatives, at any time, box office statements received from the theatre (or theatres, as the case may be) in which the Play is presented by the Partnership. The General Partner agrees to furnish financial statements to the Limited Partners and the Department of Law of the State of New York pursuant to the provisions of Article 23 of the Arts and Cultural Affairs Law and the regulations issued by the Attorney General thereunder. The General Partner further agrees to deliver to the Limited Partners all information necessary to enable the Limited Partners to prepare their respective federal and state income tax returns;

(ii) render in connection with the theatrical productions of the Play such services as are customarily and usually rendered by theatrical producers, and devote as much time thereto as he may deem necessary, and manage and have complete control over all business affairs and decisions of the Partnership with respect to all productions of the Play;

(iii) have the right to apply for and receive an exemption from any applicable accounting requirements set forth in Article 23 of the Arts and Cultural Affairs Law of the State of New York or in the applicable regulations promulgated thereunder, as such law or regulations may be amended from time to time;

(iv) be entitled to reimbursement by the Partnership upon Total Capitalization for all out-of-pocket expenses reasonably paid or incurred by them in connection with the discharge of their obligations hereunder or otherwise reasonably paid or incurred by the General Partner on behalf of the Partnership;

(v) have the right to amend this Agreement from time to time without the consent of any of the Limited Partners (A) to add to the duties or obligations of the General Partner, or surrender any right or power granted to the General Partner herein, for the benefit of the Limited Partners; (B) to cure any ambiguity, to correct or supplement any provision herein which may be inconsistent with any other provision herein, or to add any other provisions with respect to matters or questions arising under this Agreement which will not be inconsistent with the provisions of this Agreement; and

(C) to delete or add any provision of this Agreement required to be so deleted or added by the staff of the SEC or by a state securities commissioner or other government official, whether United States or foreign, which addition or deletion is deemed by such authority to be for the benefit or protection of the Limited Partners.

(b) Notwithstanding anything to the contrary contained herein, this Agreement may not be amended without the consent of all the Limited Partners who would be adversely affected by an amendment that:

(i) modifies the limited liability of a Limited Partner;

(ii) alters the interests of the Limited Partners in the allocation of profits or losses or in distributions from the Partnership; or

(iii) affects the status of the Partnership as a partnership for federal income tax purposes.

TWELVE: In the event that the General Partner finds it necessary to perform any services of a third person, the General Partner may, if he so desires, receive the reasonable compensation for such services that a third person would have received for the services rendered.

THIRTEEN: The Limited Partners shall not have the right to demand and receive property other than cash in return for their Capital Contributions. In the repayment of Capital Contributions, the dividing of profits or otherwise, except as provided in Paragraph FOURTEEN hereof, no Limited Partner shall have priority over any other Limited Partner.

FOURTEEN: The General Partner may arrange for the deposit of bonds required by the Actors' Equity Association or any other union or organization or theatre guarantees, without, however, reducing the proportion of Net Profits payable to the Limited Partners. Such arrangements may provide for obtaining such bonds or guarantees from Persons who may not be Limited Partners upon terms which require that prior to the return of Limited Partners' Capital Contributions, or the payment of any Net Profits, all funds otherwise available for such purposes shall be set aside and paid over to the Actors' Equity Association or other such union, organization or theatre, in substitution for and in discharge of the bonds and guarantees furnished by such other Persons. In the event such arrangements reduce the estimated production requirements, the General Partner shall have the right to assign from the proportion of Net Profits allocable to the Limited Partners, to the Person contributing such guarantee or security, a share not greater than the amount that would otherwise have been allocable to the Capital Contribution required for the for the respective bonds, provided, however, that in no event shall the shares of Net Profits payable to each Limited Partner hereunder be less than the proportion that would otherwise have been payable to such Limited Partner had the amount of the respective bonds been contributed by the Limited Partners as part of the Total Capitalization.

FIFTEEN: Capital Contributions, in the discretion of the General Partner, may be used to pay Running Expenses, Other Expenses and Production Expenses.

SIXTEEN: (a) The General Partner shall have the right to admit Additional Limited Partners and/or permit Limited Partners to increase their respective interests in the Partnership without obtaining the consent of any Limited Partner, until the Partnership has sold fifty (50) Units. A Limited Partner may not assign his Interest without the prior written consent of the General Partner, and no assignee of a Limited Partner shall have the right to become a substitute Limited Partner in the place of his assignor without such consent, or further assign such Interest.

(b) All references herein to Limited Partners shall refer as well to Additional Limited Partners and all terms and conditions governing Limited Partners shall also govern Additional Limited Partners.

SEVENTEEN: The General Partner shall have the unrestricted right, in his sole discretion, to co-produce the Play with any other entity and to enter into any agreement, in connection therewith, including partnership agreements or joint venture agreements; provided, however, that no such co-production or similar arrangement shall decrease or dilute the Interests of the Limited Partners.

EIGHTEEN: In the event that the General Partner at any time shall determine in good faith that continuation of the production of the Play will not benefit the Partnership and should be abandoned, he shall have the sole right to make arrangements with any Person to continue the run of the Play on such terms as the General Partner may deem appropriate and beneficial to the Partnership, or to abandon the same.

NINETEEN: (a) In the event the General Partner shall desire the Partnership to organize a company or companies in addition to the original one, to present the Play in the British Isles, the United States and Canada, or any other part of the world (if the right to produce the Play in such areas accrues to the Partnership), then the General Partner shall have the right to do so and may utilize Partnership capital or Net Profits to do so. The General Partner may invite Limited Partners to contribute to the capital of such companies, but nothing contained herein shall be construed to obligate the General Partner to accept the contribution of a Limited Partner for such purposes.

(b) The Partnership may also enter into one or more agreements with respect to the disposition of British production and subsidiary rights of the Play with any partnership, corporation, or other firm in which the General Partner may be in any way interested, provided that such agreement shall be on fair and reasonable terms. The General Partner shall also have the unrestricted right to employ a producer or manager for such British production, to pay him an amount the General Partner deems appropriate and to give such person production billing either as a co-producer or associate producer.

(c) In addition, the General Partner alone or associated in any way with any person, firm or corporation, may produce or co-produce other productions of the Play in other places and media, and may receive compensation therefore without any obligation whatever to account to the Partnership or the Limited Partners; provided, however, that the Partnership shall be entitled to receive from any such producing entity, the customary fees and royalties payable to it, if any, as producer of the original Play in connection with such other productions.

(d) The General Partner shall have the right in his sole discretion to make arrangements to license any rights in the Play to any other party or parties he may designate, provided the Partnership receives reasonable royalties or other reasonable compensation therefore, and, provided further, that the Partnership shall not be involved in any loss or expenses by reason thereof. In the event of any such license of rights the General Partner may render services to the licensee in connection with exploitation by the licensee of the rights so licensed.

TWENTY: If, upon the termination of the Partnership, any production rights of the Play for the United States and Canada, with or without the physical production of the Play and with or without the Partnership's interest in the proceeds of the subsidiary rights of the Play, are purchased by the General Partner, the amount paid by such party or parties shall be the fair and reasonable market value thereof, or an amount equal to the best offer obtainable, whichever is higher.

TWENTY-ONE: The General Partner shall be entitled to receive a producer's management fee equal to two percent (2%) of the gross weekly box office receipts of each company presenting the Play under his authority and control which will be reduced to one percent (1%) until recoupment of the total production cost in accordance with a royalty formula set forth in the Production Contract. The General Partner shall also be paid a weekly cash office charge in the sum of $400 for each such company. The aforementioned cash office charge shall be paid to the General Partner beginning no sooner than two (2) weeks before the commencement of rehearsals of each company presenting the Play and ending no later than two (2) weeks after the close of each such company.

TWENTY-TWO: The General Partner has acquired the exclusive option to produce the Play within the Option Period in an Off-Broadway or Middle theatre pursuant to the Production Contract. If the producer has produced the Play as provided herein the Authors agree that the Producer shall receive an amount equal to the percentage of net receipts (regardless of when paid) specified hereinbelow received by Authors if the Play has been produced for the number of consecutive performances set forth and if before the expiration of ten (10) years subsequent to the date of the last public performance of the Play in New York City, any of the following rights are disposed of anywhere throughout the world: motion pictures, or with respect to the Continental United States and Canada, any of the following rights: radio, television, touring performances, stock and amateur performances, foreign language performances, condensed tabloid versions, so-called concert tour versions, commercial and merchandising uses, and audio and video cassettes and discs: ten percent if the Play shall run for at least twenty-one consecutive paid performances; twenty percent if the Play shall run for at least forty-two consecutive paid performances; thirty percent if the Play shall run for at least fifty-six consecutive paid performances; forty percent if the Play shall run for sixty-five consecutive paid performances or more. For the purposes of computing the number of performances, provided the Play officially opens in New York City, the first paid performance shall be deemed to be the first performance, however, no more than seven paid performances shall be counted in making this computation. Producer will only be entitled to subsidiary rights income from Productions not produced or licensed by the Producer. A copy of the Production Contract is on file at the offices of Legal Counsel for the Partnership.

TWENTY-THREE: The General Partner represents that the following percentages of gross weekly box office receipts of the Off-Broadway production of the Play will or may be payable by the Partnership:

The Author's "full royalty" shall have the following meaning: 1. Six (6%) percent of the gross weekly box office receipts until recoupment of the total production costs; 2. Seven and one-half (7 ½%) percent of the gross weekly box office receipts after recoupment of the total production costs. The Author's "reduced royalty" shall mean one-half of the full royalty before recoupment, i.e. three (3%) percent of the gross weekly box office receipts. If all royalty recipients including the Producer with respect to the Producer's fee, with the exception of the star(s) billed above the title, similarly reduce their respective full royalties by at least one-half then until recoupment of the total production costs the following shall apply:

1. Each full royalty due less the amount of the respective reduced royalty shall be payable only from 50% of the "weekly operating profits", to the extent that there are weekly operating profits.

2. Such payments shall be made to each of the respective royalty recipients proportionately (based on the full royalty amount prior to recoupment) up to but not in excess of the amount of each respective full royalty.

To the extent that such 50% of the weekly operating profits is insufficient to pay the Author and the other royalty recipients their full royalties, the difference between that amount actually paid and the amount of the respective full royalty shall be deemed to be a "deferred royalty." After recoupment of the total production costs, the royalty recipients will be paid their full royalty which shall be deducted from operating profits as an operating expense, and any deferred royalties shall be proportionately recouped by such royalty recipients proportionately from 25% of the weekly operating profits.

The Producer's fee and the cash office charge will be in an amount as set forth in paragraph TWENTY-ONE above.

The Director, Choreographer, Lighting, Scenic and Costume Designers have not yet been engaged; however, it may be assumed that the Director may receive 3% of the gross weekly box office receipts, the Choreographer may receive 1% of the gross weekly box office receipts and the Lighting, Scenic and Costume Designers may be entitled to an aggregate of 1% of such receipts. The same royalty pool formula accepted by the Authors and the Producer will be proposed to the other royalty participants.

TWENTY-FOUR: The General Partner represents that he has engaged Bob Bob 1234 W 45th Street, New York, New York 10018, to perform the services of general manager in connection with the Play, as more fully set out in the Offering Circular.

TWENTY-FIVE: The estimated weekly budget (including fixed

operating costs of $49,208) for the run of the Play at a theatre with a seating capacity of approximately 499 seats is approximately $61,284 at full capacity (weekly operating profit of $34,000). The theatre will gross approximtely $95,000.

TWENTY-SIX: All monies raised from this offer and sale of syndication interests shall be held in a special bank account in trust at The Bank of Banks 551 West 44th Street, New York, New York 10017, until actually employed for pre-production of production purposes of this particular theatrical production or until returned to the investor or investors. The General Partner will have the sole discretion as to whether such funds shall be maintained in an interest-bearing account. Prior to Total Capitalization, the Capital Contribution of a subscriber may only be employed for pre-production or production purposes if specifically authorized by such subscriber.

TWENTY-SEVEN: Any Limited Partner who shall sign this Agreement under the category entitled "LIMITED PARTNERS AUTHORIZING IMMEDIATE USE OF FUNDS AND WAIVING REFUND" shall not be entitled to reimbursement of his Capital Contribution in the event Total Capitalization is not raised. By so signing, a Limited Partner specifically authorizes the General Partner to utilize his Capital Contribution for Production Expenses incurred prior to Total Capitalization. The General Partner shall not accept Capital Contributions from prospective subscribers who desire to sign this Agreement under the caption "LIMITED PARTNERS AUTHORIZING IMMEDIATE USE OF FUNDS BUT NOT WAIVING REFUND" to the extent that such contributions exceed the aggregate net worth of the General Partner. Each Person executing this Agreement as a Limited Partner in any other category does not waive the return of his Capital Contribution in the event fifty (50) Units are not sold.

TWENTY-EIGHT: Each of the Limited Partners and each of the Additional Limited Partners does hereby make, constitute and appoint the General Partners his true and lawful attorney-in-fact in his name, place and stead, to make, execute, sign, acknowledge and file (1) the Certificate of Limited Partnership of the Partnership, including therein all information required by the Laws of the State of New York; (2) any amended Certificates of Limited Partnership as may be required pursuant to this Agreement; (3) all certificates, documents and papers which may be required to effectuate dissolution of the Partnership after its termination; and (4) all such other instruments which may be deemed required or permitted by the laws of any state, the United States of

America, or any political subdivision or agency thereof, to effectuate, implement, continue and defend the valid and subsisting existence, rights and property of the Partnership as a limited partnership and its power to carry out its purposes as set forth herein.

TWENTY-NINE: This agreement may be executed in one or more counterparts and each of such counterparts, for all purposes, shall be deemed to be an original, but all of such counterparts together shall constitute but one and the same instrument, binding upon all parties hereto, notwithstanding that all of such parties may not have executed the same counterpart.

THIRTY: Any dispute arising under, out of, in connection with, or in relation to this Agreement, or the making or validity thereof, or its interpretation or any breach thereof, shall be determined and settled by one arbitrator in New York City pursuant to the rules then obtaining of the American Arbitration Association. The arbitrator is directed to award to the prevailing party reasonable attorneys' fees, costs and disbursements, including reimbursement for the cost of witnesses, travel and subsistence during the arbitration hearings. Any award rendered thereon may be entered in the highest court of the forum, state or federal having jurisdiction. The provisions of this Paragraph THIRTY, or any other provisions of this Agreement, shall not, however, operate to deprive the Limited Partners of any rights afforded to them under the securities laws of the United States of America.

THIRTY-ONE: Each of the parties to this Agreement acknowledges and agrees that one original of this Agreement (or set of original counterparts) shall be held at the office of the Partnership, that a Certificate of Limited Partnership and such amendments thereto as are required shall be filed in the Office of the County Clerk in the County of New York, and that a duplicate original (or set of duplicate original counterparts) of each shall be held at the offices of the Partnership's Legal Counsel, and that there shall be distributed to each such party a conformed copy thereof.

THIRTY-TWO: This Agreement contains the entire agreement between the parties hereto with respect to the matters contained herein and cannot be modified or amended except by written agreement signed by all of the parties.

THIRTY-THREE: Except as otherwise expressly provided herein, no purported waiver by any party of any breach by another party of any of his obligations, agreements or covenants hereunder, or any part thereof, shall be effective unless made by written instrument subscribed to by the party or parties sought to be bound thereby, and no failure to pursue or elect any remedy with respect to any default under or breach of any provision of this Agreement, or any part thereof, shall be deemed to be a waiver of any other subsequent, similar or different default or breach, or any election of remedies available in connection therewith, nor shall the acceptance or receipt by any party of any money or other consideration due him under this Agreement, with or without knowledge of any breach hereunder, constitute a waiver of any provision of this Agreement with respect to such or any other breach.

THIRTY-FOUR: Each provision of this Agreement shall be considered to be severable and if, for any reason, any such provision or provisions, or any part thereof, is determined to be invalid and contrary to any existing or future applicable law, such invalidity shall not impair the operation of or affect those portions of this Agreement which are valid, but this Agreement shall be construed and enforced in all respects as if such invalid or unenforceable provision or provisions had been omitted, provided, however, that the status of this Partnership, as a Partnership, shall not be prejudiced.

THIRTY-FIVE: This Agreement shall be binding upon and inure to the benefit of the parties hereto and their respective executors, administrators and successors, but shall not be deemed for the benefit of creditors of any other Persons, nor shall it be deemed to permit any assignment by the General Partners or Limited Partners of any of their rights or obligations hereunder except as expressly provided herein.

THIRTY-SIX: Each of the parties hereto hereby agrees that he shall hereafter execute and deliver such further instruments and do such further acts and things as may be required or useful to carry out the intent and purpose of this Agreement and as are not inconsistent with the terms hereof.

THIRTY-SEVEN: This Agreement and all matters pertaining thereto shall be governed by the laws of the State of New York applicable to agreements to be performed entirely within the State of New York.

THIRTY-EIGHT: By his signature appended to this Agreement, each Limited Partner represents and warrants that together with this Limited Partnership Agreement, he has been furnished with offering material contained in an Offering Circular, as same may be amended.

IN WITNESS WHEREOF, the parties hereto have executed this Limited Partnership Agreement on the day and year first above written.

AS GENERAL PARTNER

_____

BILL BOE

STATE OF NEW YORK)
          :
COUNTY OF NEW YORK)

On this   day of   , 1987, before me personally appeared BILL
BOE be known and known to me to be the individual described in and
who executed the foregoing instrument, and he duly acknowledged to
me that he executed the same.

_____

LIMITED PARTNERS

LIMITED PARTNERS WHOSE CASH CONTRIBUTIONS MAY BE USED ONLY UPON FULL CAPITALIZATION

Printed Name: _____

Social Security No.
and/or Employer I.D. #: _____

Home Address: _____

Home Telephone No.: _____

Business Address: _____

Business Telephone No.: _____

Amount to be Contributed: $ _____

_____
Signature

LIMITED PARTNERS WHOSE CONTRIBUTIONS ARE OTHER THAN CASH

THE FOLLOWING SIGN THE FOREGOING AGREEMENT AS LIMITED PARTNERS, BUT IN LIEU OF A CASH CONTRIBUTION AGREE TO MAKE THEIR CONTRIBUTION BY GIVING, OR CAUSING TO BE GIVEN, THE FOLLOWING DESCRIBED OBLIGATION OF THE FOLLOWING FACE AMOUNT:

Printed Name: _____

Social Security No.
and/or Employer I.D. #: _____

Home Address: _____

Home Telephone No.: _____

Business Address: _____

Business Telephone No.: _____

Amount to be Contributed: $ _____

_____
Signature

LIMITED PARTNERS

LIMITED PARTNERS AUTHORIZING IMMEDIATE USE OF FUNDS
BUT NOT WAIVING REFUND

THE FOLLOWING SIGN THE FOREGOING AGREEMENT AS LIMITED PARTNERS AND AGREE THAT THEIR CONTRIBUTIONS MAY BE USED FORTHWITH BY THE GENERAL PARTNER FOR PRODUCTION OR PRE-PRODUCTION PURPOSES. THE UNDERSIGNED DO NOT WAIVE THEIR RIGHTS OF REFUND OF ANY PORTION OF SUCH CONTRIBUTION EXPENDED FOR SUCH PURPOSES AND RELY ON THE GENERAL PARTNER TO REFUND THEIR CONTRIBUTION IN THE EVENT THE PRODUCTION IS ABANDONED PRIOR TO FULL CAPITALIZATION OF THE PARTNERSHIP. SUCH REFUND IS, THEREFORE, CONTINGENT UPON THE GENERAL PARTNER'S FINANCIAL ABILITY TO MEET THIS OBLIGATION. THERE IS A RISK THAT BY EXERCISING SUCH CONSENT THE UNDERSIGNED MAY SUSTAIN UNLIMITED LIABILITY FOR ALL DEBTS ARISING PRIOR TO FORMATION OF THE LIMITED PARTNERSHIP. THE UNDERSIGNED OBTAIN NO ADVANTAGE BY ENTERING INTO THIS AGREEMENT.

Printed Name: _____

Social Security No.
and/or Employer I.D. #: _____

Home Address: _____

Home Telephone No.: _____

Business Address: _____

Business Telephone No.: _____

Amount to be Contributed: $_____

_____
Signature

LIMITED PARTNERS

<u>LIMITED PARTNERS AUTHORIZING IMMEDIATE USE OF FUNDS</u>
<u>AND WAIVING REFUND</u>

THE FOLLOWING SIGN THE FOREGOING AGREEMENT AS LIMITED PARTNERS AND AGREE THAT THEIR CONTRIBUTIONS MAY BE USED FORTHWITH BY THE GENERAL PARTNER FOR PRODUCTION OR PRE-PRODUCTION PURPOSES. THE UNDERSIGNED WAIVE THEIR RIGHT OF REFUND OF ANY PORTION OF SUCH CONTRIBUTION EXPENDED FOR SUCH PURPOSES IN THE EVENT THE PRODUCTION IS ABANDONED PRIOR TO FULL CAPITALIZATION OF THE PARTNERSHIP. THERE IS A RISK THAT BY EXERCISING SUCH CONSENT THE UNDERSIGNED MAY SUSTAIN UNLIMITED LIABILITY FOR ALL DEBTS ARISING PRIOR TO FORMATION OF THE LIMITED PARTNERSHIP. THE UNDERSIGNED OBTAIN NO ADVANTAGE BY ENTERING INTO THIS AGREEMENT.

Printed Name: _____

Social Security No.
and/or Employer I.D. #: _____

Home Address: _____

Home Telephone No.: _____

Business Address: _____

Business Telephone No.: _____

Amount to be Contributed: $ _____

_____
Signature

APPENDIX I

Offering Circular for SEC Regulation and Exemption

OFFERING CIRCULAR*

$250,000 maximum ($200,000 minimum) in Limited Partnership
Interests
in
THE SMART LIMITED PARTNERSHIP
A Limited Partnership to be formed to finance, produce and present
Off-Broadway (in a theatre with approximately 285 seats) the new
musical play presently entitled:
SMART (The "Play")
THE UNITED STATES SECURITIES AND EXCHANGE COM-
MISSION DOES NOT PASS UPON THE MERITS OF OR GIVE
ITS APPROVAL TO ANY SECURITIES OFFERED OR THE
TERMS OF THE OFFERING, NOR DOES IT PASS UPON THE
ACCURACY OR COMPLETENESS OF ANY OFFERING CIR-
CULAR OR OTHER SELLING LITERATURE. THESE SECURI-
TIES ARE OFFERED PURSUANT TO AN EXEMPTION FROM
REGISTRATION WITH THE COMMISSION; HOWEVER, THE
COMMISSION HAS NOT MADE AN INDEPENDENT DETER-
MINATION THAT THE SECURITIES OFFERED HEREUNDER
ARE EXEMPT FROM REGISTRATION.

---

*The dollar amounts, the time period, and percentages set forth in this sample circular are typical.

	Price to Public	Underwriting Discounts or Commissions[1]	Proceeds to the Limited Partnership[2]
Per Unit Maximum	$ 5,000	—	$ 5,000[3]
Per Unit Minimum	$ 4,000	—	$ 4,000
Total Maximum	$250,000	—	$250,000
Total Minimum	$200,000	—	$200,000

Pre-Formation Limited Partnership Interests ("Limited Partnership Interests") are being offered by Ira Ira residing at 123 West 45th Street, New York, N.Y. 10011 ("the General Partner"). The ultimate issuer will be THE SMART LIMITED PARTNERSHIP, when formed (the "Partnership"), whose address is 123 West 45th Street, New York, New York 10011 and whose telephone number is (212) 789 0123. All monies will be held by the General Partner in a Special Account at Citibank, 46th Street & 3rd Avenue, New York, NY 10163 until the total capital contributions are raised.

THE DATE OF THIS OFFERING CIRCULAR IS_____.

1. This offering has no underwriters.
2. Before deducting expenses payable by the Issuer related to this offering, which are estimated at $15,000.
3. Aggregate Pre-Formation Limited Partnership Interests are not actually divided into a specific number of units and monetary amounts. For purposes of convenience, they may be considered to consist of 50 "Units" of $5,000 per Unit.

Date of Commencement of proposed sale to public: As soon as practicable following the filing of the Notification Form 1-A relating to this offering and terminating May 30, 1988.

THESE SECURITIES INVOLVE A HIGH DEGREE OF RISK AND PROSPECTIVE PURCHASERS SHOULD BE PREPARED TO SUSTAIN A LOSS OF THEIR ENTIRE INVESTMENT (See "RISK FACTORS").

THIS OFFERING CIRCULAR MAY NOT BE USED FOR A PERIOD OF MORE THAN NINE (9) MONTHS. THEREAFTER, THE ATTORNEY GENERAL OF THE STATE OF NEW YORK DOES NOT PASS ON THE MERITS OF THIS OFFERING.

NO DEALER, SALESMAN OR ANY OTHER PERSON HAS BEEN AUTHORIZED TO GIVE ANY INFORMATION OR TO MAKE ANY REPRESENTATION OTHER THAN THOSE CONTAINED IN THIS OFFERING CIRCULAR, AND IF GIVEN OR MADE, SUCH INFORMATION OR REPRESENTATIONS MUST NOT BE RELIED UPON AS HAVING BEEN AUTHORIZED BY THE GENERAL PARTNER. THIS OFFERING CIRCULAR DOES NOT CONSTITUTE AN OFFER TO SELL OR A SOLICITATION OF AN OFFER TO BUY ANY OF THE SECURITIES OFFERED HEREBY, TO ANY PERSON IN ANY JURISDICTION WHERE SUCH OFFER OR SOLICITATION WOULD BE UNLAWFUL.

TABLE OF CONTENTS

SUMMARY OF THE OFFERING CIRCULAR

The Partnership will be formed for the purpose of producing and presenting the Play and exploiting and turning to account the rights at any time held by the Partnership in connection therewith (see "THE PARTNERSHIP"). It is currently anticipated that the Play will open Off-Broadway in New York City on or before May 30, 1988.

The Partnership will be formed upon or prior to the sale of 50 Units and the receipt by the General Partner of capital contributions totalling $250,000 (or such lesser amount as the General Partner determines is sufficient to produce the play but in no event less than $200,000) (see "RISK FACTOR #5") by the filing of a duly executed Certificate of Limited Partnership in the Office of the Clerk of New York County. The Certificate shall be filed as soon as possible after the execution of the Limited Partnership Agreement by the General Partner and at least one limited partner ("Limited Partner"). The Limited Partners will receive 50% of the net profits of the Partnership and the General Partner will receive 50% of such profits.

The Partnership shall terminate upon the occurrence of any of the following: (i) the Bankruptcy, death, insanity or resignation of an individual General Partner or the dissolution, cessation of business or Bankruptcy of a corporate General Partner; (ii) the expiration of all of the Partnership's right, title and interest in the Play; (iii) a date fixed by the General Partner after abandonment of all further Partnership activities; or (iv) any other event causing the dissolution of the Partnership under the laws of the State of New York. Notwithstanding the foregoing, the Partnership shall not be dissolved upon the occurrence of the Bankruptcy, death, dissolution or withdrawal or adjudication of incompetence of a General Partner if all of the remaining General Partners elect within 30 days after such an event to continue the business of the Partnership.

The Partnership's plan of operation is: (a) to engage in pre-production activities with respect to the Play; (b) upon completion of pre-production activities, to engage in rehearsals of the Play; (c) during the rehearsal period, to begin the promotion and publicity for the Play; and (d) to produce and present the Play. For further information with respect to these matters, see "USE OF PROCEEDS."

Since the Partnership has not yet been formed, there are no income, expense or other financial statements of the Partnership presently available. For information with respect to the risks to subscribers in connection with this offering, see generally "RISK FACTORS."

THE PARTNERSHIP

The General Partner shall organize the Partnership as a New York limited partnership to raise capital contributions totalling $250,000 (or such lesser amount as the General Partner determines is sufficient to produce the play but in no event less than $200,000) and for the purpose of producing and presenting the Play and exploiting and turning to account the rights held by the Partnership therein. The capitalization requirement is, in the opinion of the General Partner, sufficient to mount a production of the Play in an Off-Broadway Theatre containing approximately 284 seats.

If 50 Units have not been sold by May 30, 1988 (the date to which the rights to produce the play have been extended in accordance with the agreement of May 30, 1986), the offering will cease and all capital contributions theretofore received will be returned with accrued interest, if any, except capital contributions which have been expended by consent of individual subscribers who have waived their right of refund (see "RISK FACTOR #5").

The General Partner will have sole and complete authority over the management and operations of the Partnership. The General Partner in his sole discretion may purchase Units of Limited Partnership Interests in the Partnership and participate therein as a Limited Partner. However, at present the General Partner has not determined whether he will so participate as a Limited Partner or the extent of any such participation. The General Partner will assign to the Partnership, upon formation, certain rights in the Play which he has acquired on behalf of the Partnership. Upon formation, the Partnership will assume all obligations and liabilities incurred by the General Partner in acquiring such stage production and all other rights assigned to the Partnership. For additional information on the rights acquired by the General Partner and the division of proceeds therefrom, see "PRODUCTION AND SUBSIDIARY RIGHTS."

The executive offices of the Partnership will be: c/o Ira Ira, 123 West 45th Street, New York, New York 10011, telephone number: (212) 789-0123, unless otherwise designated by the General Partner.

RISK FACTORS

(1) Based on the "Review of the 1985–1986 Theatrical Season" released by the New York State Department of Law, of the Off-Broad-

way productions subject to New York State's Theatrical Syndication Financing Act during the 1985–1986 Season, —— productions reported losses and unrecovered costs.

(2) Based on Partnership capitalization of $250,000 and the estimated weekly expenses for the production of the Play, (see "USE OF PROCEEDS" and "ESTIMATED WEEKLY BUDGET"), and assuming the Play is presented at prevailing box office scale in a 285 seat Off-Broadway theatre with potential gross weekly box office receipts of $45,000 the Play must run for approximately 14½ weeks (116 performances) to a full capacity house in order to return to the Limited Partners their initial capital contributions, or for a longer period of time if presented at less than full house capacity. Based on a Partnership Capitalization of $200,000 the play under such circumstances must run for a period of twelve (12) weeks (96 performances) to a full capacity house in order to return the Limited Partners their initial Capital Contributions. The substantial majority of the plays produced for the Off-Broadway stage during the 1985–1986 Season failed to run for 12 weeks. Of those that did, few played to capacity audiences throughout their run.

(3) There is no assurance that the Play will be an economic success even if the Play receives critical acclaim.

(4) These securities should not be purchased unless the subscriber is prepared for the possibility of total loss and is able to afford such total loss. The sole business of the Partnership will be the production of the Play. In such a venture the risk of loss is especially high in contrast with the prospect for the realization of any profits.

(5) An individual subscriber may agree to the use of his capital contribution prior to full capitalization of the Partnership, and either retain or waive his absolute right of refund in the event of abandonment prior to the production of the Play. A subscriber who agrees to earlier use may sustain unlimited liability for production debts incurred prior to formation of the Partnership. Subscribers waiving refund may lose all or part of their respective investments, without a production of the Play having been presented, if insufficient funds are raised to complete the offering, or if the offering is not completed for any other reason. Subscribers not waiving refund must rely solely on the ability of the General Partner to reimburse them for their expended capital contributions, which might exceed the assets of the General Partner and result in a total loss to such subscribers. There is a distinct disadvantage to waiving such refund because persons who do so risk the loss of their entire investment even if the Partner-

ship is never formed or the Play is abandoned prior to production.

(6) In the event the capital contributions raised through this offering are insufficient to produce the Play as contemplated, the General Partner may advance or cause to be advanced, or may borrow on behalf of the Partnership, additional capital. Such advances or loans are to be repaid prior to the repayment of the capital contribution of any Limited Partner. Such advances or loans might result in a considerable delay in the repayment of capital contributions, or in a complete loss to subscribers if such loans or advances equal or exceed the revenues from the production of the Play.

(7) If the Partnership receives an exemption from the requirements of filing certified accounting statements, pursuant to the New York Arts and Cultural Affairs Law, Limited Partners may be furnished with unaudited financial statements. The General Partner has not, as of the date of this Offering Circular, applied for such exemption or determined whether such applications will be made.

(8) Contributions other than cash may be accepted in the form of guarantees or bonds as may be required by Actors' Equity Association, theatres and other unions or organizations, as such contributors will receive the Limited Partnership Interest allocable to the amount of bonds or guarantees contributed, and furthermore, shall have the right to be reimbursed in full prior to the return of capital to other Limited Partners.

(9) The General Partner has not previously produced a theatrical stage production, and is under no obligation to devote his full time and efforts to the Partnership's activities (see "THE GENERAL PARTNER"). This fact may affect his ability to successfully manage the production of the Play.

(10) The General Partner will receive a share of box office receipts for each week during the run of the Play, as well as other remuneration [see "COMPENSATION OF THE GENERAL PARTNER (Producer)"], and he may continue to present the Play regardless of whether the Partnership realizes any profit.

(11) No market presently exists for resale of the Limited Partnership Interests and it is unlikely that one will develop. Limited Partners may not assign their interests without the consent of the General Partner.

(12) If 50 Units have not been sold on or before the expiration of the initial option period, or by such date to which the General Partner has extended the option period (see "PRODUCTION AND SUBSIDI-

ARY RIGHTS"), the capital contributions of the Limited Partners shall be returned promptly, with accrued interest, if any, except there shall be no return of capital contributions expended with the consent of the individual subscribers who have waived their right of refund.

(13) Partnership net profits previously distributed to the General and Limited Partners, and capital contributions previously returned to the Limited Partners (including accrued interest returned, if any), may be recalled by the General Partner for the purposes of paying any debts, taxes, liabilities or obligations of the Partnership.

(14) The General Partner, in his sole discretion, may create one or more reserves from Partnership income for the financing of one or more additional companies of the Play. As a result, the distribution of Partnership income to the Limited Partners, as a return of their capital contributions or as net profits, or both, could be delayed, and if such additional company is not financially successful, ultimately reduced.

(15) The General Partner has not contracted for certain key elements of the production, including the director, choreographer, general manager, scenic, lighting and costume designers, and the theatre.

(16) In any year in which the Partnership shall report net profits, a Limited Partner will be taxable for his proportionate share of such net profits, whether or not such net profits have been distributed to such Limited Partner.

(17) The General Partners have the right to cause additional persons, firms or corporations to become General Partners at any time prior to the formation of the partnership. In this event, an offer of rescission will be made to those investors who invested before the additional general partners are added.

(18) The General Partner shall have the absolute right to abandon the production of the play.

THE OFFERING

Each of the 50 Units of Limited Partnership Interests is being offered to the public at a purchase price of five thousand dollars ($5,000), for a Partnership capitalization of $250,000. Fractional Units may, however, be issued by the General Partner. Subscribers of Units and fractional Units shall each be entitled to receive that proportion of 50% of the Partnership's net profits which their respective capital contributions bear to the total capitalization of the Partnership. Purchasers of fractional Units will be entitled to the same rights and be subject to the same obligations as purchasers of Units. The General Partner may purchase Units and will be treated as a Limited Partner to the extent of his respective purchase of such Units. In his sole discretion, the General Partner may permit certain capital contributions to be made by the posting of required performance bonds on behalf of the Partnership. The persons posting such bonds shall participate as Limited Partners and shall be entitled to a share of net profits of the Partnership based on the cost of such bonds had they been posted directly by the Partnership.

Offers to subscribe to Limited Partnership Interests are subject to acceptance by the General Partner. A capital contribution shall be payable at the time of execution and delivery to the General Partner of the Limited Partnership Agreement by the subscriber. All monies raised pursuant to this offering shall be held in trust by the General Partner in a special bank account at Citibank, 46th Street & 3rd Avenue, New York, NY 10163 until actually employed for preproduction or production expenses. Prior to the sale of 50 Units, the capital contribution of a Limited Partner may only be employed for preproduction or production expenses if specifically authorized by such subscriber. If 50 Units have not been sold prior to the expiration of the option period, May 14, 1986 (see "PRODUCTION AND SUBSIDIARY RIGHTS"), all capital contributions will be promptly returned to the Limited Partners, with accrued interest, if any, except to the extent used pursuant to specific instructions permitting the use of a subscriber's funds and waiving right of refund. Limited Partnership Interests will be offered to the public by the General Partner on behalf of the Partnership, through the use of the mails, by telephone and by personal solicitation.

A copy of this Offering Circular and of the Limited Partnership Agreement for The Smart Limited Partnership shall be presented to each potential subscriber. A potential subscriber desiring to become a Limited Partner in the Partnership must sign the Limited Partnership Agreement and indicate the amount and category of the capital contribution being made, as well as the subscriber's actual residence address (or principal place of business of a corporation, partnership, association or other entity) and social security or employer identification number. Each executed Partnership Agreement should be forwarded to the General Partner at the Partnership address and must be accompanied by a check or money order made payable to The Smart Limited Partnership in the full amount of the capital contribution indicated on the subscription form.

With respect to the capital contributions of Limited Partners, any one of the following may also apply:

(1) An individual subscriber may agree in writing to the use of his capital contribution prior to the sale of 50 Units without waiving the absolute right of full refund on abandonment prior to the production of the Play due to an insufficiency of funds. The General Partner will be liable to such subscribers; however, such capital contributions will not be accepted in excess of the net worth of the General Partner.

(2) The individual subscriber may agree in writing to the use of his capital contribution prior to the sale of 50 Units and waive the right of refund of such contribution on abandonment prior to the production of the Play.

(3) The General Partner may accept as an investment in lieu of cash, a cash deposit for Actor's Equity, or other union bonds, or the theatre deposit.

(4) An individual subscriber may also invest in the Partnership by purchasing an assignment from a Limited Partner, provided the General Partner consents in writing to such assignment. No assignee of a Limited Partner may become a substitute Limited Partner without the written consent of the General Partner.

The General Partner reserves the right to give to any subscriber an additional participation in net profits for any reason whatever, provided such participation is payable solely from the General Partner's share of such profits, and does not affect the proportion of net profits payable to the Limited Partners.

The Partnership books and records will be maintained at the office of the Partnership, 123 West 45th Street, New York, New York 10011.

ADDITIONAL CAPITAL CONTRIBUTIONS BY LIMITED PARTNERS (OVERCALL)

There is no involuntary overcall provided for in the Limited Partnership Agreement, and if additional money is needed above the capital contributions raised, the General Partner may make funds available and must do so in a manner that will not reduce the interest of the Limited Partners in the net profits of the Limited Partnership. Any additional funds advanced or loaned to the Partnership are to be repaid prior to the return of contributions of Limited Partners.

USE OF PROCEEDS

The present estimates of pre-production and production expenses, and the allocation of capital contributions made to the Partnership are as follows:

FEES:		
Director	$ 2,500	
Lighting Designer	1,124	
Scenic Designer	1,247	
Costumer Designer	500	
Design Assistants	1,500	
		$ 6,871
PHYSICAL PRODUCTION:		
Set Construction	10,000	
Props	2,500	
Costumes	2,500	
Shoes/Boots/Wigs	1,000	
Lighting	5,000	
		$21,000
TRANSPORTATION:		
Local Trucking	1,000	
Misc. Transportation	1,000	
		$ 2,000
REHEARSAL SALARY—3 WEEKS:		
Equity	7,921	
Stage Manager	1,626	
Asst. Stg. Manager	1,104	

Company Manager	2,002	
Press Agent	1,502	
		$14,155

REHEARSAL EXPENSES:
Audition & Casting	1,000	
Scripts	500	
Rehearsal Space	2,400	
NY Hang (includes crew)	10,000	
		$13,900

PRESS/PROMOTION:
Media	60,000	
Press Agent Expense	500	
Photo Call	750	
Photo Repros	250	
Window Cards/Heralds	3,500	
One Sheets	500	
Artwork	400	
		$65,900

MISCELLANEOUS:
Legal Fee	10,000	
Insurance Deposit	1,000	
Taxes/P&W	4,000	
Departmental	2,500	
Opening Party	1,000	
Misc.	2,500	
Gen Mgr—Pre Production	5,000	
Gen Mgr—Rehearsal	3,750	
Theatre Deposit	7,500	
Office Fee	1,750	
Front of house	5,000	
Closing costs	5,000	
Preliminary Theatre Expense	8,000	
Accountant	4,000	
		$61,000

TOTAL ESTIMATED PRE-PRODUCTION COSTS	$154,826	
BONDS: Equity	10,468	
ATPAM	5,400	
RESERVE	49,306	
TOTAL CAPITALIZATION	$250,000	

If the total capitalization is $200,000 instead of $250,000, the Media expense will be reduced from $60,000 to $30,000 and Reserve will be reduced from $51,806 to $31,806.

As of the date of this Offering Circular, the General Partner has advanced approximately $8,000 on behalf of the Partnership (which amounts are included in the foregoing allocation of proceeds) as follows:

FEES AND ADVANCES:
General Manager . . . . $ 1,000
Legal Counsel . . . . $ 6,000

OTHER COSTS:
Administrative & Office Expenses
(including script and cassette
duplication, long distance
telephone, and office
expenses) . . . . $ 3,000

RIGHTS:
Authors (Advances against
Royalties) . . . . $ 500
$10,500

All sums which have heretofore been, or shall hereafter be, advanced by the General Partner for the benefit and on behalf of the Partnership will be repaid to the General Partner from the proceeds of this offering upon the sale of 50 Units, to the extent that the General Partner has not been reimbursed from front money furnished for that purpose.

ESTIMATED WEEKLY BUDGET

The maximum estimated weekly operating budget prerecoupment for the Off-Broadway run of the Play is approximately $27,700 in a theatre with a seating capacity of approximately 285 seats. During weeks in which capacity audiences are not realized, the maximum estimated weekly operating budget will be reduced. (SEE BELOW for a discussion of the royalty arrangements with Author, Director, Designers and Producer.) Based on a capitalization of $250,000, a theatre capacity of approximately 285 seats, and a gross weekly potential for box-office receipts in the amount of $45,000 the Play must have a run of approximately (14½) weeks (116 performances) at full capacity (weekly estimated profit of $17,300) merely to return to the Limited Partners their initial capital contributions. Based on a capitalization of $200,000 the play must have a run of approximately 12 weeks (96 performances) at full capacity to return to the Limited Partners their initial capital contributions.

The Author's (Bookwriter, Composer-Lyricist) royalty for each production of the Play under Producer's management license or control, shall be 5% of the gross weekly box office receipts until recoupment of the total production costs and 6½% thereafter (subject to the provisions of the following paragraph wherein it is provided that under certain circumstances the royalty will increase to 7% of the gross after recoupment.)

Royalty Pool Formula

If the Author and all other royalty participants, including the Producer with respect to the Producer's fee, agree to a similar waiver of one-half of their usual royalty, the Author agrees to waive one-half of his royalty, that is two and one-half percent of the gross weekly box office receipts, until recoupment of the total production costs of production (less bonds, deposits and other recoverable items) on the express condition that: 1.) Each week's operating profits are paid directly to the investors as payment toward recoupment of such total production costs; and 2.) After recoupment of such total production costs the Author's royalty shall be in an amount equal to seven percent (7%) of the gross weekly box office receipts. Producer agreed to such waiver of one-half of Producer's fee.

The Producer's fee will be in an amount equal to 2% of the gross weekly box office receipts, which will be reduced to 1% until recoupment of the total production costs in compliance with the Royalty Pool Formula above set forth. The cash office charge payable two weeks before rehearsal until two weeks after the close of the show will be in the amount of $350.00 per week.

A percentage of gross weekly box office receipts of the Off-Broadway production of the Play will be paid to the following as indicated (an asterisk indicates an estimation), subject to the Royalty Pool Formula referred to above:

Recipient	Share of Gross Box Office Receipts	
	Pre-Recoupment	After Recoupment
Author	5%	6½%
*Director	3%	4%
*Lighting, Scenic & Costume Designers	1%	1%
General Partner	2%	2%

If the Royalty Pool Formula becomes effective.

Recipient	Share of Gross Box Office Receipts	
	Pre-Recoupment	After Recoupment
Author	2½%	7%
*Director	1½%	4%
*Lighting, Scenic & Costume Designers	.5%	1%
General Partner	1%	2%

The maximum estimated weekly fixed operating costs referred to above are based on the following allocations (pre-recoupment and post-recoupment):

Salaries	$ 6,688
Taxes	1,739
Rentals of Equipment	1,800
Advertising	5,000
Theatre Rental, Office Expense, Insurance, Attorneys Fee, and Misc.	10,160
Total	$25,387

THE PLAY

Smart is a new comedy by Bo Bo. It has two acts, one set and seven actors.

*Estimated

THE AUTHOR

Bo Bo, the Author, studied play writing at New York Academy.
As Author he will be paid a royalty of 5% of the gross weekly box office receipts until recoupment of the total production costs and 6½% thereafter. If the Royalty Pool Formula becomes effective he will be paid as Author 2½% of the gross weekly box office receipts until recoupment of the total production costs and 7% thereafter.

See "Royalty Pool Formula" supra.

THE DIRECTOR

As of the date of the Offering Circular the Director has not been engaged for the Off-Broadway or Middle Theatre Production.

See 'Royalty Pool Formula" Supra.

THE SCENIC, LIGHTING, SOUND AND COSTUME DESIGNERS

As of the date of this Offering Circular, the scenic, lighting, sound and costume designers have not been engaged for the Play. However, it is anticipated that the scenic, lighting, sound and costume designers may be entitled to receive an aggregate of one percent (1%) of the gross weekly box office receipts of each company presenting the Play under the authority or control of the General Partner. In addition, an estimated aggregate fee of approximately $4,300 will be paid to these designers.

See "Royalty Pool Formula" supra.

THE CAST

As of the date of this Offering Circular, none of the cast has been selected for the Play. The General Partner has approached certain possible cast members, but has no indication regarding the cost, availability or interest of any performer.

THE GENERAL PARTNER

See Author above. As General Partner, Bo Bo will be paid a production fee of 2% of the gross weekly box office receipts, however, if the Royalty Pool Formula becomes effective the Producer's fees will be reduced to 1% until recoupment of the total production costs.

See "Royalty Pool Formula" supra.

THE THEATRE

As of the date of this Offering Circular, a license agreement has not been entered into for a theatre in which to present the Play. A theatre is being sought which contains approximately 285 seats and which has a potential for gross weekly box office receipts of approximately $45,000 at full capacity. It is anticipated that the theatre will be entitled to receive a license fee and staff costs of approximately $6,000.

PRODUCTION AND SUBSIDIARY RIGHTS

The General Partner has acquired the option to produce the Play as an Off-Broadway (including "Middle Theatres") production, together with certain other rights to produce the Play on Broadway, on tour and the British Isles pursuant to the Production Contract dated May 30, 1986. The term of the option period will expire on May 30, 1988.

If the Producer has produced the Play as provided herein the Author agrees that the Producer shall receive an amount equal to the percentage of net receipts (regardless of when paid) specified hereinbelow received by Authors if the Play has been produced for the number of consecutive performances set forth and if before the expiration of ten (10) years subsequent to the date of the last public performance of the Play in New York City, and of the following rights are disposed of anywhere throughout the world: motion pictures, or with respect to the Continental United States and Canada, any of the following rights; radio, television, touring performances, stock performances, Broadway performances, Off-Broadway performances, amateur performances foreign language performances, condensed tabloid versions, commercial and merchandising uses, and audio and video cassettes and discs: Ten percent (10%) if the Play shall run for at least twenty-one (21) consecutive paid performances; twenty percent (20%) if the Play shall run for at least forty-two consecutive paid performances; thirty percent (30%) if the Play shall run for at least fifty-six (56) consecutive paid performances; forty percent (40%) if the Play shall run for sixty-five (65) consecutive paid performances or more. For the purposes of computing the number of performances, provided the Play officially opens in New York City, the first paid performance shall be deemed to be the first performance, however only seven paid previews will be counted in this computation.

The above computation of the General Partner's share in subsidiary rights is set forth in the aforementioned Production Contract, a copy of which is on file and available for inspection during normal business hours at the offices of legal counsel for the Partnership: Donald C. Farber, Esq. of Tanner Gilbert Propp & Sterner, 99 Park Avenue, New York, New York 10016.

The General Partner will assign to the Limited Partnership, when formed, all of the rights granted to his by the Author, including all interests in subsidiary rights and production rights pursuant to the Production contract.

COMPENSATION OF THE GENERAL PARTNER (PRODUCER)

In addition to his share of any net profits of the Partnership in the aggregate of fifty percent (50%), for which the General Partner will make no Capital Contribution, the General Partner will receive the following compensation and advantages whether or not the Partnership earns net profits:

(1) As a Producer's management fee—two percent (2%) of the gross weekly box office receipts (reduced to 1% until recoupment of the total production costs if the Royalty Pool Formula becomes effective) for each company presenting the Play under the authority or control of the Partnership.

(2) For furnishing office space and secretarial services for the benefit of all productions of the Play, the General Partner will receive three hundred fifty ($350) dollars per week for each company presenting the Play under his authority or control. This cash office charge shall commence two (2) weeks before the commencement of rehearsals and end two (2) weeks after the close of each company presenting the Play under the authority or control of the Partnership. The offices of the Partner-

ship will be: c/o Ira Ira, 123 West 45th Street, New York, New York 10011, and such offices will not be used exclusively for the activities of the Partnership. To the extent that charges received from the Partnership by the General Partner for office space and other items furnished by him exceed their own cost, the General Partner will receive additional compensation.

In the event that the General Partner finds it necessary to perform any services usually performed by a third person, the General Partner may, if he so desires, receive the compensation for such services which the third party would have received had such third party directly performed the required services. In any event, such compensation must be an amount reasonable for the rendering of such services. As of the date of this Offering Circular, the General Partner has not made any plans, arrangements, commitments or undertakings to perform services for the Partnership which would otherwise be provided by a third person. In the event that the General Partner deems it advisable, he may license theatre space from a partnership, corporation or other entity in which the General Partner may have an interest, providing that the terms of such license are reasonable and no less favorable than the terms would be if it were rented from a third person in an arms-length transaction.

The General Partner will receive no compensation, other than that stated above, for any services, equipment or facilities customarily rendered or furnished by a theatrical stage producer; nor will the General Partner receive concessions of cash, property or anything of value from persons rendering services or supplying goods to the Partnership.

NET PROFITS AND CERTAIN EXPENSES DEFINED

The following terms are defined in the Limited Partnership Agreement in the following manner:

The term "net profits" shall mean the excess of gross receipts over all "production," "running" and "other expenses," as those terms are defined in the Limited Partnership Agreement and in this Offering Circular.

The term "production expenses" shall include fees of the director, choreographer, scenic, lighting and costume designers, orchestrator, cost of sets, curtains, drapes, costumes, properties, furnishings, electrical equipment, premiums for bonds and insurance, cash deposits with Actors' Equity Association or other similar organizations by which, according to customs or usual practices of theatrical business, such deposits may be required to be made, advances to the Author, rehearsal charges and expenses, transportation charges, cash office charges, reasonable legal and auditing expenses, advance publicity, theatre costs and expenses, and all other expenses and losses of whatever kind (other than expenditures precluded hereunder) actually incurred in connection with the production of the Play preliminary to the official opening of the Play. The General Partner has heretofore incurred or paid, and prior to the inception of the Partnership, will incur or pay, certain production expenses as herein set forth, and the amount thereof, and no more, shall be included in the production expenses of the Partnership, and (but only if all capital contributions for 50 Units shall have been received) the General Partner shall be reimbursed for the expenses so paid by him individually. The term "Running Expenses" shall mean all expenses, charges and disbursements of whatever kind actually incurred in connection with the operation of the Play, including without limiting the generality of the foregoing, royalties and/or other compensation to or for the Author, business and general managers, director, choreographer, orchestrator, cast, stage help, transportation, cash office charge, reasonable legal and auditing expenses, theatre operating expenses, and all other expenses and losses of whatever kind actually incurred in connection with the operation of the Play, as well as taxes of whatever kind and nature other than taxes on the income of the respective Limited Partners and General Partner. Such Running Expenses shall include, without limitation, payments made in the form of Gross Receipts as well as participants in Net Profits to or for any of the aforementioned persons, services of rights.

The term "other expenses" shall be deemed to mean all expenses of whatsoever kind or nature other than those referred to in the two preceding paragraphs hereof actually and reasonably incurred in connection with the operation of the business of the Partnership, including, but without limiting the foregoing, commissions paid to agents, monies paid or payable in connection with claims for plagiarism, libel, negligence, etc.

As of the date of this Offering Circular, "Running Expenses" may be expected to include payment to the Author, General Partner, Designers and Director, amounting to eleven percent 11% of the gross weekly box office receipts prior to recoupment of the total production costs and 13½% thereafter (if the Royalty Pool Formula becomes effective it will 5.5% of such gross prior to recoupment and 14% thereafter). The Limited Partners' share of fifty percent (50%) of the

net profits will accordingly be attributable to roughly 89% of the gross
weekly box office receipts until such recoupment and 86½% thereafter
except that if the Royalty Pool Formula becomes effective such 50%
will be attributable to roughly 94.5% of the gross weekly box office
receipts till such recoupment and 86% thereafter. The producer has the
right to further reduce the funds available for distribution by assigning
a share of the net profits. There are no plans at the present time to assign
any such share and if it does happen it will not exceed 5% of such net
profits.

RETURN OF CAPITAL CONTRIBUTIONS—SHARE OF NET PROFITS

The Limited Partners as a group will be entitled to receive fifty
percent (50%) of any net profits of the Partnership, each in the proportion which his capital contribution bears to the total capitalization of
the Partnership. The General Partner will also receive fifty percent
(50%) of such profits. Any net profits will be distributed only after all
capital contributions have been returned to the Limited Partners and
the Partnership maintains a reserve fund in the amount of $60,000.

Before net profits are earned, all losses will be borne by the Limited
Partners to the extent of their respective capital contributions. After net
profits are earned, the General Partner and Limited Partners will bear
losses to the extent of the net profits in proportion to their respective
interests. If the Partnership liabilities exceed its assets, all Partners,
both General and Limited, will be required to return pro-rata any net
profits distributed to them, and if a shortage remains, any repaid capital
contributions as well. Even if the Play is successful, the Limited Partners may not have their capital contributions returned to them because
the Limited Partnership Agreement provides that the General Partner
may withhold net profits for investment in other productions of the
Play without notice.

If repayment of capital contributions or distribution of Partnership
net profits shall have been made prior or subsequent to the termination
of the Partnership and, at any time thereafter, there shall be any unpaid
debts, taxes, liabilities or obligations of the Partnership and the Partnership shall not have sufficient assets to meet the same, then the General
Partner shall be entitled to recall all or part of the returned capital
contributions and distributed Partnership net profits, in such aggregate
amounts and under such circumstances as the General Partner deems

necessary or advisable. Returned capital contributions will not be re-called until all Partnership net profits distributed to the General Part-ner and the Limited Partners have been recalled. If returned capital contributions are recalled, such recall shall be made ratably from all Limited Partners based upon their respective capital contributions to the Partnership, or in the case of Limited Partners who have posted bonds in lieu of making cash contributions, withdrawn ratably from the special bank accounts in which amounts equivalent to the repayment of capital contributions are to be deposited on their behalf. If dis-tributed net profits are to be recalled, such recall shall be made from the General Partner and the Limited Partners in the same proportions as they shared in the distribution of such net profits.

Payments by the Limited Partners of recalled amounts are to be made within ten (10) days after receipt by each Limited Partner of the General Partner's written request therefor. If a Limited Partner does not return his share of distributed net profits or returned capital contri-butions when due, the remaining Limited Partners shall be liable (on a ratable basis dependent upon their respective capital contributions to the Partnership) for any defaulted amounts, but in no event shall such obligation of any non-defaulting Limited Partner exceed the amount of Partnership net profits theretofore distributed to the Limited Partner and capital contributions theretofore returned to the Limited Partner and not recalled from the Limited Partner. Any residual liabilities of the Partnership must be borne by the General Partner or any other persons who may agree to bear such liabilities.

OTHER FINANCING

Except as described above, no person or entity has advanced any-thing of value toward the production of the Play.

FINANCIAL STATEMENTS

The ultimate issuer of these securities will be the Partnership to be formed. Accordingly, no financial statements are presently available. Limited Partners will be furnished with all financial statements re-quired by the New York Arts and Cultural Affairs Law and the Regula-tions promulgated in accordance with New York law, and will include, after formation of the Partnership, annual statements of operations. In cases where a lengthy period elapses after the initial expenditure of subscribers' funds, financial statements may have to be furnished even before formation of the Partnership. If the General Partner is permitted to furnish an unaudited statement, Limited Partners will not have the benefit of an accountant and will rely wholly upon the General Partner's statement for the determination of their share in any net profits.

EFFECT OF FEDERAL INCOME TAXES

It is the belief of the General Partner, that for purposes of federal income tax, the Partnership should be treated as a partnership. A tax ruling from the Internal Revenue Service as to the Partnership's status as a partnership for federal income tax purposes has not, however, been applied for, nor does the General Partner intend to apply for such a ruling. Each investor should consult his own accountant or tax advisor for the tax consequences of the investment as far as his own circumstances are concerned.

LEGAL COUNSEL

Tanner Gilbert Propp & Sterner, whose offices are located at 99 Park Avenue, New York, New York 10016, will act as counsel for the Partnership.

INDEMNIFICATION

There is no provision in the Limited Partnership Agreement or any contract, arrangement or statute under which any General Partner is insured or indemnified in any manner against any liability which he may incur in his capacity as such.

FEDERAL SECURITIES LAW

This offering of securities has been organized with the intent of qualifying for an exemption from the registration requirements of the Securities Act of 1933 (the "Act"), as amended, pursuant to Regulation

A promulgated by the Securities and Exchange Commission under the Act. These securities are not registered under the Act. Whether these securities are exempt from registration pursuant to Regulation A or otherwise, has not been passed upon by the Securities and Exchange Commission, the Attorney General of the State of New York or any other regulatory agency, nor has any such agency passed upon the merits of this offering. The securities offered hereunder may not be resold without registration under the Act or exemption therefrom.

APPENDIX J

Certificate of Limited Partnership

CERTIFICATE OF LIMITED PARTNERSHIP OF THE WARMING COMPANY LIMITED PARTNERSHIP*

WE, THE UNDERSIGNED, being desirous of forming a Limited Partnership pursuant to the laws of the State of New York, do hereby certified as follows:

FIRST: The name of the Partnership shall be The Warming Company Limited Partnership.

SECOND: The business of the Partnership shall be to furnish part of the financing of the play "The Warming of the Buns" for a New York production.

THIRD: The Partnership's principal place of business shall be located at c/o Rose Rose, 345 East 56th Street, New York, N.Y. 10021.

FOURTH: The Partnership commenced upon the date on which, pursuant to the New York Partnership Law, the Certificate of Limited Partnership was filed in the office of the Clerk of New York County, and will terminate upon the Bankruptcy, death, dissolution or withdrawal or adjudication of incompetence of a General Partner, or a date fixed by the General Partners after abandonment of all further Partnership activities.

FIFTH: After payment or reasonable provision for payment of all

*The dollar amounts, the time periods, and percentages set forth in this sample limited partnership certificate.

427

debts, liabilities, taxes and contingent liabilities of the Partnership, and
after provision for a reserve in the amount of $50,000 all remaining cash
in excess of said contingent liabilities, expenses, debts, and other liabilities, shall be distributed to the Limited Partners, at least monthly,
within ten (10) days after the end of each calender month, together with
the unaudited statement of operations herein provided for, pro rata,
until their contributions to the Partnership shall have been repaid and
thereafter all cash in excess of said contingent liabilities, expenses,
debts, and other liabilities, shall be paid to the General Partners and
Limited Partners in the same proportion in which they share in the net
profits of the Partnership.

The General Partner may use partnership capital or net profits for
financing other productions of the play in other parts of the world, if
the right to produce the play in such areas accrues to the Partnership.

Upon the termination of the Partnership, the assets of the Partnership shall be liquidated as promptly as possible and the cash proceeds
shall be applied as follows in the following order of priority: (a) to the
payment of debts, taxes, obligations and liabilities of the Partnership
and the necessary expenses of liquidation. Where there is a contingent
debt, obligation or liability, a reserve shall be set up to meet it, and if
and when such contingency shall cease to exist, the monies, if any, in
said reserve shall be distributed as provided for in this Paragraph FIVE,
(b) to the repayment of capital contributed by the Limited Partners,
said Partners sharing such repayment proportionately to their respective contributions, (c) the surplus, if any, of said assets then remaining
shall be divided among all the Limited Partners and the General Partners in the proportion that they share in the net profits.

SIXTH: Any sums paid to the Limited Partners or to the General
Partners (whether as repayment of contribution or distribution of
profits) shall be returnable to the Partnership in such manner and at
such times as are more specifically set forth in the Limited Partnership
Agreement, if and to the extent that the Partnership shall have insufficient assets to meet its liabilities.

SEVENTH: A Limited Partner may not assign his interest and no
assignee of a Limited Partner shall have the right to become a substitute
Limited Partner in the place of his assignor, without the consent of the
General Partners. Additional Limited Partners may be added until the
Total Capitalization of the Partnership is in the amount of $300,000.

EIGHTH: The net profits that may accrue from the business of
the Partnership shall be distributed and divided among the General
Partners and the Limited Partners of the Partnership as follows:

The Limited Partners shall each be entitled to received that proportion of fifty percent (50%) of the net profits which his contribution bears to the total amount raised hereby, and the General Partners shall be entitled to receive the remaining fifty percent (50%) of such net profits.

The General Partners may make an arrangement with a Limited Partner, or partners, who furnishes bond money or some part of the theatre security deposit, which gives that Limited Partner, or partners, priority over other Limited Partners in receiving the return of capital, as provided in the Limited Partnership Agreement.

Until net profits have been earned, losses suffered and incurred by the Partnership, up to the total capitalization plus any additional contributions by the Limited Partners, shall be borne entirely by the Limited Partners, in proportion to their respective capital contributions, but only to the extent of the total capitalization. After net profits have been earned, then, to the extent of such net profits, the General Partners and the Limited Partners shall share such losses pro-rata in the same proportion as they are entitled to share in the net profits of the Partnership.

NINTH: The General Partners agree to contribute to the Partnership upon its formation, by due and proper assignment, all contracts theretofore entered into or acquired by them relating to rights, services or materials necessary to produce and present the Play, including without limitation the Joint Venture Agreement, dated as of October 9, 1986, all of which contracts thereafter shall belong to and be held in the name of the Partnership which shall assume all obligations agreed to be performed by the General Partners under said contracts.

TENTH: The Partnership shall not be dissolved as provided in Fourth, above, upon the Bankruptcy, death, dissolution or withdrawal or adjudication of incompetence of a General Partner, if any of the remaining General Partners elects within thirty (30) days after such event to continue the business of the Partnership.

ELEVENTH: The names and places of residence of the General Partners and of the Limited Partners, the amount of cash contribution of the Limited Partners, and the proportion of net profits to be received by the Limited Partners are as follows:

GENERAL PARTNERS

Rose Rose
234 East 56rd Street
New York, New York 10021

Helen Helen
123 East 45th Street
New York, New York
10022

LIMITED PARTNERS

NAMES, ADDRESS AND I.D. OR SOCIAL SECURITY NUMBERS	CONTRIBUTION	PROPORTION OF PROFITS BASED ON A BUDGET OF $300,000.
Cal Cal 80 Garick Street New York, New York 10014 Soc. Sec. # 123-45-678	$15,000	2.5%
Roy Roy 987 East 65th Street New York, New York 10022 Soc. Sec. # 987-65-4321	$12,000	2.0%

IN WITNESS WHEREOF, the parties hereto have set their hands and seals this 30th day of December 1987.

GENERAL PARTNERS

_____

_____

LIMITED PARTNERS

_____

_____

APPENDIX K

Theatre License Agreement

AGREEMENT made the *25* day of *March* 1985 between *EASY THEATER CORPORATION* (hereinafter called "Easy") and *THE RISING COMPANY LIMITED PARTNERSHIP* (hereinafter called the "Producer"), for the booking of the play now entitled *RISING* (hereinafter called the "Play"), by *Sam Sam* at the Easy Theatre in New York City (hereinafter called the "Theatre"). The first preview performance will be presented on or about *April 30, 1986* (hereinafter called the "First Preview"). The official opening will be presented on or about *May 8, 1986* (hereinafter called the "Opening").

EASY

I.   (A) Easy shall furnish the Theatre properly licensed commencing *April 23, 1986* (hereinafter called "Available Date") and Producer agrees to pay Easy Dollars ($ *N/A*) per performance week (pro rata on the basis of a six-day week) commencing with the Available Date and ending on the day before the First Preview. In addition, Producer agrees the manager for the Theatre shall commence employment on the Available Date and be paid for by Producer.

(B) Easy shall furnish, but Producer will pay, *Twelve thousand five hundred 00/100———* Dollars ($*12,500.00*) per performance week (hereinafter called "Fixed Charge") in advance on Monday of every week commencing with the week during which the First Preview occurs pro rata on the basis of a six-day week for the following: General and

431

Administrative costs, depreciation, and interest amortization on mort-
gages.* The Fixed Charge is calculated on the base year *July 1, 1985*
through *June 30, 1986* and at applicable union minimums without
regard to Sundays, holidays, and other premium payments. Any increases or decreases in the Fixed Charge to Easy shall increase or
decrease the Fixed Charge payable to Easy by Producer. All payroll
items involving Easy's employees are to be paid for as set forth in
Paragraph II (B) and are not to be considered part of the Fixed Charge.
Easy shall not make any additional charge for equipment owned by
Easy and placed in the Theatre.

THE PRODUCER

II.   (A) Producer will furnish and pay for all other personnel,
services, properties and materials not herein specifically agreed to be
furnished and paid for by Easy necessary to take-in, present, and take-
out the Play as a complete theatrical production including, but not
limited to, complete cast, scenery, costumes, electrical and sound equipment, all literary and musical rights and materials, advertising, signs
and press material. If any of the items required to be furnished by
Producer under this Paragraph II(A) are to be paid for by Easy, then
Producer shall advance Easy an amount sufficient to cover such total
payments upon presentation by Easy to Producer of a written estimate
(hereinafter called "Estimate") to cover all prospective charges. By the
end of the business day of every Monday, Easy shall substantiate all
amounts expended for the previous week and the net adjustment paid
either to Producer or to Easy as the case may be, excepting Easy shall
have the right to withhold from any amounts owing Producer an
amount equal to the Estimate for the then current week if such Estimate
has not been previously paid. Failure to advance Easy an amount equal
to the estimate within twenty-four (24) hours of presentment shall be
a breach of this Agreement and Easy may, upon such failure, terminate
this Agreement.
   (B) It is the intent of the parties that Producer pay all costs of
operating the Theatre excepting charges set out in paragraph I(B). All

---

*Real estate taxes, utility charges (except as set out in Par. VII), refuse removal, telephone, general
and liability insurance, maintenance and supplies, licenses, permits, count-up charges and exter-
minating services.*

wages and payroll taxes of employees will be paid for by Producer at the greater of applicable union rates applying or a rate made during or after the engagement retroactive to the time of the engagement. The charges for payroll taxes shall be sixteen and one-half (16½%) percent of the applicable payroll. The percentage charge of 16½ is calculated on the base year *January 1, 1985* through *January 1, 1986* and any increases of these costs shall be paid by Producer.

(C) Commencing with the First Preview, Producer will furnish, pay for, and present the Play as a complete theatrical production including, but not limited to, complete cast, scenery, costumes, electrical and sound equipment, all literary and musical material, advertising and press material, and all other properties, materials and services not herein specifically agreed to be furnished by Easy, necessary for the presentation of the Play.

DIVISION OF PROCEEDS

III.   The gross weekly box office receipts (hereinafter called "Gross Receipts" and defined in paragraph IX hereof) will be divided between Producer and Easy as follows:

SEE RIDER

Easy shall keep and maintain accurate books and records relating to the Gross Receipts derived from the performances of the Play at the Theatre, and all expenses and other costs paid on account of or charged to Producer. All of such books and records shall be available for inspection by a duly authorized representative of Producer, upon reasonable notice, during all regular business hours. The provisions of this paragraph shall remain in effect for the period of one (1) year following the termination of this Agreement.

TERM

IV.   The Play will be presented at the Theatre commencing with the First Preview and continuously thereafter for eight (8) performances during each week until terminated in accordance with this Agreement. There will be *six (6)* evening performances presented *Monday* through *Saturday* evenings and *two (2)* matinees, one each presented on Wednesday, Saturday, and *N/A*   . Producer may vary this schedule with the consent of Easy, such consent not unreasonably to be withheld. Either Easy or Producer can terminate this Agreement if the Gross Receipts commencing with the *week ending July 14, 1986* for two (2) consecutive weeks be less than *Sixty thousand* Dollars (*$60,000.00*), (hereinafter called the "Stop Clause Amount"), and Easy or Producer delivers written notice to the other of such termination no later than Monday night, 6:00 P.M., following said two (2) weeks. In the event such written notice of termination is properly and timely given, the run of the Play will end at the closing of the evening perform-ance at the next Sunday. If within the week during which the First Preview occurs, less than eight (8) performances are given, then the Stop Clause Amount in this paragraph IV will be reduced, for that week, by one-eighth (⅛) for every performance less than eight (8) given during said First Preview week. Any increase or decrease of the Fixed Charge, the rates of pay of personnel, advertising rates, and/or the 16½ percent payroll tax charge will either increase or decrease the Stop Clause Amount to the extent of such change.

MINIMUM SUM

V.   The minimum sum to be paid by Producer to Easy for each week will be the amount necessary to meet Producer's obligations under paragraph I(B) and paragraph II(B) hereof (hereinafter called the "Guarantee"). If within the week during which the First Preview oc-curs, less than eight (8) performances are given, then the Guarantee in this paragraph V will be reduced for that week by one-eighth (⅛) for every performance less than eight (8) given during said First Preview week. Each week Easy's receipts, other than Easy's share of the Gross Receipts, falls below the Guarantee, Easy will have the right to retain so much of the Producer's share of the Gross Receipts as may be necessary to pay the Guarantee. If the Gross Receipts are insufficient to pay the Guarantee, Producer will pay the difference between the Guarantee and the Gross Receipts immediately to Easy. To the extent salaries (or other emoluments, benefits or payments) of union personnel furnished or shared by Easy are increased as a result of collective bargaining agreements executed prior or subsequent to the date of this Agreement but effective after the date hereof and to the extent that real estate taxes, insurance premiums, and utility charges are increased over the applicable base years the minimum Guarantee will be increased by the percentage amount of such increased payments, effective as of the date such increased payments became effective, but not before July 1, 1986.

DEPOSIT

VI.   Concurrently with the signing hereof, Producer has deposited with Easy   *N/A*   Dollars, ($ *N/A*   ) as security for the payment of all the Producer's obligations to Easy hereunder, and Easy may apply the security deposit or any part thereof to such payments. Upon such application, Producer, upon demand, will immediately restore to the security deposit the amounts thereof so applied and if Producer shall fail to do so, Easy may restore such amounts by deducting an equal amount from Producer's share of the Gross Receipts and may immediately terminate this Agreement. At the end of the run of the Play, Easy shall continue to hold the security deposit for a reasonable time in order to determine any amounts Producer may owe Easy arising from obligations hereunder. After determining such amounts, if any, Easy shall repay to Producer, without interest, the security deposit less any amounts applied hereunder. Producer shall not assign or encumber the security deposit or any part thereof and Easy will not be bound by any assignment or encumbrance thereof. If for any reason whatsoever, the Producer does not present the play as provided for in this agreement, the Producer will forfeit said security to Easy in addition to paying for any other costs incurred by Easy hereunder.

AIR CONDITIONING

VII.   For each performance that the air-conditioning system be in operation, Producer will pay Easy the sum of *One hundred and fifty—* ————————— Dollars (*$150.00*). To the extent utility charges are increased to Theatre, then the amount set out in this paragraph VII shall be increased by the percentage increase of such charges.

TAKE OUT

VIII.   If Producer does not move out the production within seventy-two (72) hours after the closing performance, then Producer will be deemed to have abandoned the production and Easy may dispose of same as it sees fit, inclusive of the right (but not the obligation) to store same at the expense of Producer. Producer will be liable to Easy for all damages sustained by Easy caused by Producer's failure to move the production and for all costs and expenses in moving the production out of the theatre and disposing of same, and for storage charges (if same be stored). If Producer will be indebted to Easy the latter may retain possession of the production and dispose of same at private or public sale, with or without notice to Producer, and apply the net proceeds toward the payment of such obligation.

GROSS RECEIPTS

IX.   The Gross Receipts referred to herein will be the receipts from the sale of tickets less admissions and other taxes and brokers' fees, commissions, group sales charges, credit card company charges (computed at 4 percent), computer sales charges, computer ticket charges, subscription fees and discounts, if any, payable upon such receipts and less any amounts which may now or hereafter contractually be required to be paid by either Easy or Producer for pension and/or welfare benefits when the source of the payments are funds representing a reduction or elimination of admissions taxes by any governmental entity. In the computation of Gross Receipts, the weekly assessment established by the League of New York Theatres will be deducted from the amount of gross weekly box office receipts and will be remitted by Theatre to the League Special Projects Account. The receipts of each performance will be ascertained by the statement of the sale at the box office, verified by the count of tickets taken at the door, and settlement will be made on each Monday for the week immediately preceding. The Treasurer of the Theatre is authorized by the parties hereto, in his sole discretion, to accept in payment for tickets, personal checks, postal savings or bank orders or other conventional orders for the payment of funds including credit cards satisfactory to Easy. All losses in the event of nonpayment or noncollection or otherwise in connection with any such orders for the payment of funds will be deemed to reduce the Gross Receipts in such amount for the performance affected thereby.

(C) Producer agrees to be solely responsible for all sums payable for Social Security, Unemployment Insurance, Disability Benefits and other charges in connection with Producer's employees.

(D) The payment by Easy of any payroll, payroll taxes and/or other charges with respect to any of Producer's employees employed by or under the direction of Producer will not constitute or be construed to constitute Easy to be the employer of any such employees. Producer is and will remain the employer of such employees for all purposes.

THEATRE CONDITION

XIII.   (A) The Producer accepts the Theatre in the condition "as is" as of the time of occupying Theatre, and any improvements, changes, alterations and/or decorations including, but not limited to, additional electrical signs, painting of the star or featured players' dressing rooms, changes in the size of the orchestra pit, seating, stage floor surface, stage traps, platforms for switchboards, booms and boxes, and outlets on balcony rails will be made and paid for by the Producer and Easy will have no responsibility with respect thereto. None of said changes, improvements, alterations and/or decorations, however, will be made by the Producer without the Producer first obtaining the prior written permission of Easy and the approval of all governmental authorities having jurisdiction thereof. Said changes will be in accordance with the rules and regulations of the New York Board of Fire Underwriters. At the end of the Play, the Producer agrees at its own expense to restore the Theatre to the same condition as it was at the time of occupying Theatre unless Easy notifies Producer, in writing, that such restoration is unnecessary.

(B) Producer will conduct the company and present the Play in full accordance with existing laws, ordinances and regulations, and will not violate any copyright laws or infringe upon the literary or other rights of any person, firm or corporation.

(C) Producer will abide by the reasonable rules and regulations of Easy as regards conduct in the Theatre and Producer will pay for all breakage and damage to property caused by any member of Producer's company.

(D) Producer will, and continue to, maintain all material brought into Theatre in a fireproof condition in accordance with the existing laws and/or ordinances, rules and regulations of any governmental authority having jurisdiction thereof.

(E) If Producer fails to promptly remove any violation placed against any of its equipment or theatrical properties, Easy may remove such violation at the expense of Producer.

(F) Producer agrees to indemnify and save Easy harmless from any and all claims based upon the violation by Producer of any of the foregoing provisions of this paragraph XIII, and in the event of the failure of Producer to comply with any of the foregoing, Easy may elect upon reasonable notice to Producer to take such reasonable action as is necessary to correct such failure (without assuming any liability therefor) at the cost and expense of Producer.

EXCLUSIVE ENGAGEMENT

XIV.   Without the written consent of Easy, except for the engagement herein contracted for, Producer agrees that it will not allow or permit the company performing the Play (or any members of the cast or any other persons) to appear, play, perform the play or any part thereof or be advertised as an attraction at any theatre, radio, television studio or theatre, club, cabaret, restaurant or other place of amusement or entertainment in connection with the Play. Nor will the Play (or any part thereof) be filmed, taped or broadcast, including advertisements of such filming, taping or broadcasting, by radio or television (including paid, cable or closed circuit television) or otherwise performed or presented, except for out-of-town legitimate theatre tryout performance prior to the engagement at the Theatre in New York City, during the run of the Play at the Theatre as herein provided for, and for a period of eight (8) weeks after the end of the run at the Theatre except that radio or television broadcasts not exceeding fifteen (15) minutes in duration may be made of the Play solely for publicity purposes. The restrictions of this paragraph will apply to the company appearing at the Theatre, and to any other company hereafter organized, except first-class company(s) presenting the Play, live, with a first-class cast and first-class director in a first-class manner in first-class theatres more than sixty-five (65) miles distant from the Theatre. The provisions of this paragraph XIV will not apply to an extension of the run of the Play, live, in a different theatre in the City of New York in the event this Agreement is terminated by Easy pursuant to the provisions of paragraph IV hereof. The foregoing provisions will not apply to any cast show album or records of the Play which are played on radio, or elsewhere under license by ASCAP or BMI. This paragraph XIV is of the essence to the contractual relationship of the parties and Producer acknowledges that Easy may obtain injunctive relief restraining any violation or attempted violation of this paragraph in addition to any other legal remedies Easy may have.

UNFORESEEN EVENTS

XV.   If the Theatre is rendered unsuitable for presentation of the Play due to fire, national or local calamity or emergency, act of God, strikes, labor disputes or other contingency or unforeseen occurrences beyond the control of Easy, Easy will not be responsible to Producer for any damages caused thereby and Easy in such event may terminate this Agreement upon twenty-four (24) hours' notice to Producer. The terms "strikes" and "labor disputes" as used herein, will be deemed to include all strikes by or lockouts of persons employed in the Theatre by either party hereto and will also be deemed to include picketing of the Theatre by representatives of any labor union having or claiming to have jurisdiction over such employees.

BOX OFFICE

XVI.   Price scale and distribution (including TDF, Twofers and other discounts) of tickets will be under the joint control of Theatre and Producer. Easy will have sole and exclusive control and supervision of the box office and its personnel. All Gross Receipts will, until such time as settlement is made in accordance with paragraph IX hereinabove, be under the absolute control, disposition and supervision of Easy. Easy will have the right to co-mingle advance sale monies until such time as settlement is made in accordance with paragraph IX and will have the right to deposit advance sale monies with a bank or invest same, and any increment, interest or profits earned thereon will be, and remain, the sole property of Easy, and Producer will not be entitled to participate therein. All tickets, two-for-one tickets and any other documents evidencing or affecting the right of admission to the Theatre, will be ordered only by Easy, with Producer's prior consent, and Producer covenants that it will not order, distribute or issue same without Easy's prior consent. Easy herewith consents to the sale of tickets to and through the Theatre Development Fund.

PLAYBILL

XVII.   Producer acknowledges that Easy has an existing contract with Playbill, Inc., which grants to Playbill, Inc., the sole right to distribute programs in the Theatre and to change the content and format from time to time. Producer further acknowledges that it is aware that the policy of Playbill, Inc., does not provide for the inclusion of the pictures of any star or other person of any show as part of the cover of the said program.

HOUSE SEATS

XVIII.   (A) In connection with the run of the Play at the Theatre, it is understood and agreed that Easy will reserve for itself and will have the right to purchase theatre tickets (house seats) for those locations for which Easy has customarily reserved or purchased such tickets in the past, as follows:

(1) For the opening night performance, 84 orchestra and 20 mezzanine seats;

(2) For each performance, for which there are no theatre parties or benefits, 26 orchestra seats and for those performances for which there are theatre parties or benefits, 14 orchestra seats.

(B) The issuance of free tickets to the press will be under the joint control of the parties hereto.

UNLAWFUL CONDUCT

XIX.   (A) In addition to any other remedies which Easy may have pursuant to this Agreement, at law or in equity, Easy will have the right upon forty-eight (48) hours' notice to Producer to terminate the license granted by this Agreement in the event that (i) Producer breaches any of the terms, provisions, covenants or conditions of the Agreement, or (ii) Easy in its sole discretion, determines that the showing of the Play may subject Easy to actions for damages, fines, penalties, revocation of license or any other legal action or proceeding by reason of copyright infringement or otherwise.

(B) If the license granted to Producer by this Agreement is terminated by Easy in accordance with (A)(i) or (ii) of this paragraph XIX or for any other cause under this Agreement, Producer covenants and agrees to terminate the run of the Play and remove Producer's property from the Theatre upon the effective date of such termination, and in the event of Producer's failure to do so, Producer will be liable for all damages, consequential or otherwise, that may be incurred by Easy. Producer expressly authorizes Easy (i) to post such notices as may in Easy's judgment be appropriate to notify all employees of the closing of the Play on the effective date of such termination, and (ii) to take such other steps as may be deemed advisable by Easy to remove Producer's property from the Theatre and effectively terminate the run of the Play, including exercising such rights as are reserved to Easy after the closing performance under paragraph VIII hereof.

(C) Until the license granted to Producer pursuant to this Agreement is terminated in accordance with (A)(i) or (ii) hereof, or is otherwise terminated in accordance with the provisions of the Agreement, Producer covenants and agrees to continue the run of the Play in the Theatre. Any interim closing of the Play for reason of holiday season, actors' vacations, actors' illnesses or other reasons without the consent of Easy will constitute a breach of this Agreement by Producer.

HANGING PLOT

XX.   Producer covenants and agrees that prior to the opening date and the commencement of any installation by Producer, Producer will submit the hanging plot to Easy for Easy's prior written approval and that thereafter and at all times during the run of the Play at the Theatre, Producer will comply with and conform to the approved plot.

NOTICES

XXI.   Any notices provided for herein will be in writing and will be effective if:

(A) Delivered by Easy in person or by mailing same to Producer, return receipt requested, at:

1172 West 12th Street
New York, New York 10000

or personally delivered to the Company Manager of the Play.

(B) Delivered by Producer by mailing same to Easy, return receipt requested, at 123 West 45th Street, New York, New York 10036, Attention: General Manager.

NO WAIVER

XXII.   All the rights and remedies of Easy herein will be deemed to be distinct and separate, nor will any mention or reference to any one or more of them be deemed an exclusion of or waiver of any of the others or of any rights or remedies which Easy might have, whether by present or future law and Easy will have, to the fullest extent permitted by law, the right to enforce any rights or remedies separately. No failure on the part of Easy to enforce the provision herein contained nor any waiver of any right hereunder by Easy, unless in writing, will discharge or invalidate such provision or affect the right of Easy to subsequently enforce same.

CONSENTS

XXIII.   Whenever the approval or consent of Easy is required by Producer pursuant to this Agreement, such approval or consent will not be deemed to be granted unless in writing.

ASSIGNMENTS

XXIV.   This Agreement may not be assigned, transferred, hypothecated or in any manner encumbered by Producer without the consent in writing of Easy, except that Producer may assign the Agreement to a corporation which is controlled by Producer, or to a limited partnership organized by Producer to produce and present the Play (of which limited partnership Producer will be a general partner). In the event of any such assignment, Producer will continue to be primarily liable for all of the Producer's obligations hereunder. Before such assignment may become effective, an executed copy of the assignment and an assumption of all of the terms, covenants and conditions of this Agreement by the assignee, in writing and in form satisfactory to Easy, will be delivered to Easy.

In the event of the transfer of title of the Theatre, Easy may assign all of its rights under this Agreement to the transferee of the title and provided such transferee assumes the obligations of Easy hereunder, Easy will be released of any further responsibility or liability under this Agreement. Easy, in the event of such transfer, may transfer any security deposited pursuant to paragraph VI hereof to the transferee and provided the transferee assumes the obligation to hold the same in accordance with the provisions of this Agreement, Easy will be released from all liability for the return of such security and Producer, in such event, agrees to look to the transferee solely for the return of said security.

LICENSE

XXV.   This is a license agreement and nothing herein contained will be deemed to constitute a joint venture, partnership or landlord-tenant relationship between the parties.

MODIFICATION

XXVI.   This Agreement contains the entire understanding of the parties. There are no representation, warranties, promises, covenants or undertakings other than those herein expressedly set forth. No waiver, change or modification hereof will be binding unless in writing executed by both Producer and Easy with the same formality as provided for in this Agreement.

HEADINGS

XXVII.   The headings of the paragraphs of this Agreement are for convenience of reference only. They do not form any part hereof and in no manner modify, interpret or construe this Agreement.

WITNESS the due execution by the parties hereto as of the day and year first above written.

THE RISING COMPANY LTD.   EASY THEATRE CORPO-
RATION

_____   _____
Robert Robert   Ben Easy
Producer   *President*

*RIDER MADE TO AN AGREEMENT DATED THE 25th DAY OF
MARCH, 1986, BETWEEN EASY THEATER CORPORATION AND
THE RISING COMPANY LIMITED PARTNERSHIP*
Inserted as to Paragraph III:

*(A) If the Theatre is operated with a seating capacity of not more than
499 seats,*

*(i) On Gross Receipts up to and including Sixty-two Thousand
Five Hundred Dollars ($62,500.00), One Hundred Percent (100%)
to the Producer;*
*(ii) On Gross Receipts over Sixty-two Thousand Five Hundred
Dollars ($62,500.00), Ninety Percent (90%) to Producer and Ten
Percent (10%) to Easy for a period of twenty-six weeks commencing
with the week after the week in which the Opening occurs or upon
recoupment of Production Expense (as defined for the investors),
whichever occurs first, and thereafter, Eighty-Five Percent (85%) to
Producer and Fifteen Percent (15%) to Easy.*

*(B) If the Theatre is operated with a seating capacity of 500 seats or
more, Ninety-two and One-half Percent (92 1/2%) to Producer, Seven
and One-Half Percent (7 1/2%) to Easy.*

Paragraph V is amended as follows:

*A. The Stop Clause Amount set out herein is applicable only when
the Theatre is operated with a seating capacity of not more than 499 seats.*
*B. If the parties agree, the Theatre will be operated with a seating
capacity of more than 499 and in such event the Stop Clause Amount
shall be renegotiated.*

Notes

CHAPTER 1

1. The copyright law was enacted in various stages beginning in 1790, when the subjects of protection were maps, charts, and books. In 1831 musical compositions were included, and on August 18, 1856, authors of dramatic works were given—in addition to the sole right to print and publish—the sole right to perform such works.

2. For a further discussion of the topic of public domain, see pages 9–12.

3. There are some exceptions to this rule. In the area of music, the copyright law provides for a compulsory mechanical license for songs that have been previously recorded. A person wishing to record a previously recorded song may do so upon providing the copyright owner with written notice of his intention to obtain such a license and thereafter paying the statutory license fee.

There is another exception called "fair use," the purpose and intent of which is not relevant to the subject of this book.

4. The play licensing companies usually control only the stock and amateur rights. If the producer intends to present a "first-class performance," he or she would, in most instances, have to get those rights from the author or owner of the work. For a definition of "first-class performance," see Chapter 2, footnote 1.

5. Normally, when a musical play is written independently (not for a movie or publishing company), the composer and lyricist will assign their publishing rights to a music publisher for purposes of further exploitation; however, the composer and lyricist will retain ownership of the remainder of the copyright, including the grand performing rights.

6. The concept of the "merger of rights" is that all contributions to a play (the basic work, the book, the music, and the lyrics) merge and become one entity for all dramatic (grand rights) uses. This will occur after the play has run an agreed-upon specified number of times, and the persons controlling such dramatic uses will also be set forth in the agreement between the parties contributing to the play.

7. This common law copyright (which is eliminated by the new copyright law

445

for works created after January 1, 1978) is sometimes referred to as the "right of first publication," since it exists until the work is first published, at which time the provisions of the copyright law become effective.

8. The word "publication" is a legal term of art and has no precise definition. The courts decide what is needed to constitute publication on a case-by-case basis.

9. Registration of the work by sending in a copyright form to Washington did not grant copyright protection. Registration was merely a method of recording the work in a public place and a prerequisite to the maintenance of a lawsuit for infringement. Publication with the copyright notice was the key to copyright protection under the old law.

10. January 1, 1978, is the effective date of the new copyright law.

11. In certain instances, the copyright term will be longer than fifty-six years as a result of the new 1978 copyright law.

12. A complete explanation of these agreements can be found in the following chapters.

13. The same title cannot be used if it has established a secondary meaning whereby the mention of the title brings to mind the producer's particular adaption of the play. This protection is derived from the law of unfair competition and not the copyright law. If, however, the title of the adaptation is the same as that of the public domain work being adapted, no secondary meaning can be established and that title is free to be used by all.

14. In any translation there is, of course, an element of adaptation of the underlying work. For the purpose of clarity, however, we will call such translation/adaptation simply a translation.

15. See Chapter 4 for a complete discussion on the reasons for a producer entering into a Dramatists Guild contract.

16. As a point of interest, an area where this occurs more frequently than admitted is in the television industry. Writers often mail scripts to producers of a television series hoping to get a writing job or to sell their script. Since the success of a television series is sometimes based on not much more than an original idea with unusual characters, the script could be an easy target for copying. If an allegation of copying arises, it then becomes a question of fact to be decided by a court as to whether just the idea was copied or enough to cause a copyright infringement. Because of this potential problem, and because there have been numerous lawsuits in this area, many television producers refuse even to look at unsolicited scripts or scripts not submitted by agents or attorneys. Others insist that the writer sign a release stating that if they happen to produce a series with the same idea, the writer will acknowledge that such idea was developed independently of his or her script and that any similarities are purely coincidental and not a basis for a lawsuit by the writer.

17. If an author conveys an interest in the subsidiary rights together with the license to an insignificant production, and if the chance for a first-class production later occurs, the needed interest in the subsidiary rights to give to the first-class production will already have been conveyed.

18. See Chapter 4 for a complete discussion of the contracts required to adapt a basic work.

19. For a discussion of the purchase of the adaptation rights for the basic work see Chapter 2—"Payments to the Author."

CHAPTER 2

1.   A first-class performance is usually thought of as a Broadway or pre-Broadway performance; the term, however, is much broader. A first-class performance is usually defined as one with a first-class cast (professional actors—that is, members of Actors' Equity), a first-class director (a director who is a member of Actors' Equity or the Society of Stage Directors and Choreographers), and a first-class theatre. Actors' Equity has a different contract for a first class theatre than for other houses. If there is a question whether a particular theatre is a first-class house, the League of American Theatre Owners and Producers or Actors' Equity could tell you. The first-class theatres are usually not used for one-night stands but for extended or open runs of plays on tour.

2.   The author or owner may own the copyright in the play, but the copyright is, in a sense, divisible. The copyright owner may, for example, grant someone the exclusive rights to present the play for a stage production, someone else the exclusive right to present the play on television, and someone else the exclusive right to record the play, etc, etc, etc. It is important for the optionee to know that the owner owns the rights being granted. It is also important to know what other grants, if any, have been made, because—as will later be seen—the optionee may be coming into other production rights in the play and other monetary interests in other uses of the play in other media.

3.   Some authors' representatives try to limit the extent of the author's liability to the producer to only those amounts which the author receives from the production of the play. This limitation is good for the author and bad for the producer, both for obvious reasons. If the play gets enjoined prior to opening, the producer's recovery is limited to only the advance he or she paid the author, whereas the exposure to liability could be extensive. This all but destroys the purpose of the clause and is usually avoided by all producers. The outcome, of course, depends on the relative bargaining power of the author and producer. The author should really be able to say, "I wrote that and I didn't steal it and I will pay you your damages if I did."

4.   Although payments for options are usually advances against royalties, sometimes the author's representative will insist that part of the payment be a fee and not such an advance. This is a favorite point for compromise. A shrewd producer might be able to convince the author or his representative to take a much smaller initial payment, which is an advance, if the larger second payment is considered a fee. For example, one might go with a total of $1500 as payment for a one-year option, with a $250 (which is low) advance against the royalties for six months and $1250 (which is high) as a fee for the second six months. The producer gets a cheap start and parts with the bigger money when he knows it is being well spent.

5.   There are theatres in New York that do not fit into the category of either Broadway or Off-Broadway. Some of them are called middle theatres, because they have over 299 seats but are smaller than the Broadway houses. Middle theatres usually have 499 seats, although some of these houses are expandable to more than a thousand seats. There are also some small theatres under 299 seats in the Broadway area. In any event, each of these theatres must make its own special deal with Actors' Equity and the other applicable unions. The not-for-profit theatres are mostly referred to as Off-Off-Broadway theatres and have problems similar to the not-for-profit regional theatres.

6.   There is marked difference of opinion on this subject. Some producers feel

strongly that the production of the play in other media increases interest in the play and extends the play's run. Others feel that any other production detracts from the play. It is my feeling that the more productions and the more publicity there is, the better it is for the original production. The timing of the other productions is the critically important element.

7. What constitutes unreasonably withholding approval? It may not be reasonable to withhold approval of a New Zealand production of the play during the Broadway run. A production in New Haven, on the other hand, could be directly competitive. Even if a movie release could compete, if the producer has earned a 40 percent interest in the subsidiary rights, it might be reasonable to permit a movie, especially if the box office of the play is waning. The movie could rekindle interest in the play.

8. Movies are different. There may be so much money involved in a movie sale that everyone's best interests will be served in making one. If the producer has earned 40 percent, it may more than compensate for any lost ticket sales.

9. It may simplify matters to think of the option payment as a fee for the rights to produce the play within a fixed period of time, and the royalty payments as a fee for the continuing rights to produce the play during its run.

10. The usual compromise is 5 percent going to 6½ percent after recoupment of the production budget, or 6 percent going to 7½ percent after recoupment.

Most important during the early weeks of a show are the waivers of some part of the royalties to help keep the show alive. The usual provision will provide for a waiver if all persons entitled to royalties similarly waive.

11. The person or persons acquiring rights to adapt the basic work may, in the first instance, be the bookwriter, the composer, the lyricist, or any combination of these.

12. The share of subsidiary income referred to is the total author's share. As will be seen later, a producer of the play may end up with some of this subsidiary income for his or her production company—as much as 50 percent. So the question is, How is the 50 percent (or whatever amount goes to the author) divided up?

13. The question boils down to this: Who is making an important enough contribution to the new work that they can claim an interest in the play and all subsidiary uses of the play? We all know some directors who have this kind of bargaining power. The person to be avoided is the producer who includes himself or his girlfriend as a creator under some label so as to unfairly dilute the others' interest in subsidiary income.

14. Any waivers are *pari passu*—that is, each party waives proportionately as to their royalty. For example, the author receives 6 percent, the director 3 percent, and the producer 1 percent (for a total of 10 percent). If the total royalties for the week in question are $10,000 (computed at 10 percent of a gross box office of $100,000), and if paying those royalties would cause the play to lose $4,000 for that week, the author would waive six-tenths, the director three-tenths, and the producer one-tenth of the $4,000 of royalties due them from the $10,000. This would make each participant's waiver $2,400 (6/10 × $4,000), $1,200 (3/10 × $4,000), and $400 (1/10 × $4,000) respectively for a total waiver of $4,000. This would also reduce each participant's royalty share for that week from $6,000 to $3,600 for the author; $3,000 to $1,800 for the director; and $1,000 to $600 for the producer.

15. The next chapter will discuss the topic of subsidiary rights for a Broadway production.

16. Although the agreement refers to the producer sharing in these receipts, as will be seen later, the producer assigns all his rights under the option agreement to the production company formed to finance and produce the play. The investors (and the producer to the extent he shares in profits) are the ultimate beneficiaries of the receipts from subsidiary rights.

17. For a first-class production, the producer will share in subsidiaries after the rights vest under the circumstances outlined in the later chapter on the Dramatists Guild Minimum Basic Production Contract. Other nonfirst-class contracts may vary to graduate the 10 percent to 40 percent between twenty-one performances and ninety-nine performances. The figures above set forth in the text are not only usual, but also fair.

18. There are, of course, exceptions. Short runs usually mean, however, that the play's subsidiary uses are less valuable. Long runs usually mean that the subsidiaries are of greater value—but there are even exceptions to this. For example, *The Magic Show* could hardly be a big stock and amateur theatre candidate, because a trained magician is required and not many groups have one.

19. There are even exceptions to this. There are some few authors and composers who are so famous and commercial that they could be financed for a Broadway production with little or no subsidiaries thrown in. The producer who argues that he needs the subsidiary income to interest investors knows, of course, that he, too, will share in subsidiaries only if the investor does.

20. Authors will sometimes ask for and sometimes (but rarely) get 10 percent for twenty-one performances, 20 percent for fifty-six performances, 30 percent for seventy-five performances, and 40 percent for ninety-nine performances. They will also sometimes succeed in counting the performances from the official opening without counting any of the preview performances.

21. An ABC ad is an ad in the alphabetical listings which appear in the *New York Times* and the New York *Post*. A teaser ad is one in which only the name of the play (and sometimes the star) is mentioned together with the name of the theatre.

22. The classic billing dilemma was occasioned by Mary Martin and Ethel Merman when they did a benefit performance on the same program. The problem was neatly solved by having the program identical on both sides, except that on one side Mary Martin's name was first, and on the other side Ethel Merman's name was first.

23. It may be provided that a determination will be made by one arbitrator rather than by three arbitrators. This will save some money, as the more arbitrators there are, the more it costs. Since an arbitrator's decision is, in fact, "arbitrary," I am not sure that a disputant will get more justice from the arbitrary decision of three arbitrators, rather than the arbitrary decision of one arbitrator.

24. There is a big difference between the author's script control on a play and the author's script control on a film script. The play author has absolute script control and the screen play author, most usually, has none. I have speculated that the difference developed historically because plays were optioned with relatively little money being paid for the option. During the early Hollywood days in the 1920s and '30s, it was not unusual for studios to hire writers, pay them huge sums of money, and put them in a room with a typewriter. Under such circumstances the film company would expect to own everything that came out of the typewriter. Film options traditionally give the producers the right to alter, change, add to, subtract from, and amend the screenplay

in any way they see fit. Of course, as was mentioned, this is not so with plays, where not one single word can be changed without the author's prior approval.

CHAPTER 4

1.   Very few Broadway plays have been produced without a Guild contract. There were good reasons for using the Minimum Basic Production Contract, because, although it was a mess to read and difficult to comprehend, it was in fact a fair business arrangement for both parties to the agreement. In fact, in some instances of a foreign author, the contract was used even though foreign authors could not be Guild members. The new Approved Production Contract will probably continue to be widely used. This is so because the Guild members will want to use the contract negotiated by their association and the producers will want to use it because it is a very favorable contract from the producer's point of view. Faced with a Sherman Antitrust Law violation (see Footnote 2) the Guild, anxious to settle the lawsuit as part of the contract negotiations, was not exactly bargaining from strength.

2.   The federal antitrust laws are intended to prevent businesses from banning together in restraint of trade. Employees may join together in labor unions. Writers are really "independent contractors" rather than employees and as such ought not be considered "employees." Their joining together in an association to collectively bargain with the producers could be considered in violation of the Sherman Antitrust Law and in restraint of trade.

3.   Historically, it is interesting to note that up until the APC was adopted in May of 1985, the old MBPC provided for a royalty of 5 percent of the first $5,000 of gross weekly box office receipts, 7½ percent of the next $2,000 of such receipts, and 10 percent of all such receipts thereafter. Broadway theatres now gross between $250,000 and $300,000 per week for straight plays. Since the shift was from 5 percent after $5,000 and from 7½ percent after $7,000, the royalty for this contract must have been (and was, in fact) established when the potential gross weekly box office receipts for a Broadway theatre was on either side of $20,000.

4.   The additional opening-night house seats are usually not necessarily in the same preferred location as the regular run-of-the-show house seats. The opening night seating plan requires both great wisdom and skill. It is necessary to accommodate (and also please) critics and investors, as well as the cast and crew's friends and relatives. This is not always an easy job—and sometimes it is not even possible.

5.   Before the attorney general of the state of New York conducted an investigation about twenty-five-years ago, some Broadway treasurers, general managers, theatre managers, and even some producers lined their pockets with extra cash from the illegal sale of theatre tickets at escalated prices. There was often collusion between the theatre owner and the producer to extract additional money from those patrons who were ready to pay exorbitant prices for the shows that were the smash hits.

The treasurer and other box office personnel would simply sell the ticket for a markup above the regular price, and since all of these transactions were cash, the amount above the box office price was segregated and divided up by the parties participating in the scam. The investors were cheated, the takers paid no tax on the money, and there were reports of huge amounts of money being collected in this fashion. Most everyone in the business knew what was happening and either paid little attention, because who wants to squeal on one's friends, or were themselves participating in the illegal skimming.

The extra money that they extracted was known as "ice" and the investigation became known as the "ice scandal."

The investigation by the attorney general, the exposure of the practice, and the introduction of computer sales has wiped out this illegal scheme, at least that is what most persons in and out of the business believe to be the fact.

6. One must be careful to make the distinction between a monetary interest and control. Although, in a sense, a monetary interest and additional production rights could both be thought of as "subsidiary rights," the usage here is only as a monetary interest. The distinction, however, is always important to bear in mind.

7. The question previously raised as to whether receipts from cassettes was included as subsidiary rights income was settled by the terms of the APC, which include the income from both audio and video cassettes as such income.

8. Some Broadway productions will be difficult, if not impossible, to present as stock or amateur productions. For example, *The Magic Show,* which needs an accomplished magician and extravagant illusions costing a great deal of money, would be an unlikely stock or amateur possibility. Local magicians may or may not be able to handle the intricate sleight of hand required, but even if they could, the cost of the illusions would be prohibitive. It is also difficult to imagine a stock or amateur production of *Cats* or *Starlight Express,* which require huge expenditures for the intricate sets.

9. As a matter of good business, I believe that all agreements in the entertainment industry should include an arbitration clause. Special provision may be included requiring quick decisions. Sometimes the agreement will name the arbitrator, such as a director, to settle artistic disputes between co-producers, and the attorney or general manager to settle business disputes between co-producers. I know there are some attorneys in and out of the business who disagree with this philosophy and insist on their day in court. I will only appeal to your sense of reason by inquiring whether you would prefer to have a theatrical dispute settled by a judge—who may or may not have any special knowledge of the theatre business—at the court's usual slower pace, or by an arbitrator who is obligated to make a quick decision and who is selected especially because of his or her having a knowledge of theatre.

10. It is not unusual for the bookwriter, composer, and lyricist to share equally the proceeds from any advances, royalties, and other income, that is, each receiving one-third. There are of course occasions when one of the parties is so important, so well known and has such bargaining power that his or her share will be more than one-third. An important composer, for example, could command and receive half of all receipts, while a lesser-known bookwriter and a lesser-known lyricist would share the other half.

11. Although the composer and lyricist control the publishing and recording rights (with the exception of the original cast album), the producer sometimes finds it necessary to solicit an investment from a publishing or recording company that would want the publishing or recording rights or at least an option of first refusal for such rights. A contract with the composer and lyricist will sometimes provide that the producer may make a deal with a publishing or recording company in exchange for an investment in the play if the composer and lyricist do not have previous commitments.

CHAPTER 5

1. A limited partnership is a statutory entity, not a part of the common law. In order to organize a limited partnership, the statutory requirements must be complied with. In New York State this requires filing a Certificate of Limited Partnership with the county clerk in the county where the partnership will have its principal office and will conduct its business. The certificate contains facts about the partners—the amount of their investment and their relationship to each other. A digest of the certificate or the certificate must be published once a week in two newspapers in the county for six consecutive weeks. In New York County, one of the papers designated by the county clerk is always the *New York Law Journal*. There is an exception to the requirement of publishing the certificate for stage productions (see page 72).

2. The Internal Revenue Service has arbitrarily determined that if the budget of the show is $2½ million or less, the assets of the corporation must be at least 15 percent of the budget, or $250,000, whichever is less. If the budget of the show exceeds $2½ million (which is highly unlikely), the total assets of the production must be at least 10 percent of the budget. If the corporation has this kind of assets, it would defeat the purpose of limiting the liability of the party; this is the reason, in almost all instances on Broadway, that the producer is an individual or individuals.

3. This kind of arrangement, of course, has built-in dangers. The insolvent individual partner would have a general partners' liability, and also general partners' authority as far as creditors are concerned, and could obligate the limited partnership to commitments that might be unwise. If the corporation has few or no assets, and if the individual partner is insolvent, some of the creditors could end up unpaid and all of the principals in the limited partnership would have defiled their reputation in a very small business where one's credit and credibility is an essential asset.

4. One Broadway producer recently offered his investors 75 percent of the net profits. Instead of the usual 2 percent or 3 percent of the gross weekly box office receipts for a producer's fee, he was going to take 5 percent of the gross weekly box office receipts. The producer was offering a bigger percentage of the net, the pie in the sky, in exchange for a larger percentage of the gross, which is real money. Bear in mind that a percentage of gross is different from a percentage of net. The producer offering 75 percent of the net to investors was giving away ice in the wintertime in exchange for real dollars.

5. An investor can give permission to use his investment before the total budget is raised. It is most usual, however, that the total budget be raised before any of the funds are used. This is to insure the investors that the play will be produced and open if their money is used.

6. Until recently it was customary to file the Certificate of Limited Partnership only after the aggregate limited contributions had been paid into the partnership. Now it is better policy to form the partnership as soon as one limited partner signs the agreement.

If the partnership does not use the words "limited partnership" in the title, or if it is not for a theatrical stage production, you must publish. Publishing the name, address, and investment information about just one limited partner can save considerable money. Since the contents of an amendment to the Limited Partnership Agreement need not be published, putting the names, addresses, and investment information about all the other investors in the amendment avoids the necessity of publishing that information.

The other reason for filing a certificate of limited partnership as early as possible is that the attorney general of the state of New York issued an opinion that the partnership is not formed until the publishing is completed. To wait until the total budget is raised might delay use of the money when it is needed, for the limited liability promised would only become effective after completion of the publishing, and that means six weeks.

7.   A well-known producer/director some years ago had to fire the director of a show he was producing and ended up directing the show himself. He could not be paid as the director because the partnership agreement made no provision for such a payment. Hence this blanket provision started appearing in agreements.

8.   There is, of course, the more important tax consideration. As was discussed under "Characteristics of Corporation for Tax Purposes," it was noted that one of the corporate characteristics is free transferability of interests. For this reason it is wise to limit assignability to make sure the partnership does, in fact, end up being taxed as a partnership and not a corporation.

9.   Some investors may object to the producer having the right to use the profits of the original production company to finance other productions. For this reason this provision may be eliminated from the agreement. Investors should realize whether or not this provision is in the agreement—and it usually is; if it is, it means that the investor is giving the producer the right to use profits from the original production to mount other productions.

10.   A producer ought to file the limited partnership certificate at the earliest opportunity, since an investor whose money is used would not enjoy the protection of a limited partner until it is filed. When the producer starts using someone else's money, such as front money, the certificate should be filed listing such investor as a limited partner. If the rest of the money is being held in escrow until the total production budget is raised, when this is done, the certificate can be amended to include the rest of the investors.

CHAPTER 6

1.   Who ends up with what depends on the bargaining power of the parties. A veteran producer would be reluctant to give bigger billing credit or more say so to a young new co-producer. If, on the other hand, the newcomer to producing brings in substantial money, he or she may make greater inroads. The bargaining power of each surfaces during the negotiations.

2.   Do not underestimate the importance of the personnel who will be used on the show. A producer may insist on having his or her own attorney or accountant and the co-producer may want someone else. In all events it is vitally important to use specialized persons who know the theatre. I have wasted hundreds of hours trying to work out agreements with some attorneys unfamiliar with theatre law and its special problems.

3.   An associate producer is known to be one who is not a general partner, and thus not responsible for the obligations of a general partner. Some money raisers want to have billing as a co-producer instead of as an associate. What they must realize is when they get the co-production credit they may be exposing themselves to the liability of a general partner.

4. From the regulations promulgated under the Arts and Cultural Affairs Law, article 23, of the state of New York.

CHAPTER 7

1. The "blue sky laws" of each state in which money will be raised must be complied with. Blue sky laws are the securities laws.

2. One may not disperse any written information to investors unless it is filed with the SEC and accepted for filing by the SEC. The SEC wants to make sure that prospective investors have a full and fair disclosure. For this reason one may not pass out reviews of a previous production of a play unless one distributes all of the reviews. To permit an offerer to distribute only favorable reviews would not be the full and fair disclosure required by the SEC.

3. As was noted above, nothing may be given to prospective investors unless copies are filed with the SEC and accepted for filing. Until the prospectus is accepted, it may not be used and the offering may not be made. It is possible to use a "red herring" prospectus on a full S-1 filing. It permits preliminary use of the prospectus with a warning in red ink that the prospectus is subject to change and the offering may not be made nor may money be accepted until the prospectus is in a form acceptable to the SEC for filing.

4. An investor may consent to his or her investment being used before the total budget is raised, may waive refund if the budget is not raised, or may opt to be reimbursed if the budget is not raised. The ticklish part of this is that an investor authorizing use of his or her investment before the limited partnership is organized may be exposed to general partner's liability until the limited partnership is formed. One of the risk factors in the offering circular calls attention to this fact (see footnote 6 of Chapter 5).

5. The offering circular can refer only to cast members who have actually been contracted to act in the play. A star's interest or desires cannot be stated. Producers are tempted to state that a big star is interested or is considering the part. *This may not be noted* unless the star has, in fact, been signed and is committed to do the part.This means posting a bond with Actors' Equity and can be an expensive proposition.

6. As was noted in Chapter 4, if the play is produced pursuant to the APC, and if the play runs long enough to vest with the producer, the production company to which the production rights were assigned will receive a share of the subsidiary rights income as detailed in Chapter 4.

7. It is most usual that persons making loans to the partnership will be entitled to recover the amount of the loan before investors are repaid. The persons making loans will usually also be paid a percentage of the profits of the company, but such percentage is payable from the producer's share of such profits.

8. Investors may not realize that the profits of the original producing company may be used to finance other productions of the play instead of being returned to them. Such a provision is most usual. If the play is successful, such profits may represent a good investment in other productions. If not successful, there would be no profits for further investment. But investors should be conscious of the fact that the producer has such authority to use any profits for this purpose.

9. Note carefully that the offering can only be made to less than thirty-six investors—not just that there are less than thirty-six investors. If there are, in fact, thirty-four or thirty-five investors, you can be assured that the attorney general of the state of New York will require evidence of the fact that the offering was not made to more than thirty-five persons. The producer is likely to be invited to testify under oath concerning the number of persons to whom the offering was made.

CHAPTER 9

1. Local No. 1, Agreement V.
2. Local No. 1, Agreement VI.7.
3. Local No. 1, Agreement VIII.
4. Local No. 1, Agreement XI.
5. Local No. 1, Agreement XII.
6. Local No. 1, Agreement XIV.
7. Local No. B—183, Agreement 3.i.
8. Local No. B—183, Agreement 3.i.
9. Local No. B—183, Agreement 5.
10. Local No. 54, Agreement 13.
11. Local No. 54, Agreement 20.
12. Local No. 54, Agreement 6.

CHAPTER 10

1. The Actors' Equity Association's Agreement and Rules Governing Employment Under the Production Contract not only outlines rules governing the employment of actors but also details the actors' responsibilities to Equity.
2. Equity agreement rule no. 22A.
3. Equity agreement rule no. 63.
4. Equity agreement rule no. 48.
5. Equity agreement rule no. 71.
6. Equity agreement rule no. 19.
7. Equity agreement rule no. 12A.
8. Equity agreement rule no. 70B.
9. Equity agreement rule no. 50A.
10. No more than two performances can be given in one day without the consent of Equity, whose consent cannot be unreasonably withheld. Rule 50A(3).
11. Equity agreement rule no. 51.
12. Equity agreement rule no. 58.
13. Equity agreement rule no. 58D(1).
14. Equity agreement rule no. 58D(1).
15. Equity agreement rule no. 61.
16. Equity agreement rule no. 58D(1).
17. Equity agreement rule no. 58D(1)(e).
18. Stage managers are entitled to overtime payment whenever the actors receive overtime payment. Equity agreement rule no. 58D(3).
19. Equity agreement rule no. 73C(6).

20. Equity agreement rule no. 16H.
21. Equity agreement rule no. 16G.
22. Equity agreement rule no. 16H.
23. Equity agreement rule no. 12C.
24. Equity agreement rule no. 12C.
25. Equity agreement rule no. 12D.
26. Equity agreement rule no. 47.
27. Equity agreement rule no. 5.
28. Equity agreement rule no. 54.
29. Equity agreement rule no. 7A(1).
30. Equity agreement rule no. 45(C). The posting of a closing notice is often used by producers as a hedge against further loss. Often closing notices are posted weekly while the producer fully expects business to improve and the show to remain open. Should the producer give notice, however, an actor may consider this notice as final and take other commitments despite the intentions of the producer. It is not impossible to lose a star actor by posting a misunderstood closing notice, thus forcing the closing of the play despite the producer's intention to run.
31. Equity agreement rule no. 31.
32. Equity agreement rule no. 29.
33. Equity agreement rule no. 74.
34. Equity agreement rule no. 12.
35. Equity agreement rule no. 74E.
36. Equity agreement rule no. 74E.
37. Equity agreement rule no. 68.
38. Equity agreement rule no. 41.
39. Equity agreement rule no. 60C.
40. Equity agreement rule no. 6.
41. Equity agreement rule no. 11.
42. Equity agreement rule no. 14.
43. Equity agreement rule no. 73.
44. Equity agreement rule no. 52.
45. Equity agreement rule no. 3.
46. Local 764 article I.
47. Local 764 article IIIw.
48. Local 764 article IIIc.
49. Local 764 article IIIe.
50. The number of dressers employed is determined by the wardrobe supervisor and the stage manager, depending upon the particular production requirements and physical surroundings of the show.
51. Local 764 article V.
52. SSD and C article 1.
57. SSD and C article 5.
54. SSD and C article 6.
55. SSD and C article 4B.
56. SSD and C article 4F.
57. SSD and C article 5C.
58. SSD and C article 7A.

59. SSD and C article 7B.
60. SSD and C article 15.
61. SSD and C article 18. Many knowledgeable theatre insiders feel that this clause is not used to its greatest advantage by producers of long-running shows, especially musicals.
62. SSD and C article 17.
63. Local 829 agreement II.A.
64. Although all designers are by contract obligated to obtain various estimates for the producer to make decisions on construction contracts, the designer will usually voice a strong preference for a particular construction house regardless of the various estimates. Designers will base this preference on previous experience at a particular house and the talent they know is available in that house to execute their designs.
65. Local 829 agreement II.B.
66. Local 829 agreement II.C.
67. Local 829 agreement IV.
68. Local 829 agreement VI.
69. Local 829 agreement VI.F.
70. Local 829 agreement VI.C.
71. Local 829 agreement VI.D.
72. Local 829 agreement VIII.
73. Local 829 agreement XIV.D.
74. Local 829 agreement IV.E.
75. Local 829 agreement IV.C.
76. Local 829 agreement X.
77. Local 829 agreement XIV.G.
78. Local 829 agreement IX.
79. Local 829 agreement VII.

CHAPTER 11

1. ATPAM Union #18032 agreement, article I, section 1.
2. ATPAM agreement, article II, section 6.
3. ATPAM agreement, article VI, section 2 and 3.
4. *Ibid.*
5. ATPAM agreement, article VII, section 3-A.
6. ATPAM agreement, article VII, section 3-B.
7. ATPAM agreement, article VII, section 2.
8. ATPAM agreement, article VI, section 1.
9. ATPAM agreement, article III, section 2.
10. ATPAM agreement, article III, section 1.
11. ATPAM agreement, article V.
12. ATPAM agreement, article IV.
13. ATPAM agreement, article IV, section 2.
14. ATPAM agreement, article IV, section 5.
15. Local 802 agreement, Fifth article.
16. Local 802 agreement, Sixth article.
17. Local 802 agreement, Third article (F)(2).

18. Local 802 agreement, Sixth article.
19. Local 802 agreement, Fourth article.
20. Local 802 agreement, Eighth article.

CHAPTER 12

1. In some instances where the show has a superstar, it is currently fashionable and financially expedient to have an extended pre-Broadway tour, sometimes for as long as two years. In fact, sometimes the show makes a lot of money on tour and never gets around to opening on Broadway. Most big superstars are not anxious to commit themselves for such a long period of time, so the long tours usually have minor superstars—that is, those who have broad box office appeal but can't command huge fees.

2. A few Broadway and Off-Broadway shows find it expedient not to have an official opening. A show with wide box office appeal may not want to run the risk of the critics if it is the kind of show the producer knows the critics would not appreciate. One show with an overabundance of sex went this route.

3. See the discussion of resident theatres as pre-Broadway tryouts, Chapter 2.

4. The *Village Voice* is sometimes a source of advertising for a particular kind of play. Because of its readership, avant-garde works, gay-life plays, and heavy, serious dramas, to mention a few, would be particularly suited for the *Voice.*

5. The last few years have produced just one exception to this rule of "never." A show was closed out-of-town before it ran out of money, but it was one of those plays with not even a remote possibility of success.

CHAPTER 13

1. The theatre availability in Manhattan is a cyclical matter. There are times when a producer has his choice of theatres. Recently, however, it's been difficult to get one, and jam-ups have been causing waits of more than one or two months. The current situation Off-Broadway is particularly critical, with an extraordinary demand for good 299- and 499-seat theatres.

Another critical problem may be presented if the star's availability does not coincide with the availability of the theatre.

2. There is a whole body of landlord/tenant law—both statutory and common law—which governs the landlord/tenant relationship. A license agreement relieves the landowner from the obligations imposed upon a landlord by these laws designed to protect tenants.

3. The theatre owner and producer, as will be seen, are in reality partners in the play's success or failure. Consequently, the theatre owner will want to have some control over the elements that could make the show a success, such as the star. The theatre may be licensed to a particular producer because of the specific star, and for this reason the theatre owner will want to be assured of that star's continued presence in the show.

4. Although the producer or the theatre owner may terminate the agreement if the stop clause amount is not raised for two weeks, the clause is really for the protection of the theatre owner. The producer has other means of terminating the agreement.

Index

Production expenses *(cont.)*
  defined, 69–70
  recoupment of, 231
Profits, 22, 110
  distribution of, 80–81
  net, 102–103, 107, 110–111
  share of, 79–80, 101–102
  sharing with director, 148
  sharing with co-producers, 90–91
  sharing with star, 148
Program insertions, 140
Property men, 129
Pro rata share, 60
Prospectus for a regulation A
  exemption, 97–98
Public address system, 221
Publication
  of Certificate of Limited
    Partnership, 86
  defined, 9
  of music, 37–38
Public domain work, 3, 9–11
  adaptation of, 11–13
  translation of, 12–13
Publicity under Actors' Equity
  Association, 167
Publicity pictures. *See* Photographs
Public relations, 128–29

R

Radio
  advertising, 47
  under ATPAM, 195
Range of production costs, 231
Recesses, 152
Record company financing, 225
Recording under Actors'
  Equity Association,
  151
Recoupment of production expenses,
  231
Red herring prospectus, 104
Refunds under Treasurers and
  Ticket Sellers Union, 135
Register of Copyrights, 4
Regulation A, SEC, 95, 97–102
Regulation D, SEC, 95

Rehearsal
  under Associated Musicians of
    Greater New York, 205
  expense money for, 158
  under Actors' Equity Association,
    150, 152–53, 154, 158
  under Theatrical Protective Union,
    132–33
  under Theatrical Wardrobe
    Attendants Union, 173
Rehearsal pianist, 182
  under Associated Musicians of
    Greater New York, 206
Renewal term, 10–11
Rental vs. fee, 219
Rental insurance, 227
Repertory
  under Actors' Equity Association,
    168
  under Theatrical Protective Union,
    131
Replacement of principal actor, 164
Residence theatre, 71
Rest periods
  under Actors' Equity Association,
    153
  under Theatrical Wardrobe
    Attendants Union, 174
Return of contributions, 80, 81–82,
  102, 110
Reviews (critical), 231
Revival of plays, 50, 51
Rewrites by author, 46
Rewriting by directors, 177
Right of first refusal for subsequent
  production, 190–91
Right of privacy laws, 14–15
Rights to assign option, 32
Rights to tour the play, 30–31
Riots
  under ATPAM, 196
  under Treasurers and Ticket
    Sellers Union, 137
Risk to investors, 99
Road tour opening, 153
Rodgers and Hammerstein Library,
  4